A History of Utah's American Indians

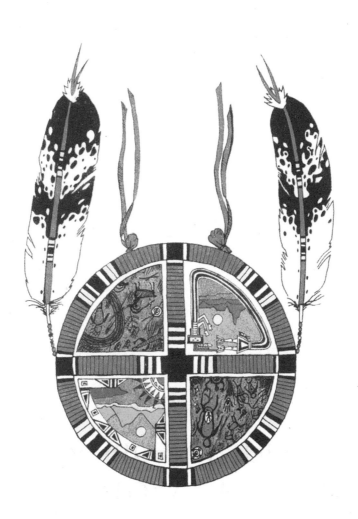

A History of Utah's American Indians

Edited by Forrest S. Cuch

with chapters by
David Begay
Dennis Defa
Clifford Duncan
Ronald Holt
Nancy Maryboy
Robert S. McPherson
Mae Parry
Gary Tom
and Mary Jane Yazzie

2003
Utah State Division of Indian Affairs / Utah State Division of History
Salt Lake City

ISBN 978-0-913738-49-8
Library of Congress Catalog Card Number 00-133020

Utah Division of Indian Affairs   Utah Division of State History
324 South State Street   Suite 500   300 Rio Grande
Salt Lake City, Utah 84114   Salt Lake City, Utah 84101-1182

Distributed to the book trade by
Utah State University Press
Logan, Utah 84322-7800

The paperback edition reprint of this book is made possible through a grant
from the George S. and Dolores Doré Eccles Foundation.

Book and cover design by Richard Firmage
Cover and frontispiece art by Dallin Maybee

Preface

Allan Kent Powell

The commemorations of the Utah Statehood Centennial in 1996 and the Sesquicentennial of Utah Settlement in 1997 were cause for reflection not only on these milestones in Utah's history but also for a reexamination of the people, events, and movements that constitute Utah history. To this end, several projects were launched prior to the commemorations; they included a one-volume Utah history encyclopedia, a one-volume history of Utah, a four-volume comprehensive history of the state, and a twenty-nine-volume county centennial history series. All of these projects were designed to provide careful accounts of how Utah has developed from prehistoric times to the present. Other books, films, and projects looked at particular aspects of the Utah experience. They included Utah's struggle for statehood, Utah's literary legacy, the Mormon Trail and overland travel to Utah, the state's natural heritage, and what Utahns thought about themselves and their state through an essay project, known as "Faces of Utah," that involved contributions from thousands of the state's residents.

With a combination of great pride in the history and heritage of their peoples and concern that their story might be ignored or misrepresented, Utah's American Indian leaders proposed their own commemorative project—a one-volume history of the American Indian experience in Utah. The history would be a collaborative effort between Indians and non-Indians, but it ultimately would recount how Utah's American Indians have celebrated and interpreted their past from the earliest days to the present. This would not be another non-Indian perception of the past that would ignore the Native American audience, but rather a telling of the past from the perspective of Utah American Indians. The book, it was hoped, would provide a written account that could help all generations of American Indians understand their rich and diverse heritage while also giving non-Indians a useful perspective on both their separate

and shared pasts. The ultimate goal was neither to condemn nor to judge; rather, it was to instruct and enlighten.

When asked by Governor Michael Leavitt in 1993 about their legislative priorities, Utah's Indian leaders placed state funding for the American Indian history project near the top of the list. The governor and the legislature concurred, and a $20,000 appropriation was made during the 1993 legislative session to the Division of State History (Utah State Historical Society) for the project. As sister agencies within the Department of Community of Economic Development, the Division of State History and the Division of Indian Affairs entered into a partnership to produce the book, with Wil Numkena, director of the Division of Indian Affairs, as project director and general editor for the volume. In 1997 Wil Numkena resigned as director of the Division of Indian Affairs to return to his home on the Hopi Reservation in Arizona to work in the Hopi Tribe education program. His successor, Forrest S. Cuch, embraced the project wholeheartedly and assumed the duties of general editor for the volume. The Public History section of the Utah State Historical Society provided support and assistance.

This volume is the first of six history initiatives identified by the Division of Indian Affairs. They include: Indian History Research; curriculum development of Utah Indian History for the public schools, including the integration of Indian History studies into the school core curriculum and the training of teachers to teach Indian History; public and educational lectures; Indian oral history projects; and audio-visual Indian history projects. This book provides an essential foundation from which to undertake these other initiatives.

The book project was launched with the establishment of an advisory committee made up primarily of representatives from Utah's Indian tribes. The committee made recommendations as to content to be included and potential authors. After considering several options, the committee recommended that the effort concentrate on producing one volume, which would include a thorough introduction followed by chapters for each of the six Utah Indian tribes. A summary or concluding chapter that focused on major issues and problems facing Utah's American Indians at the end of the twentieth century and also considered urban and non-reservation Indians would end the volume.

An initial goal of the committee was to identify and secure the participation of American Indian historians and writers for the project to ensure that the volume reflected clearly an Indian perspective and interpretation of the Native American past. This was accomplished in great

part by Forrest Cuch working as the general editor for the volume and four of the chapters having been written solely by American Indians. Two chapters were collaborative efforts by Indian and non-Indian writers, the other three chapters were authored by non-Indians working closely with representatives of the tribes and groups about whom they were writing.

This volume, then, represents some of the realities of writing American Indian history and history in general. Not all members of a group perceive or interpret their history in exactly the same way. While there is usually agreement about most of the basic facts, the importance that one event or experience has over another, the implications that developed from certain actions, or the role of one individual or group in certain developments are all subject to differing interpretations. Therefore, just as is the case with the history of all Utahns, it is impossible to write chapters about Utah's American Indians that can be said to contain a consensus of everyone's views about their past. Still, it is important to ask: Can non-Indian historians do justice to Indian history and write with both sympathy and accuracy about another people's past? Only well-informed readers can answer that question for themselves about this book. However, each of the non-Indian contributors to this volume has used oral histories from tribal members as well as written documents and records from the respective tribe. They also have reviewed their chapters with members of the respective tribes to ensure that the chapters contain what those members believe to be the essence, or at least an accurate representation, of their history.

As the authors and committee members met, a list of suggested topics was developed for inclusion in each chapter. These topics included: creation legends and stories; first non-Indian contacts; a chronological summary of important events; present-day and certain future issues and concerns; the roles, contributions, and impacts made by the tribes on the larger community, area, state, and nation; and consideration of such topics as religion, politics, education, folkways, family life, social activities, and economic issues. One of the greatest challenges to the authors was to condense the complex and diverse history of the tribes into a chapter-length narrative. In this sense, the chapters that follow represent a beginning point much more than an ending point in understanding Utah's first residents. Some chapters also are written on a more personal level, evoking in a more lyrical manner themes important to the author, rather than attempting a more dispassionate chronological unfolding of events of conventional historical importance.

More than five hundred years have passed since the first encounter between Indians and non-Indians took place with the arrival of Christopher Columbus in what quickly became known as the New World. Throughout those five hundred years disease, pestilence, war, atrocities, greed, discrimination, relocation, intolerance, and misunderstanding have characterized many of the actions and attitudes of non-Indians to the peoples they found inhabiting this vast hemisphere. Most North American Indian tribes faced extinction as their populations dwindled in the face of this encounter. That tribes like the Goshute, Navajo, Paiute, Shoshone, and Ute have survived and now flourish to some measure is an important lesson for a planet where ecological disasters threaten in many forms. As their histories tell us, these tribes have long endured and will continue to endure. They have always been and will continue to be an important part of Utah's history. What greater gift can they offer all Utahns than an understanding of their story?

The chapters that follow will enlighten and enrich readers with knowledge about cultures that stretch back to the ancient past. Special thanks is extended to the Utah State Legislature and Governor Michael Leavitt, who recognized the importance of this project and appropriated the necessary funds to undertake the research and writing and to provide copies to each public school and library in the state.

—Allan Kent Powell

Contents

A Ute Indian photographed by a member of the John Wesley Powell ethnographic expedition in 1873–74. (Utah State Historical Society—USHS)

Introduction

Forrest S. Cuch

The day will come, when a white people will set foot on the eastern shores and claim this land as their own. They will build a white house near the shore from where they will govern their people. Upon establishing their government, they will raise a banner upon a flag-staff, on top of which they will place the spirit of the Hopi (Indian) people, this will be a sign to us that the Creator will keep his promises to us. This people, the "Bahana", will scatter our people, seek to destroy us down to the last child, and bring upon us diseases that we have never known before.
—(Oral History of the Hopi Prophecy)

My understanding of ancient American Indian philosophy is that there is purpose for all things and that there are no accidents in this world. To many, it was no accident that the ancestors of the Hopi, the pre-Puebloan (Anasazi) people, once inhabited the area today known as the state of Utah. I also think it was no accident that my friend and predecessor, Wil Numkena, was Hopi, and a person of great wisdom and esteem. His vision, dedication as an educator, and love for the Indian people of Utah made this book possible. To him we all owe a debt of gratitude for this major accomplishment. I, and many others, will always appreciate his role in making this book possible and his contributions to our state.

The Hopi people claim there are four worlds of human passage. We are nearing the end of the third world and entering the fourth. In many ways, this book reflects this transition. We, the indigenous people of Utah, have endured great suffering during these times but are now coming forth in our development. The time has passed for non-Indian people to speak for us about "our past," about "our history." It is now time for us to bring forth the truth as *we* know it to be, and share it with others. Through bringing forth the truth, and through earnest discussions about it in our

schools, and with our neighbors, we will truly heal our wounds and take our rightful place in society.

Presenting the truth is necessary to dispel the myriad myths surrounding Utah history. One of the most obvious but prevailing myths is that "no one" (or no people of importance) lived in this area prior to Mormon settlement. Knowledge of pre-Mormon human presence in this area must hereafter be vital to any endeavor of educational enlightenment and postures of advanced learning by our citizenry. Furthermore, the belief must be eliminated from our consciousness that Utah's American Indians were treated better than "other Indians" outside our state boundaries. In its place must be found the facts, suggesting that the treatment of the American Indian in the state of Utah was rarely different from what occurred in surrounding states. In some cases, treatment of the Indians was better; but, in the case of the Bear River Massacre, for example, treatment was even more harsh and severe than what was experienced by Indians residing in other states.

For the most part, the histories of Utah's American Indian tribes have not been considered a viable and integral part of the history of the state of Utah. They have been treated as addenda or commentary rather than official textbook documentary. To quote Will Numkena, "Non-Indian authors have traditionally been the writers of Indian history. Therefore, it is their perceptions, understandings and views reflected in those writings. The reader is given a one-sided perspective without presentation of the Indian experience." In other words, until this time, Indian history has been written by the conqueror, with little or no regard for those conquered.

In the following pages, the reader will have an opportunity to view six tribal histories as perceived by members of those tribes in consultation with local scholars. Each author has used written and oral sources to tell the respective stories of each tribe. Their histories reflect a series or combination of differing aspects, stories that are thought-provoking yet tragic, awe-inspiring yet plain, simple yet complex. Clearly, groups have a common thread binding them all together, but each has its own distinction, its unique history and perspective.

A common perception is that all Indians are the same, when, in fact, Indians are a very diverse group. There are over 540 federally recognized Indian tribes in the United States and over 340 languages of Indian people currently still in use. The tribes differ in so many ways: different customs, practices, clothing, housing, and foods. Also, however, although many differences exist, Indian tribes also have many commonalities: high

A Shoshone mother and her two children. (Courtesy Mae Parry)

value placed on family and spirituality, nuclear family and extended family and extended kinship structures; similar tribal spiritual philosophies; a high regard for the elderly, who sometimes serve as the educators and second parents; and many more.

The following chapters provide a rare look into American Indian history from an Indian perspective—one that has been ignored because it is unwritten and is based on oral tradition. To quote Will Numkena again, "Generally speaking, scholars and publishers do not give the cre-

Paiute Jim, his wife, and two children. (USHS)

dence to oral Indian history afforded European folk tales and oral history because they apply Euro-American standards—if not written in black and white, oral history does not deserve validation. By featuring tribal oral histories in this volume, the readers are provided several unique creation stories, explanations for life-ways, rituals and traditions, including tales of [first contact with the white man] and early interactions between Indians, explorers, soldiers, and settlers."

It has only recently been determined (or the truth has escaped us) that neither Columbus, Cortez, nor the English colonials ever "discovered" America. The Western Hemisphere was discovered thousands of years before them by American Indians. Nor did early explorers find America to be an exotic untouched wilderness. Rather, all explorers on both continents encountered real live people and thriving civilizations. Columbus encountered kind and loving people, the Tanoan people, living on an island utopia that is yet to be equaled—and he quickly vanquished them into slavery. Cortez encountered an incredible civilization marveled about to this day. The English colonials found evidence of an

Indian population estimated at between thirty to forty thousand who lived in tree-bark structures, managed the land, and excelled in agriculture, as evidenced by expansive fields of corn. Both of the latter groups possessed written forms of language—the Aztecs and Mayans used stone tablets and parchment scrolls, the Delaware (Leni Lenape) wrote their tribal history in pictographs on wooden tablets, while the Algonquian and Iroquoian people portrayed their histories on sacred wampum belts.

Beginning with Columbus and the ensuing colonial contacts, the precedent would be set in America for Indians to be treated as separate and sovereign nations. It goes without saying that, if Indians were here prior to the colonial nations, their forms of government and independent sovereign status preceded the colonials as well. The Iroquois nations would also suggest that "democracy" preceded the colonials via the Iroquoian Confederacy—their governing council referred to as the "Council of Fire" and their constitution referred to as "The Great Roots of Peace." In other words, the sovereign status of the American Indian tribes was in place prior to the arrival of European colonists and is solidly lodged in history.

Indian sovereign status was reflected, then and now, through a legal instrument referred to as a "treaty." Treaties between the colonials (soon to be the United States of America) and the Indians came about as a result of wars between them. As American settlers appropriated to themselves more and more Indian land, fighting between the nations occurred. Some treaties were ratified by the U.S. Congress, some were not, and some treaties and land settlements were the result of executive orders of the president of the United States. One of the primary terms and conditions specified in most treaties was the understanding and provision that large amounts of Indian land were to be exchanged for government services to the Indians and peaceful relations between them. It was the treaty process that established the unique political status and nation-to-nation relationship Indian tribes presently possess with the United States. Many treaties between the U.S. government and Indian tribes continue to be honored and enforceable to this day.

Another important aspect of U.S. government relations with Indian Tribes was changing federal Indian policy. The first federal policy era, referred to above, was the Treaty Period of 1789–1871, when treaties were entered into with the Indians. Following this came the Reservation Period of 1871–1887, when the United States removed tribes from their aboriginal lands onto reserved sections of land called reservations. Next came the Allotment Period of 1887–1934, during which time the United

States attempted to break up reservation land holdings by assigning plots of land from 40 to 160 acres to individual Indians considered heads of households. The next period was called the Reorganization Period of 1934–1953, during which time the U.S. government attempted to establish governments for tribes resembling their forms of government. The Howard-Wheeler Act mandated establishment of tribal governments with constitutions and governing bodies, soon to be called tribal councils.

Ironically, following this period to reorganize tribes came the Termination Period of 1953–1970, a time when the federal government disenfranchised and disestablished many tribes. In 1954, under the prodding of Senator Arthur Watkins of Utah, Chairman of the Subcommittee on Indian Affairs of the Senate Interior and Insular Affairs Committee, a number of termination bills for specific tribes were enacted. The bills attempted to integrate Indians into mainstream American society. They proved to be of benefit to land-grabbing non-Indians but a miserable failure resulting in poverty for those tribes terminated, with the loss of thousands of acres of land on the part of individual Indians and their tribes.

The Self-Determination Era of 1970–1994 recovered some of the losses of the previous period. Under the Self-Determination policy, federally recognized Indian tribes were granted the authority to plan, develop, and operate (through contract with appropriate federal agencies) programs serving Indian people. The policy proved to be a refreshing change to prior oppressive policies and set the stage for the next and current policy mandate, the Self-Government policy. The Self-Government policy is a refinement of the previous policy and provides additional authority to tribal governments to prioritize and configure their own appropriations to meet their needs.

Writing this volume is important to the State of Utah, not only because it recognizes and validates the history of the various Indian tribes but also because it makes this information available to schools, libraries, and the general public. A written history including Indian perspective and the blending of Indian oral traditions and experiences with non-Indian written accounts is a major contribution to all people. This text provides a glimpse into traditional Native American life prior to the coming of the pioneers, into experiences of first contact with the white man, and into personal family perspectives, the ravages of war, and mistreatment of Indians by the pioneers and by the state and federal governments. It is apparent, not all has been well for Indians in the history of Utah.

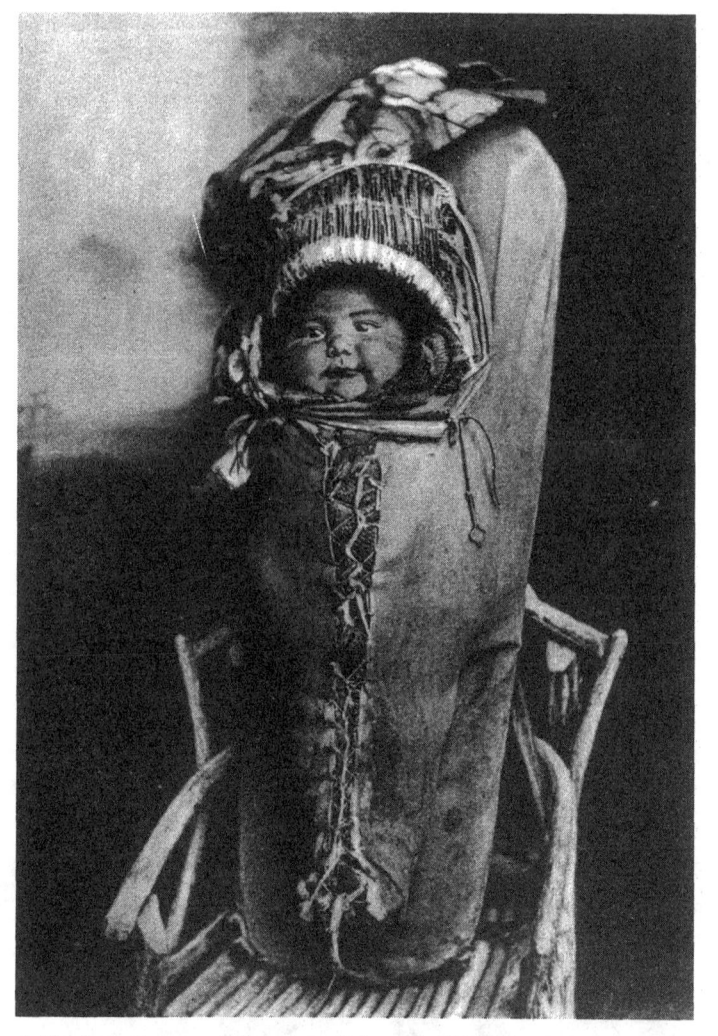

A Ute baby in a traditional cradleboard. (USHS)

All Utah tribes have experienced their moment of great suffering. For the Shoshone, it was, as mentioned above, the Bear River Massacre of 1863. For the Utah Utes, it was forced removal in 1865 from their beloved Utah Valley into the arid Uinta Basin. For the Goshutes, it was broken promises and removal from traditional sacred lands. For the Navajo and Paiute, it was countless skirmishes with Mormon settlers in southern Utah. The Paiute suffered again late in their history, when, dur-

Hoskaninni Begay and his grandson photographed in 1939. Hoskaninni Begay was the son of Hoskaninni (Haashkéneinii), who crossed the San Juan River in 1863 to escape the round-up of Navajos and the Long Walk to Fort Sumner in eastern New Mexico. (USHS)

ing the 1950s, they were terminated from federal assistance and their reservation lands were taken from them.

In many ways, some of Utah's Indian tribes continue to suffer from traumas of the past. The Shoshone have not recovered from the Bear River Massacre; they continue to suffer from limited land-base, scattered and substandard home sites, intertribal political strife, poverty, poor health, and ineffective educational programs for their children. The Confederate Tribes of Goshute Indians continue to struggle with lands having limited natural resources. The Skull Valley Goshute have encountered external and internal conflict and strong resistance to proposed development on their lands. The Paiute continue to struggle to restore much of what was lost following the termination era. The Ute continue to experience difficulty adapting to complexities and sophistication required in developing their natural resources. The Navajos along with the other tribes face issues of development and equity. This history seeks to restore hope and healing to all Utah tribes and to promote improved relationships with their non-Indian neighbors.

This text is organized to provide the reader with information and themes which include creation stories, traditional Indian beliefs, oral history, first non-Indian contacts, the Indian experience, historic events of significance, and present-day issues impacting Indian tribes. Authors include Dennis Defa, with the assistance of Milton Hooper (Goshute) on the Goshute tribal history; Clifford Duncan (Northern Ute) on the Ute tribal history; Ron Holt and Gary Tom (Paiute) on the Paiute tribal history; Robert McPherson, with the assistance of Mary Jane Yazzie (Ute Mountain Ute) on the White Mesa Ute history; Nancy Cottrell Maryboy (Dine') and David H. Begay (Dine') on the Navajo (Dine') history; and Mae Parry (Northwestern Shoshone) on the Northwestern Shoshone history. We respectfully honor and acknowledge the contributions of Vyrie Gray (Goshute), who passed away prior to the completion of this publication. Thanks to those who assisted in other ways includes Janet Smoak and Kent Powell of the Utah State Historical Society and Richard Firmage for the design and editing of this volume.

Presently, Utah Indian tribes are faced with many challenges in the areas of economic development, natural resources, unemployment, education, health, environment, high crime, and substance abuse. Successful tribal governments will invest in developing human resources as much as in developing natural resources, for many of the problems identified above have a direct effect upon family, children, and the elderly in particular. Regarding the future, tribes that are wise will maintain sovereign

political status with the U.S. Congress and both federal and state governments. They will put forth long-range planning strategies for tribal programs and services, and initiate intertribal partnerships with other public groups and the private sector. They will strengthen relationships with state governments and put into effect policies building upon those relationships. The political relationships, decisions, and agreements will influence effectiveness in deliberations and interactions with state and federal agencies on behalf of their constituents.

Many Indian people have long believed that through nature, with its expression and glory, all other connections are made—the vital link with our true God, our Creator. The ancient people of this land maintained this connection with nature. The teachings of these people, as, for example, through the Hopi prophecy above, demonstrated this vital link. This wisdom is evident in the warnings of the Hopi traditionalists, descendants of the Anasazi, who urge us to keep life simple and remember two things: Love one another, and love the earth.

These ancient prophesies may be significant to modern times—to non-Indian people as well as to Indian people. Perhaps the wisdom of ancient prophesies will provide direction for the future. From the ancient high plains symbolism (found in the "Medicine Wheel") to the Hopi prophesy, perhaps a new direction can be found for all of mankind.

And so it is with this newfound wisdom and enlightenment from the ancients that we look forward to this new millennium. Once we discover that we truly are brothers and sisters—that the world is one community for all—we can begin to discover our true essence, our beauty, and what we, as enlightened beings, truly have to offer. It is when our world becomes safe that we can begin to develop our true potential and make this world into heaven on earth.

In closing, I think it is important to note the most important legacy of the Utah American Indians: Despite widespread attempts at genocide and often full-scale extermination campaigns against us by the dominant culture, "we continue to exist." We continue to live as a people with a distinct and beautiful culture, worldview, and way of life. "We are still here! And we do not plan to be leaving … not real soon anyway."

—Forrest S. Cuch (Ute)

A History of Utah's American Indians

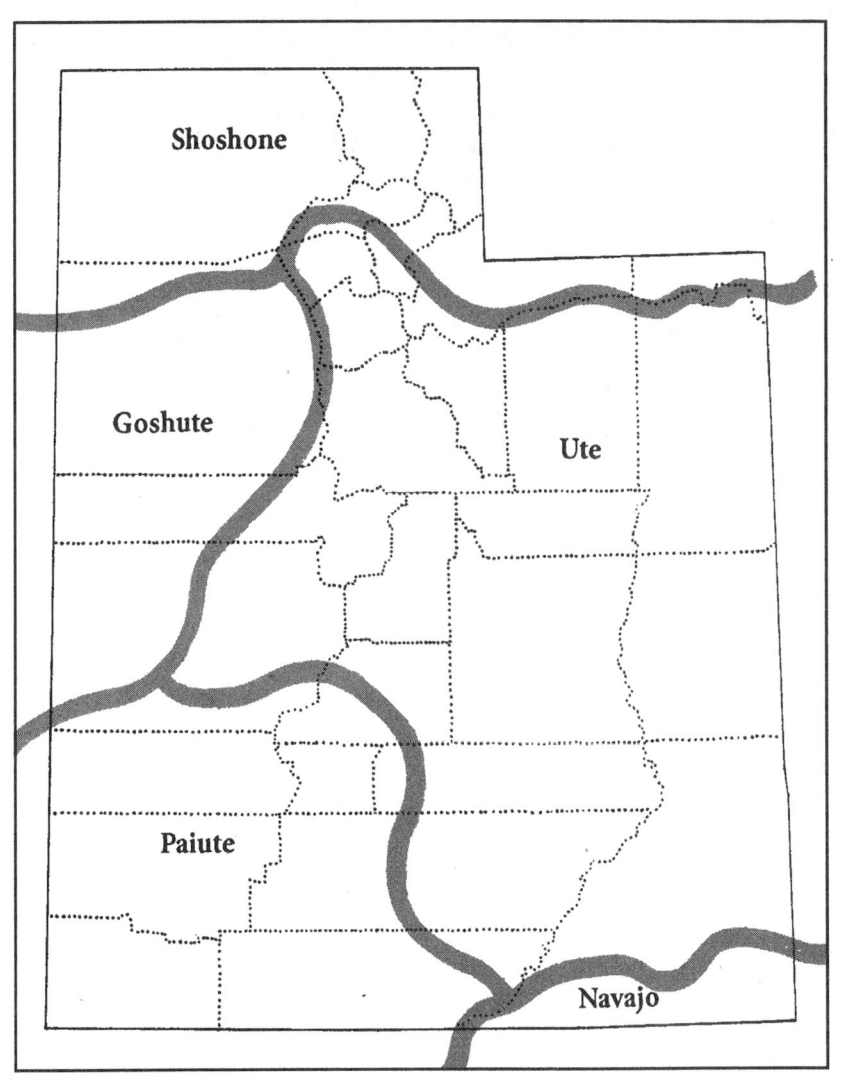

Map showing approximate general territory of Utah's Indian tribes just prior to white settlement in 1847. Note that not only are boundaries inexact but also there was some interaction and use of adjacent territories by members of virtually all tribes.

Setting the Stage:
Native America Revisited

Robert S. McPherson

The writing of Native American history can be said to have started when Christopher Columbus first waded ashore on San Salvador Island in the Caribbean. It has continued ever since. What preceded his arrival—the prehistoric phase of Native Americans—has generally been left to archaeologists and anthropologists to decipher and explain from physical remains. The initial contact, post-contact, and contemporary phases are the realm of historians, who write in keeping with longstanding conventions of their own trade. In both instances, facts, dates, and interpretation generally are presented from an Anglo American perspective that has evolved over centuries.

What this has meant to the Indian people is that rarely, if ever, has their view been predominant, if it has even been known. Calvin Martin, a noted Indian historian, put it this way: "We presume to document and interpret the history of a people whose perception of the world for the most part eludes us, whose behavior, as a result, is enigmatic.... To ignore the Indian thoughtworld is to continue writing about ourselves to ourselves."[1] This has been especially true until recently.

Within the last twenty-five years, there has been a perceptible shift in the tide of writing that now insists on a more balanced treatment of the Indians' view of events. However, this is at times a difficult thing to achieve. Native Americans in the past have been slow to come forth with their own story for a number of reasons, including fear of retribution, a desire to leave the past behind, reticence to speak as an individual for a group, and the belief that certain events are sacred, personal, and not to be divulged for public view. Whatever the reason, when one considers how much has been produced about these people, there are relatively few tribal histories written or sanctioned by Native Americans.[2]

In the following pages, the reader will encounter six tribal histories composed either by Native Americans or their representatives. Each au-

Part of Chief Washakie's village encamped near South Pass in the Wind River Mountains. Photo taken by William Henry Jackson in 1870 while he was with the Hayden Survey. (Utah State Historical Society—USHS)

thor has used both written and oral sources to tell the story of the tribes living within the boundaries of Utah. The tribal histories are complex, as they speak of persistence and change, the past and the present, diversity and unity. What will be recognized early on is that there are common threads woven throughout each tribal account; but these may assume a different cultural pattern. Thus, each group enjoys a distinct identity.

Among the most prominent of these threads is a religious worldview that ties these people of Utah to a living, sentient creation. Their world is one of power, filled with holy beings who either help or hinder those who interact with them. Unlike most Anglo Americans, who separate themselves from a world they divide into animate and inanimate objects, the Indian worldview sees the land as an interconnected whole— with rocks, trees, animals, water, clouds, and a host of other participants in a circle of life.[3] Human relationships exist with non-human entities, bonded by a mutual respect for the role each plays as a part of nature.

An example provided by the Navajo illustrates this type of connection between the land and its creatures, a characteristic viewpoint shared by all of Utah's tribes. To the Navajo, deer were animals treated and hunted with respect. They were controlled by certain gods who made them avail-

Navajos taking sheep to water in Monument Valley. (USHS)

able for man's use. Before leaving for the hunt, men participated in a sweat bath to purify themselves and to encourage the holy beings to give them the best meat. Ritualized behavior circumscribed the hunt, making the act of killing a deer a sacred event recognized as good by both the animal and the gods.

The disposal of entrails and other parts not used by the hunter was also treated in a ceremonially prescribed manner to insure that new deer would be plentiful. Failure to do so could affect the amount of rainfall, since Navajo people believed that deer were in close contact with the holy beings who controlled moisture. Because deer lived in the mountains, they were protected by thunder and lightning; their antlers were not brought home since they attracted electrical storms; and, because they fed on sacred, medicinal plants, to eat their meat was to ingest medicine.[4] This type of thinking and practice is pervasive throughout traditional Native American life.

The roots of this worldview, so different from that of most Euro-Americans, lies embedded in religious beliefs. In order to understand how these Native American practices began, one must return to the creative period of time, when the earth was "soft" and creatures talked and acted like humans. The gods were close, visible, and involved, establishing the laws and forming the world for the People—the term many dif-

ferent groups used to identify themselves, using, of course, the appropriate word in their own language. Rivers and canyons, mountains and deserts, lakes and caves took their place in an orderly universe recognized and utilized by the tribes. Plants, insects, fish, and wildlife made their homes under the direction of the gods. The territory in which these creatures lived was bounded by familiar landmarks given to the bands and tribes by the holy beings.

A survey of any Utah map quickly testifies to the intensity of this relationship between the land and its early inhabitants. The state's name itself comes from the Ute tribe. Other Ute names on maps include Wasatch (signifying a mountain pass or low place); Oweep (grass) Creek; Cuberant (long) Lake; and Ouray, Peteetneet, and Santaquin (Ute leaders). From the Paiutes come Panguitch (fish), Parowan (harmful water), Paunsaugunt (place of beavers), and Parunuweap Canyon (roaring water). The Goshutes added Oquirrh (wooded or shining) Mountains, Onaqui (salt) Mountains, and Tintic (a Goshute leader). Both Washakie and Wanship were Shoshone leaders, while the Navajo have provided Cha (beaver) Canyon, Oljato (moon water), Nasja (owl) Creek, and Peshlikai (silver) Fork, among many other names on the land.[5]

To the Indians of Utah, these were places for hunting, fishing, gathering, and worship. They were sites where the People could contact the supernatural through ceremonies to invoke protection and sustain life through a holy means. A covenant based upon respect for these unseen powers, coupled with an intimate knowledge of the land, motivated the People to live within the guidance given them during the time of the myths.

This word "myth" holds a variety of meanings central to understanding the difference between the Native American and Anglo views of the world. To the former, the word defines a truth that is real—sometimes tangible, sometimes intangible—but always considered to be a powerful force in explaining why things are the way they are. Because this explanation is derived from a religious belief, faith and knowledge are mutually supportive in their explanations of physical and social relations. Victor Turner, an anthropologist who has studied the force of myths in society, calls them "the powerhouses of culture." They define and guide people through the uncertainties of life.

The general understanding of myths by most non-Indian Americans is far different. Although biblical teachings are prominent in Anglo culture, there is a far greater dependence by most people on scientific methodology and practices to explain the physical world. This has led

white people to view myths of other peoples as amusing tales without true substance, powerless ramblings or fairytales about the supernatural. Superstition is considered to be the basis of myth. Factual proof, recorded events, and material culture—although intermixed by many with Christian dogma—have been a much more comfortable means of explaining the past for general Western culture. Thus, truth is considered to be something objectively discoverable through logic and observation. This stands in contrast to the Indian's view of truth as a preexisting framework, partially revealed in myth to help interpret phenomena. This dichotomy in thinking has characterized relations between native peoples and Euro-Americans throughout the Americas, including Utah.

What, then, does this non-native worldview say about the evolution of cultural development in Utah? Archaeologists and anthropologists have sketched a fairly complete picture of what they believe happened before the historic tribes appeared. Although there is disagreement on dates and the interpretation of some factual evidence, there is general agreement among researchers on the sequence of events. A very brief synopsis of this analysis of prehistory follows.

Portions of the eastern Great Basin, western Rocky Mountains, and northern Colorado Plateau, which comprise the state of Utah, were the setting for the Archaic cultures that lasted from roughly 9,000 or 8,000 B.C. to the beginning of the Christian era (A.D. 1). Although there were climatological variations during this time, including more water and vegetation than are now found in the state, much of the semi-desert environment as it now appears was similar at the start of the archaeological record at the end of the last Ice Age, around 8,000 B.C. Over this long period of time, Native American groups have survived in an austere environment that required an intimate knowledge of the land and its resources. As Jesse D. Jennings, noted scholar of Utah's prehistory, said: "The key to understanding prehistoric Great Basin human adaptation lies in the recognition of a myriad of microenvironments.... Instead of being the uniformly uninviting desert so often visualized, the Great Basin consists of hundreds of special and often rich environments where a widely varying mix of desired plant and animal species was available for harvest."[6]

The first period of human habitation in this environment (from roughly 9000–7500 B.C.) is known from scanty remains preserved in rock shelters such as Danger, Smith Creek, and Deer Creek Caves. Most of these sites were located on the margins of lakes and sources of water, some of which have since disappeared. Knife blades, projectile points,

Paiute Indians living on the Kaibab Plateau playing the game of "Ni-aung-pi-kai" or "Kill the Bone," now referred to as "The Hand Game." Photograph taken by John K. Hillers of the Powell Expedition sometime between 1871 and 1875. (USHS)

milling stones, and fire pits indicate a hunting-and-gathering lifestyle, much of which focused around sources of water.[7]

The next period (7500–4000 B.C.) is characterized by a more diverse use of ecological zones, ranging from high to low altitudes, for hunting and gathering. Seasonal occupation of various areas and a greater variety in diet resulted. Twined basketry, grinding stones, animal nets, and the spear thrower (atlatl) with dart were some of the simple but effective tools invented and made to work the environment. Excavations at Hogup Cave indicate how effective this lifeway was. The remains of four species of large mammals (deer, antelope, mountain sheep, and elk), thirty-two species of small mammals, and thirty-four species of birds have been

found there, indicating that they were part of the diet of the cave's inhabitants. Add to this thirty-six different types of plants, and one can see a widening variety in the diet of these early inhabitants of the land.[8]

The final phase of this Desert Archaic Culture lasted from about 4000 B.C. to the beginning of the Christian era and is characterized by a large expansion of people into peripheral areas in the uplands and a decreased emphasis on living near lakes and basin areas. The diet of these people became more restricted in both plant and animal varieties, indicating a reduction in marshland habitat that forced these Native Americans to utilize other areas of the environment. At the same time, the bow and arrow replaced the atlatl, increasing their efficiency in hunting.[9]

But there were even greater changes on the horizon, starting around 400 B.C. in the eastern Great Basin—the beginning of horticultural societies. The raising of corn, and later beans and squash, now offered an alternative to the more traditional hunting and gathering activities. From a strictly utilitarian perspective, domesticated plants increased the carrying capacity of the land. People could now better determine the amount of food available for their use and, if environmental conditions cooperated, could harvest not only what was needed immediately but enough to store for the future. As with many cultures in Native America, a slow revolution in lifestyles occurred, giving rise to a variety of sedentary cultures.

One of the most impressive prehistoric cultures in America was that of the Anasazi, found in the San Juan River drainage of the Four Corners region and extending into southwestern Utah and southern Nevada.[10] This culture appeared in approximately 1000 B.C. and descendants are believed to live today in the historic pueblos along the Rio Grande and in the villages of Hopi, Zuni, and Acoma. The prehistoric ancestral pueblos have been generally subdivided into two major categories—Basketmaker (early and late) and Pueblo (Periods I, II, and III; examples of the later Periods IV and V are not present in Utah). This archaeological classification scheme is based on changes in technology, art, and subsistence patterns.

The relationship between the late Archaic and the early Basketmaker groups is unclear. Early Basketmaker life developed a technology centered on shallow pithouses, and it included circular storage pits, skillfully crafted baskets and sandals, feather and fur robes, and a greatly expanded tool kit. The people made their homes and stored their food in the rock overhangs of the canyon floors or amid the juniper and pinyon groves of the higher lands above. Their lifestyle still reflected a partial

Chief Kanosh lived from 1821 until 1884 and is buried
in the town of Kanosh, Millard County. (USHS)

orientation to the hunter-gatherer tradition in that the people seasonally
moved to various sites to harvest their foods (although they returned to
their villages to care for their crops), continued to use the atlatl for hunting, and foraged for wild plants as a supplement to their main diet of
corn and squash. Bell-shaped underground chambers and shallow slab-
lined storage cists located in protective rock alcoves held not only food
supplies but also the Anasazi dead.

The Late Basketmaker Period started around A.D. 450 and is distin-
guished from the earlier phase by the introduction of beans, stone axes,
pottery, and the use of larger, more elaborate pithouses with internal
storage facilities and antechambers located to the south or east of the
main room. These houses may be found alone, in small clusters, or in
groups of a dozen or more dwellings. Other innovations during this phase
were the appearance of pottery—gray utility and black-on-white painted
ware—as well as the bow and arrow to replace the atlatl.

By A.D. 750 the Anasazi reached the next stage of development, that
of Pueblo I. As the name suggests, there were some significant changes in
their dwellings, although elements from earlier phases persisted. For in-

Chief Washakie of the Shoshone Tribe is seated in the center of this group of Indian leaders. (USHS)

stance, the Anasazi now built their homes above ground in connected, rectangular blocks of rooms, using rocks and jacal (a framework of woven saplings and sticks packed with mud) for construction materials. One or more deep pithouses have been found in each of the building clusters and may have served a ceremonial function. These rooms were equipped with a ventilator shaft that brought in fresh air, deflected it around an upright stone placed between the shaft and the firepit, and then evacuated the smoke by the entryway in the roof, a technique utilized by the Anasazi for the remainder of their stay in the Four Corners region. In Pueblo II times this structure became the common kiva.

The Pueblo II phase started about A.D. 900 and lasted for approximately the next 250 years. A change in climate in the general region provided an increase in precipitation, higher water tables that affected springs and seeps, and temperatures more conducive to agriculture. The Anasazi reacted by moving from clusters of populations in strategic locations to a far-ranging decentralization. Satellite worksites and living sites fanned out from the larger concentrations of people. At no previous time had there been as many settlements spread over so much of the land.

The final stage of Anasazi occupation in Utah, Pueblo III, occurred between about A.D. 1150 and 1300. The general pattern of events is characterized by a shrinking or gathering of the dispersed communities into a series of larger villages in areas that were more defensible. Large communal plazas, tower clusters around springs at the heads of canyons, more carefully crafted building techniques, and decreased regional trade relations are indications that Anasazi society was undergoing rapid and significant changes.

Archaeologists argue about what caused these cultural shifts and the subsequent abandonment of the area by the Anasazi. Some people place the cause on environmental factors such as prolonged drought, cooler temperatures, severe arroyo cutting, and depleted soils. Others suggest that the area was invaded by nomadic hunters and gatherers, ancestors or precursors of the historic Ute, Paiute, and Navajo peoples. Pueblo mythology points to internal strife and the religious need to purify the group through migration and pilgrimage to a new land in the south. No single explanation satisfactorily answers all of the questions; however, by A.D. 1300 the Anasazi had left the San Juan River drainage area and moved south to places coinciding with their descendants' present locations.

A less spectacular, but just as interesting, group of Native Americans called the Fremont lived in much of southwestern, central, and northern Utah contemporaneously with the Anasazi.[11] Their origin, shrouded in the mists of the past, does not necessarily suggest they were close relatives of their neighbors the Anasazi. Some archaeologists suggest an influence by the Mogollon people farther south in New Mexico and Arizona, while others believe the Fremont sprang from indigenous roots in the Great Basin. The earliest dated sites discovered thus far are in northern Utah. Certainly those who lived closer to the Anasazi adopted many of their architectural, economic, and social patterns. As one moves farther north, there appears to be a general decreased dependence on farming and an increased reliance on hunting and gathering of foodstuffs.

This mobile lifestyle did not encourage the same florescence in the making of fine polychrome pottery, clustering of homesites, or intricate social and religious relations suggested by Anasazi ruins. Small settlements, rarely much larger than twenty homesites, varied in construction from pithouses made of wood and dirt to slab-lined or adobe homes. Many of these were tied to seasonal use.

These Fremont structures reflected these people's ties to their environment. Food gathering depended upon the resources of a specific area

Utes dancing. (Marriott Library, University of Utah—U of U)

(such as marsh, mountain, desert, and basin habitats), indicating a people willing to travel and not totally dependent on corn. Regional variations in these patterns have led to a sub-classification system that includes southwestern Utah, central Utah, Great Salt Lake, Uinta Basin, and eastern Utah groups. (The dividing line between the Fremont and Anasazi in southeastern Utah generally follows the Colorado River.) Like the Anasazi, the Fremont culture ceased to exist in an identifiable form around the same time—A.D. 1300.

One question often raised is what type of relationship, if any, did these two groups have with the historic tribes that soon filled the vacuum left by their departure. The Navajo have the most fully developed body of lore that outlines their interaction with the Anasazi. Briefly, the Navajo speak of their relations with the Anasazi in the worlds beneath this one; relations which continued after the People emerged into this, the Glittering World. Friendly associations eventually soured, giving rise to a period of conflict that ended in the supernatural destruction of the Anasazi because they fell into disfavor with the gods. Anasazi ruins and artifacts are now generally avoided by Navajos because of the powers contained within. However, some Navajo clans today claim ancestral ties with this prehistoric culture.[12]

Chief Ta-va-puts of the Uintah Utes, photographed by John K. Hillers of the Powell expedition 1873–74. (USHS)

The Utes, Paiutes, Goshutes, and Shoshone, on the other hand, show respect for the Fremont peoples and their sites, and some claim a vague relationship; but they do not have as complex a knowledge and teachings about them as the Navajo do about the Anasazi. This is one area where further research can reveal a Native American perspective not found in the archaeological record.

One reason that these tentative ties have not been pursued more actively is that there is still disagreement about whether these historic cultures were ever contemporaneous with the Anasazi. Language studies have been used to provide part of this answer. With the exception of the Navajo, who will be discussed shortly, all of the tribes in Utah belong to the large Uto-Aztecan language family and are part of its Numic-speak-

ing branch. Linguists place this group's place of origin in southern California, and most agree that by A.D. 1000 some Numic speakers were roaming into the Great Basin area of Nevada and Utah. By the year 1300 they had spread into Colorado.[13]

What may be perceived as a fairly straightforward migration of people, however, is not that simple.[14] In southern California at present there are three branches within the Numic family: Western, Central, and Southern, represented by the Mono, Panamint, and Kawaiisu people,respectively. Even though these people live in close proximity, their languages have some significant variation. Each of these linguistic branches, in fact, is closely related to those languages of tribes living in the Great Basin and Colorado Plateau—a distance of more than one thousand miles. Thus, the Panamint in California share close linguistic ties with the Shoshone and Goshute, the Kawaiisu with the Utes and Southern Paiutes, and the Mono Indians with the Northern Paiutes. According to Uto-Aztecan linguist Brian Stubbs, "This shows that the three groups (Western, Central, and Southern Numic) first separated in Southern California, then their language changed separately for a few centuries before some of each of the three groups later spread out into the Great Basin."[15]

How much difference in speech is there between these three Numic branches? Perhaps the best way for a non-linguist to understand this is through a comparison. Within one of the branches, say between the Southern Paiute and Southern Ute, there would be differences in dialect and rate of speech, but generally, members of the two tribes would be conversant, perhaps comparable to an American and an Englishman trying to communicate. If one compares languages of different branches, for instance the Southern Utes with the Shoshone, problems of understanding increase dramatically. Difficulty in comprehension is now similar to that of an American attempting to understand a Dutch person (both languages belonging to the same Germanic branch of the Indo-European language family). Thus, each Numic-speaking group faced a linguistic challenge if it ventured too far afield from its home territory.

The Navajo were in a totally different situation, belonging to another language family—the Athabascan. As will be pointed out in their chapter, the Navajo are believed to have come from Canada and Alaska to the north and to have arrived in the Southwest either at the same time, or, more likely, shortly after the Numic-speaking people. In terms of history and culture, they saw themselves in opposition with their neighbors the Utes, and to a lesser degree, the Paiutes. With a few exceptions, the

Utes were considered traditional enemies and the Paiutes friends and a source of labor. The main body of Navajos generally lived south of Utah in the future states of New Mexico and Arizona. Thus, they did not maintain strong relations with any of the other Numic-speaking tribes.

By the time of first contact with Europeans, all six of Utah's tribes were living in their general historic locations. This is not to suggest that there would be no major shifts once the white man exerted force—take, for example, the push of Northern Utes from Colorado into the Uinta Basin—but only that the tribes had adopted a specific area they considered to be theirs. As the prehistory phase of Utah's story closes, its written history opens. This is where many of the following tribal histories start.

Each group has its own separate narrative to share. Before looking at the individual stories, one might do well to consider some of the major trends in Utah Indian history and compare them to what has happened in the broader context of Native Americans in United States history. Relevant questions include: Just how similar or how different was the Native American experience in Utah? What factors caused any differences to exist? And what lessons can be derived from the historical record?

The Spanish were the first Europeans to have a significant impact on the tribes of Utah. Their physical presence was limited to an occasional entrada of exploration from their centers to the south, the expeditions of Juan Maria Antonio Rivera (1765) and Fray Francisco Atanasio Domínguez and Fray Silvestre Velez de Escalante (1776) being the most notable. From these expeditions came the first known written descriptions of Native American groups living within the future state. To historians, these accounts are invaluable.

But the Spaniards' most important contribution to the Indian people came in the form of the horse. The dispersion of these animals began in the early 1600s, spreading out from New Mexico to the north and east in an arc that first introduced them onto the Great Plains and then into the Great Basin. By the early 1700s, all of the tribes in Utah had some access to the horse, some adopting it as a means of transportation, others accepting it as a source of food.

In some instances, the horse became a dividing force between various groups that had heretofore shared the same language, culture, and values. Take, for instance, the Southern Paiute and the Southern Ute or the Goshute and the Shoshone. Both pairs of Native American tribes were closely related linguistically and shared a comparable technology. The big difference between the peoples was in where they lived and what

that environment could support. To the Paiute and Goshute, who hunted and gathered over a more austere territory, the horse appeared as a tasty addition in the food quest. Indeed, in some instances the horse competed for the same plant foods utilized by these people, and so they would want to eliminate the competitor.[16] Also, Paiute and Goshute lands in southwestern and west-central Utah did not provide sufficient grass to sustain large horse herds, while the kinds of animals that were hunted generally did not lend themselves to a chase on horseback. Compare this to the situation of the Utes and Northern Shoshone, who hunted herds of buffalo and deer and who could draw upon the richer resources of the mountains and valleys of eastern and northern Utah and the southern portion of Idaho. They were able to adopt a lifestyle more like that of Plains Indians—a tepee-living, buffalo-hunting, horse-wealthy warrior society.

The differences between the Numic-speaking groups may have been accentuated by the introduction of the horse, but nothing encouraged large-scale warfare between the groups. True, at times the Shoshone fought the Utes and Paiutes, and the Utes preyed upon the Paiutes as a source of slaves to trade to the Spaniards and Mexicans, but most of the traditional enemies of these groups lay to the north and east of the Rockies, home of the Blackfeet, Arapaho, Comanche, Sioux, and other Plains tribes. Relations within the confines of Utah were usually peaceful, with a number of areas serving as general use among groups for hunting, gathering, and winter encampments.[17]

In 1821, newly independent Mexico inherited from Spain a vast territory that stretched from California to Colorado, encompassing the future state of Utah. For the next twenty years, Mexico would hold title to the land but do very little with it other than to allow trading expeditions into the territory and cast a wary eye on the influx of American mountain men traversing streams in search of beaver. By 1830 the Old Spanish Trail connected Santa Fe, New Mexico, to Los Angeles, California, the main trail entering the state near Monticello, then passing through the future locales of Moab and Green River and Sevier Valley before exiting to the south in the Cedar City region. For Native Americans this 1,100-mile route brought trading groups traveling through the valleys of the Colorado Plateau and over large stretches of the Great Basin. It served as a conduit that introduced desirable trade goods. At this point in their history, the Indians were in control of their destiny and could selectively choose what they accepted from white men. This, however, was about to change.

In 1847, a year before the area that is now Utah went from Mexican control to that of the United States, a large contingent of Mormon pioneers entered the Salt Lake Valley. Up until this time, the region had been a place through which white travelers passed but in which few remained. Now, this valley, which had been shared by both the Shoshone and Utes, came under the plow of a determined lot of people—members of the Church of Jesus Christ of Latter-day Saints. What followed will be discussed in the chapters of this book. It should be asked at this point, however, if this experience was different for the Indians of Utah, or was it simply a continuation of the pattern of the westward movement of white immigrants encountered by other tribes across the nation.

Historians are mixed in their response. Certainly there were similarities in what and how some events unfolded. For instance, once the settlement process took on a feverish pace, its impact on Native American hunting and gathering practices in the territory soon proved disastrous. In a region like the Great Basin, where resources such as grass, water, and arable land were often restricted to relatively few locations, it was only natural that both Indian and settler would utilize them. In the broadest sense, the contest for resources between the two cultures was no different from what the Powhatan confederacy faced with the first colony of Jamestown, Virginia, during the early 1600s.

One certainly cannot miss the disruption to the native cultures in the future state of Utah. Everything seemed to conspire against them, from the cattle and horses that destroyed traditional food sources, to the loss of lands important in economic and religious practices, to the intense cultural biases that colored their daily relations with the newcomers. And, as with other Indian groups, ranging from the Pequot in Connecticut to the Sioux at Wounded Knee, the Utah Native Americans would share some dark, bloody pages of history. The 1863 massacre of some 250 Northwestern Shoshone encamped on the Bear River (just over the border in Idaho) testifies to that.[18]

The results of this frontier period were also similar to what had transpired elsewhere. The Native Americans lost their land, were placed on reservations, and then were either ignored or pressured into accepting the tenets of white civilization. This also fostered a mixed outcome— some people choosing to walk the white man's road while others were determined to remain true to their traditional culture. In both instances, these paths led to prolonged periods of social, economic, political, and cultural disruption in the lives of individuals.

Yet, there is another side to the Utah Indians' story—some things

Ute Indians at Whiterocks posed for this photograph with their shinny sticks used in a Ute game somewhat like field hockey. (USHS)

that make it unique in the annals of frontier history. The most notable difference is the presence of large numbers of members of the Church of Jesus Christ of Latter-day Saints (Mormons) and their settlement of the Great Basin and Colorado Plateau region. In one sense, the Mormons fled problems in their own larger society by moving to a place they considered free for the taking; then, either intentionally or unintentionally, they created an even more disheartening set of problems for the people already living here. It did not take long to set this process in motion.

Before looking at the events, one should consider certain beliefs of the Mormons. A great deal has been written about the Book of Mormon with its suggested ties between the scriptural "Lamanites" and the Indians encountered on the frontier.[19] From a purely ideological point of view, the Mormons believed that the Indians were a remnant of a people who fell out of grace with God, were given a dark skin as a sign of their spiritual standing, and who now lived in an unfortunate condition awaiting restoration to an enlightened state.

The church's position was that it would serve as the vehicle by which these people would be raised both spiritually and in this world. Although it was patronizing from a cultural perspective, these beliefs led to the oft-quoted sound economic Indian policy of Brigham Young that it was

Paiute Indians at Koosharem. (USHS)

"Cheaper to feed the Indians than to fight them."[20] Assistance, not resistance, would set the tone of relationships. Mormon men called and appointed as special "Lamanite missionaries" would learn the language, work with different Native American groups, convert, and then lead them into the fold of Christ's church. That was the plan. What happened in practice was often at odds with this and was often met by cultural and armed resistance.

Unlike many areas of western settlement, Utah, in its earliest stages, was engulfed by a systematic flow of pioneers who looked to a central organization for leadership. The U.S. Census of 1850, taken three years after the Mormons arrived and each decade thereafter, shows just how efficient this migration was. In 1850 the white population was 11,380; subsequent ten-year periods showed dramatic increases—to 40,273 (a 254 percent increase) in 1860; 86,786 (116 percent) in 1870; 143,963 (66 percent) in 1880; and 210,779 (46 percent) in 1890.[21] In 1847, as the advancing frontier moved to Utah in the guise of the first Mormon wagon train, there was an estimated Indian population in the future state of 20,000.[22] While these demographic estimates on both sides are dwarfed by comparison to the influx of people during the California gold rush of 1848–49, for instance, the impact on the scarce resources was great, and Native American tribes in the Great Basin felt it. The resulting competition proved to be all too one-sided.

The movement into areas peripheral to Salt Lake City was just as inexorable and organized as the initial entrance of the Mormons into the territory. From 1847 to 1857 there were sixteen cities and towns established within territory claimed by at least one of the Utah tribes except the Navajo.[23] Some of these towns were established for a short time only, like the Elk Mountain Mission (Moab, 1855) which soon closed because of Ute hostility; but the Moab area was permanently settled some two decades later. The end result of this movement was to push the sinuous tentacles of civilization deep into the hunting and gathering grounds that had been utilized for hundreds of years by the native peoples. As their resources diminished, so too did their patience.

Mormon theology and practice joined together to form an Indian policy that allowed for variations in response from each tribe. The Paiutes, for example, would provide the largest number of Mormon converts and adopted children of all of the groups in the last half of the 1800s. The Utes, on the other hand, waged two costly wars—the Walker War (1853–54) and the Black Hawk War (1865–68)—that the struggling settlers could hardly afford. The Shoshone and Goshute followed similar forms of resistance, although lesser in their scope.

The Mormon response to these conflicts has received differing reviews from historians, some insisting that they were waged with a stern but fair justice, tempered with love and understanding. Others have argued that once the initial spark ignited the conflict, attitudes of destruction and hate found on every other frontier became prevalent in Utah— there was no difference between Mormons and non-Mormons when it came to meting out the white man's view of justice.[24] Readers will have to determine for themselves how they see this issue.

On a more positive side, there were times when Indians were actively sought as allies in answer to external pressures being placed on the Mormons. A prime example of this is found during the late 1850s, as the settlers of southwestern Utah became increasingly concerned with events associated with the Utah War and the advance of federal troops under Colonel Albert Sidney Johnston. As early as January 1858, Mormons met with Navajos, Utes, and Paiutes to form an alliance that could oppose federal forces if they entered southwestern Utah.[25] While nothing concrete came of these efforts, it does indicate an interesting reversal of traditional frontier practices. Certainly the earlier Mountain Meadows Massacre, in which Mormons and (perhaps) Paiutes killed more than one hundred California-bound emigrants in this region in 1857, could show the potential effectiveness of this type of alliance.[26]

There were, of course, more peaceful relations and a desire of many Mormons to help the Indians as their natural resources diminished. The creation of four farms in Millard, Sanpete, Utah, and Tooele Counties was designed to help move the Indians toward greater self-sufficiency as they shifted from their traditional economies. This project eventually proved to be ineffective, but it had the blessing of both federal and Mormon officials. As Utah came under increasing federal control, however, the quality of Indian relationships generally assumed the form of government relations found in other parts of the West during the nineteenth century.

In the 1870s, federal policy began to coalesce into a more consistent program of change for the Indian. The next sixty years were filled with government initiatives that first grouped and then moved Indians onto reservations with resident agents; divided various tribes among Christian denominations for proselyting purposes; encouraged farming or simple skilled labor as a way of life; sent children to reservation schools or boarding schools as part of a systematic attempt at acculturation to Western culture; and created a series of legal codes designed to erase elements of the native culture. Indian resentment, underground resistance, and a general failure of many government programs followed.

Of all of the federal programs of this era, the most damaging was the allotment period (1887–1933), during which the government attempted to replace tribal land ownership with individual ownership of land parcels and sell any remaining lands to non-Indian people. The vehicle by which this was to be done was the Dawes Severalty Act of 1887. As an incentive, Indian adults received somewhere between 40 and 640 acres, depending on the suitability of the land for farming. This property, supposedly, enjoyed a protected status that forbade its being sold by the individual for twenty-five years, at the end of which time the owner would be recognized as an American citizen. (Blanket citizenship for Native Americans was not received until 1924 under the Snyder Act.) In reality, however, large chunks of both tribal and individual lands soon were sold. One example will suffice. Between 1890 and 1933 the Uintah-Ouray Reservation lost 523,079 acres through the Dawes Act. Add to this another 973,777 acres removed in 1906 as part of the Uintah National Forest, and one can begin to understand why this era in history was so difficult for Native Americans.[27]

A respite from the loss of lands and assault on Utah Indian cultures occurred in 1934, when Commissioner of Indian Affairs John Collier introduced the Indian Reorganization Act. Among this bill's accomplish-

Connie Mack on the left with an unknown person. (U of U)

ments was the creation of tribal governments for self-determination; the stopping of the allotment process and the restoration of some of the lost lands; the development of reservation schools that encouraged pride in Indian culture; permission to return to Indian religious practices; an improvement in health care; and various programs to foster the growth of economic self-sufficiency. For most of the tribes in Utah, the Reorganization Act could not have been better news. The Navajo, however, proved to be an exception. This was not because of the above changes, some of which they wholeheartedly accepted, but because of the loss of their animals during the livestock reduction program. This overshadowed all else for them.

While the 1930s and 1940s brought increasing benefits to Utah's Indians in the form of greater recognition and more employment—especially associated with the war industries of World War II—the 1950s would swing the pendulum of change in the other direction. House Concurrent Resolution 108, passed in 1953 and championed by Senator Arthur V. Watkins of Utah, attempted to end the trust relationship between the federal government and the tribes, thus mainstreaming Native Americans into the dominant society. In Utah, these efforts translated into termination of the Southern Paiute Tribe and of the mixed-blood

Five Ute leaders on horseback. (U of U)

Uintah-Ouray Utes.[28] Other tribes were more successful in their struggle to fend off the loss of lands and community.

The foregoing discussion provides an overview of events to be encountered in the following chapters. Specific information about six different tribal experiences lies ahead, with each author emphasizing what he or she feels most important in these very complex histories. The final chapter will provide a survey of contemporary Native American events in Utah. But, in spite of the complexity and change, the reader will find the constant theme of the people's love for the land and their desire to maintain their cultural identity. These two ideas are inseparably intertwined, threading throughout these tribal histories.

The Northwestern Shoshone

Mae Parry

In early historic times the Shoshone Indians were a large nation of Indians who lived and traveled over an extensive territory that included parts of Idaho, Utah, Nevada, and Wyoming. Usually groups of extended families traveled together in varying numbers according to the season and the purpose of their gathering. Groups came together in larger encampments at different times during the year to trade, socialize, and sometimes for protection against enemies.[1] The Northwestern Shoshone Indians have always lived in northern Utah and southeastern Idaho. They were nomadic gatherers, hunters, and fishermen.

The Eastern Shoshone lived in the Wyoming area. Chief Washakie was recognized as the head chief among most of the Shoshone bands at the time of the entry of the Mormons into the Salt Lake Valley.[2] Washakie was known throughout the western country as one of the most able chiefs and had several sub-chiefs under his leadership, each of whom had between 300 and 400 Indians in their bands. Chief Pocatello was the leader over the Fort Hall area Shoshones. Other Northwestern Shoshones traveled under the leadership of Chief Sagwitch Timbimboo, Chief Bear Hunter, Chief Sanpitch, and Chief Lehi. They believed that a friendly relationship was possible with the pioneers. As a result, the Mormon pioneers and their leaders were initially welcomed into the Shoshone country. Warning of the Latter-day Saints' wagon train reached Great Basin area tribes in advance of their arrival into the Salt Lake Valley. The reports characterized the LDS as friendly and said that they were not known to have shot at Native Americans. On July 31, 1847, Shoshone tribal leaders, including Chiefs Sagwitch and Bear Hunter, met with LDS leader Brigham Young in Salt Lake City to advance their territorial claims.[3]

Shoshone Lifestyle

The Northwestern Shoshone traveled with the changing seasons. They

looked upon the earth not just as a place to live; in fact, they called the earth their mother—it was the provider of their livelihood. The mountains, streams, and plains stood forever, they said, and the seasons walked around annually. The Indians believed all things came from Mother Earth.

Linguistically, the Shoshone, Paiutes, and Bannocks are related under the term *Neme* (the People). Prior to white contact, the Neme groups formed small extended-family groupings that traveled extensively as semi-nomadic hunter-gatherers to survive in the harsh environment of the Great Basin desert. Horses, guns, white contact, and disease destroyed this social organization, resulting in more formal tribal identities and band loyalties. Pre-contact identities did exist according to the influence of horse ownership and resource use. What became the Northwestern Shoshone bands were part of those groups that had traveled largely on foot in a delicate balance of living off the land and that, when horses became available, joined the buffalo hunting groups in annual harvests. The expression *So-so-goi* means "those that travel on foot."[4] The old ones called the Shoshone by that name. Before horses became available to the Northwestern Shoshone, they used dogs and manpower to carry their belongings. Small children learned at an early age that they were expected to share in the burden of moving. They were given small bundles to carry on their backs. Later, Ute and Navajo Indians came into the Northwestern Shoshone territory for trading purposes, exchanging horses for skins and pelts.[5] With horses available, travois were adopted, which made moving and travel much easier. Mothers and grandmothers rode the horses. The children rode on top of the goods piled on the travois. Tepee poles served as poles for the travois. When the poles became too short from wear after being pulled new poles were cut.

Shelter for the Northwestern Shoshone Indians was provided by the use of tepees, green houses, and sometimes caves. The tepee cover typically was made from ten to twelve buffalo hides. The cover was stretched over from twenty to twenty-five poles erected in a cone shape. There was a smoke hole left at the top which had flaps designed to regulate the hole according to wind direction. The tepees were well ventilated and cool in the summer and, with a fire, were warm in the winter. On the floor of the tepees were backrests and bedrolls. Clothing, medicine bags, shields, bags, and other articles hung from poles. Tepees were decorated with drawings of animals, birds, or abstract designs. Great dreams or acts of bravery could be recalled in drawings on the tepee.

A spiritual leader would pray and dedicate the new dwelling. He would normally pray before the poles were covered that the occupants

A Shoshone dwelling photographed by William H. Jackson on 10 October 1878. (Utah State Historical Society—USHS)

would have a happy life together in the dwelling, that no evil thing would enter through the door opening, and that the dwelling would always be open to the hungry, fatherless, and aged. Since the people were nomadic, the tepee was a very practical dwelling because it could be easily transported.

In the summer, dwellings were often made from green leafy branches placed over a pole framework.[6] Willows, quaking aspen branches, reeds, and tall grass such as wheatgrass were used in making summer shelters. These dwellings were temporary and could be left behind as moves were made to other areas. Caves also were used as shelters and temporary dwellings. Bath houses or sweat lodges were erected to be used as places for spiritual experiences as well as for personal hygiene.

Rabbit skins braided like rugs were made into quilts.[7] Buffalo robes served as blankets and, in some cases, as floor coverings. Deer hides, elk hides, and bear skins also served as bed coverings. Dried moss also could be woven into blankets. Woven sagebrush and juniper bark as well as boughs and cattail fluff served as mats and mattresses.

Campsites were selected to be near fresh water and in a location protected by trees, willows, shrubs, or brush. Sagebrush was often used as camp windbreaks. The winter campsite where the Bear River Massacre occurred is an example of how terrain was used as a weather barrier. The

deep embankments sheltered the camp from wind and the stand of willows in the river bottom protected against heavy snows.

Shoshone people were not wasteful: they gathered no more than was needed for their use. They killed just enough game for their family and camp, and almost every part of the animal was used as food, clothing, or shelter. The Shoshone never killed game for recreation or for the pleasure of killing.

Shoshone women loved to socialize as they went in groups to gather seeds. Willow baskets, winnowing pans, and hitting sticks were used. As they gathered seeds such as sunflower, wild rice, and mustard, they shared news, traded recipes, and sang. Gathering seeds was a hard task at times. When seeds were scarce, a woman might spend an entire day gathering enough for only one family meal. Digging sticks were used for digging out roots and bulbs. Vegetables were normally plentiful. Ground potatoes, camas, sego lily, wild garlic, cactus, and other bulbs and roots were harvested. Berries of all kinds were picked in the mountains and fields. Wild honey was gathered in the fall.[8]

Eggs were gathered in the marshes and fields. At times, fish were an important part of the Shoshone diet. The people would move into the area of Salmon, Idaho, to fish. Spears, fishing poles, and baskets were used in catching fish. The Shoshone caught and dried salmon for winter use.

Meat was a very important item in their diet. Many Shoshone people traveled in western Wyoming and Utah to hunt buffalo, elk, moose, and pronghorn. The meat was sun dried for winter use. It was very important to get the big game, for it meant the difference between feast and famine. It also meant clothing and shelter for the people.

In western Utah and eastern Nevada, remnants of sagebrush corrals could be seen as late as the 1930s. These corrals were used by Shoshone hunters. They would drive deer into the corrals to facilitate their capture for food and clothing. Larger animals like moose and elk were harder to kill. Sometimes they were driven over cliffs or chased into large pits near watering holes.[9] Rabbit hunting was done during summer and winter. Rabbits could be snared, shot with bow and arrow, or clubbed in deep snow. Squirrels, woodchuck, and other small animals also were harvested. Ants and locusts were utilized as food. Ducks, geese, grouse, doves, chukars, and many smaller birds also served as food.

In the spring, summer, and fall the Northwestern Shoshone traveled around southern Idaho, western Wyoming, and Utah. In the spring many plants were harvested and eaten fresh, as food supplies always ran low

over the course of the winter. Cattails were eaten when they first appeared in the spring; parts of the stock are edible and the roots were dried and ground into meal and prepared as mush or into cakes. Wild onions and "Indian Carrots" were eaten both raw and cooked. Wild roses produced blossoms that were eaten raw, and the rose hips or red fruit were eaten raw for a snack. Cacti saved many Indian lives when food became scarce after a long winter. Cactus plants were sometimes dug from the snow. The buds and sometimes the joints were eaten in spring. The plant was baked in firebed ashes, peeled, and eaten.

During the summer and fall months the Northwestern Shoshone spent their time gathering seeds, roots, and berries for family use. Seeds like the mustard and sunflower were ground into meal and eaten as mush or were sun dried and prepared as bread. The mustard seeds were also mixed with water and used as a drink; mustard seeds from the Idaho area were considered to be not as bitter as those in other places. Berries like chokecherries, buffalo berries, serviceberries, gooseberries, and strawberries were eaten fresh or sun dried for storage. Most berries were very sweet and could be used as a beverage when mixed with water.

Late summer was root digging time. Bitterroot can look very similar to noodles and when boiled becomes very soft. It was cooked with meat to make soup. Sego lily and other bulbs were also used in stews and dried for use in the winter. Ground potatoes look like very small potatoes and have a taste similar to sweet potatoes. Also in late summer and early fall other plants were gathered to store over winter. Thistle grows along streams and in the fields. It has tall stalks with gray-green prickly leaves and purple flowers. The stalks were picked and peeled; they are crunchy and have a taste similar to that of celery. Squash and corn were both introduced to the Northwestern Shoshone by the Utes. Both could be dried for winter use and were boiled together to make a meal.

Around the middle of October, the Northwestern Shoshone people traveled into western Utah and eastern Nevada to gather pine nuts. The nuts were an important part of their food supply and were a rich source of protein. The Indians prepared pine nuts in a variety of ways, and they were an excellent food. The nuts were ground up as meal, roasted in their shells, and even eaten as dessert.

The pine nuts usually were winnowed and ground once they were gathered. In order to winnow, a quantity of nuts was placed in a winnowing pan. The nuts were tossed vertically so that they could be caught as they fell. The wind blew the pine needles and empty shells away and the good nuts fell back into the pan. The nuts were cooked until they

A group of Shoshone Indians. (USHS)

started popping and the shells were then cracked. The nuts were winnowed again to remove the shells and then placed on a flat or concave rock and ground to a fine meal. The meal was used in making gravy, soups, in baking, and in salads or deserts.

Drinks were prepared from a variety of plants. Common drinks were peppermint tea, rose tea, and Mormon (or Brigham) tea. Rabbitbrush, sagebrush, and milkweed had parts that could be chewed as gum.

Tanned animal skins were the primary clothing material. Men and women worked to produce clothing all year round. The skins from elk, deer, and antelope made the best dresses or suits. As many as seven hides from the pronghorn antelope, three or four hides from deer, or two large elk hides were required to make one dress. Dresses and suits were decorated with shells and animal claws and teeth. Bones and porcupine quills were also used. Sinew from animals was used for thread. Sagebrush and juniper bark were used to make capes, blouses, and leg coverings.

Moccasins were made from deer, elk, and moose hides. Rawhide was the preferred material for the soles, being much longer wearing and better able to protect the feet when walking through rocks and rough places. Sometimes moccasins were lined with juniper bark.

Head coverings or bonnets were made from animal skins. Rabbit and bear skins were commonly used. Lynx caps were made for younger

children. The skin was tanned very carefully, so that when worn the head covering looked like a natural lynx. Bonnets were decorated with owl, hawk, and eagle feathers. Eagle feathers were considered the finest of all. Weasel skins were used on eagle bonnets and sometimes tied on braids. Sometimes white weasel skins served as neckties. Beaver, otter, and mink skin were often used as hair ties.

A headdress known as a roach was traditionally worn by men and fancy dancers. This headdress was made primarily from porcupine hair, with the base being made from deer hair. The winter hair of the deer was best to work with, as it was longer and stronger. When clothing made from skins got wet it had to be removed and vigorously rubbed and stretched until it dried to a soft condition. It was best to actively wear wet moccasins until they became dry to maintain their softness.

Lifeways

In early times marriage was arranged for nearly all Shoshones. Sometimes an older man would go to the home of parents of a newborn girl and ask permission to marry their newborn daughter at some future date. If the parents liked the man and knew him to be a good provider, they were sometimes agreeable. Many times the parents were not agreeable and refused the arrangement, especially if they knew the man to be cruel or a poor provider.

In another approach to marriage, a man would send a gift to the desired girl's parents. It might be a horse or several horses; it could be skins of all kinds, deer meat, or other food supplies showing him to be a good provider. If the parents agreed, the marriage was arranged. This arrangement was not considered a wife purchase; rather, it was considered compensation for the loss of her services to her parents.

Sometimes to add interest to the marriage process they would stage a tug of war. The bride to be would be dressed in well-made buckskin clothing that would not tear or fall apart. The mother of the girl and the prospective mother-in-law would come together, with the girl between them. Tugging on the girl would begin, with the mother pulling one way and the mother-in-law pulling the opposite direction. The winner was the one who pulled the girl across the line. The girl was required to go with the winner.[10]

A marriage ceremony in those days was conducted by a spiritual leader. He gave the couple rules to live by, among which they were counseled to be true to their mate at all times. They also were counseled to be chaste in thought and remember their marriage vows. They were told to

avoid breaking up their marriage. Sometimes the spiritual leader would pull hair from both the bride and groom and tie it together. The bound hair was taken by a relative to a hiding place. If later the couple could not get along and wanted to divorce, they would first have to find the hair and untie it.

Indian children, like all children, loved to play. Their toys were made of materials available to them such as sticks, rocks, clay, and balls made of stuffed rawhide. A skill they liked to develop was tracking. Play for the children was only done during short periods between fulfilling their family obligations. The children were expected to work hard and to share the family burdens. Love of children was a dominant characteristic of the Northwestern Shoshone and physical punishment was never employed.

Older children had the responsibility of caring for their younger brothers and sisters. They helped dress, comb hair, feed, and play with the younger children. Other duties included gathering and carrying wood, water, berries, and seeds. They were expected to help care for animals if they had any and help with the cooking when they were older. They were responsible for caring for elderly grandparents and for running many errands. The children were considered to be responsible and important members of the family unit, and they were taught to love Mother Earth as the provider of all things. Most of the time, Indian children developed strong bonds with each other which remained with them throughout their lifetime. This was particularly true between family members.

Indian children were taught at an early age to be hospitable. They were taught that guests were assumed to be cold, tired, or hungry, and they were to be fed. Upon departure, a guest was to be given a gift, with nothing expected in return. Children were taught to honor and respect their parents and grandparents and were advised that wisdom and knowledge come with age. Teaching and storytelling fell mainly to the elderly grandparents. The oral history, legends, and customs of the tribe were passed on in this way.

Many Shoshone bands occasionally would gather together and compete with each other in a variety of games. The Franklin, Idaho, area was centrally located in the Shoshone country. Bands of the Northwestern Shoshone gathered in this area for meetings and winter sports as well as for summer fun and games. They took part in foot races, horse races, a game similar to hockey, dancing, and other activities. They also made flutes, drums, and darts. In the winter, dried deer hides were used for sleighs. In the summer, the children would dig foxholes along the banks of the Bear River and play Indians at war. Over the years the foxholes got

larger and deeper as the children played their games. (It has been mistakenly reported in history books that such children's play holes were rifle pits quickly dug as defensive pits against Colonel Patrick Connor's soldiers at the site of the Bear River Massacre.)[11] They would also fish in the river.

Winter time was storytelling time. Stories were told to children with a purpose more important than just recreation. Since the Indians kept no written record, many stories embraced the history of their people and were repeated many times to ensure accuracy. Children were good listeners and were taught never to interrupt the storyteller. Children were expected to stay awake during the storytelling. If one fell asleep during the telling, the storyteller stopped speaking and ended the session. Stories and tribal history were memorized by young people.[12]

The Bear River Massacre

The Franklin, Idaho, campsite was a natural protected place for the Shoshone Indians to spend their winters. Land along the Bear River there was in a natural depression and was thick with willows and brush that provided shelter from the wind and winter blizzards. In addition, there were natural hot springs to provide warm water. With adequate fuel and natural protection, their tepees were kept warm and the people were content.

Often, members of the Eastern Shoshone band and those from Pocatello's band would assemble at the Franklin area with the Northwestern Shoshone for meetings, fun, and games. They would compete with each other for prizes. In early January 1863 one such gathering was held—a Warm Dance. The object of the Warm Dance was to drive out the cold of winter and hasten the warmth of spring. If Colonel Connor had known of the Warm Dance custom, he could have had the opportunity to kill thousands of Indians instead of hundreds.

Following the celebration of the Warm Dance and after the visiting bands of Shoshone had left, the Northwestern group began settling into their normal routine. It was at this time that several incidents of trouble arose between the Shoshones and the white settlers of the area. A few Shoshone troublemakers stole some horses and cattle belonging to the white settlers. They headed north and along their way killed one of the cattle for food. The three men involved were known as One-Eyed Tom, Zee-coo-Chee (Chipmunk), and Qua-ha-da-do-coo-wat (Lean Antelope).[13]

About the same time, some miners and Shoshone got into a fight

and the miners were killed. The Shoshone involved were not from the Northwestern Shoshone group but from Chief Pocatello's band. The miner's horses and belongings were taken into Pocatello's part of the country. These murders of George Clayton, Henry Bean and, in a separate incident, John Henry Smith were the catalyst for action. Colonel Conner decided to move against the Northwestern Shoshone as a result, and Chief Justice John F. Kinney of Utah Territory issued a warrant for the arrest of Chiefs Bear Hunter, Sagwitch, and Sanpitch.[14]

The third incident that the Shoshone believe led to their massacre was a fight between some white youths and Shoshone youths. Two whites and two Shoshones were killed. Again, the Shoshones involved were not of the Northwestern Shoshone band. To the white authorities and settlers, Indians were Indians, and there was never any inclination to distinguish between the locals and those who came from other bands.

Because of these three incidents, many of the Northwestern Shoshone were getting restless and concerned. They felt that trouble was brewing and could soon break out. The settlers around Franklin, Idaho, were beginning to call the Indians "stealing savages" and "beggars." They did not seem to understand that the Indians were also human beings with feelings and emotions like anyone else. Many Indians were becoming bitter and defensive and began to feel that what was theirs was being taken away little by little. The territory which had been theirs for untold number of years was being taken away. The encroachment of the white settlers into their lands threatened their very existence. They felt that there would soon be no place for them to pitch their tepees. They were starting to feel like prisoners in their own country. Many began to feel like trapped animals who would have to fight for their lives to the end.[15]

On the night of January 27, 1863, an older man by the name of Tin-dup foresaw the calamity which was about to take place. In a dream he saw his people being killed by pony soldiers. He told others of his dream and urged them to move out of the area that night. Some families, believing the dream of Tin-dup, heeded his warning and quickly moved. As a result, the lives of those families were spared from the terrible massacre that soon followed.[16]

In the meantime, a white friend of the Shoshone—the owner of the grocery store in Franklin, Idaho—came to the camp and informed them that the settlers of Cache Valley had sent an appeal to Colonel Connor in Salt Lake City to come and settle the Indian problem. It was apparently the desire of the settlers to completely get rid of the Northwestern Band of Shoshone. Because of the information from the white friend, the

A photograph of the Bear River Massacre site, showing the location of the Shoshone encampment along Battle Creek, the ford used by soldiers to cross the Bear River, and the direction of their attack. (USHS)

Shoshone knew the soldiers were coming. The Shoshone, however, fully expected they could and would negotiate a peaceful settlement of the problems with Colonel Connor. No preparations had taken place to defend their position against an assault. What the Shoshone did not know was the murderous intent of the colonel to kill the entire band of men, women, and children. Connor is reported to have said "nits make lice," meaning that it was his intention to kill all Indian children and babies before they had a chance to grow to adulthood.

Chief Sagwitch, being an early riser, got up as usual on the morning of January 29, 1863. He left his tepee and stood outside surveying the area around the camp. The bluff above the river to the southeast appeared to be covered with a steaming mist. As he continued to watch, the mist appeared to lower along the bluff. Suddenly Sagwitch realized what was happening—the soldiers from Camp Douglas in Salt Lake City had arrived. Planning to meet and negotiate with the soldiers, but not knowing exactly what to expect, Sagwitch started calling to the sleeping Shoshone. The Shoshone quickly gathered their bows, arrows, and tomahawks. A few men had rifles and a very limited number of cartridges. Some of the Shoshone were so excited that they gathered whatever was in sight to use as shields and weapons. Some picked up their woven-willow winnow pans and baskets as if to use them for shields.

The site of the Bear River Massacre, also known to some as the Battle of Bear River. This later photograph shows the area where the Indians were camped. (USHS)

Chief Sagwitch shouted to his people to refrain from initiating any hostile action. It was his intention to meet with the military people and negotiate the delivery of those few troublemakers to the military. He thought the military man was perhaps a just and wise leader. He did not want the Shoshone band to suffer tribulation and perhaps death for the actions of a few renegade visitors. Many of the Indian men ran toward the river and dropped into the snow. They knew the people of the band were not guilty of anything, but experience had taught them to be wary and ready to defend themselves. They had experienced other situations where they had had to fight for their lives. Some had dropped into the holes the children had dug along the river bank. Never did these grown men foresee the need to be using children's play foxholes to await a possible military conflict.[17]

Negotiation was never in the mind of Colonel Connor and his troops. Connor had not the remotest inclination or desire to conduct an investigation. It probably never entered his mind to determine the guilt of those responsible for the trouble. In his mind, if there was Indian trouble, all Indians were the perpetrators. Whether the problem was caused by one Indian or two, the whole band—men, women, and children—were guilty by association.[18]

Connor had given the orders early. The soldiers came down the bluff and charged across the river, firing their rifles as they came. It was their

intention from the very beginning to kill every living person and destroy the Shoshone camp. The Shoshone tried to defend themselves, but arrows and tomahawks did little against the rifles and side arms of the soldiers. The Shoshone men, women, children, and babies were being slaughtered like rabbits, butchered by Colonel Connor and his troops.

The massacre started early in the morning, most of it along the riverbanks and among the willows. The Bear River, which had been lightly frozen a short time earlier, was now starting to flow. Some Shoshones were jumping into the river and trying to escape with their lives by swimming across. The snow was now becoming red with blood. The willows that were being used as hiding places were bent down as if in defeat. The old dry leaves which had been clinging to the willows were now flying through the air along with bullets.[19]

Ray Diamond, a nephew of Chief Sagwitch, was successful in his escape attempt. He swam across the river and found shelter in the hills to the west. He lived to be more than one hundred years old, and he told and retold of the Bear River massacre of his people to the younger generations until the time of his death.[20] Some Shoshone women jumped into the river and swam with babies on their backs. Most of them died. One Shoshone woman named Anzee-chee jumped into the river and took shelter under an overhanging bank. By keeping her head above water under the riverbank, she was saved. When it became safe for her to do so, she watched the massacre from her hiding place while trying to tend the wounds she had received to her shoulder and breast. Anzee-chee carried the scars from her wounds for the rest of her life and would often show them to the young Shoshone children as she related the account of the massacre to them. She also told of losing her own small baby to the river during her escape. The child drowned and floated down the river among other dead bodies and blood-red ice. One man swam with his buffalo robe upon his back. Soldiers shot at him, but the bullets appeared not to penetrate the buffalo robe.

Those few Shoshone still alive called to Chief Sagwitch to escape with them. They no longer had any means to defend themselves. Their arrows and few bullets had long since been spent. Most of their people had been killed. After having two horses shot from under him and receiving a bullet wound to his hand, Sagwitch escaped by riding a horse across the river. Another man reportedly escaped across the river by holding onto the tail of Sagwitch's horse.

A most cruel, inhumane killing was that of Chief Bear Hunter. Knowing that he was one of the leaders of the Northwestern Shoshone Band

the soldiers whipped him, kicked him, tortured him in other ways, and finally shot him. Through all this the old chief did not utter a word. To him crying and carrying on was the sign of a coward. Because he would not die easily or cry out for mercy the soldiers became very angry. One of the military men stepped to a burning campfire, where he heated his bayonet. He then ran the bayonet through the old chief's head from ear to ear. Chief Bear Hunter went to his death a man of honor. He left children behind and a wife who witnessed the event from a hiding place in the willows.

Yeager Timbimboo, whose Shoshone name was Da-boo-zee (Cottontail Rabbit), was a son of Chief Sagwitch. He was about fifteen years old at the time of the massacre. He remembered the event well and lived to tell about it. He retold the story several times a year and relived the scene in his memory. Over the years, the history of this event became imprinted upon the minds of friends, relatives, and grandchildren. The grandchildren memorized the story and could repeat it without deviation. Yeager told of being very excited and apprehensive, as any young boy would have been during the fighting. He felt as if he was flying all around from here to there without knowing a destination. He dashed in and out among the whizzing bullets but luckily was not hit. He heard cries of pain and saw death all around him. The young Shoshone boy kept running around until he came upon a little grass tepee that was so full of people that it was actually moving along the ground. Inside the grass hut Da-boo-zee found his grandmother, Que-he-gup. She suggested they go outside and lie among the dead. She feared the soldiers would set the grass tepee on fire at any moment. The boy agreed and they crept out of the hut to lie among the dead and pretend to be dead. "Keep your eyes closed at all times," his grandmother whispered, "maybe in this way our lives will be saved."

Yeager Timbimboo and his grandmother lay on the freezing killing field for many hours. At the end of the fighting, the soldiers were moving among the Indians in search of the wounded, to "put them out of their misery." Yeager, being a curious boy, could not keep his eyes closed; he just had to see what was taking place. His curiosity nearly cost him his life. A soldier came upon him and saw that he was alive and looking around. The soldier stood over Yeager, his rifle pointing at the young boy's head. The soldier stared at the boy and the boy at the soldier. A second time, the soldier raised his rifle and the young boy felt certain it was his time to die. The soldier lowered his rifle but a moment later raised it for the third time pointed at the boy's head. For some reason, the sol-

dier could not bring himself to pull the trigger. He lowered his rifle and walked away. What went through this soldier's mind will never be known. Perhaps a power beyond our comprehension stopped this soldier from killing young Yeager so that the true story of this massacre could be written. Yeager Timbimboo got the scolding of his young life. His grandmother reminded him that he was supposed to remain motionless with his eyes closed and pretend to be dead. He had disobeyed and it had nearly cost him his life.[21]

Soquitch (Many Buffalo) Timbimboo was a grown man at the time of the massacre. He was the oldest child of Chief Sagwitch. His memory of the event was very vivid. After having nothing left with which to fight, Soquitch jumped on a horse with his girlfriend behind him. Bullets were fired in their direction as they tried to escape to the hills. One of the bullets found its mark and the Indian girl fell dead off the horse, shot in the back. After determining the girl was dead, Soquitch kept going and finally reached safety. He dismounted from his horse and sat down by an old cedar tree that was concealed by some brush. He proceeded to watch the aftermath of this terrible massacre which Colonel Connor and the white settlers later called the "Battle of Bear River." To this young man, this was the most cruel event he had ever witnessed. The Shoshone camp which hours earlier was thriving, peaceable, and quiet had vanished from the face of the earth.

Toward evening the massacre field was nearly silent, except for the cries of the wounded soldiers being carried away. The Northwestern Shoshones who had escaped watched from the hills as the soldiers left with their wagons, upon which they had put their dead and wounded. Official reports from the army listed fourteen soldiers killed during the fighting and four more died later from wounds received. As they drove off, the wagon wheels made a very mournful sound as they squeaked along the frozen snow. The Shoshone had done some damage to the military with what little they had to fight with. The Shoshone fought bravely, mostly by hand.[22]

The military said the fighting lasted four hours. The Shoshone claimed that the military was there the whole day. Soldiers spent the remainder of the day murdering those who were found alive on the battlefield who "were killed by being hit in the head with an axe ... to end their suffering in mercy." Individual soldiers also took whatever they could find of Shoshone property abandoned by those who escaped. After the Shoshone were massacred, the soldiers burned their tepees and gathered their food and clothing and also burned it.[23]

By nightfall, the Shoshone who had escaped the carnage were cold, wet, and hungry. There was no food to be found. The soldiers had done an efficient job of scattering all of the food on the ground and setting fire to it. All of the tepees except one were burned to the ground. The lone standing tepee had been shot through so many times it looked as if it were made of net. This was the tepee of Chief Sagwitch and his family. After the soldiers had left, Chief Sagwitch made his way to his tepee and found his wife lying dead. There beside her was an infant daughter who was still alive. Sagwitch requested others who were with him to take the baby girl from her mother. They then put her in a cradle board and hung it on the branch of a nearby tree. He hoped that a kindhearted settler would find the infant girl, care for her, and raise her. He knew that without nourishment from her mother and under the bleak conditions they faced the infant would otherwise have no chance to survive.

The Shoshone could not believe what had just taken place. Sagwitch was a very shocked and stunned man, stricken and sad at heart. He mournfully gazed at the scene of the carnage. Just the day before, the camp had been a happy place. He remembered the many seasons the Northwestern Shoshone had spent in and around this favorite place on the Bear River. The Shoshone realized that they could not hold proper burial services for their dead. As an alternative, many of the bodies were thrown into the still-flowing Bear River. A water burial was better than leaving the bodies for animals to eat. At this time, a sad reality of life was indelibly impressed upon Sagwitch: there were different worlds in which people lived. One group was greedy and seemed to want everything, while the people in his world wanted only to live and travel around their aboriginal lands as they had done from time immemorial. One group made their wishes and desires come true by making themselves conquerors. His group, because of the other's genocidal policies, became part of the vanishing Americans.

As darkness fell upon the camp, a large fire was seen nearby in the hills to the west. A voice was heard to call, "If there are any more survivors, come over to my campfire and get dry and warm." The surviving Shoshone in the area gathered at the campfire. They were tattered and torn in body and in spirit. Almost every one of them had suffered wounds. All of the men, women, and children were in a dazed condition. Their eyes were glazed and their faces looked hollow. They were just starting to realize the magnitude of the tragedy which had so recently taken place. An old medicine man moved among the wounded and sick doing what he could without much success.

A Shoshone man photographed by William H. Jackson in the 1870s. (USHS)

As they warmed themselves at the fire and dried their clothes, some related the stories of their escape. A small Shoshone boy by the name of Be-shup (Red Clay) told of his survival. He had chosen to remain in the small wheatgrass tepee that was moving along the frozen ground. When he finally left the tepee, he was cold and scared and wandered around in a daze until he was found by a relative. In his cold little hands he carried a bowl of frozen pine-nut gravy. Food was so precious to this little six-year-old boy that he had clung to his bowl all day long. The boy was a son of Chief Sagwitch. His father told him that his mother was dead and his baby sister was left in a tree in hopes that she would be picked up and cared for. At this moment in his life, the little boy could not utter a word or cry—he was bewildered, frozen in grief, and in shock.[24]

The morning after the massacre, the few Shoshone who remained looked at their destroyed village in horror and disbelief. They now saw things they had not noticed the night before. The ground was covered in various colors. There was red from the spilled blood, black from the fires of their tepees and food, and brown from the many seeds and nuts which had been scattered over the ground. There were also blue and purple areas made up from their dried berries. There were also partly burned tepee poles remaining from the fires the soldiers used to keep warm. After observing the depressing scene, the remaining group decided to make their way to other members of the Northwestern Band who were wintering in the Promontory, Utah, area.

Word of the massacre at Bear River quickly spread to other Indians across the region. Northwestern Shoshones living near Brigham City, Utah, soon became aware of the tragedy. Two Shoshone women rode from Brigham City to Promontory to spread the news to other tribe members. They had gone into mourning for their dead friends and relatives. Poe-be-hup Moemberg and her friends cut their long braids and slashed the flesh of their arms and legs. This was the custom after the death of close relatives and friends.[25]

A few days after the massacre, Chief Sagwitch, being a man of great honor, wanted the horses stolen from the white settlers to be returned to them. He sent his oldest son, Soquitch, along with a cousin, Hyrum Wo-go-saw, and a nephew, Ray Diamond, to retrieve the stolen horses. They went into Chief Pocatello's area and returned with the horses. The stolen cattle had been killed and eaten and thus could not be returned. The horses were returned to the settlers.

The surviving Shoshone told of their buffalo robes and many other things being taken by the soldiers for souvenirs and for sale. Animal pelts

Chief Little Soldier. (USHS)

were taken for trade. Tomahawks, stone axes, willow baskets, headdresses, bows and arrows, and much more were taken.

Thirteen survivors of the massacre who in later years lived out their lives at Washakie, Utah, were a living historical source of this tragic event. They were Chief Sagwitch Timbimboo, Soquitch Timbimboo, Yeager (Da-boo-ze) Timbimboo, Ray Diamond, Peter Ottogary, Hyrum Wo-go-saw, Frank Timbimboo Warner, Tin-dup and family, Chief Bear Hunter's widow (Bia-Wu-Utsee), Towenge Timbimboo (wife of Soquitch, married after the massacre), Anzee-chee, Techa-mo-da-key, and Mo-jo-guitch. There also were other survivors who lived at places other than Washakie.

Today a monument stands near the site of this infamous massacre.[26] Many Shoshones (and now many others) believe that it should proclaim the brutal facts of the massacre of several hundred men, woman, and children of a peaceful village.

The Bear River Massacre was very important to southern Idaho and Utah. It marked the ending of some real conflict between whites and Shoshone in the territory. The decimation of the Indian population allowed the settlers and farmers to encroach further into traditional Shoshone territory without fear. The Northwestern Shoshone were almost totally annihilated. U.S. Army troops under the command of Patrick E. Connor had slaughtered nearly the entire band of Shoshone because of some trouble between a few Shoshone and the encroaching whites.[27]

A few years after the massacre, the Shoshone people asked Chief Sagwitch and his cousin Ejupa Moemberg to ask Mormon church president Brigham Young for assistance, as they were starving to death. While they were gone, an uncle who was left in charge sold little Be-shup to a Mormon family for a quilt, a bag of beans, a sheep, and a sack of flour. The Mormon family raised him and gave him the name of Frank Warner. He was sent to school, where he quickly learned the English language among other studies. He graduated from the old Brigham Young Academy and taught penmanship and reading to farm families. He drove his buggy from town to town and farm to farm throughout Cache Valley. He became a member of the Church of Jesus Christ of Latter-day Saints and served two missions to Montana and Canada. The Shoshone people of the area took great pride in his accomplishments. Proudest of all were Chief Sagwitch and his family. The chief came to believe that if Shoshone children were taught and educated early in life, they could succeed in the white culture.

In the years following the massacre of their people at the Bear River the nomadic and traditional ways of living of the Shoshone people gradually began to decline. The areas where they had hunted and gathered from time immemorial were now mostly lost to them through the encroachment of the white people. Although beaten and somewhat disorganized, the tribal members still had to find ways to survive. There were families to feed and shelter to be provided. Hunting, fishing, and gathering had to continue, although in a more limited way. Contact between the Shoshone and the white settlers inevitably increased. Some of the male tribal members began working for settlers on their farms. Many Shoshone were now being baptized into the Mormon church by its missionaries.

John Moemberg, who was a tribal leader and a cousin to Chief Sagwitch, had learned the English language while working for white farmers in the Brigham City, Utah, area. During the Bear River Massacre, he was living in Brigham City and thus escaped the carnage. Moemberg was a large man and showed great intelligence in dealing with the whites. He was closely associated with, and was an interpreter for, Sagwitch.

In 1874 Chief Sagwitch and John Moemberg were camped in Cache Valley along with a group of Indians. It became apparent to them that if they were to survive as a people their only recourse was to take up some land and begin farming like the white settlers. After discussing how to proceed, they decided to send a message to Brigham Young and ask him for help in this endeavor. Sagwitch and Moemberg traveled to Wellsville in Cache County to seek the help of Frank Gunnell, a true friend to the Indians. There was no man in the acquaintance of the Indians for whom they had more respect. Gunnell in his concern for his Indian friends wrote to Brigham Young concerning their request.

In response to the letter written by Gunnell, Brigham Young sent George W. Hill to visit the Indians and see what he could do for them. From Hill's journal comes the following extract: "On Tuesday, May 26, 1874, I went to Franklin, Idaho, to organize the Indians and set them to work under Bishop Hatch. In May 1874, we commenced to gather the Indians to Franklin, Oneida County, Idaho, thinking a settlement there would be a good place to gather them. But, things not working satisfactory, it was abandoned in the Fall, after spending a good deal of time and money."

The area in the vicinity of Promontory and Corinne, Utah, had been an ancestral place of the Shoshone where they spent the winter seasons. Because of the unavoidable changes in lifestyle facing the Indians, this area now had become more of a permanent settlement. Missionaries from the Mormon church had befriended, baptized, and were teaching the Indian people how to farm and to become self-sufficient. The *Deseret News* of July 22, 1875, published an article titled "Civilization Among the Indians" in which it detailed George W. Hill's work with the Indians and his hope that the colony at the Box Elder County Cooperative Field would succeed. The *Deseret News* editors agreed wholeheartedly that this was the best path to follow.

Many of the male tribal members had gained some farming experience from working as hired hands for some of the area's white farmers. With the help of some Mormon missionaries, the Shoshone labored long and hard in the year 1875 to begin farming. They raised wheat, pump-

An encampment of Shoshone Indians near Hoytsville. (USHS)

kins, melons, corn, and potatoes. They tended and watched over their crops, pleased that what they had planted was growing well. Harvest time was approaching and the Shoshone were getting ready to gather their crops. Sadly, however, the Shoshone would not be permitted to do so.

The Shoshone were informed by some white friends that the *Corinne Telegrapher* and an unscrupulous group of Corinne workers were plotting to get them removed from their farming area. The group was spreading a false rumor that the Shoshone were preparing to attack the town of Corinne and reported this baseless rumor to the military stationed at Fort Douglas. The military, in turn, sent a contingent of soldiers to Corinne to investigate.

An article entitled "The Indian Ejectment," written by George W. Hill, was published in the *Deseret News*, August 27, 1875, detailing what happened:

Statement made by George W. Hill regarding the Indians who were driven from their grain fields and lodges on Bear River, August 12. For the last three years, Members of Sagwitch's band of Shoshones and of other tribes of Indians, had been begging of me and others to find them a location where they could have a farm and go to work and till it and live like white men. I had been requested to attend to this matter and had selected a spot

of ground between the Bear and Malad Rivers, about twenty miles north of Corinne and entirely out of the way of any settlements. Finding the labor would be too arduous to bring the water out of the Malad River in time to irrigate this season's crop, I, with the Indians, moved about ten miles south to a field where the water had been taken out by the citizens of Bear River City.

The Indians of the camp belonged principally to the Shoshones and had frequently expressed the desire to become citizens of the United States; in fact, had paid taxes in Franklin, Idaho Territory, in 1874, the taxes being levied on horses, which was the only taxable property they owned and for which they hold the receipts.

The Indians had some hundred of dollars worth of work in clearing out the ditch, making a new dam, repairing the fences of the citizens, and here a temporary camp was established and crops were planted.

This season, the Indians put in about one hundred acres of wheat, about twenty five of corn, five and one-half to six of potatoes, three to four of melons, peas, beets, and other vegetables, which, at the time of the commencement of the excitement, were just ready for harvest. In fact, the Indians were in the fields with two reapers and had just commenced harvesting when the first news of trouble reached them. This was Tuesday, August 10.

Being told by an Indian, who had been to Corinne, that soldiers were there and that the captain wished to see Mr. Hill, I started with two chiefs and my informant for that place. On the way, I met a party of gentlemen consisting of Captain Kennington, Mayor Johnson of Corinne, interpreter L. DeMars and a newspaper correspondent, and with them returned to our camp. On reaching my tent, I invited several chiefs to be present and the following conversation ensued:

Captain Kennington: Do you characterize this report of the Indians being about to attack Corinne as a lie?

Hill: I do. There is not a particle of truth in it.

Johnson: Do you mean to say that a large party of Indians did not leave camp last night to attack Corinne.

Hill: I mean to say that there was not one Indian left my camp last night to go to Corinne or anywhere else.

Johnson: Were you up and awake all night, that you know what your Indians were doing?

Hill: I was up until the Indians had all gone to sleep and their ponies were scattered all over the prairies. It was utterly impossible for the Indians to have gathered up their ponies and started for Corinne without me knowing it; besides, they never leave camp without informing me.

Kennington: There was a guard placed at the Malad River bridge last night, and it was reported to me this morning that a large body of Indians came down and when they saw the guard, they whirled and ran.

Hill: It was entirely a mistake on the part of the guard. I wake easily and there could not be a stir in camp without my knowing it.

Johnson: Do you mean to say that your Indians have not threatened to attack Corinne?

Hill: I mean to say that no Indian had threatened to attack Corinne, and I challenge anyone to give the name of any Indian who has done so, and I will immediately send for him and have the matter settled. If you, Mr. Johnson, do not know the name of the Indian, I will go with you through the camp and you can point him out to me, and I will at once have him brought in and the matter forthwith investigated. (Mayor Johnson could neither give the name nor point out the Indian.)

Reporter: Do these Indians all belong to the Mormon Church?

Hill: Yes, and a great many that are not here.

Johnson: How many Indians do you have here?

Hill: I do not know; I have not counted them.

Kennington: What are the Indians who come from distant reservations doing on the farm?

Hill: Some have come to trade buffalo robes and buckskin for ponies; others visit their relatives on the farm, in the same way other people visit their friends and relatives.

Reporter: When are they going away?

Hill: A large party has already gone. The remainder calculate on going tomorrow.

Johnson: Have you a large party here from Fort Hall?

Hill: No.

Johnson: Not from Humbolt?

Hill: None that I know of.

Johnson: Have you not had large parties from these places?

Hill: No, Never that I know of. Occasionally a small party of four or five would come in, stay probably a day or two, and go home again.

Johnson: What claim do the Indians put forward to the land?

Hill: Simply that they were the original owners and had never sold it. They make no other claim whatsoever.

Johnson: Had they ever attempted to enter any land in the U.S. Land Office?

Hill: Not that I know of.

Johnson: How much land do they claim?

Hill: Just what they need for cultivation and to pasture their ponies, not to infringe on the whites.

Johnson: Did the strange Indians from the other parts put in the same claim?

Hill: I do not know. I have never asked them.

Kennington: Where are the visiting Indians from?

Hill: There are Shoshones from Wind River and a party of Bannocks from the north of Crow Country.

Kennington: I have been informed that the Indians have cut away the dam on which Corinne depended for water. Was this the case?

Hill: It is only two miles from the dam over level country. Will you ride over and look at it? You will find that the dam has not been touched, and, like other statements, this assertion was without the least foundation in truth.

Kennington: I will take your word for it.

Hill: If you will go out on the farm, you will see the Indians hard at work harvesting, with many of the squaws and papooses gleaning, and others scattered all over the camp, while the Indian horses are grazing in every direction over the prairie as far as you can see. Did you ever, Captain, hear of Indians going to war under such circumstances?

The next day, Wednesday, Major Briant, accompanied by Captain Kennington and interpreter DeMars, visited the camp. The Major delivered his message, which was to the effect that all the Indians must leave the farm and go to their reservations before noon the next day, or he would be compelled to drive them therefrom by force.

I told the major that all the Indians who belonged to reservations had already gone, and that the Indians that were on the

farm were residents and had no reservation to go to as they never belonged to any. I also asked him if he would telegraph, to the Department at Washington, a statement that I would make and wait until an answer was received, which I would accept as an ultimatum, allow the Indians to remain where they were and on the evening of the morrow, I would meet him at Corinne to know what the reply was. The Major said he would send the statement for me, but the order must be obeyed.

I replied, "If these orders are to be carried out, I have nothing further to say. The Indians want to be citizens, cultivate the land, obey the laws and seek their protection; but, if I understand right, If they do not leave their ungathered crops and are not off the farm by tomorrow at noon, It will be equivalent to a declaration of war." The Major said he supposed so. Sagwitch came forward and asked what he had stolen, whom had he killed, what meanness had he done, that the soldiers had come to drive him away from his crops.

DeMars here began to translate incorrectly what Sagwitch had said to Major Briant, and I asked him to translate correctly or say nothing. The Major said he would be as gentle as he could. I replied, "What that term means, we well understood". This was about three o'clock in the afternoon. Immediately after, I called the Indians together, told them that it would all come out right and advised them to return to their former haunts. By sunset, not an Indian could be found in the camp. All had scattered out to wander from place to place as in former days, leaving their crops, for which they had toiled so industriously and on which they depended for their Winter's food, neither cut nor garnered.

The next day, after the departure of the Indians, a man who styled himself a "State Marshall," with three or four others of Corinne, rode into camp and stole everything to which they took a fancy. Among other things they took the chickens belonging to Sagwitch, 11 beaver traps and a muskrat trap, copper kettles, axes and rabbit skin robes, in which the Indians wrapped their children.

Once again the Shoshone were displaced—a high price to pay for civilization as expounded by the whites. The whole Corinne affair was just another cruel act by some greedy whites against the Shoshone. What a punishment for trying to learn the ways of so-called "civilized people."

A Shoshone encampment, date unknown. (Courtesy Mae Parry)

After their expulsion from their farm by the military, some of the Shoshone moved a few miles north to the Elwood, Utah, area to be with other Shoshone who were already living there. Others continued to travel farther north to the Fort Hall reservation, to stay with relatives there for a period of time. Some returned to Cache Valley to wander in areas they had previously called home. It has been reported that, upon a request by the Shoshone, a letter was sent to the President of the United States concerning their expulsion from the Corinne farm. This, however, proved to be a useless endeavor.

The Shoshone, however, were not abandoned by their good friend George Hill. During the winter of 1875–76, Hill visited the Shoshone in the various groups residing in different places to give them encouragement and instructions. He encouraged the Shoshone to again settle in an area between the Malad and Bear Rivers, east of what is now the city of Tremonton, Utah. In the spring of 1876 some of the Shoshone entered land under the Homestead Act, hoping that by doing so they would avoid another Corinne experience.[28] At about this time, Isaac Zundel was called by the LDS church to labor with the Indians. The objective was to teach the Indians farming and industrial practices, encouraging them to become self-sufficient and industrious citizens.

Other white families were called by the LDS church to settle among the Indians on what had now become known as the Malad Indian Farm.[29] Again, crops were planted. It has been reported that in 1877 there was one hundred acres of wheat planted along with smaller acreage of vegetables. In addition, lumber was being obtained with which to build houses. Early in 1878 Moroni Ward with his family moved to the Malad Indian Farm to provide further spiritual and cultural guidance as well as instruction in farming. Machinery had been acquired and land ownership had been established.

Even though the farming experience in this area generally had been very positive, there were still some drawbacks. Among them, the surrounding area was being gradually settled by white people, and attempts to obtain water from the Malad River for irrigation had proved to be unfeasible for a variety of reasons. Also, the size of the land holding was considered to be too small for the number of Indians that were expected to inhabit the farm. Consideration was being given to once again settle the Indian band in Cache Valley. This idea was discarded in favor of moving the Indians and the farming operation to an area called the Brigham Farm in the Malad Valley. This location was still in Utah, about twenty miles south of Malad, Idaho, and about four miles south of Portage, Utah.

The land was purchased from the Brigham City M and M Company, which at that time was managed by Mormon leader Lorenzo Snow. A house and a granary had already been built at a location on the farm, which was about two miles south of what was to become the permanent location of the Washakie settlement. In 1880, Isaac Zundel, who was assigned as president of the mission, moved into the house, and a few families of Indians camped around the home in their lodges and tepees. This area became the home of the Northwestern Band of Shoshone Indians for the following eighty years. The settlement was named after the respected Shoshone leader Washakie.[30]

Washakie

In the following year, 1881, the LDS church purchased additional farming land from the Merrill brothers of Portage just to the north of the farm acquired from the Brigham City M and M Company. Some of the buildings and the granary were moved about two miles north to the new site, which was to become the permanent settlement of Washakie.[31]

Under the direction of Isaac Zundel, Alexander Hunsaker, and Moroni Ward, the Shoshone at Washakie began to make some real

Chief Washakie. (USHS)

progress. A canal carrying water from springs in Samaria, Idaho, had been started by farmers from nearby Portage. The LDS church acquired part ownership in the project for use on the Washakie farm. Shoshone Indians from the community pitched in and were responsible for much of the construction of the canal which was to bring water to Washakie for irrigation of farm crops. The canal remains in use today.

A sawmill and lumber business also was started. The first sawmill in the area was built by the Shoshone in the mountains near Samaria.[32] The second sawmill was built in the Elkhorn Dam area of Idaho. The Shoshone worked very hard in the operation of the sawmills. Large quantities of lumber were manufactured. Profits from the mills were rein-

Planting potatoes at Washakie in 1903. (Courtesy Mae Parry)

vested into machinery to manufacture lath and shingles. A wood planer also was purchased. Wood building products from the operation were being sold throughout the entire area. For the first time in their lives the Indian people began to profit from their labors, but continued success was not to be. First, they began to lose lumber from theft. Second, over a period of time, both sawmills burned to the ground under suspicious circumstances. The Shoshone believed that arson was the cause of the fires. This meant a loss of their investment as well as a great amount of lumber.[33]

The Shoshone community saw a need for additional building materials. As a result, a brick kiln was erected near a spring in the foothills of the mountains east of the Washakie settlement. The Shoshone who worked at the kiln scratched their names into a slab of rock adjacent to the kiln. They were Ammon Pubigee, Ona Johnny, Charley Broom, Quarrich Wongan, and James Brown. The Shoshone workers made and baked bricks in their kiln and a brickyard was established at the Washakie townsite. Some Shoshone became carpenters and bricklayers. Two large multi-level brick homes were the first to be built entirely by the Indians under the guidance of their white leaders.[34]

In addition to farming the land on the church farm, the Shoshone at Washakie acquired land in their own names under three separate acts of

Congress. Under the Citizens Homestead Act of May 30, 1862, four Shoshone residents of Washakie acquired homesteads. Under the Winnebago Act of 1881, twenty-seven Shoshone acquired land. Under the Indian Homestead Act of 1884, twenty-five-year trust patents were issued by the United States in trust for six additional Shoshone residents. Three additional allotments of an unknown type also were issued, for a total of forty to Washakie residents.[35]

In a communal project, the Shoshone Indians at Washakie purchased a herd of sheep. It has been reported that at one time the herd numbered several thousand head. Profit from the sale of wool and lambs enabled the people to buy additional farm machinery and equipment. The sheep project came to an end, however, when many of the sheep were lost due to exceptionally hard winter weather and the loss of the remainder of the herd to theft.[36]

In 1882, just two years after settling the village of Washakie, a school was established. The first teacher was James J. Chandler. The first lessons taught to the Indian students were of necessity very elementary. Chandler taught the students nursery rhymes and simple songs, presumably to acquaint them with the English language. The students learned to read from a primer and to write their names. The students ranged in age from quite young to young adults. Among the early students between 1882 and 1900 were Willie Ottogary, Charlie Broom, Don Carlos Hootchew, Quarrich Wongan, Ona Johnny, James Brown, Neatz Broom, Eliza and Amy Hootchew, Eliza Ottogary, O-ha-qa-sue, Mu-da-wa-a-ze, and Annie Comesevah. All of these students eventually became leaders in the community.

After Chandler, other teachers came to the Washakie school, including Lorenzo Hunsaker, Foster Zundel, William Anthony, and a Mr. Lillywhite, who probably came from the Salt Lake City area. J. Edward Gibbs came from nearby Portage and, after leaving the community as a teacher, maintained a lifelong relationship with the Indians. Following him was Caroline Perry, a good teacher who earned the respect of her students. Ivy Bird Hootchew, a student of Perry, recalled her school days at Washakie: "She was a good teacher; if there had been more like her, we would have amounted to something. Our teacher, Miss Perry, recognized our various talents and let us know we had wonderful gifts to give."

A Miss Young came from Ephraim, Utah, around 1913. She was a very interesting person who took her teaching seriously. Her students were taught basic reading, writing, and arithmetic. She was remembered most of all for her musical talents: she played the piano and organ and

Thinning beets at Washakie. (Courtesy Mae Parry)

had a beautiful singing voice. A Miss Harris came from nearby Portage and was quite well acquainted with the Indians and their customs. She was quite small in stature but nonetheless was able to handle any disciplinary problems which arose. Some of her students recall being chastised with her ruler. Virgil Atkinson came from Clarkston, Utah, and taught basic subjects, just as the previous teachers had done. At this time, most of the students dropped out of school after completing the third grade. Vida Ward, the daughter of LDS bishop George M. Ward, had grown up in the community and had the advantage of knowing her students well. Dolores Hoganson came from Logan, and teaching at Washakie was her first assignment after completing her college work.

In the 1920s a new Washakie school building was erected. It was an improvement over the old white church building which until this time had served for school classes. The building had one large room with modern desks as well as two storage rooms and living quarters for the schoolteachers. Many windows were built into the schoolroom, and a large bookcase where all of the books were kept was built into one wall. For the first time swings, slides, and other playground equipment were brought in and a sandbox was welcomed by the younger children. First through eighth grades were now taught in the school.

A group of Shoshone schoolchildren at Washakie. (Courtesy Mae Parry)

Mr. and Mrs. William Fowler were the first teachers in the new school. Students ranged in age from six years through the late teens. The curriculum began to resemble that of the other county schools. Alvin and Ida Harris from Portage were the second set of teachers to teach at the new school. They were well acquainted with many of the Shoshone in Washakie. In addition to teaching the basic subjects, emphasis was placed on public expression and speaking in front of the class. The telling of Indian stories, legends, and customs became an almost daily occurrence. Programs were prepared and presented to the community.

Legrand and Martha Horsley came from Brigham City and made school interesting and fun for the students. They made a special effort to get acquainted with all members of the village. Martha Horsley was an accomplished musician and had a beautiful singing voice; she taught more modern and popular songs to the students. The couple took the time to participate in community events and also arranged programs to be taken outside of the community to broaden the experience of the Shoshone students. As a result of their efforts, the students seemed to be progressing further and faster in their education. Ralph D. and Delsa Olsen had just married when they came to teach at Washakie. The young couple exhibited extraordinary interest in teaching their young students. They tried to make learning fun as well as a rewarding, successful experience. They tried to broaden the experience of their students by letting them see many things outside the community.

For years the community thrived, but population began to decline with the onset of World War II and the availability of better-paying jobs elsewhere. By the early 1940s so many had moved away from Washakie that the number of residents in the community dwindled to the point that a school in the community was no longer feasible. The few students remaining were bused to the school in Fielding, Utah.[37]

End of the Washakie Farm

The relationship between the Washakie Indians and the LDS church also began to decline in the 1940s. After seventy years of close relationship on the farms at Corinne, Elwood, and Washakie, the number of Shoshone families began to decline. Many of the younger people became involved in the world war. Older people found employment in the defense industries established to support the war effort. After the war few, if any, moved back, as their opportunities seemed better elsewhere. Involvement in the Washakie farm declined to the point that on December 31, 1959, only three Shoshone Indians were working on the project.

During the summer of 1960 most of the remaining dilapidated homes of the Shoshone, which appeared to be abandoned but were not, were burned to the ground in preparation for the sale of the church farm. Some Shoshone families had possessions in the homes such as appliances, bedding, and personal papers that were burned. This action resulted in bitter recriminations from some of the Shoshone, who believed the LDS church had defaulted on a promise that Washakie and the use of the farm would be there for the Shoshone in perpetuity. A relationship which began in 1874 had ended.

The Shoshone families whose homes were burned to the ground met in 1974 to discuss their losses when the farm was closed. They were asked to express themselves as to their feelings about the loss of their homes and what should be done to compensate them for their losses. The following are excerpts from that meeting, transcribed from a tape recording in June 1974.[38]

Testimony of Geneva Alex Pacheco

It was in June and I was scraping my deer hide at my home in Washakie, Utah, when I saw Mr. LaMar Cutler start a fire by Elias Pubigee's home. The fire was coming toward my mother's gooseberry patch and toward my home. Mr. Cutler's fire was coming down the ditch and along the fence line. I asked Mr. Cutler what he was doing and he informed me that he had orders from Stake President Smith to burn all this down. I told

him that it was too bad, but he was not going to burn my place up. I told him we were paying taxes on this property and it was ours. I further told Mr. Cutler if he wanted to burn something to go elsewhere and burn. We exchanged unpleasant words. I also told him not to set foot into my yard as there is a boundary line here. Again I told him to go and he said O.K. and moved his fire along the ditch past my place and over towards the canal. A few days later, Mr. Cutler came over and asked me for my mailing address. I gave it to him. About a week later, I received a letter from the church attorney, Mr. McConkie. The letter requested me to get out of my house by the 3rd of June of that year. It also stated for me to take all my lumber and anything else that was mine and move on. I still have the letter I received from Mr. McConkie. I also saw Everett Neaman's old house burn down. It went up as if it was a gasoline fire. This home was burned by Vernon Lamb and Mr. Snow. Vernon Lamb also fenced our driveway up. We went to our home and could not get into our yard. He made us a gate. I do not know if we had any water rights, but when Fullmer Allred was at Washakie, he would let us water our garden with water from the canal. After Mr. Allred left, we didn't see any more water.

Testimony of Leona Peyope Hasuse

We have always lived in Washakie. One summer we went on a visit to Bannock Creek, Idaho. While we were there, my mother got sick and died. Because two of my sisters live at Bannock Creek, my son Richard and I stayed longer at Bannock Creek after mother's death. I told my son that we had a home at Washakie and were going back soon. Everything we had was in our home. We lived in the Kippie Norigan home. We came back to Washakie and would go back to Bannock Creek for visits. This was our way of life. We lived a few months here and a few months there. Washakie was always our home. We liked the celebrations on the Reservation, so spent the biggest part of each summer at Bannock Creek. When things quieted down, we always came home. During one of our visits at Bannock Creek, I was informed that my house had been burned down. I was informed by Amy Timbimboo.

As soon as I could, we drove to Washakie and viewed our burned home. All my personal papers had gone up in flames.

An encampment of Shoshone Indians from Washakie in Logan for a celebration in 1908. (Courtesy Mae Parry)

Such things as records of my people, birth certificates, all my church records and other important papers. My blankets, clothing, mattresses, beds, stove, dishes, cupboard, refrigerator, table and chairs, and even our food was gone. As I stood looking at my burned stove and metal beds and my refrigerator sitting in the ashes, I cried. I mean, I cried out loud. I felt real bad. I was never notified by mail or any other way that my place was going to be burned.

We went back to Bannock Creek, Idaho, as there was nothing left for us at Washakie. On the Reservation we are not allowed to hunt or fish. We are considered as Mormon outsiders. We are like visitors. I would like to say that although the church has done me wrong, I do not hold a grudge against them. I still believe in all the teachings of the church. I still have my faith and it has not been broken. One day at Fast Meeting while I was bearing my testimony, I told of my home being burned down and of my faith in the church and of not hating the church for what they have done to me. After church one of the white members asked me why I didn't give up my membership in the Mormon

church and go elsewhere. I told this lady I was raised in the Mormon church and have lived its laws and rules all my life and was not going to give it up just for this. My faith is strong. I am not angry at the church. I am only hurt very deeply. While I lived at Washakie, my neighbors were Neitze Broom and Amy Broom. They lived next door to me in the red brick house. Across the road lived Nellie Tootewana and Minnie Woonsook. All these people are dead now and all their homes are gone too. Minnie Woonsook's home was burned the same summer as mine. My neighbor to the east was my brother Evans Peyope. He lived in our family home. This home was burned also. I have been hearing that maybe the church is going to buy us some land for another Washakie. I hope it comes true but I feel I will not live long enough to see this come true. My son Richard may see it come true some day and may even come back to the new Washakie to live.

Testimony of Evans Peyope

I lived in the old Jacob Peyope home. I cannot remember where I was when my home was burned down. I heard some talk in June about my home being burned. I drove to Washakie from Bannock Creek, Idaho, and found there was no home. It was burned. I said "darn, someone has burned my house down." Everything was black. I was angry, but what could I do. My bed and table were gone. I had no place to call my home now so I went back to Bannock Creek, Idaho and stayed with my sisters. I never really left. I was just visiting around like the rest of the Indians. My plans were to return again. On the reservation I am not allowed to hunt or fish. Sometimes I fish though. I live by eating rabbits and small fowls. I can hunt. I am another one of those Mormon outsiders. My sister Leona and I both lost our homes. If it is possible, I will take cash as I am very old now and cannot keep up a home. I am past 68 years old.

Testimony of Elias and Alice Pubigee

Alice: I was so busy visiting around on the reservation, I was not aware my house had been burned down. One day we came home and our house was gone. Amy Timbimboo came over and we all stood around and cried. We were never informed our house was going to be burned. We received no letters. The only thing

that made us suspicious was LaMar Cutler's questions all the time. Every time he saw us he would ask us when we were going to move for good to Idaho. I asked him why he wanted us to move. I also asked him if he disliked us. He said he liked us but raised the question about moving again. It seemed as if he asked the same thing every other day. When my husband was watering in our yard, Mr. Cutler told him to quit watering. I told my husband to ask Mr. Cutler if he disliked us so much. My husband only laughed and stopped his watering. Then Mr. Cutler informed us we were going to be moved. I cannot remember when the burning took place.

Elias: Mr. Cutler also burned an old car of mine. It was in running condition and had a good engine in it.

Alice: When I saw everything was burned, I said to my husband, "I wonder who ordered this done." I looked around and when I saw our car sitting there all burned black I started to cry. Although my home may have looked like a shack to some people, it was my home. It was the place we remembered and always returned to. Many of our things were still there. Being Indians, we did a lot of farm labor. We left in the spring to thin beets; in the summer we picked fruit, and in the fall we did beets and other things. When things quieted down we always came home. So you can see we were gone away almost half of the year. We always knew where our home was. It was at Washakie. We have seen Lamar Cutler going around burning along ditch banks that always seem to burn toward houses. We saw the scene described by Geneva Alex Pacheco. At this time he almost burned one of our other houses. A house that we got from Seth Eagle. We bought a log house at Bannock Creek, Idaho, and have purchased a little land to move this home to. No longer can we come to Washakie, but every time we pass through we cry and feel bad. This was our hometown. We had things here but they are all gone now. Since our home was on church land maybe they felt they had a right to burn it down. We still feel bad. We are living at Bannock Creek, Idaho, and are going to church there. We still believe in the church but it hurts when we remember what they did to us. We are not angry at the church. We still pray and pay our tithing. I was asked to serve in the Bannock Creek Relief Society. Although I cannot read or write, I am trying very hard to do as I am told. Leona Peyope is our president. This home we have

A Shoshone family from Washakie photographed in Logan, Utah, on May 6, 1909. (Utah State University Collections and USHS)

bought at Bannock Creek is for future use by our children and grandchildren. We may not live long. If the church buys us land somewhere near Washakie for another community, I am sure we will come back. We hope this comes true. Yesterday we visited the Washakie Cemetery. We did not want to go back to Idaho. It was so quiet and peaceful here. We like it here at Washakie. I feel as my husband feels. We need a home here with a lot. I cannot forget how hard I cried. I cried very loud. All my things were gone.

Testimony of Minnie Woonsook
[Minnie Woonsook died soon after her home was burned. Amy Timbimboo related her knowledge of that burning.]
My husband, Moroni Timbimboo, and I had gone to Ogden this day. When we came back to our Washakie home, we saw that Minnie Woonsook's home had been burned. In fact, it was

still burning. I got out of our car and walked over to the burning house. I saw what remained of her home. There was a burned stove and the mattress and blankets on her bed were still smoldering. The bed, being metal, was still standing up. Her cupboard was burning with her pots and pans and dishes still in it. Her clothing and other personal things were burning. A very good couch my husband and I gave her was burning away. I could not save anything. I walked over to Mr. LaMar Cutler's home. I asked him what was going on. I asked him if he knew that two tons of coal were stored in Minnie's shed. "Who is going to pay for all this," I asked. Mr Cutler said he would talk to Stake President Smith and see if they can pay for the coal. A few days later, Mr. Cutler brought a check over to me to give to Minnie. I delivered the check to Minnie and told her that her home was gone. Minnie Woonsook and her daughter had been at home just before this happened and had gone to Ogden to her daughter's home. The daughter became sick and needed care so Minnie stayed on in Ogden. Her feelings were just like the rest of the burned out Indians. There was weeping and sorrow. She had nowhere to go. One evening as Minnie was crossing Washington Boulevard, a drunken white woman hit Minnie with her car and killed her.

Testimony of Amy Timbimboo

Each time I saw the homes burn, I cried. I stood among the ashes and remembered all the people that lived in them. I watched Bishop George M. Ward's red brick house go down in flames. I was there talking to Mr. Cutler. I told him I had seen good times in that home. I saw it as a little girl. In this home many of us were married. We were happy in it. In this home, we had singing practice and business meetings. While I recalled these events to Mr. Cutler he didn't say a word but only laughed at me. I guess to him it was an old house. To us it was a home. I saw Leona's home burn too. I talked to Mr. Cutler about this also. About my own home, it was getting real lonesome now. We have never received a letter telling us to move. We have never received anything telling us we could stay at Washakie until we died. We moved our church membership records to the Portage Ward and attended church there for two years. In 1969 we moved to Plymouth, Utah. …We attended meeting, fasted and paid our honest tithing.

Shoshone members of the Washakie LDS Ward meet with Mormon church officials in Salt Lake City, April 5, 1931. (Courtesy Mae Parry)

Testimony of Moroni Timbimboo

"Since the church is burning everything around us, maybe we better move somewhere else," I said to my wife. Just as I said this, Mr. Nish from Plymouth, Utah, came to our Washakie home and said he had heard we were looking for a place to live. He invited us to visit him at Plymouth. The next day we drove to Plymouth to look around. We saw three houses. I had only a nickel in my pocket and was house hunting. I believe the Lord guided us to Plymouth and to our present home. Mr. Keith Lamb, a good friend and neighbor, must have known I was short of money. He offered to pay for our home and all he said after he had paid for our home was "pay me back when your harvest is over." We did not ask him for a loan, he just offered his help. When my harvest was done, I paid Mr. Lamb back.

Testimony of Wallace Zundel

I bought my log house from Jessie Perdash. She had moved away. I asked her what she was going to do with her house. I told her I heard rumors that the church was burning homes at

Three Shoshone leaders at Washakie in 1933. From left to right:
Ketch Toyadook, Yeager Timbimboo, and Ammon Pubigee.
(Courtesy Mae Parry)

Washakie. I cannot name any certain person who told me this. It
was being talked about by all the Indians. Jessie said there wasn't
anything she could do if the church wants to burn her house....
My wife, Hazel, and I cleaned up the house. We scrubbed the
floor and were planning to move the house. We had intended to
use this house for the purpose of tanning our deer hides.... By
my house was a shed belonging to Jessie Perdash. Also a small

trailer house. In these places were stored beds, bedding, clothing and other household items. She had a cellar too. In it was stored food and bottled fruit. Coal was stored outside of the log home. All I have mentioned were burned. Later on I asked LaMar Cutler why he had burned my house. I told him I had bought the place from Jessie Perdash. He said he would pay me the amount I had paid Jessie. In a few days he gave me a check, the kind he pays all his farm help with. Almost all these homes were built by Indians. The logs were sawed by Indians. The homes were built with Indian labor; It was theirs. I would like a cash settlement.

Testimony of Marjorie Alex Pacheco

I was one of the witnesses to the burning of Jessie Perdash's shed and trailer house and her cellar. I also saw the log house burn that Wallace Zundel bought from Jessie Perdash. It was in the fall and our men had gone deer hunting. My daughter-in-law Marilyn Alex and I were inside our house. We were living in one of the cinder-block houses in Washakie. I heard a roaring and rumbling sound outside, so we went outside to see what was going on. We saw Wallace's house on fire. The flames were shooting real high. Because the home was old and of dry logs it burned hard and fast. I decided not to tell Moroni and Amy Timbimboo. Wallace is their son-in-law. I was afraid they might run over there and try to put the fire out and in the process might get hurt or even burn up. Our hunters coming out of the canyon saw the fire also. They rode as fast as they could. They thought Everett Neaman's home was on fire. I saw LaMar Cutler burning weeds around the home when it caught fire. The next day, I told Moroni and Amy. They knew nothing about this burning up. There was no way we could have saved this place. There was no water. Wallace's house was clean and going to be moved.

On November 24, 1960, the Washakie farm was disposed of by the Church of Jesus Christ of Latter-day Saints. The farm was sold to the Peterson brothers of Roy, Utah, to become a privately owned large cattle ranch. In a gesture of compassion for the Washakie residents, the Northwestern Shoshone Band was given 184 acres of land purchased by the LDS church in the vicinity of Washakie from Milton McCrary. This land was donated to the tribe as trust lands to fulfill the federal requirement enabling residents to receive government aid.

Northwestern Shoshone Government

The Northwestern Bands of Shoshone Indians are recognized by the United States government as Treaty Indians. The Treaty of Box Elder signed in 1863 reads as follows:

Treaty with the Shoshoni—Northwestern Bands, 1863

Articles of agreement made at Box Elder, in Utah Territory, this thirtieth day of July, A.D. one thousand eight hundred and sixty-three, by and between the United States of America, represented by Brigadier-General P. Edward Connor, commanding the military district of Utah, and James Duane Doty, commissioner, and the northwestern bands of the Shoshonee Indians, represented by their chiefs and warriors:

Article 1. It is agreed that friendly and amicable relations shall be re-established between the bands of the Shoshonee Nation, parties hereto, and the United States, and it is declared that a firm and perpetual peace shall be henceforth maintained between the said bands and the United States.

Article 2. The treaty concluded at Fort Bridger on the 2nd day of July, 1863; between the United States and the Shoshonee Nation, being read and fully interpreted and explained to the said chiefs and warriors, they do hereby give their full and free assent to all of the provisions of said treaty, and the same are hereby adopted as a part of this agreement, and the same shall be binding upon the parties hereto.

Article 3. In consideration of the stipulations in the preceding articles, the United States agree to increase the annuity to the Shoshonee Nation five thousand dollars, to be paid in the manner provided in said treaty. And the said northwestern bands hereby acknowledge to have received of the United States, at the signing of these articles, provisions and goods to the amount of two thousand dollars, to relieve their immediate necessities, the said bands having been reduced by the war to a state of utter destitution.

Article 4. The country claimed by Pokatello, for himself and his people, is bounded on the west by the Raft River and on the east by the Porteneuf Mountains.

Article 5. Nothing herein contained shall be construed or taken to admit any other or greater title or interest in the lands embraced within the territories described in said treaty in said tribes or bands of Indians than existed in them upon the acqui-

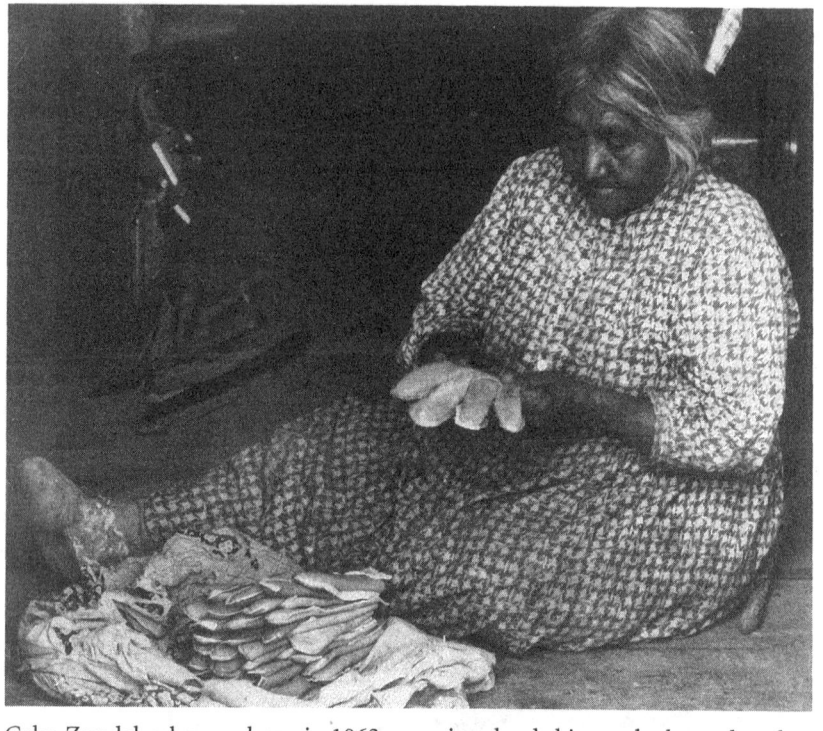

Cahn Zundel, who was born in 1863, examines buckskin work gloves that she made. (Courtesy Mae Parry)

sition of said territories from Mexico by the laws thereof.

Done at Box Elder, this thirtieth day of July, A.D. 1863....

The treaty was never fully adhered to by the United States government.

After the settlement at Washakie became a viable community where the Northwestern Shoshone Indians living in Utah became settled and self-sufficient, the concept of Indian chiefs faded away along with the Shoshones' nomadic way of living. White leaders gradually took much of the leadership responsibility. This was particularly true with respect to the religious and community affairs. The relationship of the tribe to the United States government was somewhat dormant for a period following the year 1900. The Shoshone Indians at Washakie were almost totally ignored by the United States government. Most other tribes were settled on Indian reservations and were more or less governed by agents of the Bureau of Indian Affairs.

Although the leaders were no longer called chiefs, leaders among the

Four generations of a Shoshone family. (Courtesy Mae Parry)

Shoshone Indians at Washakie continued to exist. The knowledge that the white settlers and soldiers had illegally taken their lands continued to trouble many of the Shoshone. Under the primary leadership of Willie Ottogary, along with other prominent Washakie leaders, a group of Indians decided upon court action to find relief. As a result, attorney Charles H. Merillat and Charles J. Kappler and Joseph Chez, associate attorneys, initiated a lawsuit against the United States government for the unlawful taking of Indian lands. In 1930 the Northwestern Band brought a claim for the taking of areas it contended were recognized by the United States in the 1863 Box Elder Treaty. This case finally ended in the Supreme Court of the United States where it was lost in a split decision. In Northwestern Shoshone v. United States, 324 U.S. 335 (1939) the United States Su-

preme Court held that the 1863 treaty was a treaty of friendship only and did not constitute a recognition by the federal government of any right, title, or interest in the territorial claims of the tribe.

Although they lost the case, the action helped result in the United States Congress establishing the Indian Claims Commission Act on August 11, 1946, which gave all of the Northern and Eastern Shoshone the opportunity to press their claims for compensation for the taking of aboriginal lands. Eventually, the claim of the Northwestern Band of Washakie became consolidated with claims from the Shoshone-Bannock tribe at Fort Hall, Idaho, and with the Eastern Shoshones in the Wind River area of Wyoming. The Indian Claims Commission concluded that the Northwestern Band of Indians were a party to the 1868 Treaty of Fort Bridger and, as a consequence, their claim to aboriginal lands was recognized.

On February 13, 1968, the Indian Claims Commission entered a final judgment in the amount of $15,700,000 to settle the consolidated claims. The acreage involved in the settlement as determined by the claims commission was for 38,319,000 acres. This number was reduced by the acreage involved in the Fort Hall and the Wind River Reservations. Compensation was paid at just under fifty cents per acre. After negotiations with the other tribes involved in the settlement, the sum of $1,375,000 was awarded to the Northwestern Band of Shoshone. Deducted from this amount were certain offsets owed to the United States government, attorneys' fees, and a $100,000 compromise deduction to reach an agreement with the other tribes involved in the various claims. The final amount was distributed on a per-capita basis to those properly enrolled in the tribe, as published in the Federal Register on May 17, 1972. Finally, that August, 221 members received payment as a result of the claim. Ninety-six members received checks, while money was placed in Individual Indian Money accounts (IIM accounts) for 125 members.

Leaders of the Northwestern Band who were engaged in getting restitution from the United States government included among many others Thomas Pabawena, Enos Pubigee, and George P. Sam, none of whom lived to see the fruits of their labor. All had died by the time the claim was settled, and all are owed a debt of gratitude by those of the tribe who eventually benefited from their efforts. Leaders of the tribe prior to and at the time of the settlement of the claim were Lee Neaman, Frank Timbimboo, Wallace Zundel, and Mae Parry. Frank Timbimboo and Mae Parry traveled to Washington, D.C., to testify before the Court of Claims of the United States Congress in support of the Shoshone claim.

In 1957 some members of Congress introduced a bill to terminate the special relationship and remove from wardship status 60,000 Indians in eight states. Senator Arthur V. Watkins from Utah, chairman of the Senate Indian Affairs Subcommittee, sought the action to terminate, among others, five Indian bands in Utah, including the Northwestern Band of Shoshone of Washakie, Utah. This action was vigorously opposed by the Northwestern Band at Washakie and its leadership. Through the timely and assertive action of the leadership of the Northwestern Band and many others named in the act in the form of a protest to Congress, termination of the band was avoided.

On April 29, 1987, the Bureau of Indian Affairs conducted a "Secretarial Election" for the adoption or rejection of a constitution for the Northwestern Band of the Shoshone Nation. The constitution was adopted by a vote of sixty-one in favor and six against, in an election in which at least 40 percent of the ninety-three people entitled to vote cast their ballots. Kenneth Neaman and Jennifer Davis were tribal leaders involved in negotiating with the Bureau of Indian Affairs to establish a constitution and gain greater recognition from the United States government. Frank Timbimboo was selected as chairman of the first seven-member tribal council elected following adoption of the constitution. Tribal chairmen who followed Timbimboo were Larry Neaman, Leonard Alex, Joe Louis Alex, George Worley, and, as of February 1995, a new term for Joe Louis Alex. As of May 1995 the tribe staffs two offices to serve the tribal members. One office is in Blackfoot, Idaho, to serve those living in the Fort Hall vicinity, while a Brigham City, Utah, office serves tribal members living in the northern Utah area.

In January 1995, tribal enrollment of the Northwestern Band of the Shoshone Nation numbered 454 members. Nearly all of the them live in northern Utah and southern Idaho, with a few other members scattered throughout the United States.

In the late 1990s members of the Northwestern Shoshone Band began efforts to acquire a 6,400-acre ranch straddling the Utah-Idaho border near the 184 acres the band owns near their former town of Washakie, land that currently only houses the town's cemetary. Hopes are high that this would attract members to the area, with developments planned for a ranch, truck stop, and hotel. Efforts are underway to obtain federal funds (and perhaps donations from other sources) to purchase the land, with plans to establish a new reservation.[39]

The Goshute Indians of Utah

Dennis R. Defa

The Goshute Indians live in a little known and sparsely populated portion of the state of Utah. There actually are two Goshute reservations, the largest of which is the Deep Creek Reservation located on the Utah–Nevada border about sixty miles south of Wendover, with a portion of the reservation in each state. The second, and smaller, reservation is located in Skull Valley in Tooele County, about ninety miles west of Salt Lake City. Most people who visit this region of the state view it as a harsh, hard, and unforgiving place and wonder why anyone would choose to live there. However, for the Goshutes this desert region is home and they view it much differently than does the casual visitor. Before white Americans moved into the region, the Goshutes knew the land intimately and took from it all they needed to sustain life. As efficient and effective hunters and gatherers, they understood the fragile nature of the desert and maintained a balance that provided for their needs without destroying the limited resources of their arid homeland.

At the time of their first contacts with whites, the Goshute people lived in the desert regions southwest of the Great Salt Lake. Exact boundaries are difficult to determine because of the nature of the land and the proximity of other peoples, but early chroniclers and surveyors provided some written descriptions of the general Goshute homelands.

Captain James H. Simpson located the Goshute from the Great Salt Lake to the Un-go-we-ah Range, or Steptoe Mountains, in Nevada. Howard Egan believed they inhabited the area extending from Salt Lake Valley to Granite Rock in the West Desert, and from Simpson's Springs to the Great Salt Lake Desert.[1] A treaty with the Indians in 1863 defined the boundaries of the Goshute Indians:

Article 5. It is understood that the boundaries of the country claimed and occupied by the Goship tribe, as defined and de-

scribed by said bands, are as follows: On the north by the middle of the great Desert; on the west by Steptoe Valley; on the south by Tooedoe or Green Mountains; and on the east by Great Salt Lake, Tuilla and Rush Valleys.[2]

The English traveler Sir Richard F. Burton wrote that Egan Canyon, Nevada, was the western limit of the Goshutes. George M. Wheeler believed the limits of the Goshute territory extended from the Sevier Lake Desert west to the mountains bordering Spring, Steptoe, Sierra, and Goshute Valleys, and south to about 38 degrees latitude; however, anthropologist Julian H. Steward was of the opinion that this latter boundary was "certainly too far south."[3]

Whatever the exact boundaries may have been at the time white people begin entering the Goshute domain, the region lies entirely within the Great Basin. The Great Basin is not one large cup-shaped depression; instead, it is a series of more than ninety basins which are separated from each other by some 160 mountain ranges. These mountains have a north-south orientation and vary in length from about thirty to one hundred miles. The highest mountain ranges reach altitudes of from 8,000 to 12,000-plus feet; they are separated by desert plains lying at altitudes from near sea level in the southwest to 4,000 or 5,000 feet in the north—the area inhabited by the Goshutes. The Great Basin is relatively uniform in its principal characteristics and can be defined precisely on the basis of its interior drainage, having no outlet to the sea.[4]

A quality common to virtually all of the Great Basin is aridity, resulting from a number of factors that include the rain shadow caused by the Sierra Nevada, the distance of the Basin from the ocean, and latitudes unfavorable to recurrent storm patterns. Because of this lack of precipitation, the flora and fauna of the Great Basin, if compared with most other areas of North America, are not especially abundant. The Goshute domain is topographically considered to be a steppe and desert area broken by a number of small mountain ranges. These mountains average about 7,000 feet in elevation, but it is common for some of them to extend to 10,000 feet, and, in one case, the Deep Creek Mountains, there are two peaks greater than 12,000 feet in elevation. The valleys between these ranges are from 4,000 to 6,000 feet in elevation and are floored with gravel, silt, sand, and salt. One portion, the Bonneville Salt Flats, is almost pure salt and is almost barren of plant life.[5]

The Great Salt Lake Desert is the least favorable portion of the Great Basin for human habitation. Because none of the valleys have an outlet

to the sea, they become receptacles for water and debris washed down from the mountains. The Goshute portion of the Great Basin has no real rivers, and the springs that exist form in the higher mountain regions only to sink into the desert sands. The majority of the 10,000 square miles that comprise the Great Salt Lake Desert are a barren salt flat that today is still perceived as having little economic promise. Only in the higher mountain regions are conditions favorable for the survival of plants and animals, and it was in these areas that the Goshutes acquired most of their resources.[6]

Before the white invasion of the Goshute homeland, the Indians were largely concentrated in small camps in a crescent area around the southern half of the Great Salt Lake Desert. This area is among the most forbidding in North America and offered the resident Indians few resources needed for survival. Because of this lack of resources, it has been estimated that in the time prior to white contact the population could have been no more than one person for every forty square miles of territory.[7]

A large portion of the Goshute population, now as in the past, has been concentrated near the Deep Creek Mountains on the Utah-Nevada border near the present-day town of Ibapah. The Deep Creek Valley is some 6,000 feet in elevation and is separated from the Great Salt Lake Desert by the Deep Creek Mountain Range. The highest peak in this range is Haystack Peak at 12,020 feet, and it is also the highest point in the traditional Goshute country. Immediately west of this mountain is a valley that is drained by a small stream known as Fifteen-Mile Creek. It is joined by another small stream known as Spring Creek in the vicinity of Ibapah.[8] From the confluence on, the stream is known as Deep Creek. The stream moves northward, passing through a portion of the Deep Creek Mountains and terminating as a sink on the Great Salt Lake Desert.

Other important areas of Goshute activity were Simpson's Springs, Skull Valley, and Tooele Valley, which was also the eastern limit of the Goshute domain. Skull and Tooele Valleys are typical of the Great Basin; Tooele Valley is bounded on the east by the Oquirrh Mountains, with Mount Lowe being the highest peak, at 10,572 feet.[9] The Stansbury Mountains separate Skull Valley from Tooele Valley, and the highest peak in this range is Deseret Peak, at 10,976 feet.[10]

The Goshute Indians are part of the larger Shoshonean (Numic) speaking groups that live in the Intermountain West; whether speaking individually or collectively they all refer to each other as *Newe* (the People), considering themselves still connected by an ancient common ancestry. No one knows how long the Goshute people occupied the area where

An unidentified Goshute Indian who lived in Skull Valley, photographer and date unknown. (Courtesy Utah State Historical Society—USHS)

they lived before they were first contacted by white people. The Goshute believe that they have always lived there. Scientists, using a number of dating methods, have arrived at some controversial dates of what they believe was a Shoshonean arrival into the Great Basin from the Death Valley region of California.[11]

From their first contacts with white Americans, several different terms have been used to identify the Goshute people. Various spellings such as Go-shutes, Go-sha-utes, Goship-Utes, Goshoots, Gos-ta-Utes, Gishiss, Goshen Utes, Kucyut, and Goshute appear in historical reports, letters, and other communications. The name Goshute comes from the native word *Ku'tsip* or *Gu'tsip*, meaning ashes, desert or dry earth, and people. The term *Kusiutta* is considered more proper linguistically and is used by both linguists and present-day tribal members. It is native in origin and is not an arbitrary label placed upon the people by whites, although Goshute will be used here, as it is the most widely used and accepted American variant.[12]

Several Indian groups live in the desert areas of the states of Utah and Nevada: Paiute, Goshute, Western Shoshone, and Ute. Pioneers and explorers encountered small groups of Native American wanderers of various tribes devoting their energies to survival in the west's harsh environment. By gathering foods, using baskets for utensils, and wearing woven rabbitskin robes, these people survived in an area where very little survived. Lacking the strength of numbers to engage in warfare, the peaceful and scattered people living in sagebrush wickiups or caves were often indiscriminantly called "Digger Indians" by whites who observed them digging for roots, tubers, bulbs, and even small animals. They also ate insects and other small creatures that did not appeal to the palates of white observers.[13]

Father Pierre-Jean de Smet witnessed a communal grasshopper hunt among some "diggers" in the late 1830s or early 1840s, but it is not clear if these people were Goshute or Paiute. Whichever group Father de Smet visited, the method of the communal hunt would have been the same. De Smet noted:

> They begin by digging a hole, ten or twelve feet in diameter by four or five feet; then, armed with long branches ..., they surround a field of four or five acres, more or less, according to the number of persons who are engaged in it. They stand about twenty feet apart, and their whole work is to beat the ground, so as to frighten up the grasshoppers and make them bound forward. They chase them toward the center by degrees—that is, into the hole prepared for their reception. Their number is so considerable that frequently three or four acres furnish grasshoppers sufficient to fill the reservoir or hole.[14]

Because of its geographic location, the Goshute culture has long been recognized as the least complex of any to be found in the Great Basin region. They generally lived at a minimal subsistence level, with no economic surplus on which a more elaborate socio-political structure could be built. Their isolation also contributed to the lack of cultural diversity, because they were removed from other centers of American Indian civilization. The Goshutes were not located in an area where they could acquire ideas outside their own domain as readily as did many other Indian groups in North America.[15]

The Goshutes exemplify the historic Great Basin desert way of life perhaps better than any other group because of the condition of their territory. An example of their exploitative skill is found in the use of wild vegetable foods—the Goshutes knew and used at least eighty-one species. From forty-seven species they took seeds, twelve yielded berries, eight provided roots, and twelve were used for greens.[16] Grass seeds were gathered in flat tray-like baskets by knocking or raking them with beaters, and, if there were surpluses, they were stored near the harvest area. One of the most important foods in the entire desert region was the nut from the pinyon pine. Although the crops were not always an annual occurrence, a good crop assured the bands of a good winter, and winter camps were made near the harvest and storage places. If there was a crop failure, the Goshutes were forced to move to other locations or faced starvation.[17]

When their stored surpluses were exhausted, the Goshutes were forced to leave their winter camps in search of food. With the arrival of spring they were able to eat the new plants as greens, and by early summer they collected the available seeds and fruits in the valleys and flatlands. By the end of summer, roots and tubers had matured. Surpluses were always hidden in storage as a precaution against other food source failure. Then, in the fall, all the bands moved to nearby mountains to harvest pine nuts; and, if the usual area did not produce a crop, the family groups moved on in search of other areas where trees were bearing the nuts.[18]

The day-to-day economic activities of the Goshute Indians were organized on efficient lines, with the family being the basic economic unit. All work was divided on the basis of sex, and the family was virtually self-sufficient. Women and girls gathered seeds, prepared foods, and made clothing, baskets, and some pottery, while the men hunted larger game, made tools, wove blankets, built shelters, and helped women in rodent catching, burden bearing, and in collecting raw materials. The family was highly mobile. Larger groups did assemble briefly several times a

A Goshute mother and her child. (USHS)

year when food sources such as rabbits or pronghorn were available in quantities enough to be hunted. The pattern of life made any strong central tribal development impossible, and there was a limited feeling of solidarity. The Goshute had no hereditary chiefs. Instead, the bands chose a local wise man as leader, but he possessed little tangible political power.[19]

The scarcity of resources in the arid Goshute homeland was a primary contributor to scarcity in other areas of Goshute life. There were few ceremonies in comparison with those of many other Indian groups. The round dance was known, however, and was primarily used to obtain assistance in making seeds grow; much less often it was used as a social

dance. The kinship system of the Goshute was not complex. Descent was determined by both lines of both the father and mother. Marriage rules were just as simple, allowing an individual to marry a cross cousin. The marriages were informal, usually being arranged at a festival. Children were named after events, their birthplace, other favored locations, animals, or any characteristics the infant displayed. For example, it was told that a Goshute man received the name of Blackbear because even as a newborn he had an unusually dark complexion.

Just about everyone had some knowledge of medicinal herbs and compounds. Shamans were responsible for special medicinal treatment and the use of the sweat bath or sweat lodge. The Goshute sweat bath was done without water; hot rocks and coals were covered with earth and the patient would lie on top. The shaman was considered to have the power to heal and was able to treat serious illnesses. A man could receive these healing powers as a gift given by the "Little People" or "Little Man," or he could receive this power through dreams. These healing powers did not have to be sought, they could be a gift if one chose to keep them. Religion before the present Native American Church or the Church of Jesus Christ of Latter-day Saints, which many present-day tribal members belong to, consisted of shamans who were able to heal the sick, foresee coming events, give protection against curses from one's enemies, and give personal guidance throughout life.[20]

The nature of their environment required that the Goshutes have few material possessions. The Goshutes had no horses, and only those tools and utensils necessary for food acquisition were made. These tools had to be light and durable because they were carried on all moves. Because of this requirement for mobility, Goshute material possessions consisted of baskets, pots, simple clothing, a grinding stone, flint knives and scrapers, and personal items such as ornaments. Personal dress consisted of an apron, a basketry hat, sometimes moccasins, and a woven rabbitskin robe in winter. Housing was also uncomplicated. If shelter was needed, a small, round sagebrush bower called a wickiup was constructed. More permanent houses, if built, were usually larger, sturdier versions of the wickiup.[21]

The family was not always the maximum economic unit in hunting. When taking game such as pronghorn, rabbit, deer, mountain sheep, and, under certain conditions, waterfowl, fish, and even insects, collective effort increased what an individual hunter could acquire. The length of these hunts and the number of people involved varied. For the Goshute and their neighbors the Western Shoshone, game generally was so scarce

that these cooperative hunts lasted only one to two weeks, at maximum six weeks. The participants rarely comprised more than two dozen families.

Hunting complemented gathering. Game provided not only essential foods but skins for clothing and materials for implements. With smaller game, such as rodents or insects, hunting was organized along family lines, with both men and women participating. Large game was usually taken by men, while women gathered vegetable foods. A hunter shared large game with other members of the village, but the family unit usually was able to provide most of its needs without assistance. Pronghorn and deer were driven into corrals or towards waiting hunters, while rabbits were driven into woven nets.[22]

Several plant and animal species occurred in such abundance during short periods of time that even when they were not taken cooperatively, numbers of families were attracted to their locations. The most important of these species were pine nuts, which, as mentioned, often played a major role in the Goshutes' choice of winter campsites. Crickets and grasshoppers, which were sometimes taken cooperatively as well as by single families, could also bring a number of family groups together.

These ecological factors varied in different parts of the area, but plant harvesting was the main subsistence activity for the Goshutes and Western Shoshones, game being relatively scarce. For the greater part of the year, families had to travel alone or in small groups and harvest a large area. They commonly ranged twenty miles or more in each direction from their winter village, and their itinerary, though usually repeated each year, was not always fixed. Seasonal variation in rainfall, and consequently in crop growth, frequently required that they alter their foraging routes.[23]

The most permanent association of families was at winter encampments. These were sites where certain families habitually remained during the months when vegetable foods could not be obtained. Necessary conditions for such winter campsites included accessibility to stored seeds (especially pine nuts) and water, sufficient wood for house building and fuel, and the absence of extremely low winter temperatures. These conditions were most often fulfilled in the mouths of canyons or within the pinyon pine and juniper belt in the mountains, although sometimes broad valleys near fishing streams were chosen. Whether they were scattered at intervals of several hundred yards to a mile along streams, were situated at springs on mountainsides, or were clustered in more dense colonies depended upon the quantity of foods which could be gathered and stored

The remains of a fence built by the Goshute Indians as an antelope corral.
(Vyrie Grey Collection, Marriott Library, University of Utah—U of U)

within convenient distance of each camp. In some places, families had to camp alone; elsewhere as many as fifteen to twenty could congregate.

The cooperative hunts of the Goshutes did not permit permanent associations of families for several reasons. First, these hunts lasted only while the quantity of meat taken was sufficient to feed the assembled crowd, possibly a few weeks. Second, alignment of families for hunting was often different for each species of game. Pronghorn and rabbit were the most important species in the area occupied by the Goshute, but they often were found in different parts of a valley. Moreover, the important hunts were held only where there was an antelope (pronghorn) shaman or rabbit-drive director; not every valley had such men. Therefore, for communal hunts, families traveled from their village or from where they happened to be gathering seeds to the most convenient location and often cooperated with other groups of people on successive hunts. They might join families from across their valley for a rabbit drive, go to a neighboring valley to hunt with its residents in a pronghorn drive, and associate with immediate neighbors to hunt deer in their own mountains. If their local pine nut crop failed, the next year they might be thrown into association with still other people for such hunts. Because the territory exploited by different families was variable as well as overlapping, ownership of a food area would have been impractical. Individual ownership of land was not found among the Goshutes.[24]

Another important event which took place during the winter months was the gathering of Goshutes to share their myths and stories.[25] Myths could not be told in the summer; in fact, it was considered dangerous to do so. Hawks and coyotes played many of the main roles in Goshute mythology. The coyote was feared, and even if the Goshutes were starving, they would not eat its flesh. One tale relates that an argument between Coyote and Hawk was responsible for creating the Deep Creek Mountains.

> It was Hawk who made the Deep Creek Mountains. Hawk was angry. It must have been because someone [Coyote] was fooling around with his wife. He flew up high, then dashed himself against the mountain (Mt. Wheeler) and broke it all up. It made all these mountains around here.[26]

In addition to animal myths, the Goshute told stories of *pa'ohmaa*, "Water Baby," who could be heard crying at night but disappeared when the sun rose, and *toyaneweneen*, "Little Man," who gave shamans power. Games also were played in the winter and included a hoop-and-pole game, hand game, and races.

The Goshute Indians were able to utilize almost everything that their limited environment could offer. The efficient manner in which they were able to take what they needed without upsetting the delicate balance of the desert helped ensure their survival. Although there were periods of drought when sufficient food sources were sometimes scarce, the Goshutes survived. It was not until white people began to encroach upon their lands and disrupt their lives that this natural balance was destroyed.

First White Contacts

The harsh desert conditions of the Goshute homeland provided an effective barrier against white encroachment until the middle of the nineteenth century. Direct white contact was rather sporadic until about 1850, but the Goshutes were in constant contact with their native neighbors. The period from 1827 to 1846 can be broken into three divisions, based on the people encountered: slave traders, trappers, and early immigrants.

Before 1827, Goshutes had probably never seen a white man, but they certainly knew of their existence from information and some trade goods received from their closely related neighbors, the Western Shoshone. The first indirect contact with whites came through other Indian peoples bordering the Goshute homeland. The Indian group to the

A coiled water jug made by an unknown Deep Creek
Goshute. (U of U)

east and south was the Utes, and they made occasional forays into the
desert for the purpose of capturing slaves to be taken south and sold in
New Mexico.[27] These early slave raids, however, were only a prelude to
what the Goshute Indians faced in the period between 1830 and 1859.

With the beginning of the 1830s, American and British fur-trapping
companies were nearing their zenith in the Rocky Mountains, so there is
little wonder that a group of these trappers is given the credit of being
the first white men to enter into the Goshute homeland. The first recorded white men to actually see the Goshute Indians were three trappers, a group led by Jedediah S. Smith.

Smith and his company of men spent the winter of 1826–27 in the
vicinity of the San Jose Mission, California, and in the spring of 1827
Smith tried to cross the Sierra Nevada in the area of the Stanislaus River
as he returned east. On his first attempt to cross the mountains, Smith
and his party were stopped by mountain snow. On his second try, Smith
was accompanied by only two men, Robert Evans and Silas Gobel, seven
horses, and two mules. This small group was successful in crossing the
mountains, after losing two horses and a mule.[28]

A coiled basket with bead design woven into it, made by a Deep Creek Goshute in 1939. (U of U)

Once the barrier of the Sierra Nevada was overcome, Smith and his two companions headed for the shores of Bear Lake for the trappers' rendezvous of 1827. Smith took a direct route to Bear Lake and, because of this, he was able to provide the first written description of a trip through the heart of the Goshute homeland. His relevant journal entry of June 22, 1827, begins after they had just crossed the Utah line near present-day Gandy, moving north along the base of the Snake and Deep Creek ranges. This area was Goshute country.

Jedediah Smith's description of the area was vivid and helps illustrate the whites' belief of how barren and desolate the Indians' homeland was. Smith and his two companions crossed that inhospitable portion of the Great Basin and eventually reached Bear Lake, but their suffering was great. Lack of water and lack of game made their passage across the desert very difficult. At one point, Smith wrote, "Robert Evans laid down in the plain under the shade of a small cedar being able to proceed no further." Smith and Gobel could not help Evans, so they left him and proceeded on in hopes of finding water and returning for their exhausted friend.

They found a spring, and Smith noted; "Just before we arrived at the spring I saw two Indians traveling in the direction in which Evans was left, and soon after the report of two guns was heard in quick succession." Smith saw smoke coming from the direction of Evans and, becoming concerned, took a small kettle of water and returned to the aid of his friend. Evans was found alive, was quickly revived, and the three men continued on their trek.[29]

The two Indians Smith saw moving towards Evans were Goshutes, and this encounter was the first recorded contact between Goshute people and white Americans. This section of Smith's journal provided the first description of Goshute country, and it also provided a warning to the other trappers who read its description and passed that on to others—all avoided the country south and west of the Great Salt Lake. This had the effect of maintaining the state of isolation that had characterized the Goshute Indians to this point.

Whether these men were the first whites to go through Goshute country or merely the first to write about it is really not known. Charles Kelly, a Utah writer, had been told of a similar experience. Kelly quotes Isaac K. Russell in *Hidden Heros of the Rockies* that:

> For years after Smith's journey, the Piute Indians of Skull Valley, Utah, repeated the tradition that the first white men they ever saw were three who staggered, almost naked, in from the western desert, and were half crazy from breathing alkali dust.[30]

The belief is that these three men were Smith and his companions. However, stories of this nature were common with the Goshutes, and in such a country there were doubtless many people who found themselves in a similar situation after Jedediah Smith, and perhaps even before.[31]

There is no reason to believe that other whites did not travel through Goshute country in this early period, but no written accounts have come to light to lend support to this statement. The next mention of the Goshute people is in the early 1840s in the journal of Osborne Russell. Russell never actually saw a Goshute Indian, but while in the area of the Great Salt Lake he stayed with some Utes, and it was from these people that he obtained his information. Russell wrote:

> During my stay with these Indians [Ute] I tried to gain some information respecting the southern limits of the Salt Lake but all that I could learn was that it was a sterile barren mountain-

ous Country inhabited by a race of depraved and hostile savages who poisoned their arrows and hindered the exploring of the country.[32]

Although there were trappers all around the Goshute country, few apparently ever wandered into their arid homeland. Beavers were rare in Goshute country, so there was little reason to enter the area in hopes of obtaining plews. Those trappers who did enter the Goshute country, and it seems there were only a few, had no substantial effect on the Indians.

The first Euro-Americans to have a direct effect on the actual day-to-day existence of the Goshute Indians were slave traders from New Mexico. The practice of capturing and selling Indian slaves was long established when the Goshutes began to feel the effects. Spanish colonists started taking Indian slaves as soon as they began settling portions of the New World. The descendants of these early Spanish slaveholders later extended the practice of slavery to include the Goshute Indians.

In 1821 Mexico won its independence from Spain and emerged as an independent nation. Trade restrictions with the United States ended and exchange quickly began along the Santa Fe Trail between Missouri and New Mexico. In the 1830s a regularly used trail between Santa Fe and Los Angeles was soon developed called the Old Spanish Trail.[33] It was this trail that brought the majority of the Mexican slave traders to Utah, where they soon interacted with and victimized the Goshutes.

The trail itself was first projected during the Spanish period. The Spanish, during their northward expansion, had established two lines of settlement: one along the northern Rio Grande in New Mexico and the other along the Pacific coast with the establishment of missions. It was believed that if these two areas of colonization, separated by some 1,200 miles, could be connected, Spain could dominate a vast land area and add substantially to her empire. This impetus gave birth to the concept of the Old Spanish Trail.[34] It was not until the 1830s, however, that contact of any regularity was established between Santa Fe and Los Angeles.

The Old Spanish Trail was used primarily for trade, and this was limited to what could be carried by a horse or mule, because wagons never crossed the full length of the trail. Horses and mules were the primary items traded; but guns, powder, blankets, knives, to name only a few of the many goods, were also bought and sold. The most pernicious aspect of the Old Spanish Trail, however, was the market it established for Indian flesh—the buying and selling of Indian slaves became an economically important aspect of the trail.

Weaving a basket preparatory to the pine-nut gathering season.
(U of U Library)

Slaves from a large portion of the Great Basin were captured or bought and then were sent south and west into New Mexico and California. The Goshutes were no exception. Captured women and girls usually found their way into the more wealthy households as domestic servants, while men and boys were put to work on ranches and farms. The need for

A carrying basket with canvas bottom. (U of U)

labor in these areas was acute, and this was one of the primary reasons for the economic success of forced servitude.

It was because of the importance of the slave traffic that economic penetration northward was first undertaken by New Mexican traders. Long before the Old Spanish Trail had been blazed to California, Spanish explorers had marked out many paths to the tribes of the Great Salt Lake Basin region in hopes of obtaining furs and slaves.[35]

In 1852 the Utah Legislature tried to end the enslavement of Indians by enacting a law for the relief of the victims. The law's preamble noted that the practice of slave raiding was of long standing:

> ... from time immemorial the practice of purchasing Indian women and children of the Utah tribe of Indians by Mexican traders, has been indulged in and carried on by these respective

people, until the Indians consider it an allowable traffic, and frequently offer their prisoners or children for sale.[36]

The majority of Indians sold into servitude belonged to the Paiute groups that lived in the desert regions south and west of the Great Salt Lake. Like the Goshutes, they were sometimes known as "Diggers" because they dug roots and tubers and lived in what was considered a generally harsh environment that yielded little food. Their peaceful and simple mode of living made them easy prey for their Ute neighbors and New Mexican slavers. Goshutes and Western Shoshone people also were captured and sold into slavery by well-mounted Utes, who occasionally entered their country, captured women and children, and sold them along with Paiute captives.

One important result of the opening of the Old Spanish Trail was that the commerce enhanced the power and position of the Ute Indians. Different bands of Ute Indians ranged in New Mexico, Colorado, and much of Utah. Ute Indians had been on friendly terms with the Spanish for many years, and had acted as middlemen in the slave commerce. With the opening of the Old Spanish Trail their involvement increased. The Mexican slave trade flourished between 1830 and 1854, and it was during this period that the Goshutes suffered the most.

Both the Pahvant Utes, who lived to the south of the Goshutes, and the Timpanogas Utes, who lived around Utah Lake, appear to have made raids into the Goshute country to capture women and children. Children were always sought because they were more tractable and could more easily be trained as menials by their Mexican owners.[37] Demographic figures do not exist, but it is not difficult to understand the effect a population drain of any type could have on the already limited number of Goshute Indians. It is little wonder, then, that as late as 1859 Captain J.H. Simpson was able to record: "The fear of capture causes these people [Goshute] to live generally some distance from the water, which they bring to their 'kaut' [camp] in a sort of jug made of willow tightly plaited together and smeared with fir-gum."[38]

The third group of white people to contact the Goshutes were the early immigrants passing through the Goshutes' domain on their way to the West Coast. The opening of the Oregon and California Trails in the early 1840s initiated a regularly traveled trail system across the continent, and thousands of people found it possible to make their way to the fertile lands of California and Oregon. By 1846, Utah was being crossed by an increasing number of immigrants on their way to California; but

most immigrants passed far to the north of the Goshutes' country, and just a few crossed south of the Great Salt Lake and braved the forbidding desert to the west.

John C. Frémont had crossed the northern portion of Goshute country in 1845. In 1846 Lansford W. Hastings crossed in an easterly direction from California to Fort Bridger in southwestern Wyoming, later promoting this route as Hastings Cutoff. He then tried to persuade immigrants to follow this shorter route. He was able to convince some people by pointing out what seemed to be the irrationality of traveling northwest from Fort Bridger, Wyoming, to Fort Hall, Idaho, and then beyond Fort Hall turning southwest to reach the Humboldt River and then on to California. Hastings believed that a more direct wagon route could be opened south of the Great Salt Lake.

Hastings Cutoff, as it became known, went south of the Great Salt Lake and then west across the desert area to later intersect the Humboldt River in Nevada. This trail not only crossed some of the most inhospitable land in North America but also crossed the northern portion of the Goshute homeland. The first group to utilize this shortcut was the Bryant-Russell party in July and August of 1846. They were a small group, with light equipment, who passed along the cutoff with little difficulty and reached the Humboldt River safely. Shortly afterwards, the Harlan-Young company followed, the first to take wagons on the route. A journal of their crossing may one day be found, but to date their experience can only be followed through the diaries of a group which followed a short distance behind. This group was led by Heinrich Lienhard, and the journal which he wrote in German gives some insight into the crossing of the Great Salt Lake Desert by both companies. By far the most celebrated and best known of the immigrant companies which passed over the Hastings Cutoff in the summer of 1846 was the fourth group—the ill-fated Donner-Reed party.[39]

The effects of this initial white contact were many and varied. Two groups, the trappers and the immigrants, seemed to have had very little initial influence on the Goshutes. However, the third group, the slavers, made quite an impact upon them. The actual effect of the slave trade on the Goshute and Western Shoshone can only be speculated upon because of the lack of hard evidence. The slavers did not distinguish between Paiute "Diggers" and Shoshone "Diggers," and, because of this, much confusion exists as to what groups were being raided. Many of the Indians described as Paiutes could well have been Western Shoshone or Goshutes. In later years, as white American penetration into the Goshute

homelands increased, there was very little information recorded on this group of Indians.

To summarize the contact mentioned, in 1845 John C. Frémont and his exploring expedition passed through the northern portion of the Goshute domain on their way to California. Frémont made no mention of the Goshute people.[40] In 1846 Lansford Hastings crossed over the same area and made no mention of the Indians. In reading the journals of the early immigrants from the summer of 1846, there was very little discussion of the Indians. The only exception to this was an occasional reference to Indians who were pillaging wagons abandoned in the desert. Perhaps the limited Goshute population was an important factor, or it could be that, in an area where horses were never utilized due to the lack of resources, these men on horseback, white or Indian, frightened the indigenous people into avoiding all contact. Also, the people who had come into their country earlier had come to steal or buy their children, and this could have led to Goshute timidity. Lack of information can only lead to speculation, but it is quite clear that the Goshutes suffered a population loss primarily due to the traffic in Indian captives; because of this, they avoided contact with outside people whenever possible.

Continual White Contact

The years between 1847 and 1874 brought the Goshute Indians into continual contact with white Americans. Many changes occurred in the Goshute portion of the Great Basin as whites moved into the region as permanent settlers. In 1847 the initial wave of Mormon settlers entered the Salt Lake Valley, and the spread of Mormons throughout the region soon had a pronounced effect on the Indians.

On February 2, 1848, the Treaty of Guadalupe Hidalgo was signed ending the Mexican War. As part of the terms, the United States obtained most of the present American Southwest, including Utah and Nevada—home of the Goshutes. The Goshutes came under the jurisdiction of the U.S. government, and in the late 1850s mention of them appeared in the annual report of the Commissioner of Indian Affairs.

In the 1850s the government sponsored surveys for possible railroad and wagon roads through lands inhabited by the Goshutes. Because of these surveys, valuable information on the condition of the area's Indians was recorded. Also, a Mormon-sponsored mail route from Sacramento, California, to Salt Lake City was established that ran through the heart of Goshute country. In the early 1860s the Pony Express and the Overland Stage routes crossed the area inhabited by Goshute people.

On July 24, 1847, the vanguard of the Mormon migration entered the valley of the Great Salt Lake. The arrival of these pioneers ushered in a new era in the lives of all the Indians of the Great Basin. Cultures that had been developing for hundreds of years underwent great changes, some of which erased signs of their predecessors. The early pioneers began to try to anglicize the Indian groups as soon as they arrived in the area, attempting also to convert them to the Mormon church. After reaching the Salt Lake Valley, Mormons began to explore the surrounding area, and soon settlements were founded on likely streams and in promising valleys. A number of these settlements were on Goshute land.

The first substantial contacts the Mormons had with the Indians in the territory were with the Utes in Utah County. Relations between the Utes and the Mormons generally degenerated until in 1853 an armed conflict between the two groups broke out. Known as the Walker War, named after the Ute leader Wakara, it temporarily slowed the Mormon settlement process. The Utes were forced to retreat, however, and the Mormons claimed a victory over the hostile Indians.[41]

An important result of this war was the displacement of some of the Ute Indians. The Utes in the area around Utah Lake were forced out of that region and relocated in other areas of the territory. Some of these Utes went west into the desert and the traditional Goshute domain. Some Ute men married Goshute women and assumed leadership roles among the combined peoples. This fact had an important effect in the 1860s when hostilities erupted between the Goshutes and the white settlers.

Members of the hierarchy of the LDS church, including church leader Brigham Young, visited Tooele Valley only a few days after their arrival in the Salt Lake Valley. Tooele Valley is located about twenty-five miles west of Salt Lake City. Because there were no significant topographical barriers, Tooele Valley was easily accessible from Salt Lake City. On July 17, 1849, Brigham Young and a company of men again entered the Tooele region. They hoped to find an area suitable for the establishment of a community.

In October 1849 a company of men under the direction of Ezra T. Benson entered the Tooele Valley to begin the construction of a sawmill. This was the first permanent encroachment into Goshute territory. A dozen or so Mormon families spent the winter of 1849–50 in the Tooele region. To foster better communication and to help the colonization process, on January 28, 1850, the General Assembly of the provisional State of Deseret (as the Mormons first designated their claimed territory) ordered the construction of a state road from Salt Lake City to Tooele Val-

ley.[42] United States census records for the year 1850 for the Territory of Utah listed 152 non-Indian people as living in Tooele County.

Once settlement began in the Goshute country, it continued at a rapid pace. Soon after the first community was established in Tooele Valley, the Mormons sent people to settle the areas of Grantsville and Pine Canyon (later named Lake View). In the summer of 1851 a fort was erected to protect these pioneers from the Indians. In 1852 the town of Erda was established, which enabled Brigham Young to announce that there was a successful settlement on the west side of Tooele Valley, although the Indians had made its establishment questionable. Erda was initially settled by Ormus E. Bates and for a while was called Batesville.[43]

Fear of the Goshute Indians prompted the Latter-day Saints in Grantsville to write to Brigham Young in the autumn of 1852 and request his advice. They were afraid because the Indians in the immediate area outnumbered them. The settlers knew that the Indians had remained friendly, but they were not sure how long this could last, "as Indians are very treacherous," they maintained. They requested that a dozen or more families be sent to reinforce the settlement to help guarantee their security.[44] The request for new settlers was met, and by the time of the October general conference of the LDS church in 1853 there were 159 church members in the Grantsville area. Within two years there were 251, and, next to Tooele City, Grantsville became the leading settlement in the valley.

Tooele continued to grow and became the focal point for the settled area around it. By 1853 there were 602 LDS church members in Tooele City. With the growth of the white population came the establishment of another settlement. The community of Lake Point came into existence in 1854. The settlement was first named E.T. City after Mormon leader Ezra Taft Benson, but it was later given its present name. Initial indications were that the community could prosper; however, continued farming and irrigation raised the level of alkali in the soil, making farming difficult if not impossible. Another problem was the Great Salt Lake. In times of high water the lake could cover some of the fields of the settlers, ruining their crops. When this high water occurred, many people moved to Tooele.

Livestock were introduced into the area early in its settlement, as local valleys were used as herd grounds. By the winter of 1854–55, cattle were wintering in the north end of Rush Valley, which lies south of Tooele. During this same period a cabin was built west of Rush Valley Lake. Other cabins were built there in 1855, and a few settlers spent the winter in

This young Goshute Indian was photographed in the family's
well-cared-for garden. (USHS)

them. In early 1856 the threat of Indian attack forced these people back
to Tooele, but by April they had returned. The settlement first was called
Johnson, then Shambip, then Clover, and was finally given its present
name of Rush Valley.[45]

Up to this point all the settlements had been established in Tooele,
Rush, and Skull Valleys bordering the eastern edge of Tooele County and
the Goshute homeland. The Mormons wished to remain in rather close
proximity to their settlements in Salt Lake and Utah Counties. By 1860

the census figures showed that the population in Tooele County had grown to 1,008 non-Indians.

The last major Mormon settlement in the region was at Ibapah, or Deep Creek, in 1860. With the establishment of this community, the last of the favored regions in the Goshute homeland had been invaded. The Deep Creek region runs in a north-south direction and is approximately sixty miles south of Wendover, Utah. The primary geological feature is the Deep Creek Mountains, which catch the winter snow and deliver an adequate water supply throughout the summer months. The same years this community was established, the Pony Express began operation and one of its stations was located at Ibapah. Pony Express stations employed many of the first white inhabitants of the Deep Creek region.[46]

The settlement of Faust in 1860, Vernon in 1862, Center (later called Ajax), and then Stockton in 1864 filled in the valleys of the eastern portion of the Goshute homeland. These settlements, located south of Rush Valley, helped to solidify the Mormon occupation of the eastern portion of the Goshute homeland.[47]

Other incidents occurred during the mid-nineteenth century that helped bring permanent white contact to the Goshutes. In 1850 Utah had gained territorial status, and Brigham Young was appointed territorial superintendent of Indian Affairs. From this time on, the Goshutes were placed under the jurisdiction of the federal government. In 1853 the Mormons began to send missionaries to the neighboring Indians in hopes of converting them; however, early efforts were not directed toward the Goshutes. The Mormon settlers felt it was their duty to bring the word of God to the Indians. Settlers like Howard Egan gave the Goshute instructions in farming, and, after some initial difficulty, they became adept at it. The Deep Creek region is one of the most fertile areas on the western fringe of the Goshute domain, and it was here that a farm was set up by the Mormons to help the Indians become "Americanized."[48]

In the summer of 1854 a private mail route was opened that went through Deep Creek and then on to California. This route preceded the Overland Stage route, which soon led to the building of stations at some of the most important watering springs in the Goshute homeland. These stations eventually deprived the area Goshutes of water, herbs, seeds, fish, and waterfowl.[49]

As relations between the Mormons and federal authorities degenerated, plans were made in 1857 to send an army to crush the reported Utah rebellion. The Indians in the territory were obviously interested in the forthcoming war between the Mormons and the United States; how-

ever, they did not realize the effect its outcome could have upon them. A large group of Indians gathered in the mountainous region east of Ogden, where it appeared the battle between the Mormon militia and federal troops would take place. Daniel Jones stated that while camping at Echo Canyon, waiting for the federal troops, large groups of "Weber and Goshutes" were in the same general area.[50]

Negotiations took place during the winter of 1857–58 and a compromise settlement was finally reached. The federal army entered Salt Lake City, and a military post was established about forty miles to the south in Cedar Valley. The post was named Camp Floyd and was located on the eastern fringe of the Goshute homeland, where it played a brief but important role in Indian-white relations in the area.[51] The successful negotiation of the so-called Utah War can also be seen as the beginning of a shift of power, lasting approximately twenty years, where non-Mormon whites replaced the Mormons as the dominant white influence among the Goshute Indians.

The decade of the 1850s brought many changes to the Goshutes, and by the end of this ten-year period the non-Indian population in the Goshute homeland had reached approximately 1,000 people, exceeding that of the Indians. This large non-Indian population placed the Goshutes in a desperate situation. The Indians had long been accustomed to placing their camps near streams and canyons to take advantage of the water and food supply there. As the whites increasingly encroached into Goshute homelands, they established permanent settlements and began building sawmills and gristmills. These white settlers brought with them the idea of exclusive use of natural resources and robbed the Goshutes of many of the things they needed to survive.[52]

The Indians retaliated to this encroachment by raiding the settlements and stealing the settlers' stock. Unlike the conflict between the Mormons and the Utes in other portions of the Utah Territory, these raids never evolved into open warfare between the people of Tooele County and the Goshute Indians. The conflict with the Goshutes basically was a war of attrition, and it continued into the 1860s.

The Goshute raids began as soon as the Mormons upset the natural balance of the area. As early as 1851 it was estimated that the Indians had stolen approximately $5,000 in livestock from the Mormon inhabitants of the Tooele region.[53] The Mormon settlers reacted to this violence in a like manner and raided the Goshute encampments to retrieve stolen merchandise and to discourage the Indians from further "depredations." Jacob Hamblin, an early pioneer in the Tooele region, related that he and

some men were directed to go into the field and kill all the Indians they contacted. However, after an attempted ambush of a Goshute village failed, Hamblin and his men returned to Tooele and noted that neither whites nor Indians had sustained any casualties.[54]

An incident in 1851 revolved around the stealing of a small herd of cattle belonging to one Charles White. The animals were taken from the area around Black Rock at the south end of the Great Salt Lake. The Indians herded the cattle past Grantsville and into Skull Valley, where they killed the beef to dry the meat and prepare it for storage. Initially, the Indians were pursued by fourteen men from Salt Lake City under the command of Captain William McBride. The force of Indians was deemed too large to be dealt with by so few men, so a runner was sent to Salt Lake City for reinforcements. A force of forty men under the command of General James Ferguson and Colonels George D. Grant and William H. Kimball responded. After picking up ten additional men in Tooele, they proceeded to Skull Valley where the Indians had been located. The camp was attacked and nine Indians lost their lives. The white force sustained no casualties.[55]

The hostility increased as non-Mormons entered the Goshute country. At the conclusion of the Utah War, Brigham Young was replaced as territorial superintendent of Indian Affairs by a non-Mormon named Jacob Forney. In 1858 Forney recorded the first official account of the Goshute Indians who lived in the area around Skull Valley, writing: "I have visited a small tribe called the Go-sha-utes, who live about forty miles west of this city [Salt Lake]." He was struck by the harshness of the arid region and by what he considered to be the destitute conditions of the Indians in the region and their lack of material possessions. He continued, "I gave them some clothing and provisions. They have heretofore subsisted principally on snakes, lizards, roots etc. I made considerable effort to procure a small quantity of land for them, but could not find any with water to irrigate it."[56]

The following year, Forney had more to add relating to the Goshute Indians:

This band is a mixture of Snake and Ute, the former prepondering. A few years ago the Go-sha-utes were a considerable tribe. Their principal and only chief died about four years ago, since which they have remained broken and subdivided into small fragments, except about sixty, who have organized into a

Four Goshute boys, with the Deep Creek Mountains in the background.
(Vyrie Grey Collection, U of U)

band, and have a quiet and well disposed chief to control them.
This band is now permanently located on the Deep Creek Indian farm. The remainder roam over a region of country from
forty to two hundred miles west of this city [Salt Lake]. A concentration of them all into Deep Creek is in progress.[57]

The Goshutes caused the Overland Mail service problems by stealing stock and attacking drivers as they passed through the country. This
was one of the reasons that Superintendent Forney wanted the Goshutes
concentrated on a farm at Deep Creek. To this end, Forney instructed
Robert B. Jarvis to go to Deep Creek and then on to Ruby Valley, Nevada,
to try to restrain the Indians from committing depredations. Jarvis found
that the primary barriers to relocating the Goshutes at Deep Creek had
already been reduced because of the Mormon ranchers who had settled
in the area. The Mormons were interested in the Indians and had been
working with them for a few years.

On his way to Deep Creek, Jarvis stopped at Simpson's Springs, and
while he was there a party of fourteen Goshutes visited his camp. They
talked briefly, and then the Indians were given a few presents. Jarvis in-

structed these Indians to inform the rest of their people that he wanted to meet with them in a few days in Pleasant Valley.[58]

Jarvis was understandably disappointed when he reached Pleasant Valley and only about one hundred Indians had gathered for the meeting. He was told that the other Indians believed this meeting was a trap to kill them because they had been stealing stock from the mail company. Jarvis sent messengers to convince the other Indians to come to the meeting. Those attempts failed, however, so the conference began without them.

The election of a tribal chief and subchief was the first order of business. After this was accomplished, Jarvis told the Indians that he was sent there by the "great father," who wanted to treat the Native Americans as his children and give them a farm so they could provide for themselves. The "great father" wanted to help his Goshute children, but only if they did what he wanted them to do. Jarvis continued by asking the assembled Indians if they were willing to work like the white men and raise grain to make bread. Evidently the Goshutes found this acceptable and agreed. He also told them he had heard of many cattle being stolen and that mail riders had been attacked. Jarvis assured them that the "great father" would forgive them this time but, if depredations continued, an army would descend to destroy all of them. The newly elected chief stated that his people were friendly to the whites and would do nothing to harm them.[59]

A government farm was finally established for the Goshutes at Deep Creek and crops were planted. Almost twenty-five acres of wheat and some potatoes, beets, onions, and melons were cultivated. Things initially went well for the Indian farms in Utah Territory. In 1859 Forney reported: "The farms are well located, on rich soil, and some of the Indians have worked well, and many more manifest a desire to do so as soon as they can be fed."[60]

Unfortunately for the Goshutes, Agent Jarvis resigned shortly afterwards and the farm at Deep Creek soon was abandoned. This was just one of many incidents that frustrated the Goshutes. Most of these people were interested in agriculture, but the frequent changes in government personnel delayed the permanent establishment of the farms.

Benjamin Davies, who replaced Jarvis as the Goshute agent, reported in 1860 that "Scarcely a vestige of the improvements once existing ... was visible." He also noted that the Indians "had lost confidence in the government and the people of the United States."[61]

Other federal officials also were active in Goshute country at this time. In 1859 Captain J.H. Simpson of the U.S. Army Corps of Topo-

graphical Engineers undertook the exploration of a direct wagon route from Camp Floyd to Genoa in western Nevada. Simpson recorded many valuable observations regarding the everyday life of the Goshutes.[62]

In 1858 the route for the Overland Stage had been organized and incorporated the earlier private company. This was followed in 1860 by the Pony Express, which was abandoned the following year when the first transcontinental stage line was established. With the establishment of the Pony Express and the Overland Stage, the Indians of the Goshute country raided the area stations and stole their stock. In some instances, they killed some of the drivers and stationmasters. The stage line existed until the transcontinental railroad was completed in 1869. The railroad ran through northern Utah, but the tracks were north of the Goshute homeland. Before the railroad was completed, however, the lands of the Goshutes had been crossed by the main lines of communication between the eastern United States and the West Coast. The stage line constructed twenty-two stations on Goshute land, and the loss of resources to the Indians was appalling.[63] Benjamin Davies indicated the effects of the stage stations upon the Goshutes:

> At some of these springs were immense quantities of dark-colored fish called "the chub," about four inches in length, which the Indians used to eat in winter, but the overland California mail company has built stations for their convenience, and located men and quartered stock about those spots, and the Indians no longer visit them.[64]

Davies recommended that the Goshutes should be protected from further white encroachments, but no action was taken on this recommendation. Also, there were no further attempts to reestablish the Deep Creek farm. Because the farms were abandoned, the Indians became disenchanted and some remarked that the whites were trying to take over all their land.[65]

One of the many travelers to cross the desert on the Overland Stage was the young humorist Samuel Clemens (later famous as Mark Twain). His description of the Goshute epitomizes the attitudes of most of the whites who came in contact with them. Twain wrote:

> We came across the wretchedest type of mankind.... I refer to the Goshoot Indians.... [They] have no villages, and no gatherings together into strictly defined tribal communities—a people

whose only shelter is a rag cast on a bush to keep off a portion of the snow, and yet who inhabit one of the most rocky, wintry, repulsive wastes that our country or any other can exhibit.[66]

The Goshutes could expect little help or understanding from people who held them in such disdain.

The transcontinental telegraph had little effect on the Goshutes. The Indians occasionally were hired as unskilled labor to aid in erecting poles and transporting materials. The nature of the telegraph was such that it did not need much maintenance, so the Indians saw few whites working on the line.

By early 1860 Indian-white relations in the western portion of the Great Basin were at a critical point. The Overland Stage was constantly harassed, and some of the permanent settlements were threatened. In May of that year a detachment of federal troops was sent to the area from Camp Floyd. The commander of this unit was a Lieutenant Weed, and it later was said that the unit had "done good service against the Gosh-Yuta."[67] Many whites in the area, however, were still apprehensive due to the Indian discontent.

Goshutes attacked the mail station at Deep Creek on May 8, 1860, stealing several horses and killing one man. The next month, the station at Willow Springs, just east of Deep Creek, was also attacked. No whites were killed, but three Indians died in their attempt to overrun the station. That June the station at Antelope Springs, about twenty miles west of Deep Creek, was also attacked and burned, although its occupants escaped with their lives.[68]

The military reacted to this situation and troops were sent to quell the Indians. Lieutenant Weed and seventeen mounted men rescued a man and a boy in Egan Canyon in August 1860. The two were being held by Goshutes. When the troops attacked, seventeen Indians were killed. The Indians retaliated. Express riders were attacked, several while crossing the desert, and some ranchers reported being attacked in their camps. It was also noted that a small emigrant train was attacked in the vicinity of Egan Canyon, with all but two of the travelers being killed.[69]

With the beginning of the Civil War in 1861, Camp Floyd was abandoned by the U.S. Army. The defense of the stage and mail stations was placed in the hands of Mormons who were hired for that purpose. There are no reports of further raiding until U.S. troops returned in May 1862, a detachment of California Volunteers under the command of Colonel Patrick Edward Connor.

After Connor's troops annihilated a group of almost 300 Shoshones in southern Idaho in early 1863, he turned his attention to ending the hostile actions of the Indians along the transcontinental stage and mail route. This route had gained importance because of the gold from California and the silver from Nevada that traveled the route to help finance the Civil War. Soldiers were detached to each coach to provide protection, while others were located at stations along the route. One group at Simpson's Springs decided to undertake an expedition to kill Indians. They persuaded William Riley, one of the station workers at Simpson's Springs, to guide them six miles to the south to an Indian camp located at Coyote Springs.

The camp which was attacked was one whose leader was an important, but friendly, Pahvant Ute named Peahnamp, who was married to a Goshute woman from Deep Creek. At the time of the attack he was not at the encampment. Upon his return he found that the soldiers had been there and had killed many of his people. In response to this unprovoked attack, Peahnamp attacked a mail station and killed five or six white men. One of the dead men was William Riley, the man who had served as guide for the troops. Goshute sources state that one man escaped; other sources disagree.[70]

The situation of the Goshute at this time was best described by Amos Reed. In a letter dated December 1862, Reed reported to the U.S. Commissioner of Indian Affairs that the largest portion of tillable land in the Goshute country had been occupied by whites and that the game had been killed or driven off. In response to this loss of resources the Indians had turned to raiding the Overland Mail and stage stations. Reed was convinced that unless the Goshutes received assistance they would either steal what they needed or starve. The government reacted by giving the mail company provisions to distribute among the Indians along its route. The mail company supplied an additional $12,000 for the same purpose. It was believed that the distribution of the provisions would reduce the Indian problems on the route between Salt Lake City and Carson City.[71]

Indian attacks continued, however; during the winter of 1862–63, Goshutes continued to harass the mail stations. Three stations were attacked and three men were killed and one wounded. The stage company lost a total of seventeen stations, 150 horses, and sixteen men in this "Gosh Ute War."[72] Utah Indian Superintendent James Doty responded to these depredations by stating that they were "without the slightest provocation," and requested an increase in federal appropriations to pacify the Indians.[73]

Many of the attacks that were committed seem to have been under the leadership of Pahvant Ute Indians. The Goshutes were divided as to their preferred course of action. Some joined with the Ute leaders in raiding the stage and mail companies and ranches in the area. Others remained neutral, anticipating that the Mormons or the government would help them establish farms. A dichotomy existed, with the army reporting hostile engagements with Goshutes while the agents related stories of their peaceful disposition. One noted in 1863: "I am satisfied that not one-half the depredations committed are the work of the Goshe Utes, although they have the name and the blame."[74]

The government responded to the continued hostilities by concluding a series of treaties with the Indians of Utah and Nevada in 1863. In their treaty the Goshutes agreed to end all hostile actions against the whites and to allow several routes of travel to pass through their country which would not be subject to depredations. The Goshutes also agreed to the construction of military posts and station houses wherever necessary and that stage lines, telegraph lines, and railways could be built throughout their domain. Also, mines, mills, and ranches would be permitted and timber could be cut. The federal government agreed to pay the Goshutes $1,000 a year for the next twenty years as compensation for the destruction of their game. The Goshutes also agreed to give up their nomadic ways and remove to a reservation. The treaty was signed on October 12, 1863, ratified in 1864, and announced by President Abraham Lincoln on January 17, 1865.[75]

The treaty was not one of land cession; rather, it was an agreement of peace and amity—the Goshutes did not give up sovereignty over their land.[76] Although the treaty provided for the ultimate removal of the Goshutes, it did nothing to secure a specified area for their removal. The Goshute continued to live on their land like nothing had happened, but their hostilities toward whites ceased.

Before the treaty of 1863 had been announced, the federal government had endeavored to remove all of the Utah Indian tribes to one large reservation. On May 5, 1864, President Lincoln approved "An Act to vacate and sell the present Indians reservations in Utah Territory, and to settle the Indians of said Territory in the Uintah Valley."[77] The Uintah Reservation was established, yet, while many of the Indian groups in Utah eventually accepted removal to it, the Goshutes never did.

The treaty with the Goshutes made no arrangements for placing them on farms; however, in 1864 Superintendent Doty noted that members of the tribe were working farms at Deep Creek and at Grantsville. Because

A Goshute farmer. (USHS)

of this, he concluded that, if the government would help, the area Goshutes could become self-sufficient in farming and ranching. He believed that they wanted to settle because, "More than a hundred of them have been killed by the soldiers, and the survivors beg for peace."[78]

In 1864 the first annuity goods were due, but the goods received proved to be only a fraction of what the Goshutes actually needed. The new territorial Indian superintendent, O.H. Irish, believed the Goshute annuity should be increased to $5,000. Irish found the Goshutes peaceful, but the mail company still believed they were dangerous. If the pine nut crop failed, the Goshutes would be forced to raid the stations for needed supplies or starve. Irish believed that the federal government should give the Indians supplies which would conciliate them and protect the mail.[79]

Goshute Day School at Ibapah. (Vyrie Grey Collection, U of U)

Irish also believed that the Indians could no longer exist in their native lands. This added fuel to the government's efforts to concentrate all
Utah Indians on reservations. In February 1865 the U.S. Commissioner
of Indian Affairs was informed by the Secretary of the Interior that any
Indian group that did not move in compliance with the Act of 1864 would
not receive their treaty benefits. Later that same month, Congress passed
a law that extinguished the Indian title to land in Utah Territory in order
that it could be used by whites for farming and mining purposes.[80]

The government moved quickly to extinguish the Goshutes' title.
Commissioner William P. Dole wrote Superintendent Irish reminding
him of Article 6 of the Goshute treaty, whereby the Indians had agreed to
settle on a reservation whenever the president of the United States deemed
it expedient. The president now deemed it expedient, and Irish was instructed to work to that end.[81]

Irish met with members of the various Utah tribes in June 1865. At
this meeting Irish negotiated a treaty whereby the Indians relinquished
all rights of possession to lands in Utah Territory. It was decided that
after the Indians ceded their land title they would move to the Uinta
Basin. This move was to take place one year after the ratification of the
treaty. The government agreed to spend $25,000 annually in annuities to
aid the Goshutes for ten years after ratification. After the first ten-year
period, the government agreed to pay the Indians $20,000 for each of the

The Goshute Day School at Ibapah, in the center of the photograph. (Vyrie Grey Collection, U of U)

next ten years, and then $15,000 annually for an additional thirty years. The Goshutes were told that their "reservation" at Deep Creek would be sold for not less than sixty-two and one-half cents per acre and that the money would be used for their benefit.[82] The Senate never ratified the treaty, however, and the Goshutes remained on their lands. In 1867 Superintendent F.H. Head reported that the Goshutes did not fully understand that the Senate had to ratify their treaty, and the Indians were discouraged because it had not been implemented.[83]

By 1869 the lifestyle and culture of the Goshutes had undergone a significant change. They no longer roamed the desert as they once had, although hunting and gathering were still practiced. Most of the people had settled on farms at Deep Creek and Skull Valley and were trying to sustain a living. The federal authorities promoted this new lifestyle and did much to help the Goshutes in this undertaking. In 1869, Goshutes had put about thirty acres under cultivation at Deep Creek, and the people at Skull Valley had received the aid of a Mormon farmer named William Lee. Area Goshutes received the necessary farming implements and harvested around one thousand bushels of potatoes, beets, and carrots. However, grasshoppers destroyed the majority of their wheat crop.[84]

While this movement toward settlement was taking place, efforts also continued to relocate all the Goshutes on a permanent reservation. Perhaps the most important problem to be resolved before this relocation

could take place was the Goshutes' fear of other Indian groups. Because of this fear, in 1869 Superintendent J.E. Tourtellotte suggested that the Goshutes have a separate reservation.[85]

In the spring of 1870, Superintendent Tourtellotte noted that the Goshute Indians in Skull Valley showed a predilection toward farming. He also noted that whites were disrupting Indian attempts at agriculture as they encroached on the Indian farms and tried to obtain the land for themselves. Tourtellotte recommended to Washington that at least a quarter section of land be made available to the Goshute Indians until a permanent decision about them was made.[86] The Commissioner of Indian Affairs, Ely Parker, reminded Tourtellotte that the Goshute Indians were to be moved to the Uinta Basin and that he should accomplish this as soon as possible. Tourtellotte wrote a letter to Parker attempting to explain that the Goshutes were not culturally related to the Utes and that they refused to go and live with them in the Uinta Basin; if they had to be moved, Tourtellotte recommended that they be moved to a reservation with Shoshone Indians.[87]

The year 1870 saw the Western Shoshones being attached bureaucratically to the jurisdiction of the Nevada Indian superintendent, and Tourtellotte was interested in learning more about them. He found that a group of Goshutes were trying to farm near Egan Canyon on land belonging to John V. Dougherty. Superintendent H. Douglas reported that the government had done nothing to help these Indians and it seemed that their existence had been ignored. Dougherty allowed the Indians to work a portion of his farmland, and in 1871 they harvested a few crops. However, they remained rather destitute, and in October 1870 Dougherty appealed to the Utah superintendent to provide some supplies.[88]

Early in 1871 both Tourtellotte and William Lee were relieved of their positions. The Goshutes of Skull Valley were confused and were not sure of receiving continued assistance. Because of their respect for and confidence in Lee, they asked him to be their spokesman to the government. Lee assumed the role and wrote to the new agent, Colonel J.J. Critchlow, and tried to persuade him not to end government aid to these people. Lee articulated his fear that if aid was cut off the Goshutes would be forced to steal and hostilities might begin anew. He also informed Agent Critchlow that the Indians wanted to remain in their homelands and did not want to move to the Uinta Basin.[89]

In the latter part of 1871 the government sent George W. Dodge, with the status of Special Agent, to look into Utah Indian affairs. A meeting with the Goshutes was scheduled for January 9, 1872, and William

A mounted Goshute Indian near Ibapah in 1924. (USHS)

Lee volunteered the use of his ranch. Dodge was evidently impressed with the condition of the Goshute people, because he asked that more than $2,500 worth of supplies be sent to them. Dodge also believed, however, that the only hope for the survival of the Goshutes was in their removal to another area. He recommended that the Goshutes be sent to the Shoshone Reservation at Fort Hall, Idaho; but later he amended this request and recommended instead that all the Shoshone Indians in Utah and Nevada be sent to the Indian Territory—present-day Oklahoma.[90] The Goshute people were not interested in moving to either Fort Hall or the Indian Territory, and they remained in their homelands.

In 1873, John Wesley Powell and George W. Ingalls were appointed as special commissioners to look into the affairs of those western Indians who had not removed to reservations. In a preliminary report, they stated that the Goshutes numbered around 400 individuals and that at least some of them were farming at Skull Valley, Deep Creek, Salt Marsh, and Warm Springs. Both Powell and Ingalls agreed that white movement into the Goshutes' homeland had caused the destruction of their game and consequently forced them into smaller bands. They also felt that, for their own benefit, the Goshute people should be forced to remove to the Uinta Basin. The federal authorities agreed, and Powell and Ingalls were instructed to proceed with the removal of the Goshutes.[91]

Powell and Ingalls submitted their final report in December 1873. They concluded that there were 256 Goshutes in Utah and 204 in Nevada. The commissioners also concluded that the removal to a reservation was the best way the federal government could serve the Goshute Indians. They urged the repeal of the 1864 law that stipulated that existing "reservations" were to be sold, and that the area be opened to whites in the usual manner.[92]

The Goshute people did not remove to a reservation, however, despite the report of the Special Commission. The Commissioner of Indian Affairs asked Powell for more information on the Goshutes in 1875, and again he reported that the Indians should be removed.[93]

Due to a lack of firm government purpose, direction, and organization, the Goshute people remained in their homeland and did not remove to any reservation. The eastern groups remained in Skull Valley, while to the west the Goshutes at Deep Creek farmed on their "reservation." William Lee continued to write letters trying to obtain aid for the Indians, with the intention of helping them become self-sufficient.[94] The annuities promised in the treaty of 1863 stopped, while whites invaded the choice areas of land. The Indians were destitute and it seemed that few white people actually knew of their existence.

This condition continued on through the remainder of the nineteenth century and into the first two decades of the twentieth century. In examining the reports and correspondence of the Office of Indian Affairs, the Goshute Indians practically disappeared as far as the bureaucracy was concerned. The number of 256 Goshutes in Utah offered by Powell and Ingalls in 1873 was reported in the annual reports for every year to 1895; after this date mention of them disappears entirely. It was as if the Goshute Indians had disappeared without a trace. One reason for this is that reports from the Uintah Indian Agency listed the Goshutes

as one of the tribes inhabiting that reservation. It may have been that a few Goshutes did eventually relocate in the Uinta Basin, but the number must have been small. For the most part, the Goshutes remained at Skull Valley and Deep Creek.

For more than thirty years the whites had been filtering into the Goshutes' domain and appropriating the land. The Indians maintained their free-roving lifestyle, but towns, farms, stage and mail stations, and a military post were established at the favored locations in the desert. The Indians' food resources dwindled as the white population increased. Some Goshutes tried farming, but even with the aid of well-intentioned whites, the results were far from spectacular. As years passed, the Goshutes became more and more dependent upon the whites for many of the everyday necessities of life; and, by the mid-1870s, they were unable to reverse this dependence.

The decades between 1880 and 1920 saw an increase of white encroachment into the Goshute homeland. Miners explored the area and mining communities grew as precious metals were discovered and exploited. Ranching activities also increased, taking more land and water from the Goshute people. The most essential element in the establishment of settlements in the desert was water, vital to both the native and white people. The Goshutes had been able to camp at favorable sites in the desert whenever they chose. They had harvested seeds from plants that grew around the springs as well as the fish and waterfowl that inhabited the marshier areas. In an area where there was a comparatively small amount of water, what water existed was critical to the Goshutes' existence. With the establishment of ranches at favorable locations in the desert, the Indians were denied the essentials these areas had provided.

The ranchers affected the Goshute people in other ways, most notably in their efforts to convert the people to Mormonism. The Deep Creek region was important because it was free from federal control. Colonel Patrick Connor, a devout Mormon hater, worked to keep interaction between Mormons and Indians to a minimum. The Goshute "reservation" at Deep Creek was established by the Mormons to teach the people farming. The federal government had no jurisdiction at this "reservation" because it had played no part in its establishment. Because of this, the Mormons used the Deep Creek region as a concentration area for Indians in the surrounding country. Groups like the Western Shoshone, Ute, Northern Shoshone, and even Crow were reported congregating in the Deep Creek region to obtain instruction in the Mormon faith.

During the decade of the 1870s, the LDS church expanded its mis-

sionary activities among the various Indian groups in the territory. Missions were established among the tribes and converts were brought into the Mormon fold. William Lee, the rancher who had helped the Goshutes in Skull Valley and later served as their spokesman, was especially successful in his efforts to obtain converts. He reported that in 1874 he was able to baptize more than 1,000 Indians from the Deep Creek area. Certainly, not all these Indians were Goshutes, but a rather large number of Goshutes did convert to Mormonism.[95]

On June 2, 1874, the *Desert Evening News* described one of these baptismal services at Deep Creek. The paper stated:

> One hundred [Indians] were submerged and confirmed into the "Mormon" faith here yesterday, by Indian Interpreter [William] Lee, from Grantsville, and three others whom he deputized as assistants. Sixty minutes were consumed in the operation, a heavy rain prevailing at the time.[96]

Howard Egan stated that during the 1870s there was a general religious movement among the Goshutes in western Utah. He also reported that while his father was working a mining claim, he was involved in missionary work among the Goshute people. Egan's father may not have been as successful as Lee, but he evidently encouraged many of the Goshute people to become farmers. Egan claimed that many of the converted Indians were employed as farm laborers on the white ranches around the Deep Creek area.[97]

Mormon missionaries continued to circumvent the orders of the commanders at Fort Douglas, Utah, which prevented the Mormons from proselytizing on federal Indian reservations. The military and civilian authorities distrusted the Mormons and feared their influence among the Indians. The army had no jurisdiction over the Deep Creek "reservation," so the Mormons continued to use this region as a concentration area for their missionary activities. Native people came from other areas of the Intermountain West, from Wyoming, Idaho, and eastern Nevada. This explains why 1,000 Indians could be baptized in an area where only about 250 Goshutes lived.[98]

The missionary activity continued into the 1880s, but then it appears that the Mormons lost interest in their concentration of Indian groups at Deep Creek. Federal authorities no longer restricted Mormons from proselytizing on reservations, so there was no need to gather the Indians. In March 1883 the Church of Jesus Christ of Latter-day Saints

placed the Goshute Indians remaining around the Deep Creek area on a 1,000-acre farm that became the approximate site of the present Goshute reservation. The church held the property title for a few years and then deeded it to the Indians.[99]

After the 1880s Mormon missionary activities among the Goshutes decreased. The government failed to fill the void left by the LDS church, and the Indians were left to deal with the non-Mormon whites who began to invade their land. These non-Mormon whites came into the region for many reasons but primarily to ranch and mine in the suitable areas remaining in the Goshute domain. After the Mormon church deeded the land to the Goshute people they became vulnerable to their greedy and selfish neighbors.[100] By the time the mining boom ended in the late 1880s, the Goshute people had been effectively concentrated in Deep Creek and in Skull Valley. The Goshutes remained in these areas, eking out a living and attempting to withstand the onslaught of their white neighbors, while looking to Washington, D.C., for recognition and assistance. Ignored and forgotten, no removal policy was enforced upon the Goshutes and during the nineteenth century no federally recognized reservation was established for them.

The Reservation Period

After several decades of neglect, federal authorities finally realized the Goshute Indians would not willingly leave their homelands, so finally two reservations were established by executive orders within a relatively short period. On January 17, 1912, President William Howard Taft set aside eighty acres in Skull Valley for the exclusive use of the Goshute Indians residing there. Later, on September 7, 1919, this small reservation was enlarged by 17,920 acres by President Woodrow Wilson. The Deep Creek reservation in western Tooele and Juab Counties and eastern Nevada was created on March 23, 1914, when 34,560 acres in Utah was declared a reservation by the president. Several tracts of land subsequently have been added to the Deep Creek reservation, and its current total size is about 112,870 acres.[101]

With the establishment of these reservations by the federal government, the Goshute people were finally secure in their traditional homeland. The Goshute people now had the enormous task of establishing a way of life which included preserving elements of their traditional culture while meeting the challenges of the developing twentieth century. Along with the reservations came agents and numerous federal employees, government policies of cultural assimilation, and an attempt to or-

A Goshute hand game being played about 1930. (Vyrie Grey Collection, U of U)

der Goshute life along a white American model. As the federal government made its presence felt on the reservations, conflict occurred. Agents were not always trusted and there was a feeling among the Goshute people that some of the agents were cheating them to better their own situations. On the Deep Creek reservation, the government established a school to teach the Goshutes about white culture as well as vocational skills including carpentry, basic farming, and livestock production. Girls were instructed in basic domestic skills to be used in their own homes as well as in working for whites. Later, Goshute children were sent off the reservation to boarding schools for their primary education.

While the majority of interactions between the Goshutes and federal authorities were civil and peaceable, one incident in 1918 indicates the underlying tension between the tribe and their agent. The incident is sometimes referred to as the Goshute uprising of 1918, and it involved the refusal of a number of Goshute men on the Deep Creek reservation to comply with the Selective Service Act of May 18, 1917. That act required that all male residents of the United States between the ages of twenty-one and thirty-one register for conscription and possible service in the military. Amos R. Frank was the superintendent at the Deep Creek Agency and was also appointed the local "draft board" for the Goshutes. L.A. Dorrington was appointed as a special agent for the Commissioner

of Indian Affairs and was assigned to investigate why the Goshutes refused to register for the draft. Frank evidently had explained to the Goshutes that the conscription registration was merely a census and did not mean that they would be drafted. Frank was supposed to have told the Goshutes that as Indians they had not been given citizenship and would not be called upon to serve in the military. Frank's statements evidently satisfied no one, however, and the Goshute men refused to register.[102]

Superintendent Frank then requested that several Goshute men be arrested for inciting this draft resistance. The Goshute men were to register for conscription in June 1917, but the month came and went with no one registering. Several men were arrested and tensions between the Goshutes and federal authorities increased. Rumors from both sides of the dispute added to the tension and distrust. The Goshutes armed themselves and reportedly bought thirty cases of ammunition from the local store. However, conflict was avoided when the Goshute prisoners were released and the men agreed to register for the draft and serve if called upon. Federal authorities wanted two Goshute men taken into custody, but the majority of the draft resisters refused to surrender one of the individuals. Finally the request was withdrawn and a tenuous peace was restored.

Tensions increased again when a number of Indians from Nevada entered the reservation, with more expected. Finally, in February 1918 Special Agent Dorrington filed an official complaint against the Goshute Indians and had warrants issued for the arrest of several of the supposed ringleaders. Army troops were called in and soldiers were sent to carry out the warrants. The troops arrived and moved onto the reservation. About 100 men were detained, with six eventually being arrested. The six men were finally set free and the Goshute uprising of 1918 came to an end. Eventually 163 Goshute men registered for conscription, as rumors of uprisings continued to flourish.[103]

The Goshute uprising of 1918 serves as an example of some of the problems the Goshute people faced as they settled into life on a federal Indian reservation. This specific situation seems to have resulted in a genuine misunderstanding on the part of the Goshutes as to just what was expected of them and why. Also, the local Goshutes had a basic distrust of Superintendent Frank and his role as government representative to their people.

For the next two decades the Goshute people had to struggle with a number of important and perplexing issues. One of the most difficult

issues to address was that of governance. The Goshutes had been accustomed to living primarily in family units without a strong central leader. When the federal government established the reservations for both the Deep Creek and Skull Valley bands, officials began creating a tribal "government" that mirrored the bureaucracy in which they functioned. "Chiefs," or leaders, had to be selected and "councils" had to be established. Decisions had to be funneled through a system which seemed arbitrary and was hitherto almost completely unknown to the Goshutes. Other issues also needed to be addressed. For example, did the Deep Creek Band and the Skull Valley Band wish to remain separate entities with their own council and leaders, or did it make more sense to consolidate both the reservations into one operational unit?

While the political questions continued unresolved, physical changes were occurring on the reservations. Agriculture was to be the basic economic mainstay for both reservations. To this end, fields were cleared and planted, equipment was brought in, and the Goshutes were again given instruction on how to farm. Houses, barns, sheds, and other buildings were constructed on the reservations. Roads were improved and transportation issues were addressed. Communication with the communities surrounding the reservations was considered important to help alleviate the isolation of the Goshute people and help them on the road to "civilization." The paternalistic nature of the reservation system offended and alienated many of the Goshutes, however.

On November 25, 1940, the Confederated Tribes of Goshute Reservations adopted a constitution and by-laws for the governance of the reservations. Discussions were held between the Deep Creek people and those living in Skull Valley to see if either of the groups was interested in joining together as a single political unit. The Skull Valley Band opted to remain independent, with no official ties to the Deep Creek reservation.

The constitution of 1940 detailed tribal organizations, rules for electing officials, terms of office, and much of the present organization of both reservations. On the Deep Creek reservation, the tribe elects five tribal council members to serve for three consecutive years. The tribal council then chooses one of its five members to hold the position of tribal chairman. The tribal council governs the reservation by providing leadership in the areas of education, irrigation, health, economic development, law enforcement, senior citizens' programs, tribal administration and finance, social services programs, and wildlife and parks management. The Skull Valley people did not adopt the constitution; however, they elect a tribal council and chair. Because there are so few people

A scene in front of the Goshute Day School. (Vyrie Grey Collection, U of U)

who actually live on the reservation, their organization is somewhat different than that at Deep Creek.

Over the years, the tribal governments have worked tirelessly on behalf of the Goshute people. Attempting to create an economic base on the reservations while maintaining as much of traditional life as possible has sometimes proven difficult for the Goshutes. Unemployment and the lack of personal income have created many problems on the reservations. Alcoholism is a problem that many Goshutes have not been able to escape. As is the case at many other reservations, the lack of meaningful employment or training of Indian people has added to their feelings of isolation and neglect.

The reservations were established as agrarian communities whose primary economy was to be based on farming. Although there are some very fertile areas, especially on the Deep Creek reservation, the reservations never have been self-sufficient farming communities. The jobs created by the farms were few and offered low wages. On the Deep Creek reservation, in fact, some of the lands were leased to non-Indians in the area and the rent payments were distributed to the tribe.

In 1969 a steel fabrication operation was begun on the Deep Creek reservation under the direction of Dr. Von Jarrett of Utah State University. The enterprise built steel cattle guards for road crossings, but it eventually proved unprofitable and is no longer in operation. Many of the

A Goshute couple. (USHS)

Goshute women at Deep Creek create beautiful beadcraft, necklaces, moccasins, bolo ties, earrings, buckskin gloves, belts, and headbands which are sold commercially.[104]

The Deep Creek Band also manages an elk herd in the Deep Creek Mountains. Money is raised by providing access to hunters on a limited basis, and the tribe also contracts with a single outfitter who has access to the reservation. Money from the sale of hunting permits is returned to the tribe.

In 1976 the Skull Valley Band built and leased a rocket motor testing facility to Hercules, Inc. That company needed a remote site away from residential areas to test rocket motors built at its Magna, Utah, facility. One of the critical issues was that the site had to be isolated, away from large residential areas, yet within commuting distance to the Salt Lake

Valley. The Skull Valley reservation satisfied the requirement. The operation is still functional and lease income from this facility provides the Skull Valley Band with 90 percent of its income. The Skull Valley Band is also majority owner in Earth Environmental Services, Inc., which sells dumpsters to various governmental agencies and private industry. In 1990, the Skull Valley Band built a convenience store with judgement funds. The tribe still operates the store, called the Pony Express Station.

The Skull Valley Band is also actively pursuing the development on their reservation of a storage facility for spent fuel rods from the country's nuclear-power plants. This is a controversial project that has created a powerful, and unlikely, coalition working towards its defeat. The governor of Utah, plus numerous environmental groups, private citizens, and even the Deep Creek Band of Goshutes have stated their opposition to the development of the waste storage facility. Citing concerns for public safety and pollution, the State of Utah will do all in its power to prevent the Goshutes from proceeding with their plans.

The Goshutes see this assault from the State of Utah as just one more in a long line of attacks on tribal sovereignty. With all the chemical weapons stored by the government at its facility at Dugway, the Goshute leadership is not impressed with the state's arguments regarding public safety. The Skull Valley Band has an opportunity to create a substantial economic base that will allow its members to increase their standard of living and make a better life for themselves. A final decision has not yet been made, but both sides are actively pursuing their stated goals.

The Goshutes Today

The Skull Valley Goshute Band lives on a reservation of 17,248 tribal acres plus 160 allotted acres. Total enrollment for the Skull Valley Band is 111 members at the time of this writing, with about twenty-five living on the reservation. The majority of Skull Valley members are employed off the reservation in Salt Lake City, Grantsville, Stockton, Tooele, and Ibapah. Of the eighteen band members employed, four are earning less than $7,000 per year. Low wage rates and unemployment have a major impact on the reservation.

The reservation has a majority of its land available for grazing, but about 160 acres is irrigable. Stream water is delivered to irrigate land from a pipeline which was constructed with funds from the Bureau of Indian Affairs. In 1983 a tribal community building was built with funds from tribal judgement money and a grant from the federal government through the Department of Housing and Urban Development.[105]

The Deep Creek Goshute Band has a total of about 70,410 acres in Nevada and 37,523 acres in Utah, with eighty allotted acres, for a total of some 108,000 acres. The Goshute people still have to contend with many of the issues that have constantly been a concern to them. Issues of self-rule, economic development of their reservations, the increase in tribal standards of living, recognition by local and state authorities of Goshute concerns, and tribal law enforcement remain as important today as they long have been. The Goshutes at the Deep Creek reservation are in the unenviable position of living on a federal reservation located in two states and three counties. The jurisdictional situation can be illustrated by examining health care issues on the Deep Creek reservation. There are no permanent clinics on the reservation. Depending upon where an individual lives on the reservation, if medical care is needed, individuals have to travel to Salt Lake City, Utah, if they live on the Utah portion of the reservation, or they must travel to Ely, Nevada, if they live on the Nevada portion of the reservation. Emergency facilities are located at Wendover, on the Utah-Nevada border, some sixty miles to the north.

The Deep Creek Band is always looking at ways to improve the lives and the economic conditions of its members. Education is viewed as an essential element to improvement on both Goshute reservations. The children of the Deep Creek Band in grades seven through twelve are currently bussed to school in Wendover, a 120-mile round-trip, which is made every weekday. Negotiations are now underway with the Bureau of Indian Affairs to build a school on the Deep Creek reservation.

Another project currently in the planning stage is the building of a fish hatchery utilizing the pristine water of the Deep Creek Mountains. The Goshute want to raise both Bonneville and Lahonton cutthroat trout, which are native to the Great Basin and are remnant populations of fish that once flourished in Lakes Bonneville and Lahonton of the Pleistocene epoch. The hope is to provide fish for planting in lakes and reservoirs to provide for recreational fishing needs of residents throughout the Intermountain West.

The Goshute people are working to keep their culture alive and active. Many of their native religious ceremonies and practices have been retained, but their language is slowly being lost. On the Deep Creek reservation, most of the youth under eighteen years of age do not speak their native language, and only about one in twenty in the age group from nineteen to twenty-six speak the language. However, most tribal members twenty-six years old and older speak the native language quite fluently.

A group of Goshute Indians, date unknown. (USHS)

In 1994 there were only about seven or eight members age seventy or older on the Deep Creek reservation. They believe that the language, customs, and beliefs of the tribe should be taught to the younger generations by their families. They are firm in their belief that their native language should not be taught in a classroom. Goshute parents still teach their children their native religious and cultural practices, a role they have always held in Goshute life.[106]

Conclusion

The Goshute people are survivors. They have survived in a land that many see as a desert waste, with few resources or advantages. The Goshutes, however, see the land as their home, a home that has provided them in the past with everything they needed. They knew to take care of their home, never upsetting a delicate balance of resource utilization and replenishment, and the land took care of them. The Goshute people survived the invasion of whites, of slave traders, and fur hunters. They have survived the onslaught of white Americans, who have taken the best and most productive lands in the Goshute domain for their exclusive use.

The Goshutes have survived the unjust epithets, lies, and outright barbarity of the white invaders. When necessary, Goshutes have fought and given their lives in defense of their homes and families. Although outnumbered, the Goshutes have survived in ever smaller numbers in the more remote areas of their homeland. The Goshute Tribe also has survived the neglect of the federal government as well as its attempts to remove them off their native lands.

The Goshutes have survived the establishment of reservations and the attempt to "civilize" them and turn them into farmers. While their lives have been changed and altered, the Goshute people have remained Goshute. They have adopted many of the white man's ways, but they have done so in a typically Goshute fashion.

The Goshute people look forward to the future. They are working hard to provide the skills and support needed for the younger generation to be productive and prosperous in the modern world. They are exerting their independence and are making decisions based upon the needs of their people and reservations. No longer content to be ignored and forgotten, the Goshute people are active participants in planning and directing their future. Their tenacious approach to life, which has served the Goshute people so well in the past, ensures they will have a future, a future that is bright and lasting.

The Paiute Tribe of Utah

Gary Tom and Ronald Holt

Tabuts [elder brother/wolf] carved people out of sticks and was going to scatter them evenly around the earth so that everyone would have a good place to live. But Shinangwav [younger brother/coyote] cut open the sack and people fell out in bunches all over the world and that's why people fight. The people left in the sack were the Southern Paiutes, and Tabuts put them here in the very best place.[1]

For a thousand years the Paiute people have lived in an area that is presently known as southern Utah, southeastern California, northern Arizona, and southern Nevada. Their homeland is adjacent to the Great Basin and included the resource-rich Colorado Plateau and a portion of the Mojave Desert.

Neither the written word nor the course of historical events have been kind to the Southern Paiutes. Theirs is a story of resiliency under great pressure and of disappointment after many promises. With the encroachment of Euro-American settlers into the area came the destruction of much of their traditional culture, religion, economy, and the title to their ancestral homeland. It took less than twenty-five years of contact with the Mormon settlers to reduce the Paiute population by 90 percent and turn them from being peaceful, independent farmers and foragers into destitute, landless people who survived by doing seasonal and part-time work for the white settlers. Some Paiute groups even ceased to exist.

To further the official demise of the Paiutes, the federal government and the Mormon church made only feeble attempts to provide needed services. These attempts implemented many ill-conceived policies purported to "help the Indian tribes." In spite of all this, the majority of Paiutes never left their ancestral lands—they remained and survived the barrage of acculturation, relocation, and termination policies and prac-

tices. The Paiutes survived challenges that would have overwhelmed a less flexible people. They adapted to their changing environment yet retained their distinct identity and deep roots in southern Utah.

The Paiute Lifestyle

The Southern Paiute language is one of the northern Numic branches of the large Uto-Aztecan language family. Most scholars agree that the Numic peoples began moving into the Great Basin and Colorado Plateau about 1,000 years after the beginning of the Christian era.

Prior to their contact with Europeans the Paiutes' aboriginal land covered an area of more than 30 million acres—from southern California to southern Nevada, south-central Utah, and northern Arizona. These areas provided not only a wide variety and choice in foodstuffs but also climates that were comfortable to live in. The Paiutes knew the fragile environment intimately and were able to exist and maintain a way of life without overtaxing the resources of the land.

Their mobile lifestyle included moving frequently, primarily according to the seasons and plant harvests and animal migration patterns. They lived in independent groups of from three to five households. The largest concentration of Paiutes in Utah lived along the banks of the Santa Clara River.

Paiute housing reflected the seasonal cycles. In the summer a windbreak might be all that was required. In the winter a cone-shaped structure was made of a framework of three or four poles; branches were then leaned against the framework. The walls would then be covered with juniper bark, rushes, or other material. Starting in the 1850s, many Paiutes began to use canvas or skin teepees, adapting this Plains style of dwelling from their contact with the Utes.

Data indicates that the Paiutes were highly sophisticated botanists. They used at least thirty-two families of flora encompassing some ninety-six species of edible plants. The list would be greatly expanded were it to include the equally impressive array of medicinal plants, many of which also had nutritional value. In similar fashion, the Paiutes utilized most of the varieties of fauna found within their territory: hoofed animals, rodents, carnivores, birds, reptiles, and insects. Many Euro-Americans commented at great length on the fact that no portion of the area's fauna—from ants to deer—was overlooked as a food source. The mountains of the Great Basin provided a great source of pine nuts from pinyon pines. Lakes provided fish and other aquatic resources. The major gatherings of the pre-contact period were centered around the pine nut harvest and

A group of Paiute wickiups. (Utah State Historical Society—USHS)

the spring fish spawning time at Fish Lake. These gatherings provided a good time to catch up on news and to socialize. In many instances, mates were found at these gatherings.

Groups of Paiutes usually centered around one or more major food or water resources. Groups often used resources within other groups' core areas, and groups such as the Moapa in Nevada were often seen in Utah. This mobile existence and the lack of ethnographic data make it somewhat unclear how many bands of Paiutes existed in Utah, but at least sixteen major groups, or thirty-five smaller groups, have been identified. The major groups have been categorized by their main area of activity; they include: Parowan area; Santa Clara—three to seven groups;

A Paiute family and their home. (USHS)

Kaiparowits; Cedar City—at least two groups; Beaver Dam area; Tonoquints—multiple groups; Ash Creek—Toquer's group and possibly others; Antarianunts; Panguitch Lake; Harmony; Uinkarets; Virgin River—multiple groups; San Juan—two groups; Beaver; and Kaibab.[2]

One factor that may help account for a lack of consistency in band names is the dramatic changes that were taking place in Paiute life when data initially was gathered on their social organization. In most cases, the Paiutes did not have the population or the stable residence to be designated as "tribes" as defined by the federal government. However, with the loss of their best lands and decimation by introduced diseases due to the arrival of Mormon and other settlers, members of the various original Paiute groups coalesced to form sedentary groups.

Leadership roles also began to change with the arrival of the Euro-Americans. Major decisions were made in council meetings, with adult males, old women, and other interested persons present. The traditional Paiute leader was called *niave*. He would be identified by each community to lead by example and through a search for consensus. Although such a "chief" was not a decision maker, he would offer advice and suggestions at council meetings and would later work to carry out the council's decisions as well as other prescribed duties. White settlers assumed that the Paiute "chiefs" had more authority than they actually did. As early as 1855, Mormon settlers were "setting apart" as chiefs those Paiutes who were allied with them. The Mormon practice of appointing band leaders and backing those Paiutes who stressed accommodation with whites may have led to factional splits within Paiute groups.[3]

At the time of European contact, traditional rituals associated with childbirth, puberty, and funerals were still taking place. Paiutes prayed and conducted rituals to influence the spirits of nature and show their respect and gratitude to them. In the Paiutes' view of the natural world, there was one most-powerful spirit being, often called simply the "one who made the earth". The sun was one visible aspect of this spirit; most Paiutes made prayers to the sun at sunrise and sometimes at noon or sunset. The Paiutes also associated the mythic heroes Coyote and Wolf with this spirit, seeing the good and virtuous Wolf and wicked and silly Coyote as two necessary sides of the same all-powerful creator. Other supernatural beings such as the Thunder People and Water Babies were also part of the Paiutes' world. Each of the food and medicinal plants as well as the various game animals also had spirits, according to the Paiutes.

A medicine man was called *paugant* in Paiute, meaning "one who has sacred power." This medicine man usually had one or more animal spirit helpers. A spirit helper might be an eagle, a porcupine, a squirrel, or some other animal that the *paugant* had dreamed of or had encountered in some other mystical way. He would pray through this animal, perform magico-religious rituals with its feathers or fur, and might even capture one to keep as a pet. These animal spirits were believed to assist medicine men in healing the sick or, when applied to enemies, in causing illness and death through sorcery.

In the late nineteenth century, Paiutes borrowed the "cry" ceremony from the Mohaves and other Yuman-speaking tribes living to the south.[4] The Las Vegas area Paiutes may already have adopted this funerary-type ceremony in the era before white settlement. In the "cry," singers chant songs from evening until dawn over the course of one or more nights.

These songs belong to several sacred song cycles, including the salt song cycle, the bird song cycle, and others. Between spells of singing, relatives and friends of the dead get up and give speeches about the person. When it was first adopted, the "cry" was a separate ceremony from funerals, and often a "cry" was held to honor several people who had died over a given period. Later, the "cry" was combined with individual funeral ceremonies and was held at the same time. In some cases, a second memorial "cry" was held a year, or sometimes two years, after the funeral.

The Paiutes also enjoyed different gambling games. Most notable was the hand "bone" game, which is still played today. Two teams would sit facing each other. Each team took turns hiding one or more pairs of "bones" in their hands. "Bones" were bone or wood cylinders, one of which was marked with a stripe around the middle, while the other was unmarked. While one team was hiding the bones, that team's members would sing their own game songs to give themselves luck and discourage their opponents. The competing team would then begin to sing its songs. Using traditional hand gestures and special words, one of the members of the second team would try to guess which hand on the opposite team held which bone. Score would be kept by stick counters thrust into the ground near each team. The two teams would play for valuable stakes, such as buckskins, horses, jewelry, and other goods.

Another popular gambling game was played with stick dice—a die being a flat piece of wood colored on one side and white on the other. A player would strike the dice on hard stone, usually a metate, making the dice fly up and fall to the ground with one side up. Different combinations of plain and colored sides had different point values. Score was kept in different ways, usually by moving a counter along a row or circle of stones.

The Newcomers

Originally the Spanish considered Paiutes and Utes to be one group. They believed the area northeast of the Hopi was populated by those they called "Yutas," a term the Spanish used to refer to both the Paiutes and their neighbors to the east, the Utes. The Spanish term gave the present state of Utah its name. Paiutes and Utes both use another term—pronounced Payuts by the Paiutes and Payuch by the Utes—to refer to the Paiutes as distinct from the Utes. Up until the mid-1600s, the Utes and Paiutes essentially shared a similar way of life. Once the Utes acquired the horse, however, a series of cultural changes took place among the Utes based on the mobility provided by horses.[5] Later, the horse would

Paiute Indians perform a Round Dance on the Kaibab Plateau. Photographed by John K. Hillers of the Powell expedition between 1871 and 1875. (USHS)

prove to be devastating to their generally friendly relationship with the Paiutes, as the Utes began to raid Paiute villages and take women and children as slaves to trade in the Rio Grande Valley and in California. Other slave raids also came from the Navajos and the Spanish. This activity created a population imbalance among Paiutes of males to females and children. In 1776 the Domínguez-Escalante party from Sante Fe made the first recorded European visit to Utah Paiute lands.

Through the mid-1800s the Paiutes had encountered only a few Euro-Americans, primarily traders, travelers, and trappers. The Old Spanish Trail from Santa Fe to California flourished from 1830 to about 1850 and passed right through the middle of Paiute territory. Most of the travelers were passing through to the fertile fields of California. Eventually the traffic through some Paiute farming areas was so heavy that the Paiutes had to abandon fields that were too close to the trail. Skirmishes were few, being limited to random potshots by the intruding pioneers and the theft of some livestock by the Paiutes.

Meanwhile, in 1847 Brigham Young led a group of settlers into the Great Salt Lake area in an attempt to set up a quasi-independent state. The pioneers were members of a persecuted religious group, the Church of Jesus Christ of Latter-day Saints (LDS), commonly known as Mormons. By 1849 the Mormon population had increased to the point that they began to expand their colonization efforts. Brigham Young envisioned a string of Mormon settlements from Salt Lake City to southern California—a "Mormon corridor" that would link Salt Lake City to the sea. Young's oft-repeated Indian policy was that "it was better to feed the Indians than to fight them," although Mormons, like white settlers elsewhere, had no qualms about taking Indian lands for their own use. Upon exploring Paiute territory, the Mormons identified some good sites for settlement. Unfortunately for the Paiutes, these sites were often their core living and foraging areas.

Mormon theology came as a two-edged sword for the Paiutes. According to Book of Mormon teachings, Indians were seen both as a chosen people and as a cursed people. Many Mormons believed that the Paiutes had to be "civilized" before they could be "saved." It seemed that their Indian culture was considered to be a major stumbling block to their salvation. One of the major points of contention with the Mormons was that the Paiutes and other tribes should not worship symbols such as the sun, stars, and moon.

The lives of the Paiutes shifted dramatically as Mormons became full-time residents in Paiute country in 1851. The Paiutes utilized various adaptive strategies in an effort to keep their population and culture intact. However, their lifeways were to be altered ecologically, economically, and socially. The influx of settlers also brought large numbers of domesticated livestock to Paiute country. This livestock was allowed to graze anywhere, and eventually overgrazing would take its toll on the Paiutes' food sources. Now, not only was the land being taken but also the seeds that provided a significant portion of the people's diet were being consumed. Much of the Indians' culture was lost or significantly changed.

One of the main reasons for Mormon expansion was that more land was needed to house the many new converts coming to the region. Mormon colonization of Southern Paiute lands was rapid. By the end of 1858, eight years after colonization efforts began, Mormons had established eleven settlements in Southern Paiute territory. The best farmlands and sources of water were taken for the new Mormon towns. The industrious Paiutes were hired to provide much of the labor needed to create the

new settlements. They helped prepare the fields for planting and performed various domestic chores. The Mormons, in turn, provided new sources of material goods, food, and agricultural knowledge.

The Paiutes viewed the Mormon settlements with mixed feelings. The Mormon presence provided some protection from the depredations of the wagon trains and the slave raiding of the Utes, Navajos, and Mexicans. But the Paiutes would have been less accommodating if they had understood the sheer magnitude and devastating consequences of Mormon settlement. Prior to 1851, the Paiutes had adapted to the many changes brought on by the Euro-Americans as they passed through Paiute country. But the worst period for the Paiutes in southern Utah and Nevada was the decade or so following Mormon settlement. During those years, the Mormon settlers themselves suffered from epidemics of diseases such as cholera, scarlet fever, whooping cough, measles, mumps, tuberculosis, and malaria. Since Paiutes were frequently living near the settlements, they soon contracted these diseases but had less acquired immunity to them. Some Paiute groups during this time experienced more than a 90 percent drop in population.[6]

The Mountain Meadows Massacre

One of the most controversial results of Mormon-Paiute interaction in the decade following Mormon settlement of the area was the reported collaboration of individuals of the two groups in one of the most horrific events of early Utah history—the Mountain Meadows Massacre, in which more than one hundred California-bound emigrants were attacked and then treacherously murdered in the area southwest of Cedar City in early September of 1857.

The tragic event still remains somewhat clouded in mystery despite some extensive and valuable treatment by historians.[7] The whole story does not need to be retold in detail here, as it is commonly available; but it is important to note that many Paiute leaders (among others) believe and claim that, contrary to most published accounts, Indians did not participate in the initial attack on the wagon train nor in the subsequent murder of its inhabitants.

The basic account, current for decades now, essentially maintains that Indians initially attacked the wagon train—most likely under urging or encouragement from local Mormon leaders—but that the emigrants were able to repel the attackers after some loss of life and injury. The Indians then were said to have appealed for assistance from area Mormons, who perhaps on their own determined to take advantage of

Two Paiute men. (USHS)

the situation involving perceived antagonists in those emotionally charged times following the zealous Mormon Reformation of 1856 and the prospect of war with federal troops looming on the horizon—the so-called Utah War of 1857–58.

The common history continues that local Mormons approached the beseiged emigrant wagon train under a flag of truce and convinced the

Ta-peats, a Paiute Indian who lived along the Virgin River near St. George. This photograph was taken by John K. Hillers of the Powell expedition sometime between 1871 and 1875. (USHS)

emigrants to surrender their weapons, promising in return a safe escort out of the area. The desperate emigrants agreed, only to be slaughtered by their would-be protectors a few miles away, it again being claimed that Native Americans helped take part in this brutal act of treachery.

Accounts collected by the Paiute Tribe call into question this recounting of events, claiming that in great part Paiutes have been wrongfully blamed for assisting in something that was not of their making. Some of the interviews collected were with decendants of area Paiutes of that time, but the interviews suffer from the limited vocabulary and command of

English of the tellers plus a garbling of facts generally characteristic of such long-range reminiscences. Excerpts from a couple of these interviews are presented below. The interested reader can consult the Paiute Tribe for more complete transcripts and accounts.

One interview was conducted with Yetta and Clifford Jake on November 18, 1998. Mr. Jake started the interview by introducing himself and stating that he was eighty years old. He then continued:

> I used to chop wood for the old man Isaac Hunkup and his sister.... He was telling me a story, telling me what they see and what they hear also. And the Mountain Meadow massacre and Paiute didn't know anything about what was taking place over there. They were calm and quiet. They didn't know nothing about nothing. There was two brothers that come to the pine valley, hunting deer.... But what he was telling me was that they were there camping out there in the mountain. In the morning during the day [they] heard a gun, like popping, popping like a firecracker. So they went up on the mountain. There was a wagon train the people where people were shooting and killing the wagon train people, is the way he used to tell it. Oh, my goodness! Two guys were still waiting when they got down, they got everything, everything. Even their houses, the wagons were tipped over, they had some cows and sheep and the pigs and chickens and the womenfolks also. They got womenfolks. They were running around and getting shot there. They were watching from a knoll. Them two guys. "Oh, my god," they said, "they are killing them people." They said that "I don't see no Indians around here," he said. No Indians live around this area. This is their hunting place, not the pine valley.
>
> So, anyway, they got down, they got all of those things. Those things they took away from the settlers, the wagon train. And they talked together. "Let's follow the rim about a mile, a couple of miles, away from them, see what they are going to do." So they went. They took all of them people that [were] massacring the wagon train. They went over towards the east. They followed them quite a ways from they followed them till they get to the place to where they are going to change their clothes. So, anyways, they followed them clear to New Harmony. From there they sneak up on them about a half mile. They watch them and they watch them. They sit there. They clean theirselves; they took off their

Indian outfits off—clothes, Indian clothes. And they were white
people. Them white people, they washed themselves up and
cleaned themselves. They were white people that done it. And
they said, "Let's get going," they said. "Let's get going to warn
them other people down to Sham [the Paiute encampment]."
They traveled to get there as fast [as] they can. I don't know if
they were on a foot or on a horse. But, anyway, they made it
down there ... to get a hold of them Indians, house to house. I
want them to be aware. We are going to [be] blamed for something that we didn't have happen. For those people, for shooting
them wagon train. Better beware. They said they got really scared.
After awhile during that day one of the guys from the younger
Indians they saddle up their horse and warn the people around
the area. Clear to Cedar City and ... maybe Moapa too. So be
ware; we are going to get blamed, going to get blamed for what
those white people did. There were no Indians in that massacre....

The authority came down. They got there. They said Indians don't leave their dead like this. They started blaming the Indians for it. The Paiute Indians around this area, they didn't know
anything about what happened over there. They didn't even know
nothing. There weren't no Indians around that place there....
That's what takes a place that time. Us Paiute nation got blamed
for that.

An interview in December 1998 with Will Rogers also provided interesting commentary. He said in part:

...they gathered some Indians up there; I don't remember how
much he said, five or six. Well, anyway, them that thing was coming down on the way on this side there was lot of people over
them, them that man John Seaman I was telling about he was
looking at them white people—they were white people—they
were these Mormons, they were going to massacre that, uh, that
wagon train. And then he said, "I wonder what they gonna do?"
they didn't tell them people what they was going to do, you know.
Well, anyway, they did no Indians went down there, he said; them
four guys stayed on that mountain, on that little mountain up
there, and watched them guys kill them people—they killed all
of them off they said, they killed all of them off. That time they

were going to go down there, but they won't let that Indians go down there, you know, after it happened; they said it took about, he said it took about three [or] four hours I think he said, you know, to shoot them people all. Some of them were half-dead, some of them wasn't even dead. And, uh, there was lot of that silver dollars was there; them little coins, silver dollars, those big as a silver dollar, two-hundred-dollar gold piece, gold piece was about a silver dollar. Well, anyway, from there they were going to get some them Indians you know they were going to get some that thing, they wouldn't let them have any 'cause that that was, uh, it was something no good, you get sick. "Don't get it, don't get anything," he said [they] told them Indians.

That that man, he didn't go down there, he said that John Seaman he got scared but only three guys went. But, anyway, he watched all those people die off. It was this white man's doing it dressed up as Indians; there were about, I think he said it could have been forty-five or fifty he said; you know he didn't count them people.

Gloria Bulletts Benson, who helped conduct the interviews, summarized some of the important points found in the interviews in a memo to Paiute Tribal Chairwoman Geneal Anderson. Most importantly, she stressed that there were no Paiutes involved in the killings, according to the accounts of the interviewees. Paiute involvement was limited to hearing and watching from a distance the killing of the emigrants and some of their animals, and the robbing of the possessions of the dead. Some Paiutes reportedly followed the killers towards New Harmony and saw them take off their "Indian" clothes and bury and/or divide some of the stolen goods. Paiutes were told to avoid the area and not pick up any of the scattered money, as it was "bad medicine." Area Paiutes were afraid that they would be blamed for the massacre and sent word of it to surrounding band areas to warn others.[8]

A book published by the Kaibab Paiute Tribe in 1978, *Kaibab Paiute History, The Early Years* by Richard W. Stoffle and Michael J. Evans, included commentary on a photograph: "Dan Bullets noted that *Tunanita'a* [John Seaman's father] was picked up by John D. Lees's group traveling to the Mountain Meadow Massacre. One other Paiute accompanied the group, but neither was allowed to participate in the killing. *Tunanita'a* found a gold coin after the massacre but the Mormons took it away from him, saying it was bad medicine for him to have it."

Three Paiutes at their wickiup, photographed by John K. Hillers in 1872. Note the woman seated at the grinding stone. (USHS)

Additional information important to historians is found in the oral history of Sybil Mariah Frink that was gathered by her son John E. Scottern and her granddaughters Ruth Scottern and Gyppe Scottern and great-granddaughter Patsy Ruth Carter Iverson. A brief summary of relevant points follows.

Sybil was born in Missouri in 1838. She and her family were early members of the Church of Jesus Christ of Latter-day Saints. Her parents died, but she traveled to Utah with her grandmother and married Byron Warner in 1854, when she was sixteen. Before she married she lived at

the fort in Fillmore and learned some of the Paiute language and Indian ways. She moved with her husband to Harmony, and was there at the time of the Mountain Meadows Massacre. One evening she overheard her husband and other men at her house discussing plans to wipe out the Fancher party wagon train. "She said nothing, fearing for her life. At a later date, these fourteen men met at her home, painted their faces, and dressed themselves as Indians." She followed them at a distance and reportedly watched the massacre from some bushes. Only a few small children were spared, and it is said that Sybil even cared for some of them until they were claimed by authorities later and returned to relatives.

Her husband is said to have discovered that she knew of the treachery and that he threatened to kill her if she ever told of it. She later divorced him in about 1865 and reportedly either left or was excommunicated from the LDS Church, although she remained in the territory, serving as a nurse and midwife. She married Timothy Scottern in about 1866. She died under mysterious circumstances in 1906 after being summoned to a remote location to care from the sick. Some have seen a conspiracy or vengeance in her mysterious death.[9]

Although much about the massacre remains shrouded in mystery, resulting in intense speculation and controversy even up to the present, the Native American claim that few, if any, of their people were involved in the massacre in any way has seldom been heard or accorded a fair presentation. Though some things in the interviews and accounts cited here are confused and could have their critics, elements of them certainly are plausible and deserve serious consideration in attempts to understand that tragedy. The fact that so much evidence, including relevant pages from the journals of many settlers, has been lost or destroyed, testifies to many Native Americans and their sympathizers that much of the official history cannot be considered to be complete or truthful. However, there is certainly some evidence that Indians with base camps on the Muddy and Santa Clara Rivers were involved at least in the initial siege of the wagon train.

Skeptics of Paiute involvement point to other interesting facts. According to historians, Paiutes had not been known to attack wagon trains, confining their activities to the rustling of stray cattle or other livestock belonging to emigrant parties.[10] The fact that the Mormons assigned some blame to them has been seen by some as merely an attempt to put their own culpability in a better light, to protect both their reputation and themselves from prosecution. Paiutes claimed that they had nothing to do with the initial attack, and, even after some Paiutes answered a

summons from Mormon leaders to come to the area, their assistance was non-existant or minimal, one reason being that they did not have the weaponry to attack the emigrants, who were equipped with long-range rifles. Critics also point out that it is highly unlikely that Mormons would supply the Indians with firearms and ammunition when their own supplies of both were limited and they were facing the threat of federal action.[11]

Paiutes were not prosecuted by federal officials for the massacre, and, although most Mormons successfully avoided prosecution, John D. Lee was eventually apprehended, tried, convicted, and executed for his part in the affair. Many then and to the present have felt that Lee became a scapegoat to end further prosecution efforts against other Mormons.

Relationships with Early Settlers

The Mormon settlements continued to grow, and newer arrivals, some less tolerant, came to the region. Prospectors and miners came in search of precious metals, coal, and lead. The remaining lands of the Paiutes soon were being taken. Soon, enough Mormons had moved into the area that they no longer needed or desired Paiute labor. By the 1870s, the Paiutes who lived near the region's settlements had become destitute.

Justification for taking land was given by the Mormon church and its members, including the idea that the Indians were not making efficient use of the land and therefore the Mormons had the right to take it over because they could support more people by their methods of agriculture than the Indians could. Although their theological view saw the Indians as potential converts and chosen people, the common pioneer view of the Paiute was as a savage and beggar. The Mormons assured their dominance over the Paiutes and the other Great Basin Indians through a combination of physically displacing them from the resources necessary to sustain their aboriginal lifestyle and dealing with them according to an attitude that has been called theological paternalism.[12]

In 1856–57, agent George W. Armstrong became the first official governmental contact person for the Southern Paiutes. His first act was to attempt to establish two farm sites for the Paiutes totaling 1,200 acres. However, nothing came of this recommendation.[13]

In 1865 a series of treaties was negotiated with the Indians of Utah. These treaties virtually would end the Indians' claim to any and all land and remove them to a reservation in the Uinta Basin. The Paiute leader Tutzegubet, who had become friendly with the Mormons, signed this treaty. He was to receive "one dwelling house," five acres of plowed and

This Paiute Circle Dance was photographed by John K. Hillers between 1871 and 1875. Most of the dancers are wearing rabbitskin robes. (USHS)

fenced land, and one hundred dollars per annum for the term of twenty years.[14] Upon his arrival at the reservation he also would receive oxen and farming implements, a high price indeed for the some 30 million acres of land to which the Indians were supposedly relinquishing their claims.

Life on the reservation would have posed additional problems for the Paiutes. The Utes were continuing their practice of stealing Paiute women and children, yet officials expected the Paiutes to move to the same reservation to which the Utes had been moved. Attempts to re-move the Paiutes from their homeland were a complete failure. The situation with the Paiutes grew worse; despite their theological status in Mormonism as a chosen people, they came to be considered no more than a nuisance that the Mormons felt compelled occasionally to feed.

In 1873 John Wesley Powell and George W. Ingalls headed a special commission to look into the problem. The commission identified 528 Paiutes left in Utah and suggested that they be moved to the Moapa res-ervation in nearby Nevada. Money for such a move was scarce, however, and the Paiutes refused to leave their homeland.

The first Paiute reservation came into being during this period. Anthony Ivins was mayor of St. George and ran cattle in the "Arizona Strip" country. However, hungry Paiutes were stealing from his livestock operation in the Mt. Trumbull area. When Ivins found them in his way, he utilized federal channels to get himself named a "Special Indian Disbursing Agent," serving from 1891 until 1893, and removed the Shivwits from their homeland in northern Arizona to southern Utah. Through his efforts the first Paiute reservation was established in 1891 on the Santa Clara River west of St. George.[15] This began a new phase in Paiute history, with the Indians now dependent on both Mormon church charity and the federal government's good will. The Paiutes who had originally been residents of the reservation area were either dead or had moved—most to the Moapa reservation in Nevada or to Cedar City. This fact illustrates the devastating effects of white colonization, since the the Virgin and Santa Clara Rivers had been the riverine core of the Paiute homeland and its center of densest population. The new reservations would prove to be too small and have too few resources for the Paiutes to sustain themselves from them.

Ivins purchased land and farming equipment for the Indians at Santa Clara with a $40,000 congressional appropriation. The reservation was formally established by the government in 1903. In 1916 President Woodrow Wilson issued an executive order which expanded the size of the reservation to its current 26,880 acres. Three other Paiute reservations soon followed. The Indian Peaks reservation was established on August 2, 1915, and was enlarged between 1921 and 1924. The reservation consisted of 10,240 acres of rough rocky land mostly covered with juniper but which also yielded large quantities of pine nuts from pinyon pines. The Indian Peaks Band was composed of remnants of the Parogoon, Pahquit, and Tavatsock bands.[16] Their ancestral land blended into the traditional Shoshone lands, and some intermarriage with Shoshones was not uncommon. Their land stretched from Indian Peak into Nevada. Isolated, they were the last group to become dependent on whites. They lived some seventy miles northwest of Cedar City in five log homes.

The Koosharem Band of Paiutes/Utes was established in 1928, and their reservation was enlarged in 1937. These people considered themselves Utes and were possibly a remnant of the Fish Lake Utes. Their ancestral homeland stretched from Richfield to Escalante. They were under de facto control of the local Mormon church—Sevier Stake—which also was trustee of their water rights until the Paiutes sued for those rights in 1958.

A bearded Paiute Indian with his bow and arrows, photographed by John K. Hillers between 1871 and 1875. (USHS)

Kanosh would be the last reservation to be formally established in Utah until 1984. It was created in 1929 and was expanded in 1935 and 1937. The Kanosh Band members were descended from the Pavant Indians who inhabited the Corn Creek area near Fillmore at the time of the arrival of the Mormons. Earlier, several attempts to no avail were made to remove the Pavants to the Uintah Reservation.

The last group of Utah Paiutes to achieve offical status was the Cedar City Band. As early as 1899 the federal government appropriated money to buy land for the Cedar band; however, no lands were purchased and the money was returned to officials. In 1919 the Cedar City area Paiutes were administrated to as a "scattered band" out of the Goshute reserva-

This Paiute Indian was photographed in the vicinity of St. George by John K. Hillers between 1871 and 1875. (USHS)

tion to the northwest. They had use of eighty acres of land for farming plus five and one-half acres they lived on. Consequently, they were encouraged to move to either the Indian Peaks or the Goshute reservation; but, once again, they were too attached to their homeland to leave.

Because many deaths from tuberculosis had taken place, attempts were made by the government to move the Paiutes in 1924, and money was appropriated to purchase nine lots in Cedar City. Two months later, however, William Palmer wrote an article for a local paper saying that the government refused to do anything for the Paiutes. Some city officials thought that the Indians could be made into a tourist attraction. On December 15, 1926, the Paiutes moved to property purchased for

them by the Mormon church, which retained title to the land. Their old camp, shacks, and belongings were burned and the Indians were moved to their present location near the Little League ballpark in Cedar City.

Continued efforts to help the Paiutes were sporadic and disorganized. William Manning, then the director of the Music Department at the Branch Agricultural College (now Southern Utah University), organized an "Indian show" in order to raise money to buy blankets and clothing and provide the local Indians with a bit of cash. In the early 1920s Manning wrote of the Paiutes' lifestyle:

> Each family lived in a little one room shack which was their kitchen, bedroom, and living room. Around the walls ranged bed rolls in the day, and at night the floor was covered with beds, especially if company came. Food was prepared on a small stove and eaten from a small table with the pot or frying pan set in the middle. Each helped himself out of the pot with his fingers, and at on the floor, the room being too small for very many chairs.[17]

Federal Paternalism

The federal government did establish two schools for the Utah Paiutes: the Shebit day school in 1898 and a school near Panguitch in Orton, Utah, in 1901, which was moved to Shivwits in 1908. Once the federal government became involved, it too would impact the lives of the Paiutes through its Indian policies, some of which had been made for Eastern tribes. The Paiutes would be subject to rulings which might not fit their situation. One such opinion was that of early Supreme Court Chief Justice John Marshall, who described American Indians as "domestic dependent nations" in the Supreme Court case of the Cherokee Nation vs. Georgia in 1831. The argument of the time was that, while the tribes retained rights as independent political powers, they were subordinate to the United States and were becoming dependent on the United States for their welfare and existence. The Indians had the right to occupy their lands until the federal government chose to extinguish their title. This situation brought with it the notion that the "white man's burden" was to civilize the Indians. Of course, this brought other players into the process such as Mormons, other religous denominations, eastern Indian sympathizers, and Congress. Matters of interpretation of "trust responsibility" were part of the political and social climate.

One of the first Indian policies to affect the Paiutes was the allotment of tribal lands to individuals under the Indian Homestead Act of

1875. There basically were two approaches to Indian affairs: the gradual approach and the immediate approach. Senator Henry Dawes favored the gradual assimilation of Indians into white society through gradual allotment. On the other hand, many land speculators, reformers, and homesteaders favored the immediate allotment of all reservation land. The Dawes Severalty Act of 1887 served as a compromise. Indian lands were divided up into individual plots and, after an initial twenty-five-year "trust" period, they would become liable to taxation. Lands declared "surplus" would then be sold to the whites.

By 1934, the national tribal land base had been reduced by about 86 million acres through white acquisition. Under this allotment system the Koosharem and Kanosh bands experienced change: at Koosharem, 400 acres in three allotments were patented between 1904 and 1913; at Kanosh, 1,840 acres were patented in twelve allotments in 1919–20. These allotments served as a core of Indian-owned land around which the Paiutes/ Utes could organize their work and other movements. The allotments also served to mark land for potential Indian ownership. When the reservations were established at Koosharem and at Kanosh they were adjacent to the allotments. Allotment gave the Indians land where before they had only squatters rights. By the time the allotment policy had reached the Paiutes, and the BIA attempted to fulfill its trust obligations, the federal government was trying to eliminate reservations. This was reflected in the establishment of only four small reservations by executive order between the years 1891 and 1929. They not only were small but also contained little irrigable land or water rights.

On January 1, 1927, the BIA consolidated several offices and put six small reservations and four Indian settlements under the jurisdiction of the Paiute agency located at Cedar City. The young superintendent was Dr. E.A. Farrow, who had previously worked at the Kaibab Paiute Reservation just across the border in northern Arizona. Also during this period the Indian Peaks Band moved to Cedar City.

Many factors during this period would affect the lives of the Paiutes. In October 1929 the stock market crashed, ushering in the era known as the Great Depression. The low point came in 1933 when the American banking system virtually collapsed. The Depression era, however, actually benefited many Paiutes by providing some federal projects they could take advantage of. The Paiutes overall economic condition seemed to improve. Because their annual yearly income had averaged between $150 and $200, the more dependable incomes many were now able to earn on federal programs seemed a real luxury.

Kwi-toos and his son were Paiute Indians who lived along the
Virgin River in the vicinity of St. George. They were photographed by John K. Hillers of the Powell expedition between 1871
and 1875. (USHS)

The Depression brought at least one Mormon church–sponsored
project to the Paiutes: church leaders gave William Palmer $500 to de-
velop an arts and crafts business for the Paiutes. Articles such as gloves,
moccasins, beaded bookends, and bows and arrows were created for sale
to tourists and local whites. Palmer stated that, "During these times when
there has been no work for them, this bit of employment has gone far
toward supplying actual living necessities. They know that the church
has furnished this money and they are grateful to them for it." Palmer
claimed that by reinvesting the original $500, he was able to provide $1,107
worth of employment in approximately one year.[18]

Termination

Termination was one of the government's poorly conceived policies to acculturate and assimilate the Indians. It seemed to be a carryover from the Dawes Allotment Act of 1887. Many whites believed that tribalism was the major stumbling block to the assimilation of Indians into the mainstream society and that the Indians should not be treated differently from other citizens. With this in mind, the federal government set out to "terminate" from federal trust relationship those Indian tribes deemed ready to survive on their own. The Utah congressional delegation was heavily involved in seeing termination become a reality. As has been mentioned, the acculturation process would continue, although the loss of land also continued for the Indians. Budget constraints and the eventual abolishment of the Bureau of Indian Affairs were among the reasons that made termination a popular idea with many non-Indian Americans.

The implementation of the policy of withdrawal of services and trust status was based on a four-step process: withdrawal of federal trusteeship; relocation of Indians to urban centers; creation of a claims commission to liquidate land claims and thereby eliminate any further reason for tribal allegiance; and the progressive dismantling of the BIA. One important person behind termination in the late 1940s and early 1950s was Senator Arthur Watkins of Utah, who grew up near the Uintah-Ouray Reservation. The former director of the War Relocation Authority (WRA), Dillion Myers, who had been responsible for removing 110,000 Japanese-Americans from the West Coast to concentration camps in the interior was now the Commissioner of Indian Affairs. Myers was appointed in 1950 and quickly appointed some of those who had served with him at the WRA. At a meeting including Senator Watkins and Orme Lewis, Assistant Secretary of the Interior, on February 27, 1953, a strategy for termination was developed. Without consulting any Indians, the men decided that termination was to be rapid process in which services were to be transferred from the BIA to the various states; tribal assets would be redistributed to individuals or tribes as groups, and trust responsibility for tribal lands would be transferred; tribal income and funds were to be disbursed on a pro-rata basis; and legislation would be passed for the "rehabilitation" of the Indians and their integration into the dominant society.

The Southern Paiutes of Utah were not mentioned in Assistant Commissioner Zimmerman's 1947 report on Indian readiness for withdrawal or in House Concurrent Resolution 108.[19] Zimmerman's criteria for ter-

mination included degree of acculturation, economic resources and educational level of the various tribes and their members, the willingness of the tribe to be terminated, and the willingness of the state to assume responsibility for services. The Southern Paiutes did not qualify in any of the aforementioned areas, yet they were the first group to be considered for termination and, to some degree, served as the model for the withdrawal hearings and the implementation of termination in later tribal cases.

There were many reports that showed how ill-prepared the Paiutes were for termination. During the process there were promises made and meetings held to placate the Southern Paiutes. The Goshutes also were being considered for termination but spoke out against it. It is still a mystery how and why the Paiutes ended upon the list of tribes to be terminated. Many scholars agree with Mary Jacobs when she speculates that: "perhaps Senator Watkins, already a strong believer in the merits of termination included these small groups from his own state because of his own convictions and for encouragement to other legislators to terminate Indians in their own states."[20] Another factor was that the Paiutes were receiving little federal assistance anyway and had little political influence to oppose the process.

One last meeting was to take place before the termination legislation was to be signed. It was held in Fillmore, December 30, 1953, with the Paiute bands; Skull Valley and Kaibab Indians were also there. Senator Watkins extolled the benefits and advantages of termination, claiming it would: 1) release the Indians from government control; 2) help everyone see how well Indians could take care of their own affairs; and 3) provide full citizenship to Indians in which they would get all the benefits available to them from the state and county governments. The Paiutes were advised twice during the meeting that the bill was not final and that they could make changes and suggestions. It was said that the bill would be changed to conform with "any recommended and approved adjustments." At no time did any of the officials mention anything but the benefits of termination, and, most importantly, at no time were the Paiutes asked if they wanted to be terminated in the first place. Clifford Jake, Indian Peaks spokesman, spoke out against termination and was told to sit down, shut up, and mind his own business.[21] Promises continued to be made, such as no limit on the planting of wheat; there also was a promise by an oil company that urged the band to accept termination and then grant the company an oil lease on Kanosh land. Neither of these promises materialized.

Me-kwi-uk and his daughter were Paiute Indians living along the Virgin River in the early 1870s. Photo by John K. Hillers. (USHS)

Hearings were set for the termination bill on February 15, 1954, in Washington, D.C. The bill was moving unusually fast through the legislative process. Gary Orfield has documented how Senator Watkins dominated the hearings and forced termination of the Utah Paiutes, writing, "only Watkins of the five Senate members was present for more than one hearing."[22] Orfield also underscored the lack of concern for the living conditions and dependence of the tribal peoples about to be "set free." Arguing for termination in the meeting on May 4, 1954, Watkins presented an incredible view of the degree of Paiute assimilation and a distorted account of their history. This left the testimony in favor of termi-

nation a maze of contradictions. Through all this the Paiutes were without money to travel to Washington, D.C., to voice their opposition. Telegrams were sent in opposition by the Kanosh Tribal Council and the Koosharem Tribal Council, and these were followed by opposition from the Indian Peaks and the Shivwits bands. However, these protests came with no particular organization, and there was also the fact that there was disunity within some bands. This indicates that the Paiutes themselves were not adequately informed by the federal government as to the implications of withdrawal of the trust relationship. Even though the Paiutes clearly did not meet the criteria for termination, the legislation sped through Congress, and on September 1, 1954, President Eisenhower signed Public Law 762, the bill terminating the Paiutes, after just one and one-half years of BIA preparation.

Next came the implementation of the law. It now became evident just how much the Paiutes were dependent on white advice in the early 1950s, especially concerning legislation and tribal business ventures. In a letter to Rex Lee, area director Harry Stevens suggested that $50,000 be allotted to prepare the four Paiute bands "to earn a livelihood, to conduct their own affairs and to assume their responsibilities as citizens."[23] The Paiutes were given until February 21, 1957, to prepare themselves for the end of the recognition of their special status as Indians. In order to facilitate this transition, the Bureau of Indian Affairs established a three-pronged support system composed of the BIA Withdrawal Office in Cedar City; an educational/vocational training program administered by the University of Utah (based on relocation); and the national BIA relocation program. The Indian Claims Commission would serve as an integral part of the termination effort, which was presented as holding the future promise of wealth in exchange for the Paiutes giving up all claims to their homelands.

The BIA Withdrawal Office in Cedar City included Director Wesley T. Bobo; a realty officer, Frank M. Scott; and a clerk/stenographer. The Cedar City withdrawal office was not established until August 1955, and Scott did not arrive until December of that year. From the Paiute viewpoint, therefore, nothing had really happened since they had been scheduled for withdrawal; from the BIA viewpoint, almost an entire year of the three years allotted was lost due to funding and administration problems. From November 1955 to June 1957 Bobo and Scott were engaged in an intensive effort to explain and discuss the implications of the termination bill with area Paiutes. Once again the resiliency and adaptability of the Paiutes was evident as they adapted to the changes being thrust

upon them. The BIA offered the Paiutes various options for the disposition of their land: a trusteeship for their property could be created; the tribal property could be sold and the proceeds distributed on a per-capita basis; or the property could be divided into individual parcels. It is indicative of the poor quality of the Paiute reservation lands that no acceptable bids were made (estimates of an acceptable bid in the case of the Shivwits reservation varied from $1.00 to $2.65 an acre). The Indian Peaks property was finally sold to the Utah Fish and Game Department for $39,500 to serve primarily as an antelope reserve.

In implementing the withdrawal of the federal trust responsibility, one of the duties of the BIA was to designate a trust authority to assume responsibilities for the land and for Paiute minors. The convoluted logic of termination insisted that, although the Paiutes were deemed ready to be released from the federal trust relationship, another trustee had to be selected for them. First Security Bank officials had been approached but were not interested. The Utah Attorney General ruled that the state could not assume trusteeship.[24] On June 20, 1956, W.T. Bobo met in Salt Lake City with William J. Fitzpatrick, vice-president and trust officer of Walker Bank and Trust. The meeting was originally to ascertain whether Walker Bank would be interested in serving as trustee for the "subsurface rights and monies which we may have for transfer." Walker Bank was selected as trustee without regard for the wishes of the Paiutes; as a result, the Paiutes left the trusteeship of the BIA, but their meager resources entered the trusteeship of a bank.

Although the Paiutes had received minimal services from the Bureau of Indian Affairs, now they were totally ineligible for any services. The federal government would no longer take an active interest in them and they were left in the care of the local authorities. The period between 1957 and 1975 was characterized by general neglect on the part of the State of Utah for any but the most basic needs of the Paiutes. This was a time of growing hopelessness and social and economic decline for the majority of the Paiute people. By all accounts, increased mortality rates, unemployment, and alcoholism were rampant among the Paiutes during this period. The bad economic times shattered families, and children were often raised by relatives or by whites.

For the terminated tribes, the true impact and meaning of federal withdrawal of trust responsibility became increasingly clear. They suffered the loss of land, federal expertise and legal protection, federal health and education funds to individuals, and training, housing, and business grants. The tribes and individuals were faced with taxes and the loss of

Two Paiute children, Mon-su and Su-vu-it, photographed in the vicinity of St. George by John K. Hillers in the early 1870s. Note the coyote-hide quiver with arrows in the foreground. (USHS)

the limited sovereignty they had enjoyed under the earlier Indian Reorganization Act.

Life Under Termination

Almost immediately after Public Law 762 took effect Congress began to speak in favor of economic development instead of termination.[25] Secretary of Interior Fred E. Seaton in a 1958 radio speech abandoned the policy of unilateral termination of tribes.

In the aftermath of the decision to terminate the Southern Paiutes the BIA did make some attempts to relocate and rehabilitate them. The

Ta-peats stands in front of his wickiup near the Virgin River.
Photographed by John K. Hillers between 1871 and 1875. (USHS)

BIA assumed that Indians had to overcome the common attitude that they were lazy, dirty, ignorant, submissive, and unfit for anything but subservient labor in the white man's fields. The BIA contracted with the University of Utah in July 1955 to implement a relocation/job training plan. The contract included Ute Indians from the Uintah-Ouray Reservation. Like so many of the policies that affected the Paiutes, the University of Utah project disrupted lives but did not last long enough to produce any lasting results. In fact, of the fourteen Paiutes who participated in the Adult Vocational Training through Relocation program, not one stayed away from the reservation or finished the training.

Denied federal welfare, education, health, and employment assistance after 1957, the Paiutes found themselves plunged even deeper into poverty and despair. Memories of termination-period experiences were common among survivors, who recounted increased alcohol use and the early death of others. The medical consultant's report, by Dr. Glen Leymaster, listed problems among the Paiutes of obesity, tuberculosis, an "extreme degree" of malnutrition among young infants, as well as sanitation and sewage-disposal problems. Tuberculosis was a continuing problem, and it had been the cause of about one-third of recorded Paiute deaths between 1889 and 1926.[26]

The LDS church also began to make a more conscious effort to spend more time and resources pursuing Indian converts—two proponents of such a policy being George Albert Smith and Spencer W. Kimball. In 1947 an Indian placement program began on an informal basis when a Navajo girl came to live with an LDS stake president, Golden Buchanan, of Sevier County. Official church sponsorship of the program followed in July 1954.[27] In 1957 William Manning organized a Cedar Indian Branch. Other branches were established at Richfield (by Judge Reed Blomquist), at Shivwits, and at Kanosh.

The Indian Claims Commission Act of August 13, 1946, created a special commission to which tribes could bring their outstanding grievances against the United States. This was brought about because an 1863 statute barred claims by Indian tribes based on treaties. Although there were many problems with the Indian Claims Commission, it would give the Paiutes an opportunity to receive compensation for land of theirs that had been taken. Since the 1865 Paiute Treaty had not been ratified by the Senate, any claims to land had to be predicated on exclusive immemorial possession, because joint use was not recognized in the claims act. The Paiutes plight was reported by William Palmer, acting as a representative of the mayor of Cedar City; the Cedar City Chamber of Commerce; and the president of the Parowan Stake of the LDS church at a meeting in Washington, D.C., with Commissioner William Brophy. Palmer continued his role as adviser by contacting Ernest Wilkinson, who with Felix Cohen was an author of the claims act. The promise of payment for lost land appeared early in the 1950s, but the tortuous legal process took so long that actual payments were not made until more than twenty years later.

The Paiutes joined with other bands to pursue their claims. There was some maneuvering by the Justice Department to weaken the individual tribal cases through consolidation and to remove lands from settle-

ment that had traditionally been jointly utilized by two or more groups. Because there were some time limitations and the federal government wanted to eliminate any further claims,there was some incentive to reach a compromise to move the process more quickly. This approach, however, allowed for no appeal from the Indians to either the U.S. Court of Claims or to the U.S. Supreme Court, as did the normal land-claims process. The attorneys negotiated a compromise that represented the Southern Paiute and Chemehuevi tribes. The precise value of the Paiute land was never determined, since the compromise included both Paiute and Chemehuevi lands; but the payment consisted of $8.25 million for 29,935,000 acres of land—thus, the Paiutes were to be paid about 27.5 cents an acre for their land. The Wilkinson law firm was advised informally by the ICC that the compromise was fair and would probably be accepted if first approved by the Indians and the Department of the Interior.[28] Each band was advised by the attorneys that the compromise was the best deal for their land and future. On January 18, 1965, the Southern Paiutes were awarded the sum of $7,253,165.19 for about 26.4 million acres of land, or 27.3 cents per acre.

After the settlement was accepted, however, another delay faced the Paiutes while it was determined how to administer and distribute the settlement. Once again, white paternalism would play a part in the lives of the Paiutes. Several individuals and groups, including the governor of Utah, went on record against per-capita payments to the Indians. A survey by Leonard Hill indicated that, "the basis of the concern is the fact that these people generally are impoverished, uneducated, unemployed, and inexperienced in handling money of amounts expected to be disbursed from the claim."[29] Neither the State of Utah nor the BIA wanted to accept responsibility for oversight of the claims funds; this was especially true in the case of the four terminated bands. Attorney John Boyden played a major role in these negotiations as the attorney of record for the case (Docket No. 330) and as the chair of the Utah Governor's State Board of Indian Affairs. In the end, the Paiutes had renounced, at least in the eyes of the federal government, their rights to over 29 million acres; in return, they had gained only a relatively small monetary payment.

Termination saw people unprepared on all sides. It took some people at the BIA until 1965 to realize that the Indian Peaks and Cedar bands were two different entities.[30] One of the studies used to establish early land use and occupation also suggested how poorly the Paiutes were prepared for being terminated. For many Paiutes the land claims money that was supposed to facilitate their entry into the white world was soon

These Paiute Indians on the Shivwits Reservation in 1933 were playing a card game, using buttons, needles, pins, and other small items to make wagers. (USHS)

gone, and they were left with nothing: no land, no money, no trust relationship, and no expectations for a brighter future. Some Paiutes did improve their lives by remodeling their homes, and some new homes were even built. The land claims process also increased Paiute political activity and awareness. In many ways, the claims case laid the groundwork for the 1980 restoration of tribal status to the Paiutes.[31] Talk for reinstatement began as early as 1958. In many ways, it seems that termination set the Paiutes twenty-five years behind many other tribes.

Many Paiutes continued to work as unskilled laborers, doing seasonal farm work, and some found better work on the railroad. By this time, the traditional knowledge base had deteriorated to the point that less than half of the Paiutes spoke fluent Paiute, very few were tanning deerskin, and very little storytelling or weaving of baskets and cradles was taking place. Social gatherings were very infrequent. Alcoholism began to affect more and more of the Paiutes, physically and socially. This contributed to a low life expectancy of only forty-two years during the early 1980s for Paiute males. The education drop-out rate ranged between 40 percent and 60 percent, with only an eighth-grade attainment level possible for most. Social and health services were almost non-existent. Many Paiutes were still living in substandard homes; but once again the Paiutes proved their durability and adaptability.

Restoration

Although the talk of reinstatement of tribal status for Native Americans began as early as 1958, the first real effort came in 1973 when petitions were circulated among the bands calling for the restoration of tribal status. Utah State Director of Indian Affairs Bruce Parry contacted BIA area director John Artichoker and then met with Morris Thompson, Commissioner of Indian Affairs, in Phoenix, Arizona. Both were supportive of restoration efforts, and a report was drafted by Mary Ellen Sloan, a law student working for the regional Solicitor's Office. Her nine-page memo essentially established that the Paiutes had never met the criteria established for termination and that promises made by Senator Watkins were not kept. The report also provided a policy statement on some of the errors and evils of termination.

In 1975 an Indian attorney named Larry Echohawk was approached by a member of the Paiute Tribal Corporation Board and by Bruce Parry to initiate the legal process required for restoration. Many meetings were held during 1975 to discuss the advantages and disadvantages of restoration and various forms of tribal government. The Menominee Restoration Bill then in process was watched in hopes that it would provide a useful precedent for Paiute restoration. Much support was given by the Paiute bands and some was also received from local entities and the BIA. The records of the meetings held made it obvious that the Paiutes were overwhelmingly in favor of reinstatement of federal status. Utah Senator Frank Moss requested that the BIA draft proposed legislation. Senator Moss and Congressman Gunn McKay, both Democrats, were ready to introduce and support the legislation when Moss was defeated by Republican Orrin Hatch in 1976.

The original 1975 draft version of the restoration bill provided for each Paiute band to be restored as a separate political entity, which was essentially its pre-termination status. After some discussion concerning sovereignty, population, and culture, a third draft of restoration legislation was prepared in 1976 which proposed to include all the bands under one tribal government. Newly elected Senator Orrin Hatch and Congressman Dan Marriott became the supporters needed in Congress.

In 1978 Mary Ellen Sloan, who would later join the Echohawk law firm and be its lead attorney, was asked by Larry Echohawk to write legislation to create a federally recognized tribal entity for the Paiutes. The bill, which was similar to the Siletz Tribe Restoration Bill, accompanied by a study for a plan for a Paiute reservation, was presented to Senator Hatch. In July 1979 the first meeting of the Paiute Restoration Commit-

tee was held. This group was formed in order to lobby for the Paiute cause. The committee was composed of the Paiute Tribal Council and various influential Utahns from diverse backgrounds. Tactics included encouraging individuals with contacts to write letters of support, make phone calls, and to encourage latent Mormon support and sympathy for the Paiutes. Historical and other materials were compiled to support the Paiute claims that they had suffered unjustly as a result of termination.

The essential strategy devised by Sloan and the committee was one of legislative advocacy.[32] This approach was utilized and refined throughout the process that led to restoration of tribal status and was applied, with some brilliance, during the reservation phase of activity, which followed restoration. The strategy was basically a search for support (mostly in the form of letters) from influential third parties. There was little interest in (although also little serious opposition to) restoration from the white population in southern Utah. But there was opposition from conservative circles to the idea of the inclusion of a reservation plan.

On August 29, 1979, Senator Hatch held a meeting at Southern Utah State College, in Cedar City, to assess opinion on Paiute recognition. At this meeting, several Paiutes (forty to fifty were in attendance) spoke strongly in favor of restoration, the need for a land base for their people, and of discrimination suffered by Indians from local whites. Several examples of blatant discrimination against Paiutes were cited. This testimony seems to have convinced Hatch that the Paiutes were in need of his help. The president of Southern Utah State College noted that the Paiutes, because of their terminated status, were unable to attend college, whereas Indian students from recognized tribes were eligible for tuition and other assistance. Speakers also included county commissioners of Duchesne and Uintah Counties (invited by Hatch), where the Uintah and Ouray Reservation was located, who spoke strongly against restoration and made comments that the Paiutes and others felt were racist. The lessee of the Shivwits grazing land also spoke in opposition of a reservation.

Bruce Parry and Mary Ellen Sloan made a whirlwind tour of southern Utah, meeting with the Paiute bands prior to House hearings on the restoration bill (H.R. 4996) in order to gather statistics on the current socioeconomic status of the Paiutes. This information helped to document the deplorable condition of many Paiutes after termination. This brief survey concluded that Paiute per-capita income was $1,968, in contrast to the $7,004 per-capita income of the average citizen of Utah.

A serious lobbying effort by the Paiute Restoration Committee, with the aim of including a reservation plan in the restoration legislation, cul-

"Beaverad-Utah Indian, Age about 100 Years"
Milford, Utah.

This photograph of Beaverad, a Paiute Indian
reported to be nearly one hundred years old, was
taken in Milford about 1910. (USHS)

minated when JoJo Hunt, staff attorney for the Senate Select Committee
on Indian Affairs, developed a series of fifteen amendments to a bill sponsored by Senator Hatch that included a provision for new reservation
lands to be selected and presented to Congress within two years of restoration. The committee chair approved this version, and it was adopted
through the acquiescence of Senator Hatch; even with the provision for
a reservation plan, he did not kill the bill.

Despite initial opposition from the Office of Management and Budget, which had asked for further study without offering any money to
fund it, the restoration act, Public Law 96-227, was signed by President
Jimmy Carter and became law on April 3, 1980.

The Paiutes received a good deal of local support for the restoration of the trust relationship; but when it came to receiving reservation lands, such support often ended or became more covert. Throughout the entire reservation planning process, it was made abundantly clear that the Paiutes had the support of the local personnel of the Bureau of Indian Affairs. This support began at the Phoenix Area Office and was especially strong at the Paiute Restoration Project Office, which was established at Cedar City in November 1980 in order to implement the restoration legislation. On June 1, 1983, Interior Secretary James Watt signed a measure giving final approval for the Cedar City office to become a field station serving all of the Paiutes in Utah, Arizona, and Nevada. Full-scale operations began on October 1, 1983, when the field station began to function as a Southern Paiute mini-agency.

Reservation Selection

The restoration act required the secretary of the interior to present proposed legislation for a Paiute reservation to Congress by April 3, 1982. The Paiutes were faced with a monumental task, as they had to elect a six-member interim council, establish a membership roll, write a tribal constitution and by-laws, and then elect a council under the constitution. An interim council was elected on May 31, 1980, and a constitution was adopted by the tribe on October 1, 1981. An official tribal membership roll listing 503 members was finished by August 1981. Reservation planning began under the interim council with a September 1980 meeting with Utah Governor Scott Matheson. The interim council was replaced by the newly elected tribal council on October 24, 1981. The fact that the Paiutes were able to accomplish all of this within such a compressed timeframe was a tribute to their leaders and to their hard work.

Then came the most exciting, controversial, and certainly most frustrating aspect of the restoration: the reservation planning and selection. Land selection was difficult.[33] Virtually all of the good land in southern Utah was in private hands. Lands managed by the Bureau of Land Management were marginal, and, while some U.S. Forest Service lands contained valuable minerals, they were either leased to or under the watchful eye of powerful interests. With only 503 members, the Paiute population was small and almost destitute, and they seldom voted. Certain LDS church leaders were asked to help with the reservation effort as the morally right thing to do, with the end objective of raising the living standard of Paiutes. Emphasis was placed on the Paiutes' desire for self-sufficiency and the need for good reservation land in order to accom-

Young Paiute pupils assemble in front of their school in Panguitch. (Marriott Library, University of Utah—U of U)

plish this goal. Pressure also was brought to bear on the Utah congressional delegation and local political leaders during this phase through personal visits, editorials, letters, and phone calls.

As various local and political opposition to reservation planning mounted, the support of Senator Hatch waned. One point of contention was that the Indians were being given special treatment not available to the general population, being "given something for nothing." The general white perception was that the Indians were being given land, not that the land was being restored to its rightful previous owners; also involved was the Mormon tenet that some form of work is necessary from those receiving assistance. After many heated and emotional meetings, five parcels were dropped from consideration. While the restoration legislation called for the land selection from "available public land", some officials in the U.S. Forest Service and other opponents maintained that forest lands were "not available." However, in 1956, some Uintah National Forest land had been returned to the Ute tribe, and, in 1974, 100,000 acres of national forest land had been put in trust for the Havasupai Indians of Arizona.

By 1984, tribal council members were resigned to take whatever was offered to them; their mood was one of melancholy powerlessness. The Paiute Tribal Council found itself in the familiar position of taking something with the assumption that it was better than nothing. In the end, H.R. 2898 provided the Utah Paiutes with 4,770 acres of land, less than one-third of the 15,000 acres that the restoration legislation allowed them to select. They could have followed the example of the Western Shoshonis and refuse to settle; however, this possibly would have netted them nothing. H.R. 2898 also authorized a trust fund of $2.5 million, with 50 percent of the interest drawn for tribal government expenses and economic development projects.

Paiute Indians Today

All the ingredients seemed to be in place for the Paiutes to be a "bureaucratized" people who could function amid the red tape and legalities of today's society. Efforts and energies now were needed to provide direction and leadership for the future success of the Paiutes. Internal squabbles, however, would hinder their progress, as some Paiutes had learned the bureaucratic system all too well. The Paiute leadership of the 1980s proved to be able and sophisticated. The tribe has been well served by strong leaders (within the Paiute context) and capable staff. During the restoration and reservation phases, interfamilial and band conflicts were somewhat muted; however, during the latter part of the land-acquisition process, internal squabbles began to increase, which made progress and continuity a bit more difficult. More and more conflict was evident as families sought the help of tribal, BIA, and state agencies in matters pertaining to food, shelter, medical care, education, and jobs.

Since restoration in 1980, the trend has been toward the contracting of functions previously the responsibility of the Bureau of Indian Affairs. The Utah Paiutes now contract almost all of their services; therefore, the direct supervision of their lives by the BIA is minimal. There is still a definite tendency of many tribal members to depend heavily on tribal government and services. The Paiute tribal government acts as a surrogate for the BIA and has become the continued focal point for Paiute aspirations and frustrations. Turnover in the tribal council has been high.

Although health care has improved dramatically since 1980, major problems still exist; for example, 95 percent of tribal deaths from 1981 to 1984 were alcohol related. The tribe hired an alcohol intervention specialist. In 1984 the tribal health department estimated that 68 percent of their people's health-care needs were not being met, and the life expect-

ancy of a Paiute male in 1984 was forty-two years. Improvements were made, however, and by 1989 not only were most private physicians in southern Utah available to tribal members but also there was a special clinic held at the tribal office building once a month. Dental, eye-care, diabetes, well-baby, and general clinics are held. Travis Parashoonts noted: "Prior to 1980, we had three deaths to every birth. We were a vanishing tribe, slowly going into extinction. Restoration gave us access to health service and we reversed those figures in three years."[34]

Education has been and continues to be a high priority with the Paiutes. After restoration they immediately hired a director of tribal education. Prior to 1981 about 40 percent of Paiute children dropped out of school by eighth grade, and only eight Paiutes had attended college in the previous ten years. Now, however, the drop-out rate has stayed in the single digits from 1982 to the present. By the spring of 1982, forty-four Paiutes were either attending college or vocational school. Desire for education is evident in the fact that of those between eighteen and forty years of age, 71 percent have participated in higher education or vocational training. Unfortunately, however, some progress remains to be made: only about one in three has finished his or her degree or training programs, and, of those, only about one-half have actually been able to find work in their field.[35] Tribal leaders have worried that, as their children graduate, they may find that the few jobs available in southern Utah are closed to Paiutes because of prejudice. This would force the best and brightest of the young Paiutes to find work away from their traditional homeland.

The Paiute Economic Development Committee was established in 1984 to seek out economic development enterprises closer to home. A sewing plant was established at Kanosh that employs twenty to thirty people (primarily Paiute women).[36] In the summer of 1989, a Cedar City warehouse was refurbished to establish a second sewing plant. Plans are currently underway to build a natural-gas, turbine-powered power plant, and possible development of a golf course, both slated for the Shivwits reservation.

Unemployment and underemployment still plague the Paiutes. In 1988, for example, with a labor force of 137 potential workers, seventy-seven were unemployed at some point during the year, and fifty-two were said to be actively seeking work.[37] Nonetheless, there is now a core of college-educated Paiute professionals of both sexes who can act as role models and help provide the lead in escaping the customary poverty conditions of many Paiute Indians.

Three Paiute women with a baby in a beautifully crafted cradleboard. (USHS)

The Koosharem Band has begun to benefit from the parcel of land at Joseph; five house trailers have been located there and twelve HUD homes have been built. The tribal administration has done an excellent job of acquiring HUD housing for tribal members at Cedar City, Shivwits, and Joseph.

Since they reacquired a landbase during the 1980s, the Paiutes have become more visible throughout southern Utah. In 1981, to celebrate their restored trust status, the Paiute Indian Tribe of Utah instituted a Restoration Gathering, to be held in June of each year. This celebration has become a major contemporary social event in the Paiute calendar. The gathering marks the restoration of federal recognition of the Utah Paiute tribe and includes a princess pageant, ball games and hand games, and a parade through downtown Cedar City.

The effort that goes into producing and participating in this event creates pride and solidarity among the participants. The intertribal aspects, such as the dance contests and the hand games, create an opportunity for the Paiutes to meet other Native Americans and exchange information and songs. One of the primary benefits of the Gathering is its visibility; it provides an opportunity for the Paiutes to express their ethnic pride and say to the Anglo community that they are proud of of their accomplishments and of who they are. The Paiute people never left their homeland, nor do they ever intend to leave.

Antero's encampment in the Uinta Valley, photographed by John
K. Hillers of the John Wesley Powell expedition in 1873–74.
(USHS)

The Northern Utes of Utah

Clifford Duncan

Creation and Migration Stories of the Utes

The story of Sinauf, the god who was half man, half wolf, and his brothers Coyote and Wolf has been told many times in tipis and wickiups. According to Ute legend, these powerful animal-people kept the world in balance before humans were created. After Sinauf made people, humans took responsibility to care for the world, and in time they created many stories of their predecessors. These stories became the basis of Ute history and culture and defined the relationship of Ute Indians with all living elements, both spiritually and physically.

Most often the stories were told during the winter months. As snow drifted in under the tipis through little gaps, children scrambled to cover the drafts. By the fire sat the elder, the storyteller. His listeners sat in a circle, bundled tightly in warm buffalo or rabbit robes, waiting eagerly for him to begin what could be a long night of stories. There were tales of acts of courage during summer's skirmishes and bravery during the fall hunts to be added to the tribe's oral history. But, always a favorite was the story of how the *Nuche*—the Utes—first came to be.

"Far to the south Sinauf was preparing for a long journey to the north. He had made a bag, and in this bag he placed selected pieces of sticks—all different yet the same size. The bag was a magic bag. Once Sinauf put the sticks into the bag, they changed into people. As he put more and more sticks into the bag, the noise the people made inside grew louder, thus arousing the curiosity of the animals.

"After filling his magic bag, Sinauf closed it and went to prepare for his journey. Among the animals, Coyote was the most curious. In fact, this particular brother of Sinauf was not only curious but contrary as well, opposing almost everything Sinauf created and often getting into trouble. When Coyote heard about Sinauf's magic bag full of stick people, he grew very curious. 'I want to see what those people look like,' he

thought. With that, he made a little hole with his flint knife near the top of the bag and peeked in. He laughed at what he saw and heard, for the people were a strange new creation and had many languages and sons.

"When Sinauf finished his preparations and prayers he was ready for the journey northward. He picked up the bag, threw it over his shoulder and headed for the *Una-u-quich*, the distant high mountains. From the tops of those mountains, Sinauf could see long distances across the plains to the east and north, and from there he planned to distribute the people throughout the world.

"Sinauf was anxious to complete his long journey, so he did not take time to eat and soon became very weak. Due to his weakness, he did not notice the bag getting lighter. For, through Coyote's hole in the top of the bag, the people had been jumping out, a few at a time. Those who jumped out created their families, bands, and tribes.

"Finally reaching the *Una-u-quich*, Sinauf stopped. As he sat down he noticed the hole in the bag and how light it was. The only people left were those at the bottom of the bag. As he gently lifted them out he spoke to them and said, 'My children, I will call you Utikas, and you shall roam these beautiful mountains. Be brave and strong.' Then he carefully put them in different places, singing a song as he did so. When he finished, he left them there and returned to his home in the south."[1]

Other myths tell of the creation of diversity in the land and how various creatures chose their own special places. They also tell how animals and people lost the ability to communicate with each other, drifting into different lifeways.

Lifeways

In pre-horse days, Ute family groups lived largely independently of others. Interfamily cooperation was limited to a few activities. Some activities were directed by a leader, who was "Chief" only as long as the activity needed supervision. Men and women who acquired reputations for wisdom, spiritual power, healing ability, or success in hunting or warfare were consulted. When food resources were abundant enough to enable a number of families to live in the same village, there was a village leader. His authority was limited to suggestions; he had no authority to enforce his suggestions.

Men hunted and fished, made ropes, bows, and arrows. They read the stars of the sky and the geography of the land while traveling the seasonal circuit of the family's territory. Some were also shamans, song-singers, or temporary leaders. Those who displayed skill in hunting and

A Ute brush wickiup used as a summer dwelling. (Marriott Library, University of Utah—U of U)

defending the People were admired. Women gathered foods and prepared them, sewed and repaired clothing and shelters, hauled wood and carried water, prepared medicines for the sick. Children were loved, fondled, and amused with toys, stories, and songs.

The acquisition of the horse enabled the Utes to travel more widely in search of foods and to transport that food from farther distances. Thus, the People could gather in larger villages for longer periods of time. As groups grew larger, some leaders acquired more followers, although none had authority over all aspects of Ute life. They were considered leaders because people chose to follow them, not because they chose to govern.

The Ute people followed the cycle of the seasons. Each group traveled within a specific territory in search of food, returning to their hunting and gathering areas year after year. In general, the pattern was moving to deserts and valleys during the winter and to mountains in the summer.

When the gathering season began, families would leave their winter villages and go out into the hills and desert valleys. Ute women gathered and dug cactus, various barks and seeds, and roots and tubers. Many of these plants and seeds were dried, placed in baskets, and stored in pits

A Ute summer dwelling. (USHS)

dug in the ground and then covered with earth. To gather the seeds, the women made finely woven baskets.

During the gathering season, the men kept busy either helping with the gathering or hunting small desert animals. The men set deadfalls to catch a few rodents, squirrels, or birds to supplement the diet. They also used a method of setting fire to brush and killing the animals that emerged. The time of summer harvesting was especially good for the Utes. The seeds, berries, and roots were plentiful. It was a time when families could get together for hunts and festivals and gossip about their winter adventures.

Fall was the time when seeds had to be stored, meat had to be dried, clothing had to be made and repaired, as did utensils such as pouches and bags, baskets and water jugs. This was also the time of great large-game hunts, including some for buffalo. Many families would get to-

Sai-ar's encampment and tipi in the Uinta Valley. Photographed by John K. Hillers, 1873–74. (USHS)

gether, feasting and preparing for the hunt. The hunters would ride out to find and bring back as much meat as they could carry. When the men returned, there was another gathering, with gambling, singing, and courting. These hunts were very important socially.

When the snow came, the People left their homes in the hills for the warmer flatlands. Women assembled their supply of seeds, roots, pine nuts, and dried berries and put them into storage pits. They piled meat on willow racks at the top of their tipis and hung jerky from the poles. They stored willows for making baskets, fiber, and string. They also stored great bunches of rabbitskin cordage for making blankets.

Throughout the winter the men hunted. They shot birds and small animals with their bows and arrows and did some ice fishing. They also trapped small rodents and birds. The People knew how to use alternate sources for food if game became scarce. The long winter evenings were

Two Ute woman at a spring in the Uinta Valley. Photographed by John K. Hillers in 1873 or 1874. (USHS)

spent sitting around the fire listening to the old ones tell stories of the creation and why things were the way they were. The Utes lived a busy but happy life, enjoying the bounty of nature.

The shelter and clothing of the Utes fit their lifestyle. Being often on the move, everything had to be either portable or disposable. The people lived in either brush shelters or tipis. The environment determined the kind of housing. In the desert where materials were scarce, they used brush or grass to make shelters. In more forested lands, there were trees for lodge poles and big-game animals for hides. These were tanned and sewn together with sinew of different animals to make the tipi's cover.

The brush and willow houses were cool in the summer but could be easily heated by an open fire just outside. One family might build several in the course of a year's travels, leaving them behind as they moved on. The tipi was portable, easily raised, and waterproof. With its wind-deflecting small flap at the top, it was well ventilated even with a fire burning inside. It was warm during the winter and cool in the summer.

Women made the clothing. In warm weather the women wore a short skirt of shredded bark or buckskin and the men wore breechcloths. In winter women wore ankle-length dresses; men wore shirts and leggings of tanned animal skins. The hides of buffalo, deer, antelope, elk, and mountain sheep were tanned and treated. Sinew thread was used for sewing. Blankets were made of rabbitskin, deerskin, buffalo skin, or of woven cloth traded from Pueblo people of New Mexico. The moccasins, shirts, leggings, and dresses used in festivities were often fringed and tied with hair or small tanned skins decorated with paint. Some of the garments were embroidered.

The Utes designated time and the seasons according to the position of the sun and the stars. Certain stars told the Ute people of the coming of the various seasons. The Jack Rabbit, as they referred to the Big Dipper, was their clock as to the time of the night. Its position also foretold the seasons.

The power of healing was an important aspect of Ute life. The *Poowagudt* (medicine man) used abilities bestowed upon him by spiritual or natural powers. The Utes discovered by experience what was good for them and what was not. To the Utes, disease was an entity, something which took possession of the person to do them harm. The *Poowagudt* was called upon to get rid of the evil. He might sit up all night with that person and conjure. Through the use of chants, drums, and spiritual objects, the *Poowagudt* discovered what the ailment was and what should be given to treat it.

These beliefs of the Ute people were based upon their tradition, taught to each generation. But contact with white society changed this. The old religion of the People is slowly dying out. The modern doctor is beginning to be accepted for his powers.

Ute Lands, Bands, and Early History

The Utes and their ancestors called the land of the eastern Great Basin and western Rocky Mountains home for hundreds of years before it was discovered and explored by Europeans. Through the Numic language spoken by the Utes and related tribes such as Goshute, Paiute, Shoshone, Bannock, and Comanche, it is possible to trace the later migrations made by these people, whose languages are part of the same language family.

The Ute relationship with the land and their love for it tied their culture closely to the earth and its abundance. The land of the Utes was about 225,000 square miles: from Fillmore, Utah, on the west to Colo-

rado Springs, Colorado, on the east, and from Baggs, Wyoming, to Abiquiu, New Mexico, from north to south. Some Ute groups ranged even farther to hunt. These 225,000 square miles contained a varied landscape which ranged from great mountain parks to arid flatlands, and from rugged canyons to high plateaus. In the north are the Central Rockies. In the south are rolling hills that level out into semiarid mesas and desert country on the west, and into flat plains on the east. To the west is the Great Salt Desert of western Utah. To the east is the grassland plains of eastern Colorado and western Kansas.

The Ute people did not use the lakes and rivers for transportation, but they did use them as a major source for food—both the fish and plant life within them and the game which congregated around them. Utes located their major campsites near the waterways. They also learned to use even the desert lands. These yielded foods, offered relief from the cold, and put distances between the People and their enemies.

In the Ute land, dozens of mountains reach above 13,000 feet. The mountains were important refuges for the Utes, particularly after they acquired horses. Ute bands traveled on horseback from the mountains onto the plains where they were able to gather food. Then they quickly returned to the mountains which they knew so well, and where pursuers from other tribes were at a disadvantage.

The Utes were scattered over the land in family groups or bands. In their search for food and shelter, each band traveled over a wide but certain familiar area. Bands often were known by the land they inhabited or the foods on which they lived. The Sevier Lake Utes called themselves Pahvant, which means "close to water." The band which resided at Utah Lake was called Tumpanawach, or "fish eaters." The Yampa River Band was called Yamparika, or "carrot eaters."

In some localities such as the valley of the Utah Lake and the lower Sevier River streams and forests provided abundant game and seeds. In these areas the Utes did not have to travel far to obtain foods; therefore, large encampments became established.

Each family group lived independently of others. However, the Ute people would travel far, especially after some acquired the horse, to meet together. Sometimes these meetings were because of necessity. More often they were social events with dances, amusements, and marriages, usually taking place in the summer. The most important gatherings, however, were religious in nature, such as the Bear Dance.

There was not a central political structure for the entire Ute tribe. Too many natural barriers separated the several bands. Also, there was

A young Ute warrior and his dog photographed by John K. Hillers in the Uinta Valley, 1873–74. (USHS)

not enough food in one area to support all the bands. But all the Utes recognized themselves to be *Nuche*, the People. They all shared a language, rites, traditions, lifestyles, and a beautiful land.

As in the creation legend of Sinauf, Ute ancestors probably migrated from the south, originating perhaps in the Sonora Valley of Mexico and moving north into what is now southern California. Over the next several hundred years, family groups and small bands fanned out to the north, northeast, and east throughout the Great Basin. As they separated and diverged, new tribes formed and languages changed.

The bands that continued north into what is now Utah, Colorado, and parts of Wyoming and New Mexico interacted enough to maintain a common language, although they lived as separate bands and even smaller family units. Leading a largely nomadic life, these small family groups hunted meat and gathered edible and medicinal plants, traveling with the seasons and taking advantage of the land's rich resources. When Europeans arrived some 500 years ago, there were at least ten distinct bands

of Utes in what is now Colorado and Utah, the latter state, in fact, named after the Utes.

The various bands included:

1) Moache—residing north of what is now Trinidad, Colorado, to the Denver region.

2) Capote (Kapota)—ranging east of the Continental Divide, south of the Conejos River, and east of the Rio Grande to the west side of the Sangre de Cristo Mountains. In the mid-nineteenth century they also lived west of the divide near the Animas River.

3) Weeminuche—lived west of the Continental Divide from the Dolores River in werstern Colorado through the Blue Mountains, including the fringe of the mesas and plateaus in the Canyonlands of eastern Utah.

4) Uncompahgre (Tabeguache)—located in an area including the Gunnision River, the Elk Mountains, and the Uncompahgre River, with what is now Grand Junction, Colorado, as their approximate western boundary.

5) White River (Parusanuch and Yamparika)—occupied the river valleys of the White and Yampa river systems, as well as North Park and Middle Park in the mountains of northern Colorado, with territories extending westward to eastern Utah.

6) Uintah—resided from Utah Lake east through the Uinta Basin to the Tavaputs Plateau in the Green and Colorado river systems.

7) Pahvant—ranged the deserts surrounding Sevier Lake, west of the Wasatch Mountains, almost to the Nevada border, mixing somewhat with Goshutes and Paiutes in southern Utah.

8) Timanogots—lived around the southern and eastern perimeters of Utah Lake in Utah Valley in north-central Utah.

9) Sanpits, or San Pitch—were in Sanpete Valley in central Utah and the Sevier River Valley.

10) Moanumts—lived in the upper Sevier River Valley in central Utah, the Otter Creek area south of Salina, and in the Fish Lake area.

11) Sheberetch—dwelt in the region around present-day Moab. This group was far more desert oriented than were the other groups. They had very little direct relationship with the Europeans until Mormons moved into the area in the 1850s. By the 1870s, the Sheberetch had been reduced by disease and war. It seems probable that the survivors joined the Uncompahgre, Weeminuche, and Uintah bands.

Three bands shared the eastern border: the Yamparika, the Paranuche (most of whom later joined the White River Band), and the Moache,

which also traded with the people of the pueblos. The Capote Band lived in south-central Colorado and north-central New Mexico. Friendly relationships with the Pueblo people were also maintained by this band. Both the Moache and the Capote Bands now occupy the Southern Ute Reservation, with headquarters at Ignacio, Colorado.

Along the present border of Utah and Colorado around the Dolores River Valley dwelt a band called Weeminuche. The members of this band are now found on the Ute Mountain Ute Reservation in the southwestern corner of Colorado, with Towaoc as their headquarters.

Dwelling in the high mountains of what is now central Colorado were the people known as the Taviwach or Tabeguache. Later they came to be called the Uncompahgre. They had few contacts with other tribes. In central Utah along the Sevier River and the western flank of the Pahvant Mountains was the Pahvant Band. In many of their characteristics they were like their neighbors the Kaibab Paiutes, and, like the Sheberetch, they were skilled at using desert areas. The Pahvant also used marsh life of the Sevier River, as well as Fish Lake and its mountain streams. They also farmed. An 1851 newspaper account noted: "Pah-van-te Indians ... reside at Corn Creek ... and have there raised corn, beans, pumpkins, squashes, potatoes, etc., year after year for a period that dates farther back than their acquaintance with the whites."[2]

Utah Lake was the most permanent location of any of the Ute communities. The group who dwelt there was called the Tumpanawach. Europeans called them Lagunas, or fish-eaters, and also the Timpanogos Utes. In addition to the fish from the Provo and other rivers which feed Utah Lake, the community had a great number of other resources. The Heber Valley, Uinta Basin, and San Pete Valley areas, Spanish Fork, Diamond Fork, Hobble Creek, American Fork, and Provo River canyons were close and abundant in resources. The Tumpanawach were the most powerful force in the area. This group was large because the food supply was great and relatively easy to obtain, making them a peaceful, happy people.

The San Pitch, or San Pete, Utes occupied land near the Sanpete Valley. Unlike the buffalo hunting Uinta-ats, Pahvant, and Tumpanawach, the San Pitch did not have horses. Some white observers described them as "exceedingly poor ... deserving of pity," and called them "Diggers," which became a term of derision. Eventually the San Pitch allied themselves with the Pahvant and went to the Uintah Reservation.

There were also smaller groups of Utes, some of whom had kinship ties with other Indians. The Cumumba, or Weber, Utes living along the Weber River intermarried with the Northwestern Shoshone. The Fish

The Ute Indian Pah-ri-ats in his native summer dress. Photographed in the Uinta Valley by John K. Hillers in 1873–74. (USHS)

Lake Utes associated with the Southern Paiutes and came to be identified as such. The Uinta-ats, later called Tavaputs, lived in the Uinta Mountains and the area along and around the Strawberry River. Pahvant, Tumpanawach, Uinta-ats, and some Cumumba and Sheberetch were gathered together at the Uintah Agency during the late 1860s and early 1870s. These groups then came to be called the Uintah Band.

Modern history began for the Utes in the early 1600s. Ute life changed dramatically when southern and eastern Ute bands acquired the horse from Europeans, who began invading the Ute lands about 1550. At first they were few in number and generally were received with kindness. But

A runner or messenger photographed by John K. Hillers in the Uinta Valley in 1873 or 1874. (USHS)

increasingly they made more impact and demands. As historian Fred Conetah wrote: "They wanted alliances, trade, and finally the land and its resources. They repaid the Utes with disease, whiskey, wanton killing, worthless items of 'civilization,' and broken promises."[3]

The first intruders were Spaniards who traveled into the area in search of souls and gold. The first Spanish expedition to approach Ute land was led by Francisco Coronado in 1539–42 looking for the legendary cities of Cibola. Coronado probably did not meet any Utes, but they may have heard of him from their southern neighbors. In fact, with their wide trade connections, the Utes probably heard about Spaniards long before.

In 1604 an expedition sent by Juan de Onate met an Indian who told of a land and a lake of Copala, located north and west. The Spaniards later called this legendary area El Gran Teguayo. The area was probably the land of the Utes, and the Lake of Copala may have been Utah Lake.

The earliest specific reference by Spaniards to the Ute people is found in published reports of the Onate expedition in 1626. Fray Geronimo Salmeron wrote that Pueblo people told him of visits before 1598 of a group of Indians called Guaguatu or Guaputa. The friar called them Quasuatas, a form of the word "Yutas," by which he and later Spanish writers called all Indians who spoke the Shoshonean dialect. Thus, the People came to be called the Utes.

In the early seventeenth century, Governor Luis de Rosas of Santa Fe reported the capture of eighty "Utikahs." In 1638 the first recorded conflict occurred between the Spaniards and Utes. Spaniards captured about eighty "Utacas," who were then forced to labor in workshops in Santa Fe. The first treaty with the Utes was made in 1670.

In 1680 the Pueblo peoples revolted and ousted the Spaniards from the area. Utes may have been involved in the fighting. Many Ute slaves and servants were freed, and Spanish horses became available in large numbers. Spaniards reconquered the Pueblo area in 1692, but they found their position more difficult. They were surrounded by hostile tribes. To protect themselves, the Spaniards began to form alliances with Indian peoples. They hoped that these alliances would create a buffer zone around their settlements.

The returning Spaniards hoped to maintain good relations with the Utes, who had been friendly to them. As enemies, Utes posed a great threat to the Spanish frontier towns. As friends, they were valuable allies against hostile tribes. But the Spaniards soon found that the once-friendly Utes were joining their neighbors to raid the settlements.

These alliances, however, were temporary, and they rarely involved more than a few bands. Warfare in the area consisted of small groups that would ride into an enemy camp to take horses, guns, and prisoners. After the raid they would retreat to their homelands. These tactics proved very effective for the Utes, who grew in strength and power throughout the century.

From about the year 1650 Apache groups began encroaching on Ute and Comanche lands. In 1706 the Utes allied with the Comanche to fight these intruders. As a result, the pattern of alliances in the area shifted. By 1750 the Ute-Navajo alliance had broken up. Navajos joined the Spanish and the Apache to oppose the Ute-Comanche alliance. About 1748 the Comanche allied themselves with the French. With access to French guns, the Comanche broke with the Utes and turned against them.

In 1749 Spaniards and Utes made peace and formed a new alliance. Peace with the Utes was important. Ute attacks had forced Spaniards to

abandon a number of their northern settlements, such as Abiquiu in 1747. And trade with the Utes for tanned deerskins and other animal pelts was important to the Spaniards. There was also the extensive slave trade. The Utes captured other Indians and traded them for Spanish horses. Although there were protests against this trade from about 1650, the practice only stopped after the United States conquered the territory in the Mexican War.

The Ute people were interested in allying themselves with the Spaniards for defense against the well-armed Comanche. The alliance proved valuable for both. After nearly thirty years of periodic fighting, the Ute-Spanish forces, with their Apache and Pueblo allies, defeated the Comanche. The Comanche moved south, and the Apache moved farther south and west. The Utes were left in control of the lands north of New Mexico.

By the 1770s, Spanish explorers and others had moved north even deeper into Ute territory in their ceaseless quest for gold. In 1776 the Uinta Basin Utes first encountered non-Indians when a Spanish expedition led by Franciscan friars Francisco Atanasio Domínguez and Silvestre Vélez de Escalante came through the area searching for a northern inland route from Santa Fe, New Mexico, to Monterey, California. It was led in part by Ute guides. The friars also also hoped to establish Indian missions throughout the area. The journal of the expedition was the first written description of the Ute lands and people. The maps by Don Bernardo Miera y Pacheco were also the first of the area.

The expedition traveled north through the Chama River Valley into south-central Colorado, and then through the La Plata Mountains to the Uncompahgre River. From there they headed into northwestern Colorado, entering the Uinta Basin a few miles south of the confluence of the Yampa and Green Rivers. Crossing the Green River, they traveled west, following Strawberry Creek to what is now Spanish Fork, and into the valley of Utah Lake. Expedition members observed that the local Utes,

> ... the Lagunas ... live on the lake's abundant fish.... Besides this, they gather the seeds of wild plants in the bottoms and make a gruel from them, which they supplement with the game of jackrabbits, coneys, and fowl, of which there is a great abundance here. They also have bison handy not too far away ... but fear of the Comanches prevents them from hunting them.
>
> Their dwellings are some ... little wattle huts of osier, out of which they have interestingly crafted baskets and other utensils

for ordinary use.... they wear ... deerskin jacket[s] and long leggings of the same. For cold seasons they wear blankets made of jackrabbit and coney rabbit furs.... They possess good features, and most of them are fully bearded.... [They have an] easy-going character.[4]

From Utah Lake the friars proceeded south and, after experiencing some dissension and bad weather, the expedition elected to return to Santa Fe, which they did by difficult travel north of the Grand Canyon. The expedition found no great treasures or large cities; but it did find rich lands and friendly Indians.

Spanish intrusion changed the Utes. Ute children captured as slaves were placed in Spanish houses as servants. Some were later returned to their own people as adults in order to provide friendly contacts for Spaniards. Some Utes thus acquired new skills and techniques. The most important effect Spaniards had on Ute life was to introduce to them the horse. The Ute bands in southern Colorado and southeastern Utah were the first to obtain horses. The more northern Ute groups acquired them later in the seventeenth and eighteenth centuries. Some Ute bands, like the San Pitch and Sheberetch who lived on fragile desert lands, never kept horses in any numbers.

Ute groups who had access to horses and pasturelands to support them became good riders. Their hunting skill and range increased. Their lives changed. With the more efficient hunting, band organization strengthened. More people stayed together for longer periods of time. There was a new emphasis on raiding, although Utes did not develop aggressive warrior societies. With the horse and the resources it made available, the Ute people grew more powerful. They traveled far out onto the eastern and southern plains and came into greater contact and competition with the Cheyenne, Comanche, Arapaho, Pawnee, Sioux, and Apache tribes. It also made them a greater threat to the Spanish settlements to the south.

In 1778, Spaniards were prohibited from trading with the Utes. This law remained in effect until Mexican independence in 1820, but many traders ignored it. Following Domínguez and Escalante, traders entered the lands of the Tumpanawach. A principal item the People had to exchange was slaves taken from the Paiute and desert Ute people. Prior to Spanish intrusion, there was a limited system of slavery among some Ute groups. However, these slaves were mostly captives gained in raiding expeditions and were often incorporated into the tribe. Spaniards, on the

This Ute girl on horseback was photographed by John K. Hillers
in the Uinta Valley in 1873–74. (USHS)

other hand, used Indian slaves to work in the mines of northern Mexico
and in the homes of Spanish colonists. To acquire these slaves, the Spanish developed a system with some Indian groups of trading horses, metal
objects, cloth, and trinkets for slaves. When the 1813 expedition of
Mauricio Arze and Lagos Garcia went to Utah Lake, Utes supposedly
insisted on selling them slaves, killing their horses when the Spaniards
refused.

The Ute people had been in a favorable position. Spaniards had little
impact on Ute territory, and the Utes acquired new items: iron pots, metal
knives, guns, and horses. With the 1820 Mexican revolt from Spain and
the establishment of the nation of Mexico, the lands of the Utes were
opened to the fur trade. The Utes established profitable trade relations
with the fur trappers who came into Ute territory. The fur rendezvous
held each summer from 1825 to 1840 were attended by Utes.

Wakara, a Ute leader known for his wide-
ranging horseback journeys from the
Wasatch Mountains west to California and
east toward the Rocky Mountains during the
1840s and 1850s. (USHS)

Even the 1829 opening of the Old Spanish Trail, a trade route which
crossed the lands of the Kapota, Weeminuche, Tumpanawach, and
Pahvant, was initially to Ute advantage. The Tumpanawach leader Wakara,
or Walker, raided for horses in New Mexico and California with mountain men Thomas "Pegleg" Smith and James Beckworth. The horses were
then driven along the Old Spanish Trail into Utah and sold to trappers to
carry their furs back to St. Louis or Santa Fe. In one raid they drove off
several thousand horses from ranches in California and were even able
to steal the mounts of their pursuers. Soon after the trail was opened, the
Utes were able to levy a sort of tribute on the caravans that went over the
trail yearly from 1830 to about 1848. By 1837 Wakara was getting wealthy
from it.

From the early 1750s, it is believed that French fur trappers and traders ventured into Ute country. American mountain men weren't far behind, and by the 1820s and 1830s the country of the Utes was becoming
quite well known. Their stories of the beautiful, rugged mountain coun-

try helped attract settlers to the West. In 1849 the discovery of gold in California brought a flood of Euro-Americans westward. Later, gold was discovered in Colorado. The resulting influx of people eventually led to the banishment of Utes from their homelands.

The 1830s was a period of prosperity for several of the Ute bands. Utes traded beaver and otter pelts and tanned hides of elk, deer, mountain sheep, and buffalo for weapons, ammunition, blankets, utensils, and trinkets. Several trading forts were established in the Uinta Basin and on Ute lands in Colorado. However, the fur trade was to prove destructive to the Indians, who became increasingly dependent on white men's goods, including liquor. The trading posts became centers of vice and drunkenness. The land was stripped of beaver and other fur-bearing animals.

The fur trade declined in the late 1830s when eastern fashion changed. The Utes complained to the traders, not understanding that they were the victims of a complex economic system. Part of their frustration at this turn of events was expressed in their burning the trading forts in and around the Uinta Basin in 1844.

Fur traders such as Peter Skene Ogden, Jedediah Smith, and Kit Carson traveled through and reported about the Ute country. Other people were sent by the United States government to explore the region. The trappers, traders, explorers, and surveyors found the routes, established the posts, and published the reports that aided and convinced miners, farmers, and ranchers to come west. These were the people who stayed and who appropriated the land of the Utes for themselves.

In 1848 the United States took California and adjacent regions from Mexico with the Treaty of Guadalupe Hidalgo ending the Mexican War. New relationships between the Ute people and the intruders developed as U.S. control was imposed. Without Indian consent, Ute lands were divided into territories of the United States. The policy of the United States was to supervise and "civilize" the Indians. The government established agencies in order to carry out this policy at the local level, to control Indian trade, and to restrain Indian hostilities. Agents conducted councils, negotiated treaties, and administered the funds for encouraging the Indians to farm and ranch. The agents were also supposed to protect the rights of the Indians.

At this time the reservation system was developing for handling the "Indian Problem." It would place the Indians on islands of land, reservations, usually within the larger areas they occupied. Lands surrounding these reservations could then be controlled by private landholders or the United States.

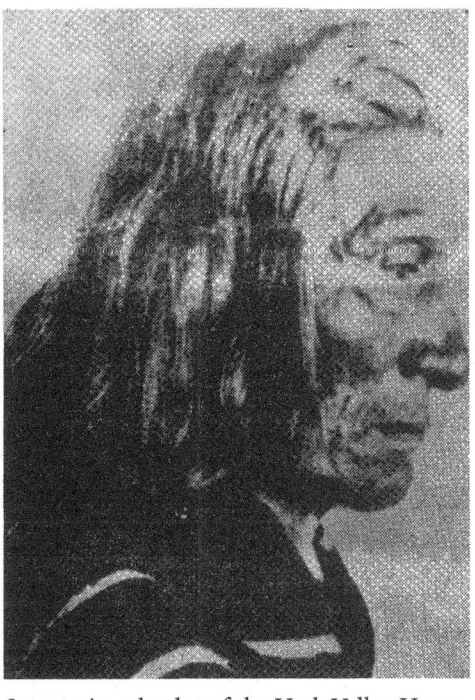

Santaquin, a leader of the Utah Valley Utes
for whom the town of Santaquin is named.
(USHS)

To encourage American settlement in Ute country and elsewhere in
the West, an expedition was sent to the Colorado Rockies in 1843 under
Lieutenant John Charles Frémont. In 1844 Frémont traveled through
Utah Ute country, leading the first official exploring and survey party
sent to gather scientific information about the area. His reports encouraged hundreds of settlers to make the trip, most notably the Mormons.

In the following years, other government explorers and surveyors
followed Frémont into Ute country. One, John W. Gunnison, returned
to work on a survey for the proposed Pacific railroad only to meet a
tragic death.

In the late 1860s and early 1870s Major John Wesley Powell entered
Ute country when he explored the Green and Colorado Rivers. He later
observed and studied the languages and customs of the Ute and Paiute
peoples of Utah, Nevada, Colorado, and northern Arizona. The photographs of John Hillers, who accompanied Powell, are an important visual record of the People. Another photographer, William H. Jackson,

accompanied F.V. Hayden on his surveys of the Rocky Mountains in the 1870s. Jackson's photographs and Hayden's maps did much to publicize the West, including the lands of the Utes.

Members of the Church of Jesus Christ of Latter-day Saints (LDS or Mormons) under the leadership of Brigham Young arrived in the Salt Lake Valley in 1847. Very soon the entire valley was being settled by Mormons. They had a particular interest in Indians and a policy of converting the Indians and encouraging them to become farmers. However, they also wanted the land and resources. Indians in the way were pushed aside.

The initial arrival of the Mormons in the Salt Lake Valley did not bother the Utes too much because the valley was considered neutral territory or a buffer zone between the Utes to the south, the Goshutes to the west, and the Shoshone to the north. Indeed, the Utes perceived that the Mormon presence created an opportunity for them to trade for European goods. Many Utes considered the Utah Lake Valley, just south, to be their homeland, however. This valley provided all the natural necessities needed for survival, such as roots, seeds, berries, and a lake teeming with fish. The nearby mountains provided deer, elk, and other game. There was also plenty of lush grassland to feed their prized ponies.

When the Mormons soon expanded into Utah Lake Valley, the Utes viewed it as an invasion into their homeland and Ute-Mormon troubles began. The Mormons took Ute land as it suited them, without regard to, or any consideration of, Ute rights, typical of the attitudes of other white newcomers throughout the West that the land was theirs for the claiming. Also, in contrast to the Native American way of seeking a balance and not depleting natural resources, they cut timber excessively and over-hunted game in the mountains.

In 1849 a fort was established at present-day Provo. The site of the fort was an area which had been used by the Ute people for centuries as a major campsite. The fort lay directly in the path of several hunting trails. By 1850, Ute people had killed and stolen several cattle and horses of the fort's occupants. On 8 February 1850, fighting erupted and a number of Utes were killed. For the next several months hostilities continued. Indians raided settlements for cattle and horses. Militias were sent against them, and many Indians were killed.

In February 1851 the Utah Territorial Indian Agency was established by Congress, and some efforts were begun to aid the Indians. However, Mormons continued to displace the Indians, to drive away the game, and replace the natural vegetation. The Mormons also acted to curtail the trade in horses, slaves, and tribute between the Ute people and the Mexi-

cans. When the Mormons came in 1847 they almost immediately were confronted with the system. During the first winter, 1847–48, two children were brought to the Mormon fort to be sold. The Indians explained they were captured in war and would be killed if the whites did not buy them. Thereupon, one was bought; the one not purchased was killed. Other children were brought in, and the settlers usually bought them.[5]

With the fur trade ended and the Mexican trade curtailed, the Tumpanawach found it difficult to live from their traditional resources. Their lands were being occupied. The lakes and streams were being overfished. Their sources of independence were disappearing. The Utes were frustrated in their attempts to adjust to the new situation and began to resist. But the Utes could not defeat the Mormons. Also, retaliation for Ute raids was intense. For example, after four Mormons were killed and their bodies mutilated by Utes, nine innocent Indians were slaughtered when they came into a Mormon camp.

Protecting their homeland, the Utes retaliated by taking cattle and horses and raiding Mormon communities. There were numerous skirmishes throughout the Ute territory, and a larger conflict erupted in 1853 known as the Walker War, named after the Ute leader Wakara. Raids and skirmishes occurred throughout much of central Utah.

In the summer of 1853 a settler killed a Ute and wounded two others. Wakara and his brother Arapeen began a series of raids on Mormon settlements. During the next ten months some twenty whites and many more Utes were killed. The war, however, was futile. Brigham Young sent out word to his followers to "fort up" and to curtail the trading of arms and ammunition to the Indians. There also was factionalism among the Utes—no alliance between bands was possible. The Utah Utes were outnumbered. In the six years since their arrival, the Mormons had become the majority.

Peace was arranged by Brigham Young and Wakara at Chicken Creek in May 1854. Wakara died on 29 January 1855, a defeated man. The "Mericats" controlled his former trading areas. The Mormons were taking over his homeland and its resources and forcing his people to depend upon their charity.

Indian affairs in Utah were complicated by the mutual hostility of Mormons and federal officials. There was constant conflict as to who should administer Indian policy. In the conflict Congress neglected Utah and ignored the Indians. The United States government took over Utah without a single Ute land title settled and without any treaty of cession negotiated.

Federal officials sent to Utah Territory began charging the Mormons with using their influence over the Indians against the interest of the government. And the Mormons were increasingly successful in their missionary efforts. However, since the basic interest of the Mormons conflicted with those of the Ute people—the Mormons wanted the land the People occupied—conflict was inevitable.

In 1854 Garland Hurt was appointed to the Utah Indian Agency. Soon after his arrival in 1855 he established three Ute Indian farms: at Corn Creek in Millard County, at Twelve Mile Creek in Sanpete County, and on the banks of the Spanish Fork River in Utah County. (Also, a farm for Goshutes was established at Deep Creek.) Hurt wanted to help improve the conditions of the Indians and to control them. He planned to develop the farms into permanent reservations, established with the consent of the Indians.

These federal farms were built upon a system of Indian farms which had been started in 1851 by Mormon leaders. There were several such farms established throughout Utah. Mormons were called to provide food for the Indians and to do missionary work among them.

After some initial success, the federal Indian farm effort was interrupted by the so-called "Utah War." President James Buchanan sent troops to Utah to take control from the Mormons. Agent Hurt fled the territory. The next agent, Jacob Forney, was dismissed for mismanagement. A year elapsed before another agent was appointed. Inadequate funds finally forced the closing of the farms. Everything was sold at the Sanpete and Spanish Fork farms to keep the Indians from starving.

The Walker War had ended in 1854, but the situation remained unstable, and the continued influx of Mormon and other settlers to the region increased the pressures on the Indian inhabitants while making their struggle for survival increasingly difficult. During this time, the federal government was continuing its established practice of creating reservations. The land set aside for Native Americans was often far from the tribe's homeland and was usually bleak and almost always considered useless by whites. In 1860 Brigham Young sent a survey party to the Uinta Basin to see if it could support a Mormon settlement. The party reported the country: "[was] entirely unsuitable for farming purposes,... [was] one vast contiguity of waste, and measurably valueless, excepting for nomadic purposes ... hunting ground for Indians."[6] The area was then suggested as a site for an Indian reservation.

In 1861, responding to Mormon pressure, President Abraham Lincoln signed an executive order establishing the original Uintah Valley

Reservation in the eastern part of the territory. The reservation boundaries were simply defined as the entire valley of the Uinta River within Utah Territory. Congress ratified the order in 1864. Utah Indian Superintendent Oliver H. Irish was ordered to negotiate with the Utes to move them to the Uintah Reservation. A council of the Ute people was called at Spanish Fork Reservation on 6 June 1865. The aged leader Sowiette explained that the Ute people did not want to sell their land and go away, asking why the groups couldn't live on the land together. Sanpitch also spoke against the treaty. However, advised by Brigham Young that these were the best terms they could get, the leaders signed.

The treaty provided that the Utes give up their lands in central Utah, including the Corn Creek, Spanish Fork, and San Pete Reservations. Only the Uintah Valley Reservation remained. They were to move into it within one year, and be paid $25,000 a year for ten years, $20,000 for the next twenty years, and $15,000 for the last thirty years. (This was payment of about 62.5 cents per acre for all land in Utah and Sanpete Counties.) However, Congress did not ratify the treaty; therefore, the government did not pay the promised annuity. Nevertheless, in succeeding years most of the Utah Ute people were removed to the Uintah Reservation.

The federal government abandoned the farms but was slow in developing the Uintah Reservation. With the wild game disappearing and the whites occupying the land, the Utes were in desperate circumstances. In 1865 a Ute leader named Black Hawk began leading a series of attacks on the settlements in Sanpete County. Black Hawk was a very capable leader and was able to recruit other Utes and even some Navajos and Paiutes. The Black Hawk War was basically an intensifying of the raids that had been conducted against the Mormon intruders since 1849.

After a smallpox epidemic and near starvation in the winter of 1864–65, Black Hawk found that some Utes were willing to join him in raids on the Mormon settlements. Great numbers of livestock and supplies were seized by the resistors. Sevier and Paiute Counties were entirely abandoned, and many settlements in other counties were temporarily left. However, the effort was in vain. The Mormons continued to increase in numbers and strength. Local civil authorities and Indian agents began moving Utes to the Uintah Reservation.

The Mormons had trouble stopping the attacks and threatened a war of extermination against the Ute people. By 1865 Utah Indian Superintendent Irish acted to convince the Utes to move to the Uintah Reservation. Mormon settlers also increased in strength. In the summer of 1867 Black Hawk appeared on the Uintah Reservation accompanied by

his family. He agreed to meet with Superintendent Head. At that meeting he explained that his Indians were tired of fighting and desirous of a permanent peace. The following summer, Head held a council with several of Black Hawk's followers. They negotiated a verbal peace treaty.

In 1870 Black Hawk traveled to various Mormon settlements asking forgiveness for the attacks. He pointed out that the raids were undertaken because his people were starving. Black Hawk died that year of tuberculosis. Some of his followers continued raiding until 1872. Many of the San Pitch Utes eventually moved to the Uintah Reservation.

The Uintah Ute Reservation

The Ute people who are now called the Uintah Utes acquired that name from the area reserved for them in Utah. Many are descended from the Uinta-ats who lived in the Uinta Basin. Others are descended from Tumpanawach, Pahvant, and San Pitch people who lived in other parts of Utah. Some are even descended from other Indian groups who intermarried with Utes. The Uinta Basin is bordered by the Uinta Mountains to the north and the Wasatch Mountains to the west. Mountain streams flowed into the Duchesne and Green Rivers. The Basin was an area of good fishing and good hunting. However, there were not large numbers of Uinta-ats living in the Basin, and most of the families living there were fairly independent groups of few residents in the limited fertile areas, such as the streams at the foot of the Uinta Range.

When the traders and trappers came into the Basin in the 1820s, mounted Uinta-ats were in the area. Antoine Robidoux's post on the Uinta River caused unsatisfactory relations with the Indians. It offered traffic in women and in whiskey and served as an attractive spot to draw other intruders into Uinta-ats country. Robidoux himself became a hated symbol among the Utes. In 1844 the Utes burned his fort while he was away. The fort was then abandoned.

The Pahvant Utes lived in villages along the western flank of the Pahvant Mountains and along the Sevier River. The Domínguez-Escalante expedition met these people. They called them Barbones, or the "Bearded Utes." Their physical appearance suggests they had had previous relations with Europeans.

Whites began invading territory occupied by the Pahvant people in the 1850s. A tragic incident between the intruders and the Pahvant was the Gunnison Massacre. Early in October 1853 a group of emigrants on their way to California camped southwest of Fillmore. A small group of Pahvant people, led by Moshoquop and his father, Mareer, went to the

camp to trade. The emigrants panicked and opened fire on them, killing Mareer. With threats of revenge, the Pahvant left camp and moved northeast of Sevier Lake.

At the same time, Captain John Gunnison, with a small military escort, was exploring for a railroad route. On October 25, Gunnison and several companions traveled to explore Sevier Lake. They were noticed by members of Moshoquop's group. He decided to avenge the death of his father. At dawn the next day, Moshoquop and his followers attacked and killed Gunnison and seven of his party.

Later, six Pahvants (including one woman) were turned over by Kanosh to military authorities. The Indians were put on trial. The Mormon jurors found three men guilty of manslaughter and acquitted the rest. This verdict displeased federal officials, and Colonel Edward J. Steptoe was sent with a detail of soldiers to investigate the murders.

The Pahvant leader Tintic also opposed white intrusion. In February 1856 members of Tintic's band killed two herdsmen, stole some cattle, and moved into Cedar Valley. First a posse and then the Utah County militia were sent after Tintic, but they failed to capture him. These raids and retaliations were called the Tintic War. Tintic was killed in 1858.

The Indian farm at Corn Creek was operated by Pahvant Utes under the leadership of Kanosh. The group struggled for years to farm the area, even after it was abandoned by the federal government. Mormon settlers gave them some assistance. Superintendent F.H. Head described their efforts in 1866: "Early in the spring I procured to be plowed for those Indians … about an acre of land and furnished to them seed, grain, potatoes, and corn. They have taken the entire care of the crop, and have raised several hundred bushels of wheat, corn, and potatoes …"[7]

But in 1868 grasshoppers destroyed most of their crops. In 1869 they joined other Utes at the Uintah Reservation. Kanosh and his people did not always remain there. They continued to return to Corn Creek, where they attempted to survive by growing crops, gathering plants, hunting, and begging. The Mormons eventually baptized many of this group.

The San Pitch had few horses and depended on gathering wild seeds and hunting small game. They were fewer in numbers and were often the victims of the slaving expeditions of Spaniards and Tumpanawach Utes. The San Pitch Utes may have been a branch of the Pahvant. As they were disrupted by white settlers, they allied themselves with the Pahvant people.

There were other Ute groups who were absorbed into the Uintah Band. One such group was the Elk Mountain Utes, or Sheberetch. Their homeland was south of the San Rafael River and east of the Wasatch

Tabiuna, or Tabby. According to historian
Dale Morgan, Tabiuna was a war chief of the
Uintah and White River Utes along the
Green and Price Rivers in eastern Utah. In
1892 he claimed to be 113 years old. He died
about 1896 in the Uinta Basin. (USHS)

Range. Black Hawk's raiding party was said to have included many Elk
Mountain Utes. They were always described as having many horses which
they knew how to ride well.

In May 1855 a group of Mormons had been sent as missionaries to
the Ute people living near Elk Mountain (Moab). Several Utes were baptized. However, trouble began in September when the Indians raided the
gardens planted by the missionaries and ended only after three Utes and
three Mormons were killed. The mission was abandoned and Mormon
settlement efforts there were delayed for some twenty years. Whoever
the Elk Mountain Utes were, they had completely lost their identity by
1880 and were never referred to again as a separate group.

Many Indians were not content to remain at the Uintah Reservation.
In the spring of 1872 Tabby and Kanosh led Utes off the reservation into
the San Pete Valley to hunt and hold a Ghost Dance. They were joined by
a group of White River Utes led by Douglas. The presence of this large

group caused alarm to the settlers in Utah and San Pete Valleys. David W. Jones, a Mormon trader who had had many dealings with Indians since the 1850s, and interpreter Dimick B. Huntington convinced the Ute leaders to meet in council at Springville. The Utes expressed dissatisfaction with conditions. They complained that supplies were not available at the reservation. Tabby explained that they would as soon die fighting as starve. The federal officials sent supplies to the Uintah Agency, and the Ute leaders peacefully returned to the reservation.

Several groups moved back to their old territories in Wyoming and Colorado and attempted to survive. Some requested annuities and supplies from agencies in those areas. Others tried to continue their hunting way of life. However, by 1879 the last Ute hunting areas in Utah and Colorado were being invaded and depleted of game. The non-Indian population in Utah had grown to 145,000. Only then did the Utah Ute people begin to remain year round near their agency at Uintah. By then their numbers had decreased to about 800 from 4,500 in 1859.

Developments in Other Areas

There were also intruders on Ute lands in northern New Mexico and Colorado. In 1858 gold was discovered near what became Denver. Hordes of treasure seekers invaded central Colorado. The white population increased so rapidly that by 1861 the Territory of Colorado was organized. Hundreds of prospectors and miners moved into the area. There were several skirmishes, and the intruders began to push for relocation of all Colorado Utes on a reservation to be located on lands occupied by the Weeminuche and Kapota, with headquarters in the San Juan Mountains.

In 1865 gold, silver, and coal were discovered in western Colorado. Miners again poured onto Ute lands, followed by ranchers and farmers. Conflicts continued. Starving Utes broke into homes begging and demanding food.

Another treaty was negotiated in 1868. Federal officials dealt with the leaders of seven Ute bands. They agreed to a reservation which included one-third of the territory of Colorado—about 15 million acres. However, as with previous treaties, that of 1868 was better kept by the Utes than by the settlers and miners who continued to trespass on Ute lands. By 1870, Colorado Utes, who had been relegated to the western third of the state since the 1868 treaty, moved deeper into the high mountains, clinging to their free-roving lifestyle. Soon, however, the flood of white immigrants, prospectors, and homesteaders crimped their way of life even in the most remote mountain valleys.

In 1873 the Brunot Agreement was negotiated to deal with the gold discoveries in the San Juan Mountains. It specified that the Utes would relinquish their rights to approximately 4 million acres of mineral-rich lands in the San Juan Mountains. But even this agreement did not signal the end of conflict.

Colorado gained statehood in 1876 and its first governor was elected on a "Utes Must Go!" platform. Politics and public sentiment was at an all-time high against the Utes. The final seeds of disaster were planted in 1878 when a self-righteous eccentric named Nathan Meeker was appointed agent at White River in northwestern Colorado. Without bothering to learn the ways of the people he was supposed to assist, Meeker set about trying to turn them into farmers. He threatened the Utes that the government would take away their reservation if they did not cultivate it. He banned a favorite pastime, horse racing, had his men plow under important winter horse pastures, and even suggested the Utes shoot their fine horses. In a very short time, strife grew into open hostility.

Fearing for his safety, Meeker called for troops. When the Indians heard of this they organized and prepared to fight. Chiefs Nicaaqat, Colorow, and Jack fought the soldiers, while chiefs Johnson and Douglas led a small group against the agency in the summer of 1879, killing Meeker and his employees and capturing the women and children.

The incident swept whites into an anti-Ute frenzy that resulted in the entire White River Band being removed to the barren lands of the Uintah Reservation in Utah. With the "Meeker Massacre" as ammunition, the anti-Indian movement grew in strength. By 1881 virtually all Utes had been forced onto reservations. Several bands went to reservations in southern Colorado and New Mexico. The powerful Uncompahgres followed the White River Utes to the Uintah Reservation. In 1882 the Uncompahgre Reservation was established in Utah for the Uncompahgres. Later the two reservations were combined.

The Uncompahgre (Ouray) Reservation

The Uncompahgre Utes are named after the agency established for them in 1875 in the Uncompahgre River Valley in Colorado. They called themselves the Taviwach or Tabeguache. Their traditional homeland was the area of the north fork of the Gunnison River. Ouray was one of their prominent leaders in the mid-nineteenth century. They were gradually pushed out of their Colorado homelands.

The intruders acquired all the Uncompahgre land after the 1879 Meeker incident, although the Uncompahgre did not rebel. Ouray even

sent a message "requesting and demanding" that the White River Utes cease fighting. Ouray also sent a message to the Southern Ute advising them to remain neutral. Thus the Meeker incident was not turned into a general Ute protest. Nevertheless, as a result of the uproar caused by the Meeker incident, the leaders of the Uncompahgre were forced to negotiate and sign the Agreement of 1880. They had to give up their lands in the Uncompahgre Valley and remove to lands in Utah Territory.

In June 1881 Ute Commission members were assigned to search for a site for a new reservation for the Uncompahgre. They felt that good areas in Colorado should be left for white settlement, and thus went north and west into Utah to a site in the valleys of the White, Green, and Duchesne Rivers. The commissioners also established the Ouray Agency.

As the summer of 1881 wore on, the Uncompahgre resisted efforts to move. They claimed that they had been deceived; however, the threat of army troops convinced the Utes to start to their new reservation. A horde of non-Ute settlers waited. In three days after the troops left, the rich lands of the Uncompahgre were occupied, towns were being laid out, and lots were being sold. Chief Ouray never made the trip to Utah. He died shortly after the removal order was issued, heartbroken and suffering from kidney disease.

The Uncompahgre Reservation in Utah was established by executive order in January 1882. The Uncompahgres were shocked and dismayed. The bleak land could not have been more different from the lush mountain home they were forced to give up. They had remained loyal and friendly to the United States but were dealt with as severely as if they had not. The situation on the Uncompahgre Reservation was particularly difficult. To control the Uncompahgre, a military post, Fort Thornburgh, was built in 1881. It was abandoned in 1884. The reservation was not only remote but also bleak and dry. Only the valleys of the White, Green, and Duchesne Rivers provided small relief in a huge wasteland. The turnover of agents was rapid and frequent. The problem of the boundary line strained relations between whites and Utes.

Fort Duchesne was established about midway between the Uintah and Ouray agencies to "discipline and control" the Utes. The Indian Office in 1886 consolidated the two Utah Ute agencies. Ouray was made a subagency, and the Uintah and Ouray Agency was established at Whiterocks.

From 1882 to 1933 the Uintah, White River, and Uncompahgre Utes were forced to cope with new rules, new systems of survival, and new relationships. Often the relationship between the Utes and the surround-

ing non-Ute communities was one of racism, jealousy, misunderstanding, and exploitation. And the relationship between them and their agency supervisors was usually one of resentment.

The relationships among the three Ute groups also were often strained. This was partly because of differences in their own tradition and history but also because of federal policies. For many years the federal government treated the groups differently in terms of land and money yet forced them to coexist on an ever-shrinking land base.

Life on the reservations was difficult for the Utes. They felt caged in and alienated. Many continued to hunt in Colorado as they had always done, and their travels off the reservations angered the surrounding settlers. There were several altercations between the People and the agency personnel who controlled their lives. Despite efforts by the personnel to turn the Utes into farmers, most were not interested. Efforts to turn them into cattle ranchers failed for the most part also. The three groups all owned large herds of horses. These were the animals they treasured.

Reservation Life

The United States government policy of Indian relations was based on treating the Indian tribes as separate nations. The Indians were dealt with by the federal government, rather than the states, through diplomatic agreements. Federal officials worked out treaties and agreements whereby the citizens of the United States could secure possession of Indian lands and natural resources.

The Indian tribes agreed to give up part of their land holdings and settle in Indian country or, after 1850, on reservations. The government was to provide them with materials and training to adapt to a new lifestyle, since they could no longer range over their lands gathering, fishing, hunting, and farming. Treaties were made to "insure civilization for the Indians and peace and safety for the whites." The government acted as trustee for the Indians and was responsible for certain obligations to them.

However, the history of Indian treaties is one of broken promises. The Indians were at a disadvantage. Treaties were written in English, and often the terms were not explained correctly to the Indians. Land ownership and government systems were concepts often foreign to Indians. And the government often negotiated with persons whom it had selected but who were not the accepted leaders of the entire tribe.

There was some outright fraud or theft by agency personnel as well as reluctance on the part of the federal government and its agents to fulfill the obligations of a treaty. Indian people were often not supplied

The Ute chief Atchee, date unknown. (USHS)

with food, clothing, and utensils to replace the game and plants which were being destroyed. Indian lands were often not protected from trespass. So it was with the Utes.

However, important rights were guaranteed to the Ute people by treaties, agreements, executive orders, and legislation. These federal statutes have been the basis of claims the Utes have made against the government. Congress does have the power to change or repeal treaties and statutes; however, many rights secured to the People by treaty, agreement, and other statutes continue to be enforceable today.

The government followed a policy of bringing Indians to Washington, D.C., to impress upon them the strength of the Euro-Americans and to convince the Indians of the futility of resistance. Ute leaders were among the hundreds of delegations. The government used these trips to overwhelm them. This, coupled with their trust in the president, encouraged the Indians to give up land and property which they might have fought to retain. The first Ute delegation to go to Washington, D.C., went in February 1863.

By 1870 the Utah Utes who had not been killed by disease, starvation, or bullets were being encouraged to move to the Uinta Basin and were being pushed into one group which would become known as the

Uintah Band. They did have an advantage that the Colorado Utes did not, however, from 1871 to 1883 the agent at Uintah was an unusually capable man, John J. Critchlow. Prior to Critchlow there had been the typical rapid turnover of agents.

In his first year at the Uintah Valley Agency, Critchlow observed that his predecessors had done little to aid the Indians. "There seems never to have been anything more done for them than to keep them quiet and peaceable by partially feeding and clothing them and amusing them with trinkets," he wrote. He noted that the people were hungry from lack of adequate food. They wanted to continue their traditional ways of life and were unhappy with the treatment given them by the government.

Critchlow immediately organized efforts to expand agricultural production on the reservation. However, efforts to get the Utes to remain throughout the year to plant and harvest a crop failed. In March 1872 the White River leader Douglas came from Colorado and persuaded the Indians at Uintah to let the white men farm for them. In May hundreds of Utes gathered in the Sanpete area. The gathering was probably to hunt but was also for a Ghost Dance. This new religion promised a supernatural solution to problems. It promised that the spirits of the dead Indians would again reside upon this earth and change it into it paradise.

The Ghost Dance did not have its intended effect. The People were not joined by their dead friends and relatives, and they did not become free of the white intruders. Utes stopped sponsoring the Ghost Dance after 1872.

Not until 1879 were most of the Utah Utes located permanently on the Uintah Reservation. Critchlow was gradually able to improve the relationship between the agency and the People. That relations were improving is demonstrated by the understanding the People showed for Critchlow's problems. In 1876 when appropriations for Utah were so meager that annuities could not be given, Critchlow explained the situation. The Utes accepted it.

A real test came in 1879 with the Meeker incident in Colorado. Critchlow reported that the reservation Indians, with few exceptions, after the first excitement, "remained in a state of almost perfect peace and quiet." They even suggested that Critchlow, his family, and employees leave the agency and join them in the mountains where they were going for safety.

However, despite Critchlow's efforts, major problems continued to plague the Ute people. They were increasingly threatened with trespass on the reservation. Cattlemen allowed their herds to graze on reserva-

tion land, thereby ruining the grazing and water for the People's stock. In 1878 Critchlow reported that the Utes were afraid that the reservation would be thrown open to white settlers and that they would be removed to some other place and thus lose all their labor. He argued about the injustice of such a plan. The fears proved to be valid. The reservation was eventually opened to non-Utes.

Within a span of twenty years, Ute life had been irreversibly changed. In 1882 the Uintah, White River, and Uncompaghre Utes found themselves in the vast semiarid country of the Uintah Reservation, far from their homelands in central Utah and Colorado. The distant mountains were a constant reminder to their minds and hearts of their ancestral homes—places now vanishing beneath the fence and plow; places that had been stripped from them by a conquering people.

Though unaware of what the future had in store for them, the Utes clearly understood what treaties meant to them: every treaty that had been made with them had been broken—the promises and reality never matched. Now three different bands were forced to live together on one reservation, each bringing their own leaders, traditions, and history. This meant that in the decades to come, the bands would face the challenge of merging into one group plus adjusting to living with new nearby communities of non-Utes. Here they would have to contend with racism, jealousy, exploitation, different rules and systems, and ever-changing federal policies.

The White River Utes received a small per-capita payment from the federal government as part of a 1880 agreement for portions of land that were taken from the band. Against White River opposition, the government withheld some of the payment to cover pensions for the families of all agency and military personnel killed in the Meeker incident. The Uncompahgres also received payment for some lands taken from them. Ironically, the Uintah, who had given up part of their land to the White Rivers, received nothing.

There were other problems for the Utes. Non-Utes continued their relentless invasion onto the Ute lands. The ranchers of Heber Valley, for example, illegally used the western area of the Uintah Reservation for grazing their stock. They finally agreed to pay a fee for pasturage; however, they worked to take the Strawberry drainage area away from the Utes.

Very little land on the reservations was arable. The lands had been left the Indians because they had been rejected by settlers. However, farmers began illegally diverting water from streams of the upper Strawberry

Two Ute Indians photographed by George Edward Anderson, date unknown. (USHS)

River on the Uintah Reservation. The farmers built canals which carried water off the reservation and diverted it into Daniels Creek and thence into irrigation systems in Wasatch County. These farmers supported efforts to allot and open the reservation. Such efforts were also supported by farmers in Ashley Valley (settled by Mormons in 1878) to the east of the Uintah Reservation. By 1890 most of the good agricultural land in that area had been taken up in homesteads. Settlers began to eye the farmland controlled by the Utes.

In 1885 gilsonite and gypsum asphalt deposits were discovered on the Uintah Reservation. The miners built a road across the reservation to

the Denver & Rio Grande railroad line in order to get the minerals to market. In 1888 Congress removed a triangular "Strip" of about 7,000 acres from the eastern end of the reservation in which were located several gilsonite claims. The People received about twenty dollars per acre for the land. The "Strip" became a lawless area of saloons, bordellos, and gambling houses. In 1888 gilsonite was also discovered on the Uncompahgre Reservation.

In August 1886 Major F.W. Benteen arrived on the reservation with black soldiers from the Ninth Calvary, who were called buffalo soldiers by the Indians on account of their curly black hair. A post was built named Fort Duchense, and the soldiers stayed for nearly twelve years. The Ute people were under constant military supervision.

When the tribes were relocated to the reservation, the law provided that they would be able to return to their former homelands to hunt during certain times of the year. However, the hunting trips to Colorado created problems with white settlers that sometimes resulted in skirmishes between the Utes and non-Indians. In the summer of 1887 a large group of Uncompahgre and White River people left the reservations for their annual hunt in their old domain in western Colorado. Colorow led this group in their effort to continue a tradition. The Agreement of 1873 had stated: "The United States shall permit the Ute Indians to hunt upon [ceded Colorado] lands so long as game lasts, and the Indians are at peace with the white people." Much of this land remained as public domain. Whites used it for grazing their livestock. They opposed the Utes using it for hunting.

Incidents were fanned by the press and local hysteria into the "Colorow War." The national guard was called in. The Colorado militia attacked and killed some of the Utes as they attempted to return to Utah. They also took 600 horses, 2,500 sheep and other goods belonging to the Indians. Most of this property was never returned.

At the same time, non-Indians were intruding onto the Uintah and Ouray Reservation, taking the best bottomlands for farming, diverting water, and illegally grazing their livestock. On the east side, in the Vernal area, non-Indians moved onto the agricultural land along the Green River. White farmers petitioned Congress to enact legislation in their favor that would further shrink Ute lands.

The system by which the land was taken from the Indians was allotment. One of the mechanisms used was the General Allotment (Dawes) Act of 1887. It had been written as part of the Agreement of 1880. It provided for the allotment of tribal lands to individual tribe members.

Sowsonicut, photographed in 1898. (U of U)

The reservation land that was left over was to be declared public domain and opened to ranchers, homesteaders, and mineral speculators.

The General Allotment Act of 1887 gave each tribal member a parcel of land, then opened the reservation to non-Indians for homesteading on unallotted land. This scattered the Utes' land base, giving the reservation the checkerboard look it has today. By dispersing Ute people onto arbitrary tracts of land, it also fractured families and tribes, causing further destruction to the culture and traditions.

The theory behind the allotment policy was to "civilize" the Indians by forcing them to become independent ranchers and farmers on separate parcels of land. The fact that various Indian groups might not be oriented towards farming and ranching was ignored. The isolation of the Indian lands and the inexperience of the Indian people made intimidation by white farmers possible.

The leaders of the Uncompahgre, White River, and Uintah Utes opposed allotment. In 1895 a commission was appointed to survey and allot the Uncompahgre lands. There was not enough arable land to provide suitable allotments to all Uncompahgre, so it was decided to take the needed additional lands from the Uintah and White River Utes. This decision caused a great furor from all the groups. However, despite continued Ute protest, in June 1897 Congress passed an act requiring allotments be made on the Uncompahgre Reservation.

Appah, photographed in 1905 at the age of
fifty. (U of U)

The Uncompahgre Reservation was to be opened to settlement in
April 1898. Federal troops were called in keep order. The protests of the
People had gone unheeded. The allotments had been issued hastily, and
little consideration was made of the wishes of the Indians. Most of the
Uncompahgre continued to live on the reservation. They refused to believe the land did not still belong to them. Congress acted without the
consent of the Uncompahgre, which resulted in their protest. When they
were informed that the 1880 Agreement provided for allotments, the
Indians agreed to accept them.

In 1898 an act was passed in Congress which authorized a commission to allot lands on the Uintah Reservation "by the consent of a majority of the adult male Indians." But the Utes were strongly opposed to
making cession to the government of any of their lands. Congress then
proceeded without their consent.

In 1902–03 Congress enacted a series of laws to break up the Uintah
Reservation and allot lands to the Utes. The Ute people continued ada-
mantly opposed to allotment and the loss of land. The congressional
delegation from Utah worked hard to have the reservation opened, as
did other whites, including leaders of the LDS church. The Ute people
were not represented. Acts were passed, including one in 1905 opening
the reservation to white homesteading.

Ungacochoop, photographed in 1905 at the age of forty-three. (U of U)

The announcement of the opening started a land rush. But the land bubble soon burst. There was not sufficient water for much farming, and the terrain was difficult to farm. By 1912 many of the newcomers were destitute. Very little of the land was eventually claimed or entered by non-Utes. Also, the gilsonite and other mineral lands had been reserved to the United States.

After the opening to whites of the Uncompahgre and the Uintah Reservations, the Ute land came to be called the Uintah and Ouray Reservation. The people who lived there were then called the Uintah-Ouray Ute Tribe. The agency was moved to Fort Duchesne in 1912 when the military left the post.

Though the Utes protested the allotments and the opening of the reservation to non-Indians, their opposition fell on deaf ears. Utah Representative George Sutherland said, "Since the Uintah Reservation was created by the President and Congress, there is no need of approval from the Utes." This position was later supported by a 1903 Supreme Court decision in *Lone Wolf vs. Hitchcock.*

In protest against the allotments and land losses the Utes engaged in a final act of defiance. In the spring of 1906 an Indian by the name of Red Cap spoke to dissatisfied Ute people during a Bear Dance, saying, "The white people have robbed us of our cattle, our pony grass, and our hunt-

This photograph includes a few of the White River Utes who left Utah for South Dakota in 1906. From left to right: Willie Willie, Arapo, Dewey (Arapo's son), Duchesne George (rear), Slim Jim, and Red Cap. (USHS)

ing grounds ..." He rallied many to journey north and join up with the Sioux. Some 300–600 Utes gathered with their wagons, supplies, and horses in the area of present Bridgeland, Utah. They left the reservation and trekked northward. Some eventually spent over two years on the Cheyenne River Sioux Reservation after they learned to their dismay that the Sioux did not want to join them in their defiance. The Utes were shocked to see the powerful Sioux defeated and relegated to reservations. Some Utes worked on the railroads and found jobs in Rapid City, South Dakota. The federal government withheld rations and payments from them to induce them to return to their reservation. In 1908 the Utes were escorted back to Utah.

This "anguished odyssey" reinforced the breakdown of traditional political organizations. The leaders were defeated and discouraged. Their inability to control their destiny, to make decisions for their people in the face of white power and control, was sorrowfully demonstrated. Through the 1920s the Utes maintained hostility toward agency and government personnel. During those years they were subjected to unfair laws, acts, and policies that stripped them of land, water, and resources.

A group of Utes taken prisoner at Fort Meade, South Dakota, about 1906. From left to right: Ben Tabbysheetz, unidentified, Ta-taw-wee Chegup, Mocha, Quien, J. Scott Apputnora, Quip, Tse-uts (brother of Red Cap). (USHS)

In 1905 President Theodore Roosevelt withdrew 1.1 million acres from the original Uintah Reservation to create the Uintah National Forest Reserve. In 1906 the federal government passed an act authorizing construction of the Uintah Indian Irrigation Project. Most Indians opposed the project, while local non-Indians supported it, especially those who had established themselves within the reservation borders. The development of the irrigation system was a huge disappointment to the Utes, because, while Ute money was spent to built it, the larger portion of the benefits went directly to the non-Indians living inside the reservation. In 1910 the Utes lost a large expanse of prime grazing land in the verdant Strawberry drainage through the "eminent domain" process. Later a very low compensation was paid for the land.

The effect of the allotment policy on the Utes was disastrous. Within fifteen years the Ute people had sold or leased 30,000 acres of the best Ute agricultural land. Much of this land was then irrigated until it became alkaline. Other land was used for stock and was overgrazed.

The Strawberry Valley Reclamation Project was authorized in 1905. A reservoir site had already been surveyed in the Strawberry Valley, and the Reclamation Service requested that the Utes sell the 56,000 acres at $1.25 an acre. The People refused. Congress then passed a law in 1910

Red Cap is seated in this group of five White River Band Utes photographed in 1907. Red Cap was one of the leaders of the Utes who traveled to South Dakota in 1906. (USHS)

extinguishing Indian title to that land. The land was taken and $71,000 was paid for it into the tribal fund.[8]

The whites became partners in the use of the Uintah Irrigation System without Ute consent. There were many problems. Water was drawn off at the heads of rivers, and dams were built. As a result, the water table dropped on lands south of the Uinta Mountains where Utes pastured their cattle. Private irrigation companies drew off water higher up along the rivers, leaving Indian lands short of water. Strict rationing had to be practiced, which caused ill feelings.

The early years of the new century were grim for the Utes. Disease and hunger were prevalent. The traditional lifestyle was deteriorating and the spirit of the people was dying. Discouraged and with little interest in farming, Utes generally gave little attention to their lands given out as allotments. Some actually sold their allotment. The population had declined from 2,825 in 1882 to 1,150 full-blooded Ute Indians by 1910.

Indian Reorganization Act of 1934

That the Indians were neglected and suffered is evident in the declining population on the Uintah-Ouray Reservation. In 1890 there were

1,854 full bloods; in 1900, 1,660; in 1920, 1,005; and, in 1930, only 917. The land base also continued to shrink. Leasing and purchasing of Indian lands continued, particularly during an alfalfa seed boom which occurred in the 1920s. By 1933, 91 percent of the reservation lands of the Uintah, White River, and Uncompahgre People had been lost from their ownership. From nearly 4 million acres in 1882, the Ute people now owned only 360,000 acres.

In the 1930s the federal government made a major shift in its Indian policy, which had proven to be catastrophic to the native peoples. A Senate committee investigation into federal Indian policy resulted in the Merriam Report of 1928, which described the appalling conditions on Indian reservations, attacking the Bureau of Indian Affairs and calling for many reforms.

The Indian Reorganization Act of 1934 was intended to undo past wrongs of the federal government. It returned to the Indians control over taxation, tribal membership, and law and order on the reservation, and assured their right to self-government. It also ended further allotment of tribal land. The act, however, stopped short of abolishing the Bureau of Indian Affairs, which maintained its role as facilitator between the Indian tribes and the federal government. This severely watered down the status of Indian tribes as sovereign nations, ostensibly one of the main goals of the act.

In 1937 the Northern Ute Tribe voted in a referendum to accept the new Indian Reorganization Act and a new government structure for the tribe. It was hoped that this would finally give the Utes the opportunity to determine their own destiny. With the acceptance of the act, all bands acquired equal rights as enrolled members of the Ute Tribe of the Uintah and Ouray Reservation. The tribe drew up a constitution and by-laws that continue to be the instruments used in governing the tribe today.

The Indian Reorganization Act provided for a tribal council system of government and for the organization of business corporations to manage the development of tribal resources. However, the federal government maintained ultimate control. A Uintah and Ouray Ute Tribal Business Committee was formed under the Indian Reorganization Act. Too often, however, the committee merely did what the BIA wanted.

Reorganization did not bring about as many changes as were hoped. The People still did not control their own destinies. The Indian Reorganization Act was passed during the depths of the Great Depression. The reservation was economically depressed along with the rest of the state and nation. Much of the land which was purchased by the Business Com-

A Ute couple with their daughter, date unknown. (U of U)

mittee under the law was bought from bankrupted white farmers. Increasingly, the Utes were split into factions. Most importantly, the reorganization failed to establish a self-sufficient tribal economy.

During these years, there were problems over grazing rights. Utes grazed some of their livestock on public domain land. Not having title to the grazing lands was not a problem until the 1920s when non-Ute ranch-

ers from Colorado and western Utah brought their livestock in increasing numbers to the Uncompahgre range, especially in winter.

In 1934 the Taylor Grazing Act was passed which ended unrestricted grazing on public domain lands. Thereafter, grazing districts were established and grazing permits issued. Efforts were made to establish part of the Uncompahgre Reservation as a permanent grazing reserve for the use and benefit of the Indians. Some white stockmen supported these efforts. This way the rest of the Uncompahgre land could be declared public domain and be organized as a grazing area for white use.

By this time the Uncompahgre had about 2,800 cattle and 7,000 sheep. Federal officials supported a proposal to establish part of the Uncompahgre Reservation as an addition to the Uintah and Ouray Reservation. The rest of the land would then be available to non-Utes. The People were led to believe that the entire 1,800,000 acres were to be restored to the reservation. It came as a shock to many Utes that the area to be restored was one-third of that acreage.

In 1938 the BIA began administering the withdrawn Uncompahgre land. Use of the land was by permit only, with the fees going to the Indians. White ranchers deliberately grazed stock on the lands without permit. This brought lawsuits that were eventually decided in favor of the Utes. In the meantime, the Uintah and Ouray Business Committee, with BIA encouragement, purchased land from the Uncompahgre Grazing Reserve. In September 1941 the Interior Secretary restored to the tribe 217,000 acres of unsold lands. Another order gave jurisdiction to the Utes of acreage withdrawn in 1933 to the United States Grazing Service.

World War II caused additional hardships for Utes. There was some resistance to the forced registration for the draft. The Utes also were victims of a shrinking rural economy. Small farms became unprofitable. Many were abandoned or taken over by large agribusiness corporations.

In 1948 legislation was finally passed to extend the boundaries of the Uintah and Ouray Reservation. The Hill Creek Extension was those lands in the Uncompahgre Grazing Reserve, about one-third of the old Uncompahgre Reservation (726,000 acres).

The Indian Claims Commission was established in 1946 as part of the termination effort. Congress saw settlement of tribal claims against the United States as a necessary step to rid the government of its responsibilities for the tribes. The commission was set up to consider claims by any "tribe, band, or group of identifiable American Indians" with whom the government had not dealt fairly. Claims were filed by Ute people, among many others. In 1958 claims for land taken for the Uintah Forest

Reserve, the Strawberry Valley Reclamation Project, and mineral claims were settled. Other awards were made in 1961 and 1981. Settlements have been for more than $33 million.

Termination

In the twentieth century the Ute people have gained some money in claims and other payments, as the government finally agreed to fulfill promises it had made in treaties and agreements. Yet there were also periods of poverty. Unemployment was usually high; many remained in debt. The awards, the use of the money, and the efforts to become economically self-sufficient created problems. Factions among Utes strengthened. Traditional culture declined, and the surrounding non-Ute community often took advantage of Ute consumers.

In the 1950s the Utes were awarded $19 million by Congress in federal claims cases. The money was to be given in several payments, the initial payment being $1,000 per person. Tied to this victory for the Utes was a new federal plan that called for terminating the relationship between the federal government and Indian nations. This "termination" policy was intended to pay off Indian claims for lands lost in the treaties of the 1800s and then end all future obligation to Indian people by the government.

To prepare the Ute Tribe for termination, the government initiated a "Thirteen Year Program" designed to educate and offer plans for economic and social development. Over the next several years, 494 Northern Utes, 27 percent of the tribe, were terminated. According to one account, these were largely descendants of four non-Ute Indian women who were married to white men. These women had been adopted into the Ute tribe many years before but had adopted more of the non-Indian lifestyle than traditional Ute ways. Their children had eventually married whites as well. Others say that the termination originally resulted from a few mixed-blood family heads who wanted money in exchange for their tribal membership.

The next seven years were spent separating tribal assets between the terminated and non-terminated Utes. The terminated group formed its own corporation to manage its property, which was to remain in trust until 1964. In 1961, out of desperation for money but without an understanding of corporate finances, some of the terminated Utes began selling their stock to non-Indians. Shares which had a $1,500 value sold for as low as $30.93. (Later the federal court ruled that since the trust period had not yet expired, the stock sold still retained its full face value.) Ter-

A Ute known as Unca Sam in a wheat field. (USHS)

minated Indians throughout the United States faced similar situations and many lost valuable land and resources. By 1961 the federal government realized that the termination policy was very culturally, economically, and socially destructive for the Indians and ended the devastating policy.

Termination of the mixed bloods within the tribe did not end controversy. After the 1960s, a group of Ute people known as the "True Utes" urged that the business committee and tribal government be disbanded. They felt that it was not enough to remove the mixed Utes, government interference also must end and tribal funds not be spent on BIA-sponsored projects. The True Utes were not successful in dismantling the tribal government, but they continued to agitate for change.

The aims of the True Utes were shared by many other Utes who hoped to regain land and resources, to become economically and politically independent, and to hold on to traditional Ute values. Many have used education, technology, and government systems to rebuild their culture and society. Since the termination era, many Utes have managed to hold onto their traditional lifestyle; however, most of the economic development programs conceived during the era have failed. Further, according to many, the tribal government structure set up by the Indian Reorgani-

zation Act of 1934 is no longer adequate or effective in dealing with the complicated issues facing the tribe today. Many Utes feel that the tribal governmental system is in dire need of major revision in order to keep pace with the changing world.

Education

The Northern Ute Tribe presently has a large number of younger members, one of the tribe's greatest resources. From this group will emerge future leaders, planners, and professional people. Therefore, education will play a major role in the development process for these young people, as it has in the past. The difference is that today they must be prepared for a fiercely competitive, industrialized world, whereas in centuries past they needed to learn the skills of basic survival.

In the old Indian way of life, a child had to be properly taught survival skills. It was important to know the natural world extremely well. From an early age, children were taught the uses of many plants and what type of wood was best for wickiups, tipi poles, cooking fires, or weapons. Elders taught the young the positions of the stars in the ever-changing seasons and the myths that were the basis for their beliefs. They talked of seasonal weather patterns, lightning, thunder, and their meanings. They taught children in detail about the habits of animals, when was the right time to hunt various animals, and how to utilize every part of the kill. Youngsters learned how to harvest plants for their edible, medicinal, and spiritual properties.

Children also learned daily rituals and practices, such as how to ready oneself for each new day, rising before the sun and praying. They learned that all elements have spirit and must be treated with respect, as one would treat a person. Everything around them—the earth and the natural world—was considered related to the Utes, and children learned to revere the world.

Before the coming of the whites, the Utes were an outdoor people, and though the lessons were different, there was an immense amount of knowledge to be passed down to children. None of it was written down, of course, which made the method of learning strictly experiential.

Through the years, the Utes have been forced to adapt a lifestyle unlike the outdoor life they once led. With it, they also have had to adapt to the white man's educational process, a process which still determines eventual survival, yet in a different context and setting. While many Utes accept these changes to their historic lifestyle, many choose to maintain their traditions. For them, the difficulty lies in preserving the old and

not becoming totally assimilated by the new. This requires both having an understanding of and maintaining a delicate balance between two distinct cultures and worlds. It is understandable that many Utes would want to hold on to their old ways, as the white man's education promised to them has only recently shown any benefit.

A few off-reservation industrial schools had been successfully established and attended by Utes, such as the famous Carlisle Indian Industrial School begun in 1879 in Carlisle, Pennsylvania. The success of such schools was measured in how much Indian culture was erased from the minds and hearts of the young students. Carlisle School founder Richard Henry Pratt proclaimed in a letter to Senator Henry L. Dawes, "The end to be gained is complete civilization of the Indian ... (and) the sooner all tribal relations are broken up, the sooner the Indian loses all his Indian ways, even his language, the better it will be." The Carlisle educator set the standard for attempting to transform not only material culture—hairstyle, dress, ornamentation—but also cultural attitudes and values.

On the Uintah Reservation, the first school was opened in October 1874 by dedicated agent John J. Critchlow. His wife taught the twenty-five or so Ute children who attended. The school closed down in April 1876 because the government did not send promised funds for room and board for the students, forcing the children to travel great distances even in severe winter weather.

The school opened again in 1877 with a new teacher but closed just eight months later when the teacher resigned. It opened briefly again in 1881 with a new building, a contract with the Presbyterian church, and just twelve students.

On the Ouray Reservation, the agent built a frame schoolhouse and hired a teacher in 1883. However, that attempt also failed miserably. The fault could be found on both sides: with whites not understanding the people they were trying to teach, and with Utes not interested in taking on the ways of a people they didn't trust or respect. Adding to the problem, in 1885 Uintah and White River women joined together to openly oppose the education of their children in white boarding schools because of health concerns for the children.

Nevertheless, whites built a new boarding school in Leland (later Randlett) in 1892. That same year, they added a new building to the school at the Uintah Agency in White Rocks. Attendance remained sporadic and sparse at both schools. With the opening of the Uncompahgre Reservation in 1898 Ouray students transferred to the Uintah school. Tragically, in 1901, a measles epidemic killed seventeen of the sixty-five students.

Richard Komas, the first Ute Indian educated in white schools. Photo taken by Alexander Gardner in Washington, D.C., in 1872. (USHS)

After 1910, conditions at the school improved, the student body grew, and attendance became more consistent.

Will Carson Ryan was among those responsible for the legislation that simplified the process by which schools were paid by the federal government for their Indian students. The Johnson O'Malley Act of 1934 enabled the state, rather than the individual school districts, to sign contracts with the Education Division of the Bureau of Indian Affairs. Although this improved the funding procedure, the state school systems often used the money for general programs. As a result, from 1940 through the early 1970s, public schools failed to develop special programs for Indian students. With the closing of the Uintah Boarding School on June 30, 1952, all schools on the reservation were administered by the public school system.

Today there are public elementary, junior high, and high schools located within Uintah and Duchesne Counties that serve both Utes and non-Indians. In addition, there are university and college extension centers located within traveling distances. While most Indian children attend the local public schools, some go to boarding school off the reserva-

tion. Young Indian adults attend the local extension centers or study off the reservation.

Cultural differences and an inflexible school system continue to hamper the education of Ute children. Curriculum is insensitive of Ute culture, and inaccurate reporting of Indian history is too common. Indian students attending local public schools often find themselves facing harassment and racial discord. Communication between teachers and Indian students also can be a major problem. Indian children attending boarding schools usually fare better; unfortunately, however, the high school drop-out rate is very high among Indian students despite a concentrated effort on the part of the tribe to combat it.

Tribal members are keenly aware of their children's educational needs, and there is growing support for various educational programs through the Northern Ute Tribal Education Department. This department offers adult education classes, works with the local school district to identify problems with individual students, and supplies counselors and tutors when necessary. It also helps Ute families research, apply to, enroll, and transport students to boarding schools off the reservation. The Education Department also encourages parental involvement in the educational process, from attending Parent Teacher Association meetings to calling for conferences with school officials to attain better understanding and harmony within the school setting.

The public school system provides a basic program to help Indian children, and social assimilation through the education process is almost complete. Still, with the heightened Indian awareness of their heritage and renewal of tribal cultures over the past two decades, many children are finding that their most effective education comes from the teachings of their elders as well as from books at school.

Religion

At the turn of the century the federal government suppressed the practice of Indian religions. Christianity was to be used to assimilate Indian people and to replace the "heathen" practices of the natives. Many tribes accepted Christianity, but many Indians eventually realized that there were negative and positive aspects to this. Often the Christian religion was used by unscrupulous people to manipulate Indians for personal gain. Religious groups such as the Episcopal, Baptist, and Catholic churches that were more receptive to the Indian way of life and religion were generally received more favorably. Today, many Utes combine Christianity and traditional beliefs, practicing both to varying degrees.

The Ute Bear Dance being performed on the Uintah-Ouray Reservation, date unknown. (USHS)

Traditionally, the Utes believe that each person is connected to the spirit of all living things. This connection makes humans responsible to the earth and all of its creations. Hundreds of years ago, tribes were basically separated not by tribal names but by the language they spoke. At times, neighboring tribes exchanged rituals and ceremonies. Thus tribal traditions and cultures were products to some extent of local geography. Historically, there is no one religion or ritual belonging to the Ute Tribe. The rituals practiced by elders in centuries past varied in many ways.

One common ingredient in many ceremonies was stones laid upon the ground in a circle. Past ritual sites with stone circles can be found throughout original Ute homelands. These stone circles are individual ritual sites and are still considered sacred today. They were not used in a uniform, structured manner. Each medicine man or spiritual person who practiced shamanism had his own ritual. Generally, the circles were used for rituals benefiting the immediate family or band.

Rituals were conducted in relationship with nature and the universe—connecting all with the supreme intelligence or creator. The stones may have been used by the shaman for contacting the spirit within, to draw a particular animal spirit to the ritual, as a boundary to keep out evil spirits, or perhaps as a marker of the site.

Animals and birds have always played a large part in ceremonies of Ute medicine people. Shamans used various animal or bird powers in the form of skins and feathers for their healing rituals. Eagle feathers were and remain very sacred. Other animals and birds had their own gifts for humans, and some ceremonies were dedicated to these animals.

Bear Dance. One of the oldest traditional ceremonies belonging to Utes is the Bear Dance. Though its origin is unknown, it was probably a ritual shared by other tribes. The Bear Dance involved the entire community. It celebrated the coming of spring, with the bear coming out of hibernation; the awakening of spirits; winter returning to its home in the north; and the return of summer from the south, both summer and winter being guardians of the world.

Today, the Utes celebrate the Bear Dance in a simple form, using it as a social gathering for families, bands, and tribes. It is a good opportunity for the bands to mix and tribe members to renew bonds. Each major community of the Uintah and Ouray Reservation sponsors Bear Dances at various times during the spring.

Sun Dance. Another ceremony that has survived over the years is the mid-summer fasting ceremony—*Tah-gu-wau-ne,* meaning "standing in thirst"—also known as the Sun Dance. Though the ceremony is for men only (considered the head of the family in Ute tradition), the entire family participates. The Sun Dance today brings together those with varying degrees of traditional beliefs, and it remains a test of a man's spiritual and physical endurance. For three or four days and nights, participants fast and take no water. They dance all day long under the scorching summer sun and sleep on the dance ground. Drummers beat the drums and family and friends stay near to offer emotional support. The dance is used to make an adjustment in spiritual balance, to renew or replenish spiritual powers. Men may dance for spiritual cleansing or health purposes or for someone else who is in bad health, for spirits, or for relatives who have moved to the spirit world. Through their dreams, participants know when they can enter the Sun Dance lodge.

The original Sun Dance of the Utes was obtained from the Eastern Shoshones of the Wind River Reservation in 1890 by a Ute medicine man named Grant Bullethead. Decades before that, the Shoshone had acquired their style of Sun Dance from the Comanche, who in turn received it from the Kiowas. (Another version is that it was acquired from the Lakota, formerly known as the Sioux.) Thus, the Northern Ute Sun Dance is an example of how rituals and ceremonies were regularly exchanged between tribes in the days before European conquest.

Ghost Dance. Another important ceremony passed between tribes was the Ghost Dance, a movement that swept up many western tribes for a short time in the 1890s. It was the Indians' last desperate attempt to save their culture. The Ghost Dance was a highly sacred ceremony performed to prepare the people for the return of the buffalo and the old ways of Indian life, and the return of whites to their former countries.

On the Uintah and Ouray Reservation, Ghost Dances were most often held near White Rocks. Participants wore Ghost Shirts thought to be able to protect them from harm, even from bullets. As the Ghost Dance movement swelled among the tribes, whites grew afraid that Ghost Dancing would lead to insurrection by the Indians. Troops were called to the Sioux reservation in December 1890. There, at Wounded Knee, 300 unarmed men, women, and children of the Lakota Tribe were massacred by the U.S. Army. Shortly thereafter belief in the Ghost Dance understandably diminished.

Sweat Ceremonies. Throughout their history, Utes have used sweat ceremonies for various purposes: for healing, cleansing of the spirit, and guidance of the spirit. The sweat house is a small dome-shaped structure measuring about twelve feet in diameter and four feet high at the center. Its door always faces east. Like all Ute ceremonies, it varies according to the belief and teachings of the person who conducts it. It may be simple or very elaborate.

In virtually all sweat ceremonies, the dark, steamy-hot dome represents the womb of Mother Earth. The ritual involves bringing red-hot rocks into the sweat house, pouring water over them, praying, and singing. Once cleansed through the ceremony, participants emerge reborn into the world.

Native American Church. The Native American Church (NAC) conducts another ceremony practiced by many tribal members. The Native American Church is organized with a charter, by-laws, and officers. It is structured to meet certain standards and requirements of federal, state, and tribal laws because of its ritual use of peyote. The NAC ritual has the same basis as other ceremonies—that is, tribal traditions, culture, ceremonial ethics, and values. The ceremony takes place in a tipi, lasts all night, and includes prayer and song. The rituals provide spiritual and healing relationships with the supreme intelligence (Great Spirit). Like other ceremonies among the Utes, the entire universe becomes a living altar.

Different tribes and reservations throughout the United States, Canada, and Mexico have NAC organizations, all of which are structured

in a similar manner. The Native American Church of North America is the largest NAC organization, however, it is not recognized on the Uintah-Ouray Reservation. Instead, there is a tribal NAC organization on the reservation.

Today, ceremonies and rituals continue to play an important role in the Utes' daily lives. Certain Utes still practice individual blessings in their home. Others collect herbs and edible plants from the mountains and river banks. Collecting herbs is done with prayers, and ritual offerings are left where the herb is collected. All is done in reverence because the mountains and rivers are considered sacred.

Ceremonies practiced today help maintain the Ute culture and the people's connection to the natural and spirit world, a connection essential to their well-being.

Utes Today

From the establishment of the Uintah Reservation almost 140 years ago, the Northern Ute Tribe has made tremendous advancements into a lifestyle and culture completely different from that of their forefathers. Presently, the Uintah and Ouray Reservation covers more than one million acres in northern Utah. Enrolled member population is approximately 3,500. Three recognized bands reside on the reservation—the Uintah, Uncompahgre, and White River. Today, tribe members are centered in three major communities—White Rocks, Fort Duchesne, and Randlett—with a few scattered families in Ouray, Myton, Neola, Indian Bench, and the towns of Roosevelt and Vernal.

The daily routine of a Ute family may closely parallel that of any non-Indian household. Generally, English is spoken; homes are furnished with modern conveniences. Gone is the intimate language spoken just between women of the tribe; instead, mothers push their babies in strollers and send their children off to public schools. Families eat out at their favorite fast-food restaurant and enjoy movies on their VCRs. But for all the appearances and trappings of average American life, many Utes are still experiencing the culture shock of a conquered people.

Even though the Ute Tribe is one of the major economic contributors to the Uinta Basin and the state, the tribe experiences the lingering problems associated with having been proclaimed sovereign yet not being treated as such by county, state, and federal entities. This creates disputes between the tribe and these bodies of government over issues such as jurisdiction, double taxation, rights-of-way, and water rights. Such conflicts often wind up in lengthy and costly court entanglements.

A group of Ute Indians in traditional dress in mid-twentieth century, exact place and date unknown. (USHS)

In the past, federal treaties and policies determined the major decisions for the tribe, even though the results did not necessarily benefit the Ute people. In the 1930s, the Indian Reorganization Act (IRA), through its by-laws, created a governing body comprised of Utes and was a first step toward self-rule. But it gave the Utes a new structure of government that did not exactly fit with the history or temperament of the people. The IRA was designed to give back to the tribe its traditional beliefs and culture; however, it was, and still is, up to the Utes to refine the governmental structure and create a place for those traditions so that they may again serve as a spiritual common ground and be incorporated into the daily decisions and affairs of the tribe.

The other goal of the IRA was to give tribes complete economic independence; and that too has had its limitations. Even though the tribe functions as a sovereign entity according to the governing by-laws, the U.S. Secretary of Interior has final approval over many tribal actions. This often hinders the tribe's efforts to create economic programs. Thus, there remains a high unemployment rate among tribal members.

Still, many Indians believe that the tribe has full capability for complete economic independence if it were recognized in the true sense as

Four Ute Indians in more contemporary times showing some traditional costume elements, place and date unknown . (USHS)

being sovereign—that is, if the state and federal government viewed and interacted with the tribe in the same manner in which they treat other sovereign nations.

Presently each band has two representatives in the six-member governing body (tribal council). Council members are elected by the voting members of the tribe and serve a four-year term. Alternating elections take place every two years for one council member of each band.

By 1953, female members of the tribe began taking a more active role in politics. Today women serve on the council and also serve as committee chairpersons. In addition to being positive role models for youth, they are important contributors toward the betterment of the Ute Tribe.

The council oversees the administration of the tribe, the court system, and tribal enterprises such as the tribal cattle herd and domestic water system. An executive director oversees the administration of the accounting department, social services, resources, maintenance, education, drug and alcohol programs, and a special department devoted to the care of senior citizens.

The tribe operates on a yearly budget of some $8 to $10 million. There are also available other national programs such as Head Start which

are subsidized by government funds. Every year the general membership has the opportunity to review the proposed budget for the coming year, as well as past and present activities of the administration.

In the past, national politics and economic trends have determined what is good for the Utes. Now, a different approach is needed, based upon the needs and desires of the Ute people, as determined by the Utes themselves. With recognition and treatment from the outside world as a sovereign nation, with a strong tribal government structure founded in traditional culture, the Ute Tribe can move forward, united and free to determine its own destiny.

The White Mesa Utes

Robert S. McPherson and Mary Jane Yazzie

Billy Mike, the oldest living resident of the White Mesa Ute community, sat comfortably and slowly ran his fingers through his silver hair. The thick glasses perched upon his nose served more as a token of past vision than as an aid to see today's world. Blind in one eye, and with failing sight in the other, he moved about slowly with the assistance of a cane. His life of ninety-some-odd years had spanned a period of transition for the Ute people. At times, his mind wandered clearly over events from the past, while at other times his memory became clouded. But there was no doubt as he remembered his people's association with the land before it had been divided and controlled by the white man. He recalled, "No one really owned the land. It was like it owned us—the Ute (Nuche) people."[1] This relationship of which he spoke—of land and people—went back, according to tribal accounts, to the beginning of time, when the gods played a part in establishing the Ute's domain.

Following the creation of the world, the gods contained the people of the earth in a large sack. The Shin-au-av brothers, Pavits and Skaits, received the bag with the instructions to carry it unopened to the center of the world. However, curiosity overwhelmed Shin-au-av Skaits, who opened the bag and then watched many humans flee from its confines. Tav-woats, another god, saw what was happening, angrily resealed the bag, and took the remaining people to the only place left: the desert and mountains of the Four Corners region.[2] There he released them to settle in the area to become the Paiutes and Southern Utes—known as Nuche, Nutc, or Nunts, and translated as "The People." Various versions of this story exist; each band of Utes and Paiutes tells of how the sack was opened in their particular territory, thus creating the "homeland" of all the groups.[3]

Historic and anthropological sources paint a different picture. Based upon their studies, the Numic-speaking peoples entered the Four Cor-

ners area close to the time of its abandonment by the Anasazi, roughly between A.D. 1200 and 1300. Exactly when and where these Native Americans came from is still open to debate. Most scholars agree that the initial homeland of Uto-Aztecan speakers was in the area of Death Valley in southern California. Some 3–5,000 years ago this language family started to diversify into nine major groups known today. Numic speakers comprised one of these divisions, which includes the language spoken by today's Utes and Paiutes. Fanning out from their central location, these two groups moved northeasterly; but they remained on the edge of the Great Basin until about 1,000 years ago, when they moved rapidly into the basin and eventually onto the neighboring Colorado Plateau. Their language became increasingly diversified as splits in groups occurred, one anthropologist suggesting that the Utes separated from the Southern Paiutes 400 years ago as they settled in the Four Corners region.[4]

Today, the two languages are still mutually intelligible. Southern Utes and Southern Paiutes recognize dialectical differences in speech, one Ute informant saying that the Paiutes' language is more "clipped" or abbreviated and that the Paiutes accused the Utes of "talking fancy." This goes along with the general pattern of the Southern Paiutes' consideration of the Utes as their "fancy" cousins, who went off to the plains and learned "everything."[5]

The archaeological and ethnographic record of Ute and Paiute entrance into the Four Corners area is vague. Campsites and material remains are difficult to find and differentiate from those left by earlier peoples because of the small amount of pottery, nondescript dwellings, and limited technology necessitated by a hunting-and-gathering lifestyle. The analysis is made even more difficult by the Utes' practice of utilizing other peoples' camps and material remains.[6] Robert Euler, a noted Paiute historian, suggests that there were two migrations of Numic speakers into Nevada and Utah. The first one took place around the beginning of the Christian era, the second more than one thousand years later, around A.D. 1150, this last movement possibly causing the resident Anasazi to withdraw into larger, more defensible sites. At the same time, Paiute culture became quite stable, with few changes in lifestyle and technology until well into the late nineteenth century. Some archaeologists place the date of this entry later, during the 1300s.[7]

The San Juan Band Paiutes and Southern Utes were part of this eastward movement of people who entered present-day San Juan County. The effect the intrusion had on the Anasazi is questionable, but some authors suggest that the reason for the sudden expansion of Numic speak-

ers into the Great Basin and onto the Colorado Plateau occurred because of severe droughts during the twelfth and thirteenth centuries. Some anthropologists believe that this first could have caused relocation within, then evacuation of, those areas by the agriculturally oriented puebloans. Numic speakers, better adapted to surviving the rigors of a desert environment, filled the occupation gaps left by the migrating Fremont and Anasazi cultures. In support of this theory, it is interesting to note that the Anasazi abandoned a well-developed community at Navajo Mountain by A.D. 1270, evidence suggesting not that the Paiutes forced a withdrawal but that they could have been present when it occurred.[8]

How Southern Utes and Paiutes view the Anasazi helps to partially support this contention. They call the Anasazi the *muukwitsi*, meaning "the dead," and believe that the dead, their spirits, and spiders are interrelated. This then helps explain why spiders often haunt the ruins. Utes use the same name to refer to the Hopi, "Moqüi" (pronounced Mawkwi, not Mokee)—a term applied only to this pueblo group and which seems to have entered general usage following the Domínguez-Escalante expedition of 1776 that depended heavily upon Numic speakers for guides. According to some Ute informants, there never was conflict with the Anasazi; among other things, they shared a language that could almost be understood. The Utes also tell how they would only see their neighbors sporadically because the Anasazi appeared "like phantoms and would be seen at a distance or be heard to scream, but would disappear into the pinyon when a Ute approached."[9]

Some scholars argue that the Utes and Paiutes were not even in the region at this time (A.D. 1300). One explanation of migratory trends places Numic speakers in southwestern Utah some 430 years ago (about 1560), in southeastern Utah and southwestern Colorado 370 years ago, moving along the Rio Grande 330 years ago, and out on the Great Plains— their easternmost expansion—some 300 years ago.[10] All of these dates are speculative, but few people would argue with the point that by the 1500s the Utes and Paiutes of San Juan County were in their general historic setting.

By the early 1600s, Spanish reports indicated that there were Utes living in northwestern Arizona, north of the Colorado and San Juan Rivers, and in eastern Colorado.[11] Early accounts do not provide exact distinctions between different Numic speakers—the Utes, Paiutes, and Chemehuevi all being designated by the Spanish as "Yutas." Today, however, a clearer understanding provides knowledge of the three bands that comprise the Southern Utes. Starting from the east there were the Muache,

living in the Denver area; the Capote in the Sangre de Cristo Mountains of Colorado and south to Taos, New Mexico; and the Weenuche, who ranged from the Dolores River in the east to the Colorado River in the north and west to the San Juan River in the south.[12] All of these groups were highly mobile and visited far into the Great Basin, throughout the Colorado Plateau, and onto the Great Plains.

Some confusion concerning names exists in the historic record. Anthropologists and historians have collectively lumped the three afore-mentioned bands together under the title of Southern Utes. To the Ute people in southeastern Utah and southwestern Colorado today, however, this title properly refers only to those living on the Southern Ute reservation headquartered in Ignacio, Colorado. In this chapter, this name will be used in the broader, collective sense. The Weenuche Band's name also has been misrepresented. The literature concerning this group refers to them as the "Weeminuche," with a variety of spellings—Wimonuntci, Weminutc, Guibisnuches, Guiguimuches, Wamenuches, and others—that has evolved over the period of time since white contact. It likely was in-troduced as an inside or intertribal joke that puns on a word associated with sexual activity. For whatever reason it was started, the use of the word has become entrenched among scholars but is not accepted by many of the Ute people it refers to. Thus, the term Weenuche, describing the band of Southern Utes who inhabit southeastern Utah, is used here.[13]

The second group of Numic speakers in this area is the San Juan Band Paiute. Historically, they have been the least understood of an al-ready amorphous group. Southern Paiute territory centered in south-western Utah and Nevada, with its most eastward extension pushing into the Monument Valley region of the Utah-Arizona border. Sixteen identi-fiable bands comprise the Paiute tribe, with the San Juan Band being the only group to occupy lands south and east of the Colorado River. Per-haps this is why their name has been translated as "people being over on the opposite side," or as the "San Juan River People."[14]

William Palmer, during his interviews with Paiutes around Cedar City in 1928, found those Paiutes had only a slight knowledge of groups existing in southeastern Utah, his informants indicating that these people were called "'Nau-wana-tats,' which to the Pahutes [sic] means fighters or wrestlers. If there is a tribe of this name, the Indians interviewed think they are in the San Juan Country."[15] This vagueness underscores the fact that there was little cohesiveness between certain bands and that the area of southeastern Utah was peripheral to major Paiute activity. The San Juan Band may be subdivided into the Tatsiwinunts, who ranged over

The Utes have always been a mobile and adaptive people. Those in this photograph show their acceptance of the Plains Indian lifestyle with its dependence on horses, use of war bonnets, and distinctive beadwork. (Utah State Historical Society—USHS)

the area between Tuba City and Navajo Creek, and the Kai-boka-dot-tawip-nunts in the Navajo Mountain area.[16]

By 1935, Palmer's interest in this elusive group had peaked. Accompanied by a Paiute translator, he visited Allen Canyon, home of the alloted Ute/Paiute faction in southeastern Utah, to determine exactly how "Paiute" and how "Ute" these people were. He reported that he was "surprised, almost amazed, to find this long isolated band speaking more nearly pure Pahute than some of the clans that attend the tribal saparovan [council] every year and do much visiting back and forth every summer."[17] The sacred stories, told by an esteemed raconteur, or Narraguinip, were also identical to those of other Paiute bands.

Today, family groups such as the Dutchies, Cantsees, Lehis, and Poseys have Paiute roots that extend back to the Douglas Mesa–Monument Valley–Navajo Mountain area, while other families such as the Ketchums, Mikes, Hatches, and Eyetoos are more closely related to the Weenuche or Ute Mountain Utes living at Towaoc. Until the mid-1920s, the three main permanent camps of Numic speakers in southeastern Utah were at Navajo Mountain (Paiute), Allen Canyon (predominantly Paiute, but with a significant mix of Ute), and Montezuma Canyon (predominantly

Weenuche Ute).[18] This point should not be stressed too heavily, however, since a great deal of intermarriage, trade, and social interaction characterized all three groups.

The major distinction between the Utes and Paiutes living in this
area was cultural, not linguistic, affected by the environment and accompanying technology. There was no clear line of demarcation. Paiutes
operated in family groups, and, when resources allowed, came together
as bands. They hunted and gathered in an austere desert land, had no
centralized chieftain, no collective religious practices, and no common
goal or practice (other than survival) that would unite the different
groups. The Utes started from the same cultural roots, but with the utilization of the horse in the mid-to-late 1600s and the development of
aspects of Plains Indian culture those groups farthest east started to
change. The Weenuche, farthest to the west, were the last to adopt these
practices from their fellow tribal members. For reasons of simplicity, this
amalgamation of groups will be referred to here generally as Utes.

The interaction with the land by these people spoke of deep cultural
ties. Though they have not been as well documented as some historic
groups, the Utes placed names and endowed the land and its creatures
with significance. General descriptive names of places in southeastern
Utah include Water Canyon or River-Flowing-from-the-Sunrise (San Juan
River), Sagebrush Canyon or Crows Canyon (Montezuma Canyon), Slick
Rock Mound (Comb Ridge), Two Rocks Canyon (Cow Canyon), Bitter
Root Mountain (Sleeping Ute Mountain), and Where-the-Sun-Sets-Last
(Mount Tukuhnikivats in the La Sal Mountains).[19] Mancos (Jim) Mesa
and the Spanish Mossback mesas were said to have been "fortified strong-
holds" for the Utes, who in time of troubles would barricade themselves
within the steep, rocky slopes and walls of these mesas.[20] Blue Mountain,
Standing-Alone-Mountain (Navajo Mountain), and the La Sals have all
been identified as Ute places of worship.

There are also stories that teach values about the land. For instance,
Sleeping Ute Mountain near Cortez, Colorado, is said to be one of seven
giants who protected the Utes from other tribes' gods during the times
of the myths. He then grew tired, fell into a deep sleep, and there will
remain until he is again needed. The mountain is said to be inhabited by
supernatural beings who are appealed to through prayer and ceremony.

There are many other teachings from the Utes that look at the land
through religious or philosophical eyes. Tales are tinged with supernatural and mystical experiences that imbue the Four Corners region with a
power and sense of divine meaning pre-dating contemporary humans.

For instance, in the time of the myths it is said that the chief of all the Utes lost his wife and did not know where to look for her. Tav-woats, a supernatural being, answered his prayers by taking the man to the land of the dead to locate her. The god rolled a great magical ball of fire before them, cutting the earth and its mountains, creating a path upon which the two could walk. The husband arrived in the land of the dead, saw how happy his wife was, and returned to the living after being cautioned that he should not walk upon this trail again. Tav-woats ensured that humans kept this law by forming a river in the trail—known today as the Colorado River and the Grand Canyon.[21]

Another story tells of how the gods gave the Indians fire by placing it in every visible form. When a tree or grass burns, it is the fire coming out, and when sparks fly from a rock, it is releasing the power trapped long ago. Yet another tale tells how pieces of petrified wood are the remains of a fight between the sun and another supernatural being. The two battled on the ground and in the air; their lightning arrow shafts turned into petrified wood, while the missiles hurled by the sun remain as cobblestones. Since the rainbow was the weapon used against the sun, it is now found on the other side of the sky, away from the fiery orb. In another legend, a bear tells the Utes that he is heading to the Bears Ears country because that is where he will find "bull-grass, strawberries and good eating."[22] Thus, physical forms upon the land often held a deep mythological significance for the Utes.

Spiritual beings also reside on the mesas and in the canyons, where they either hide or show deer and elk to hunters who have prepared themselves through ritual. If these little people are seen, the individual must leave a blanket, food, or some other useful object and then depart. By saying nothing about this incident, the person is guaranteed good fortune in the future. Utes also held healing rites in what is now called Babylon Pasture, Peavine Canyon, and on the Bears Ears because of the supernatural power invested in the landscape.[23]

The People, as part of the larger ecosystem, blended the religious with the pragmatic side of survival in an austere land. Different family groups would join together for hunting and gathering. Each of these bands would have a leader, selected as a man who made wise decisions in knowing where to obtain food and how to keep the group out of trouble. The size of these groups would vary from one to ten families; but, as the People lost more and more land to white encroachment, they were forced together into smaller concentrations, primarily in Montezuma and Allen Canyons.

Each of these bands often would have a spiritual leader who understood the supernatural powers associated with the land and how to best appeal to them. He would go to these "power points" during the season of use and on behalf of his group would pray, leave an offering, and ask for help. Individual prayer by the general members of the band was also practiced, but not at the "power point" used by the medicine man.[24] Different types of spirits were believed to live in caves, rocks, springs, rivers, mountains, and other places and could provide help or harm depending upon how they are treated. These same powers as well as those associated with animals, plants, and natural phenomena such as whirlwinds, the moon, and lightning may also "transmit the high voltage of supernatural power to humble practitioners or doctors."[25] The location of specific power sites is not general knowledge and should be discussed only with those who have a need to know.

The life of a nineteenth-century Ute, before intense white contact forced drastic changes, was tied closely to the rhythms of nature. The People followed a seasonal pattern of migration that was carefully bound to the plants and animals ready for harvest in an area. Not surprisingly, water and grass played a dominant role. The people selected campsites based upon the availability of springs, streams, and rivers for drinking water, grass for livestock, firewood and trees for shelter, and lower elevations to avoid the deep snows of winter. Just as the deer moved down from the higher elevations in the late fall, the People would follow the same pattern, descending to valley or canyon floors where shelter and more abundant food were available.

This natural cycle was incorporated into the descriptive names given to the seasons of the year. For example, fall was called "leaves turning yellow," winter "heavy snow" or "hard times month," spring "snow melting," and summer "leaves coming out" or "much warmer for growing things." Three spring months had specific titles: March, "warm days beginning"; April, "green grass appearing"; and May, "mother of the two preceding months." The People started their move back to the mountains at the time "when the doves sound soft."[26]

The Utes established their winter camps in locations such as Montezuma Canyon, with its neighboring Cross, Squaw, and Benow Canyons; Dry Valley; Harts Draw; Beef Basin; Westwater and Cottonwood Canyons; Butler Wash; White and Douglas Mesas; and along the San Juan River—especially in the vicinity of Bluff and Sand Island. As the weather warmed and the grasses appeared, streams like La Sal, Deer, Coyote, Two Mile, Hop, Geyser, Taylor, and Beaver on the La Sal Moun-

tains and Spring, North and South Montezuma, Cottonwood, Recapture, and Indian Creeks poured off Blue Mountain. Numerous springs such as Dodge, Piute, and Peters also invited the Utes to scatter and camp as they searched for food.[27] Favorite areas to plant small garden plots in corn, beans, squash, and melons were in Montezuma and Allen Canyons, Indian Creek, Paiute Farms, and Paiute Canyon.

Deer played the most important part in the Ute economy. Besides providing food, the deer supplied hides to be fashioned into clothing or traded with other tribes, especially the Navajo. The People prepared a deerskin by first stitching it on a willow hoop, scraping off the fat and flesh with a serrated bone scraper fashioned from a deer leg, rubbing deer brains into the hide, rinsing it in water, re-stretching it, and, if desired, rubbing it with either a yellow root or smoking it over a fire to soften it.[28]

Favorite hunting places for deer and other large animals were Elk Ridge and the La Sal, Blue, Navajo, and Sleeping Ute Mountains, while pronghorn were hunted in the Dry Valley area. Elk, desert bighorn and mountain sheep, wild turkey, rabbits, badger, beaver, bear, and fish added to the diet. Women gathered many of the edible wild plants, including pine nuts, chokecherries, yucca fruit, Indian ricegrass, wild onions and potatoes, sunflower seeds, bullrushes, serviceberries, and raspberries.[29]

Homes reflected the needs of a mobile hunting-and-gathering society. Tepees, and later canvas tents, served as the winter home of the Utes. Construction included a four-pole base frame with ten poles total, the dwelling standing ten feet high with an average diameter of fourteen feet. Elk or deer hides stitched together, and later canvas or muslin covers, were wrapped around the frame and fastened in the front with skewers. Brush wickiups, based on the four-pole pattern or with poles leaned against a tree, provided shelter in the summer time.[30]

Exposure to sickness was an ever-present possibility for the People, whose health practices included as much religious and spiritual curing as physical, tangible medicine. Ute beliefs, for instance, centered around the shaman, usually a man, who received his healing power either through a charm obtained from an older medicine man or through dreams provided by supernatural beings. The dreams gave secret information concerning power within animals, plants, and natural elements that the shaman could invoke for good. He often learned these healing rites through repeated dreams received during the years of puberty. These supernatural teachings could not be denied, but they also could not be divulged, charging him with a lifelong responsibility of service.

A Ute Bear Dance being performed on the Uintah-Ouray Reservation in 1924 and photographed by Olive Burt. (USHS)

A typical Ute healing ceremony consisted of the medicine man using the information about paraphernalia or other measures he received in his dream to chant, pray, suck out, and otherwise exorcise the evil afflicting the sick person. Usually he performed at night, either in his or the patient's home. Stripped to the waist, the medicine man used sleight of hand, dancing feathers, and personal attacks on the illness. Inside the shaman was a small being, or *powa'a*, that directed the use of power and swallowed the sickness when it was removed by sucking from the patient. If the *powa'a* was misused or became angry it could turn on the practitioner, calling for blood and causing illness or witchcraft.[31]

Herbs and plants also played an important role in healing. Ute patients drank tea brewed from sagebrush leaves; a sore throat was treated by boiling pinyon sap with grease and then applying it externally on the neck; the roots and flowers of sand puff remedied stomach and bowel problems; spearmint leaves cured an upset stomach; and gum plant served as a cough syrup. Non-plant remedies included putting breast milk on a nursing baby's sore eyes, sugar on large cuts to stop bleeding, skunk grease on chapped hands and feet, and horse urine on pustules that broke and caused itching. Tobacco was used as a pain reliever for a decayed tooth. Later, a sore throat was swabbed with baking powder.[32] In a world domi-

nated by spirits and the possibility of physical harm, the Utes fortified themselves against the trials of life.

One aspect of the social and religious life of the People is the Bear Dance, traditionally performed in the spring. Symbolically, it was a ceremony taught by a bear to the Utes to help the animals awaken from hibernation and to strengthen the relationship between man and this very powerful creature. The brush circle in which the dance is performed is called "cave of sticks" and is constructed of cottonwood limbs, juniper boughs, and sagebrush. The structure opens to the east and represents a bear's den, while the rasping sound of a wooden stick dragged across another serrated stick represents the noises of a bear.

The Bear Dance is believed to be the only dance to have originated specifically with the Utes. Bluff, Montezuma Canyon, and Allen Canyon were the three sites where the dance was traditionally held in southeastern Utah. The gathering in the spring was a social event where young people could meet, marriage partners be selected, and elders discuss hunting and gathering plans of the various groups. The rebirth and fertility of nature were themes echoed throughout the feasting and dancing. Once the activity ended, the People dispersed to their individual group locations to hunt and gather. Today, the Bear Dance is held in the fall at White Mesa in order to accomodate dances and ceremonies to Ute people in other locations.

An important ceremony practiced by the Ute Mountain Utes to which the People of southeastern Utah have been invited and in which they have participated is the Sun Dance. Although not of Ute origin, this ceremony embodies many important teachings derived from supernatural beings. As with the Bear Dance, it is held in a cottonwood-and-brush enclosure that opens to the east. In the center is a large, erect pole with four scarves—one red to represent the earth, one yellow for the sun, white for daylight, and black for darkness—all of which are offerings to the four directions. Before dancing, men go to a sacred spot where they fast for four days to determine if the gods have selected them. If a man dreams three times about participating, it is considered that he has a special purpose in life to fulfill and will be attended by his guardian spirit. The power derived from the performance of the dance ensures that food will be plentiful, the sick and afflicted will be healed, and that supernatural beings are pleased with the sacrifice. Although this ceremony was introduced to the Ute Mountain Utes at a fairly late date—between 1890 and 1910—it has held deeply significant religious values for the People.[33]

Even in this brief survey of Ute economic, social, and religious prac-

tices, one sees clearly their dependence upon, and interconnectedness with, the land. Because of the advancing white frontier, however, control of this key factor in their life could not be maintained indefinitely. The history of the Utes in southeastern Utah attests to an initially friendly relationship with whites that changed as ownership and use of the land became increasingly challenged. Then, conflict against overwhelming odds became a way of life for the embattled Utes. Loss of the land resulted in an impoverished and embittered people. To understand this process, one must return to the earliest recorded contacts between the People and the Spanish in the Four Corners region.

In 1712 the governor of New Mexico, Juan Ignacio Flores Mogollon, forbade Spanish traders from venturing into Ute lands, which lay generally in northern New Mexico and in Colorado and Utah.[34] Not until June 1765 did Governor Tomas Velez de Cachupin grant special permission for Juan Maria Antonio Rivera to travel into Indian country. How many others had preceded Rivera is unknown, but part of the decision to bend official policy sprang from the governor's wish to find a crossing of the Colorado River, to identify the local Indian groups en route, and to determine their attitude toward the Spanish. Another reason was to discover if there was truth to the rumor that silver deposits existed in the area. This seemed possible, since a Ute named Wolfskin from that region had appeared in Abiquiu carrying a small silver ingot. More precious metals might be found, and so Rivera, in the guise of a trader with a small expedition, set out in search of mineral wealth and a trail.

Following old Indian paths, Rivera and his party arrived at the Los Pinos River in Colorado, where he found an adobe retort used to reduce the impurities in gold. Rivera took some of the bricks with him as proof, then sent four Spaniards and a Ute guide to locate Wolfskin. The party traveled from the Dolores River to Cross Canyon, then down an old Ute trail in Montezuma Canyon to the San Juan River. There they met a band of "wild Payuchis" living in ten lodges on the bank near present-day Montezuma Creek. One of the band jumped into the water and waded out to midstream where he used sign language to ascertain the Spaniards' intent. The groups established peaceful relations, and three days later the Ute leader Chino accompanied the explorers back to the main camp on the Dolores. He said that Wolfskin had recently left for his home on the La Plata River, and cautioned that the heat and lack of water would make the trip to the Colorado River in July dangerous for the Spaniards. However, he said, if they would return in the fall, he would guide them to their destination.

Rivera, happy with his discovery, went back to Santa Fe, received permission and additional instructions to find a ford of the Rio del Tizon (Colorado River), outfitted another group, and returned by a more direct route to the Dolores River. From there, the party crossed into Utah northeast of Monticello on October 6, proceeded to the base of the La Sal Mountains, then moved to Spanish Valley and the present site of Moab. The recent discovery of Rivera's detailed journal indicates that the Utes did all they could to discourage and lead astray the expedition. The Ute guide took them into the rough country of Indian Creek, Harts Draw, and part of present-day Canyonlands National Park before another Ute led them on a more direct route. The party eventually took a high trail on the western slopes of the La Sals before dropping down into Castle Creek and finding a crossing place on the Colorado River.[35]

Once he found a suitable ford, Rivera carved a cross and the words "Viva Jesus" in a cottonwood tree. His Ute guide warned that the party would now travel through lands inhabited by "child eaters," "strawheads" (so named because of their hair), and "stone people." With the promise of winter and troubles ahead, Rivera returned to Santa Fe in fourteen days' time. He left behind his cross to assert Spanish rights, while his expeditions set the stage for the next act in the drama, the Domínguez–Escalante expedition, played out eleven years later.[36]

There were undoubtedly unofficial expeditions to this area, such as the one of Pedro Mora, Gregorio Sandoval, and Andres Muniz, who reported seeing Rivera's cross in 1775; but these excursions are lost to history. Muniz, however, served as a guide the next year for Fray Francisco Atanasio Domínguez, Fray Silvestre Velez de Escalante, and seven other men as they wound their way through western Colorado in search of a feasible trail from Santa Fe to Monterey, California. The padres' account of the Indians living on or in southeastern Utah is informative. They encountered Utes who warned them about running into a Comanche war party and being killed, but the fathers replied that God would protect them. They also obtained some guides by paying each a blanket, knife, and beads to lead them to the north. One of the Utes overindulged and became so sick that he accused the Spaniards of poisoning him, until he eased his discomfort through vomiting. Other Utes willingly sold food and listened to the Catholic fathers' preaching, but often they tried to impede the journey to the north. Later, the fathers learned that some of their companions were telling the Indians to do this because they did not want to go farther. This was to no avail, as the expedition moved on as far north as Utah Valley.[37]

As Domínguez and Escalante continued down the western side of present-day Utah, they once again neared southeastern Utah and gave a description of the Indians they encountered, this time Paiutes, some of whom probably belonged to the San Juan Band. The fathers noticed how reticent these Indians were to approach them, no doubt in part because of the slave raiding and intertribal warfare that dominated their relations with other Indian groups. The Paiutes were happy to learn through an interpreter that since their enemies—the Navajos, Comanches, and Apaches—had not been baptized, they could not enter heaven and would "burn forever like wood in the fire."[38]

The fathers made special note of a group of Paiutes, whom they called the "Payuchi Yutas," east of the Colorado River. They were members of the San Juan Band Paiutes, who spoke the same language as the neighboring Paiute groups and the Utes to the east. The padres used some of their trails, reporting that they were built up with "loose stones and sticks."[39] Thus, Domínguez and Escalante were the first to provide an accurate ethnographic report of some of these early inhabitants.

The peaceful intentions of Domínguez and Escalante did little for those interested in economic gain. For instance, Muniz, who initially guided the group, smuggled trade goods along, acting expressly against the fathers' wishes. He and his brother had spent time—three to four months in some instances—trading among the Indians of the Four Corners region.[40] Such expeditions, exchanging furs, horses, guns, and slaves, caused constant consternation for the government trying to regulate Indian relations. In 1778, officials issued an edict to stem the flow of unlicensed trading activity in the borderlands. Ten men and two Indians stood trial in Abiquiu during 1783; two years later, several others were in similar circumstances for trading "in the interior of the country of the Utes in violation of repeated edicts."[41] Again, in 1812, officials passed a law to prohibit buying slaves from the Utes, and, not surprisingly, a year later seven men under Maurico Arze and Largos Garcia stood before the judge for slave trading in Utah Valley.[42] No doubt many of these expeditions—either coming or going—passed through the borders of San Juan County.

Utes, Navajos, and Spaniards continued their hostilities right through to the time of Spanish withdrawal from the American Southwest in 1821. Generally, these relations were characterized by the Spanish currying the favor of the Utes in order to use them against the Navajos. However, by the time the Mexican government faced the problem of controlling the Indians in its territory (1821–48), the Navajos had formed a friendly alliance with the Utes, much to the dismay of the settlers of New Mexico.

Reports filtered in to Santa Fe of Navajos and Utes working together to steal horses, forming alliances for slave raiding, living together in the La Plata and Sleeping Ute Mountains, and renewing friendships. Later, however, animosity again erupted.[43]

Traffic into the region built upon prior exploration, creating by 1830 a 1,200-mile route between Santa Fe and Los Angeles known as the Old Spanish Trail. Thanks to the efforts of Rivera, Domínguez-Escalante, and other less-publicized groups, this horse-and-pack-mule trail connected the interior of New Mexico with the Pacific Ocean while bypassing a section of Arizona noted for hostile Indians. Southeastern Utah hosted part of one branch of the route. It crossed the present-day state boundary at Ucolo near Piute Spring, dropped into Dry Valley, then generally followed the path of today's Highway 163 through La Sal Junction, past Kane Springs, down Spanish Valley, into Moab, and across the Colorado River to the Green River near the present town of that name. From there the trail headed generally west through Salina Canyon, out to the Sevier River, south to Richfield and Circleville, and then dipped into extreme northwestern Arizona and southern Nevada.[44]

One of the major functions of the Spanish Trail was to expedite trade, the northerly route into central Utah being the most practical. Indeed, slave and horse trading boomed during the Mexican period. Exchange of human captives and other commodities along the trail by the Utes, Navajos, and Paiutes reached an apex during the 1830s and 1840s, then declined in the 1850s. New Mexican traders were the foundation upon which this slave, gun, and horse trade was built. Entering the San Juan region in caravans as large as 300 men and "dressed in every variety of costume, from the embroidered jacket of the wealthy Californian ... to the scanty habiliments of the skin-clad Indians," the traders sought out women and children to sell in New Mexico and to exchange later for horses and blankets along the trail or in California. As much as $200 might be paid for a young girl who could be trained as a domestic, while boys were worth only half that much.[45]

Starting in the mid-1850s, the fragile Ute-Navajo alliance started to splinter beyond repair. At the same time, Mormons in southwestern Utah were feeling the effects of the attempted invasion of Salt Lake City by federal troops under Colonel Albert Sidney Johnston in 1857–58. The Mormons, fearing the worst, encouraged the uniting of Navajos, Utes, and Paiutes to serve as auxiliaries in their militia—the Nauvoo Legion. Some Utes attended meetings with Brigham Young in Salt Lake City and then sent emissaries to the Navajos, encouraging that a peace conference

An Indian couple photographed in Bluff, Utah, and identified as "Piute Indians," although they may have been White Mesa Utes. (USHS)

be held. One Ute appeared at Fort Defiance with a certificate of membership and baptism into the LDS church, alarming government authorities with this tampering in Indian affairs. The Mormons scheduled a large meeting of Paiutes, Utes, and Navajos in the Navajo Mountain area, at which time the settlers reportedly handed out guns and ammunition to them.[46]

The effects of these rumors were twofold. First, the Utes received increased annuities from the government as bribes to keep them peacefully tied to their agency. Second, it alerted agents and military authorities to new concerns in the tangled web of conflict between the Navajos, Utes, Mexicans, and Anglo peoples.

However, the reality of a Ute-Navajo alliance faded. By the summer of 1858 the Utes were operating in large numbers against their Indian neighbors in the heart of Navajo territory. The federal government, anxious to gain control over the Navajos, skillfully used the Utes to help in this process of subjugation. The military encouraged forays against the Ute's traditional enemy, saying that the Utes "appear to have inspired the Navajos with a dread not to be gotten over."[47]

On a more local level and as part of the plan to force the Navajos to surrender, military commanders encouraged general raids by Utes, Mexicans, Jicarilla Apaches, and Pueblo peoples against their enemy. In General Dixon Miles's words, "Let loose on these Indians all the surrounding tribes and inhabitants, particularly the Utahs and Mexicans, the two they seem to dread the most."[48] Soldiers reported finding large trails made by herds of Ute-captured horses headed north, while Utes started scouting for the army as "spies and guides."[49]

Working with Kit Carson, Colonel Thomas T. Fauntleroy, a former Ute agent to the Weenuche in Abiquiu, suggested that a band of 300–400 Utes could augment the six to eight companies of Mexican volunteers and spearhead the thrust into Navajo territory. Nothing would be more effective than to use them to ferret out the enemy from their camps in the deep recesses of the Chuska/Tunicha Mountains, Canyon de Chelly, and areas as far west as the Little Colorado. Indeed, field reports indicated that camps in the Navajo Mountain region and Carrizo Mountains in Arizona were already abandoned.

Carson guaranteed the eagerness of the Utes, "the best riflemen in the world," to wage war. He continued,

> I desire that I may be allowed to employ them, as they do not require pay as soldiers, but only to be supplied for a short time with provisions, until they can get well into the Indian country. I cannot but recommend this plan as it will at once have the effect to get the cooperation of a most valuable force, and at the same time employ these restless people, who otherwise must foray upon our own settlements.[50]

This was a perfect solution that gave the Utes something to do while providing for their welfare at the expense of the Navajos. They also rendered a service that was difficult, at best, for the conventional military.

As Ute pressures increased during the 1860s, the Navajos intensified their own use of Paiutes. Beyond the more mundane cooperation in daily life, the Paiutes provided a lookout service to protect Navajo camps. For instance, K'aayelii lived in the Bears Ears area, where he established a settlement of five or six hogans. To prevent surprise attacks, he posted Paiutes along the various approaches to his camp. This was also done in the Navajo Mountain area, where the Navajos were said to be "hiding behind" the Paiutes.[51]

Perhaps the most dramatic proof of Ute, Paiute, and Navajo cooperation occurred in September 1866 when a group of Capote and Weenuche Utes and a few Mexicans met to plan a trap for some Navajos who had avoided capture and were living in northern Arizona. They intended to invite the Navajos to live nearby, but when they arrived the Utes would kill the men, enslave the women and children, and capture the livestock. However, upon hearing this plan, Cabeza Blanca, a Weenuche leader, disagreed with the others, saying that he had friends among those Navajos whom he did not want to have killed. A fight ensued during which the Capotes killed Cabeza Blanca and then fled to Tierra Amarilla for protection. After exacting revenge, the Weenuche, according to a government report, "then left, joining as is supposed the Wymin and Pah Utes who had made friends with the Navajos in the meantime. The whole party of Wymin, Pah Utes, and Navajos then left that region and went to the neighborhood of Rio Dolores, Sierra Salir [La Sal Mountains], and Sierra Orejas [Bears Ears]."[52]

In 1868, with the official end of hostilities and the return of captive Navajos from Fort Sumner, a whole new set of problems confronted the Utes residing in the Four Corners area. As Civil War veterans poured into the West, mining strikes became more frequent and numerous agricultural settlements were established. The whites demanded that Indians be kept on a reservation far from civilization. The Utes refused; they wanted little to do with a livelihood primarily concerned with agriculture. They enjoyed their freedom, insisting they had performed a good service for the Americans and so should remain unmolested.

Western Colorado had always been Ute, and so the people of New Mexico urged they be expelled to this region and the Abiquiu agency be closed to the Capote and Weenuche bands. It was believed that the Muache at the Cimarron agency, "with a little management," could also be per-

suaded to leave. However, underlying the Utes' hesitance were religious beliefs. Diego Archuleta, an unsympathetic agent, explained, "These savages are possessed of the most heathenish superstitions against abandoning those places where the remains of their ancestors lie ... [and] they consider their reduction to reservations as a species of slavery."[53]

Ute Agent W.F.M. Arny even encouraged the taking of Ute lands by stating in his annual report of 1867 that several thousand white families could homestead in the area north and east of the Animas River. By establishing a reservation, the mining and agricultural resources of the region would be opened for development, and this could be "done at a comparatively small expense, for it is cheaper to dispose of these Indians in this way than to fight and exterminate them."[54] Arny felt he could move the Capote and Weenuche onto a reservation on the San Juan River for $49,500. Within a year he had the paperwork completed.

At the same time that the Navajos received their reservation on the New Mexico–Arizona border, well below the San Juan River, the Utes also obtained a reservation. On August 19, 1868, Arny met with Weenuche and Capote leaders at Pagosa Springs in southwestern Colorado. The Indians outlined what they considered desirable reservation boundaries, given the already deteriorating circumstances on their lands to the east. They wanted to be guaranteed the territory encompassed by the Grand (Colorado) and Green Rivers to the north, the headwaters of the San Juan River on the east, the Colorado River on the west, and the Navajo country to the south.[55]

The Utes begrudgingly signed a treaty in Washington, D.C., that removed them to Colorado, though the Abiquiu and Cimarron agencies did not close until 1878 when the two new agencies in Colorado were completed. What the Utes received, however, was far different than what they had asked for—all of their territory was in Colorado. Although the reservation initially included much of the upper San Juan River area, the lower San Juan in Utah remained a fringe area that no one seemed too excited about in 1868. The Four Corners area was peripheral to the white mining and settlement activities of the 1860s, staying in a twilight zone of general use by some Navajos and Paiutes but dominated by the Weenuche Utes.

This relative isolation soon changed. By the early 1870s, the estimated 700 to 1,000 Weenuche still lived by "the chase" and came to their Abiquiu agency in New Mexico only for gunpowder and lead. According to their agent, they were "very much attached to the localities" in which they lived and were characterized as "excellent shots ... great friends of our

government... and are ... reasonable and docile."[56] But they also needed to protect what they had. In 1871 the agent noted that other groups of Utes prior to that time had feared entering Weenuche country but now were overcoming this attitude and hunting in Weenuche territory, thus increasing the pressure on available resources.[57]

In 1873 the Utes signed another treaty, the Brunot Agreement, that removed massive chunks of land from their reservation, so much that by 1880 and one more treaty comparatively little remained of their holdings. Using Colorado as an example, this meant that from their original holdings of 56 million acres, the first treaty promised only 18 million acres (about 9 million to the Southern Ute and a similar amount to the Ute Mountain Ute or Weenuche). By 1934 both of these groups had their holdings reduced by various means to only 553,600 acres.[58]

Of even greater concern was the influx of white settlers, who, starting in 1878, scouted out farms and livestock ranges along the San Juan River and in McElmo Canyon, a natural thoroughfare leading from Colorado into Utah. The Weenuche Utes and Paiutes of San Juan County became increasingly uneasy about this invasion from the east, especially when Mormons added to the growing cluster of regional settlements in 1880. Add to this the probing tentacles of Navajo expansion from the south, and friction over resources became inevitable and continuous.

Southeastern Utah north of the San Juan River was public domain that the Weenuche Band of the Southern Utes considered to be theirs. Small bands of Navajos either visited or took up residence there during the 1860s, '70s, and '80s, but it was not until the mid-1880s, as the Navajo reservation expanded north, that larger populations entered to stay. When the Southern Utes and Navajos each received their reservations in 1868, one of the treaty stipulations specified that the Indians would "retain the right to hunt on any unoccupied lands contiguous to the reservation, so long as the large game may range thereon in such numbers as to justify the chase."[59] The Indians took advantage of this opportunity since neither group could survive solely on their livestock or agricultural produce. The Utes' reservation by the 1880s had shrunk from roughly one-third of Colorado to a land area only fifteen miles wide and 110 miles long in some of the most desolate territory in the southwestern corner of the state. Few alternatives, other than off-reservation hunting, allowed the Native Americans the opportunity to obtain wild game.

One of the greatest threats to Ute resources came in the guise of cattle companies searching for free-use public lands for grazing. By the 1880s four major outfits ranged thousands of cattle on the grass and

brush of San Juan canyon country. The two most important were those of Edmund and Harold Carlisle (called the Kansas and New Mexico Land and Cattle Company) and the L.C. outfit, located on Recapture and Verdure Creeks at the head of Montezuma Canyon. The size of these companies was considerable, the latter alone selling 22,000 head between 1891 and 1893.[60] Herds of this magnitude changed the quality of the environment within just a few years' time, increasing the conflict between Indians and whites. Although many of these cattle companies would rise to meteoric heights only to fail, there always was another group to step in to keep the cattle business alive.

When bands of Navajos and Utes left their reservations, they quickly encountered the stock of the cattlemen, who grazed their herds in the same places and at the same time of year as the deer. Grass, forbs, brush, and water were most plentiful on the mountains, and so it was not long before Indian agents received some blistering correspondence spelling out Native American activities. Edmund Carlisle, co-owner of the huge Kansas and New Mexico Land and Cattle Company, contacted the Southern Ute agent, reporting that the Indians were off the reservation with written permission from a local trader, that they had been firing the timberlands on the south side of Blue Mountain in San Juan County, Utah, causing severe damage, and that they not only had killed deer but also cattle. The livestock owners wanted soldiers sent to control the Utes and "other Indians." More letters followed, indicating that this hunting group, comprised of some forty Southern Utes and a similar number of Navajos, was heading west to continue its hunt. Cowboys and white citizens alike threatened to form groups to attack the Indians, and, though no organized posse moved against them, there were individual encounters that resulted in a handful of people being killed on both sides.[61]

The next few years showed little improvement in the situation. In 1885 one man complained that half of the Southern Utes were off the reservation, burning grass and killing cattle because the Indians suffered from hunger, and that he dared not hunt for fear of being killed. Whites were not the only ones concerned. The Southern Utes from Colorado entered southeastern Utah with the express purpose of rounding up the deer like cattle and either killing them or driving them closer to their reservation. The Southern Utes and Paiutes already living in Utah were greatly angered by this attempt to remove game from their territory. The first of three annual hunts started in 1884, with an estimated 300 Indians killing or wounding deer by the hundreds and drifting thousands of others to the south and east of the La Sal Mountains.

Mancos Jim was of predominantly Paiute ancestry and was a well-known figure in southeastern Utah at the turn of the twentieth century. (USHS)

By 1889 events had reached a boiling point. To settle conflicting reports, the U.S. military sent Second Lieutenant George Williams to Blue Mountain in December of that year. Although he saw no Indian hunters, he estimated that 200 to 300 Navajos and Utes had been hunting there but had returned to their reservations. He claimed that the Indians had "killed a good many deer as is shown by the number of hides they have

sold to the trader."[62] The twelve white families living in Monticello at the base of the mountain reported that the Utes hunted for hides and meat, the Navajos primarily for hides. Many of the cowmen complained that with all of the Indians chasing through the woods, the livestock had grown more wild and harder to herd.

Williams also reported a problem with too many Indian groups hunting in the same territory. Navajos and Utes did not traditionally get along well with each other, and rubbing shoulders while armed in the isolation of the mountains could lead to explosive situations. Although no conflict actually erupted between the two tribes, this was not true of the Colorado and Utah Ute/Paiute bands. One person known to history as Hatch, from Utah, got into an argument with a man named Cowboy from Colorado while camped at Peters Spring near Monticello. Apparently the friction evolved over the killing and driving away of the deer herds. Cowboy killed Hatch and the bands separated; but, when they met again in town, the men dismounted and prepared for a shoot-out amid the settlers' cabins and stores. Cooler heads prevailed, however, and both groups went their way, leaving vivid evidence of the importance of the deer herds to all Indian peoples.[63]

In the 1890s increased pressures on the Utes by their agents and an expanding Navajo population started to change the complexion of events. The Ute agent took the opportunity to show that his charges were really on the reservation and that much of the hunting was being done by Navajos but that the blame was still placed on the Utes. He even sent a letter to the Navajos and their agent saying that the Utes and their white neighbors complained about Navajos killing game both on the reservation and to its north. He ordered them to leave with all of their livestock and no longer make the Utes' land their headquarters for killing cattle and hunting deer.[64]

The Utes needed some type of economy to survive, yet they did not have the same economic base of agriculture and livestock (sheep, goats, and cattle) that allowed the Navajos to prosper. Hunting as a way of life was becoming totally impractical. Beadwork and baskets, famous crafts of the Utes, were not as stylish as Navajo rugs and never moved beyond a very local economy that produced little revenue.

Different Ute groups in San Juan County under the leadership of Red Jacket, Narraguinip, Mariano, Bridger Jack, Polk, Johnny Benow, and Posey reacted to the general deterioration of lifestyle that occurred during this and later time periods. Many of these fragmentary bands either moved to their reservation in Colorado or coalesced into what would be

recognized by the early 1900s as the Montezuma Canyon and the Allen Canyon Ute groups. Although these two factions were interdependent, the particulars of their experience varied somewhat and so will at times be treated independently in this account.

For the Weenuche living and ranging throughout San Juan County, the cumulative impact of these events was overwhelming. With Mormon and non-Mormon settlers creating homesteads on lands with critical resources and trail networks, livestock companies herding cattle on Blue Mountain and the La Sals, and the government compressing the Muache, Capote, and Weenuche into a strip of Colorado land fifteen miles wide and 110 miles long, there smoldered a growing resentment. Utes, Paiutes, and some Navajo allies reacted to stem the loss of their resources. Fights at Pinhook Draw (1881), White Canyon (1884), around Bluff, and in the La Sal and Blue Mountains erupted when the tension became too intense. Many of these better-known encounters have been written about elsewhere and do not need repeating here, but rarely are the reasons for these conflicts or the personalities involved given fair treatment.[65]

Take, for instance, the Weenuche man Johnny Benow, who lived in Montezuma Canyon. He and his associates made life miserable for area cattlemen. Edmund Carlisle wrote to the Southern Ute agent, saying Benow's people were at Paiute Springs (near present-day Monticello) and in Cross Canyon (which enters into Montezuma Canyon) "killing many cattle and burning the grass and timber. Unless something is done to check them, they will do very serious damage. The citizens talk of organizing and killing off these Utes.... Benow is the leader at Cross Canyon and Narraguinip and Mancos Jim appear so out here [in the Monticello area]."[66]

In July 1884 the government sent a troop of cavalry, augmented by a detachment, to Montezuma Creek to protect the cattlemen's stock from Indians. An earlier fracas ended with the death of a Ute over the ownership of a horse. The Indians retaliated by driving off a herd of horses. The cavalry and cattlemen went in pursuit, the result of which was the fight in White Canyon. Edmund Carlisle identified Benow as a participant in this fray and complained that some cowboys later saw Benow riding one of Carlisle's favorite horses. The rancher then requested "a fair recompense from the government for the heavy losses my company has sustained from depredations of the Ute Indians," estimated at this time as more than 150 head of horses.[67]

Each spring, summer, and fall trouble arose. Indian agents sought help from the military to bring the Utes back to the reservation. Talk of

secret organizations formed by cattlemen and settlers to rid themselves of the Indians was common, and one of these vigilante groups killed a Ute family of six as they camped on the Dolores River in southwestern Colorado. Chiefs on the reservation did not have the power to maintain control over all their charges and occasionally denied Ute involvement in altercations.[68]

The situation did not improve. A military report of 1894 states that a group of about ninety-five Utes and eighty Paiutes under Benow refused to come in to the reservation.[69] They realized what was happening in the eastern section of the Southern Ute Agency, where whites took unalloted lands not filed on by Indians; where Ute culture deteriorated through the "civilizing" processes of education, missionary efforts, and agent control; and where agriculture, not hunting, became the only practical lifestyle.

As Indian agents and Washington bureaucrats cast about for an answer, San Juan County, Utah, suddenly appeared to some as the solution, with plans to designate it as an area for the Native Americans. In 1887 Ignacio, leader of the Muaches and Capotes, agreed to look the land over, and, with a party of Utes, traveled as far as the Carlisle ranch north of Monticello before giving a final nod of approval. A year later, the government presented a plan that signed over to the Utes 2,912,000 acres, a promise of $50,000 in ten annual payments, sheep valued at $20,000, an agency, and the right to hunt in the La Sal Mountains.[70] In effect, this gave all of San Juan County, minus Navajo lands south of the San Juan River, to the Utes.

Utah ranchers and settlers were irate. The Mormons, the Carlisles, and members of the Pittsburgh Cattle Company fought back by lobbying the state and federal governments to prevent seizure of the land. The Indian Rights Association, headquartered in Philadelphia, also politicked in Washington, fearing that even if the government removed the settlers nasty friction would still ensue with the whites in Moab, that previous mining claims would still be an issue, and that there was insufficient water for large-scale farming projects. Officials of Utah Territory were even more blunt, insisting that the territory already had enough Indians.[71]

While the wrangling went on, the Utes decided to move to the area. In November 1894 an estimated 1,100 Indians with their agent, David Day, arrived in San Juan County to select new homes. Utah Governor Caleb West, the county commissioners, and interested citizens jammed with some of the Utes into the log school in Monticello. As the deliberations became more heated, a messenger delivered a note from officials in

Washington, saying the Indians had five days to go back to Colorado. The threat of cavalry convinced them to cede the point. They eventually returned to the Southern Ute Reservation, the eastern portion of which was opened to Indian allotments, with the remaining land being sold to white settlers. The western half, by 1900, became an unalloted section called the Ute Mountain Ute Reservation, with an agency in Navajo Springs (present-day Towaoc).[72]

There was little to attract San Juan Utes to Towaoc, where it was reported that "upon this vast tract of land, no water has been provided to even cultivate an acre of land, and during the summer the Indians are compelled to take to the mountains with their stock so as to find a sufficient supply of water to quench their thirst."[73] It came as no surprise, therefore, that in 1896 "the great majority" of the Weenuche were said to be "largely in the blanket and divide their time between Colorado and Utah, the latter pilgrims being the Pi-Utes or renegades who inhabit the Blue and La Sal Mountains in Utah and [who] were added to the rolls of this agency in June, 1895."[74]

The turn of the century saw virtually no change in conditions. The Utes living at Navajo Springs as well as off the reservation eked out a bare existence. No irrigation ditch existed to water the land; ration issues proved to be a lifeline that extended for only two weeks in a month; springs on Ute lands were dry by the end of summer; and agent turnover was a continuing problem, in 1900 alone there being three such changes. That same year a smallpox epidemic claimed fifty-five lives; how many more deaths went unreported is unknown. There were eight births during the same period. A year later the Indian agent warned that "a clash will eventually occur [as] is demonstrated by the fact that on several instances, serious conflicts have been narrowly averted."[75]

The Utes and Paiutes in Allen Canyon were perhaps in an even worse situation. Ever since the first settler placed his boot in the sands of Bluff or the first cattleman ran a dogy on Blue Mountain, this band of "renegades," as whites called them, played a part in each of the conflicts occurring between the 1880s and the early 1900s. In March 1914 an even more serious event took place that assumed headline proportions for six months. The problem began when a Mexican sheepherder named Juan Chacon camped with some Utes and Paiutes from the Montezuma Canyon area. Among them was Tse-Ne-Gat, also known as Everett Hatch, who spent time with both Ute factions. Chacon spent the evening playing cards and visiting around the campfire. A few days later he was found dead, and witnesses claimed Tse-Ne-Gat had killed him.[76]

Ten months later, Tse-Ne-Gat had still not surrendered. He feared his life was in danger; however, in the eyes of the law, this was not sufficient justification for not turning himself in. U.S. Marshal Aquila Nebeker, along with local helpers from Cortez, Bluff, Blanding, and Monticello, decided to arrest Tse-Ne-Gat. The newspapers set the stage for the approaching drama by saying that "Hatch has a notorious reputation as a bad man," that he "had defied several attempts to bring him into custody," that he was "strongly entrenched with fifty braves who will stand by him to the last man," and that this group had been "terrorizing" the people of Bluff.[77] The headlines a week later could almost be predicted.

According to local papers, the "uprising" occurred when the seventy-five-man posse approached the Ute camp in the early light of dawn. A startled early riser reportedly gave "whoops of warning" to awaken the others, then opened fire. Initial volleys resulted in two Indians and one white being killed, as the posse implemented "Indian strategy of the kind that one is accustomed to read in the histories of early life in the West."[78] Another group of Indians, hearing the commotion, came up from the San Juan River, approached the cordon from the rear, and started firing. The whites and Indians called a truce, the engagement ended, and the Utes fled for the wide open spaces.

Bluff soon took on the air of a besieged town. Indian agents, state officials, and the U.S. military all became involved and no doubt sighed with relief when Brigadier General Hugh L. Scott, Chief of Staff of the United States Army, was reported on his way to "attempt a peaceful settlement with the recalcitrant Piute Indians." When Scott arrived in Bluff, he made it clear that he would try to settle the issue peacefully. Two weeks later, he had "captured the renegade Indians" by meeting with them, by promising all twenty-three of them protection, and by honoring the request that the four captives—Polk, Posey, Tse-Ne-Gat, and Posey's Boy—be brought to Salt Lake City for questioning.[79]

By April, officials in Salt Lake City released all of the prisoners except Tse-Ne-Gat, who went to Denver to stand trial. Before the Ute ever entered the courtroom, the *Mancos Times-Tribune* announced that the charges against him could not be proven; but, when he was acquitted, the ire of the settlers in the Four Corners area reached meteoric heights.

The tension continued. By January 1917 the federal government wanted to find out for itself why there was continuing unrest. Special investigator Major James McLaughlin arrived in the area on January 1 and remained for eighteen days, interviewing the Indians at Towaoc, Montezuma Canyon, and Bluff. His findings, as an unbiased source, show

No Indian from southeastern Utah has gained more
notoriety than Posey, of San Juan Band Paiute
ancestry. He was associated (proven or not) with
every point of friction between the whites and Utes at
the time. (USHS)

clearly the destitute conditions and the fear felt by the Utes and Paiutes
of San Juan County.

McLaughlin hoped that the Indians would journey to the agency to
meet with him; however, James C. Wilson, an assistant of Samuel Rentz,

Major participants in the 1915 conflict photographed here include (left to right): Robert Martin (Navajo), who served as an interpreter for the government; Posey; Jesse Posey (his son); Tse-ne-gat (Poke's son); and Poke. This picture was taken in Bluff before the group traveled to Salt Lake City. (USHS)

who owned a small trading post and home in Montezuma Canyon, wrote a letter on the Native Americans' behalf saying that the trip would be too great a hardship. These Utes, he insisted, were afraid to go to the agency; many were sick, most were without sufficient clothing, many were walking barefoot in the snow and living in shelters made out of "old rotten canvas full of holes," and their horses were too worn to travel.[80] They were, however, very anxious to talk with Mclaughlin.

The inspector departed the agency and first bumped down McElmo Canyon by auto, then by wagon up Yellowjacket Canyon, and across Cahone Mesa to the Rentz trading post, where he arrived on January 9 and stayed for two days. He met with all of the adult male Indians living in the canyon, whose total population he estimated at 160, with another fifty living around Bluff. All of the Utes were enrolled members of the Ute Mountain Ute Agency at Towaoc, but all refused to live on the reservation because they felt the Indians there were unfriendly to them and would not share the land with its insufficient water. Spokesmen from the Montezuma group included John Benow, who assumed the chieftainship; George Brooks, a medicine man; and old Polk. The seven-hour con-

ference was a cordial opportunity to air past grievances. Posey with his Bluff contingent met with McLaughlin a few days later and expressed similar anxiety about moving to the reservation.[81]

The settlers in Bluff also talked to the inspector and gave him a list of suggestions that were no surprise. The basic tenor of this correspondence maintained that the Utes were a "law-unto-themselves," that they should be put on the eastern (farthest) end of their reservation, that their leaders be moved away from the main body of people, and that this roundup be conducted in the winter when the Indians were less mobile.[82]

Although McLaughlin appears to have made a favorable impression on both Benow and the settlers, his following correspondence hints that he viewed the ultimate solution to the problem to be the removal of the Utes to Colorado. Agent A.H. Symons later visited with Benow, who was waiting for the Commissioner of Indian Affairs to visit and ensure the Indians' rights to remain. The agent, on the other hand, knew that the opposite might happen and asked that his replacement be given the responsibility of moving them so that it could be blamed on the military and not him. His explanation: "If a new man were in charge here, they [Utes] would not attach the blame to him and would start with a clean slate."[83] The move, however, did not occur for a number of years.

This volatile atmosphere could only result in a final solution for both sides, in which the winner would take all. It came in the form of what has been called the "Posey War" and the "Last Indian Uprising." Briefly, what occurred followed the same pattern as previous flare-ups; but, this time, whites made a conscious effort to prevent the same results as the 1915 episode.[84] Local people tried to minimize the influence of outsiders; forces combatting the Utes mobilized quickly, not giving the Indians time to react; and the settlers did not release captive Utes until they had signed an agreement as to what lands they would promise to live on.

All of this was accomplished because of a relatively insignificant affair that started when two young Utes robbed a sheep camp, killed a calf, and burned a bridge. The culprits voluntarily turned themselves in, stood trial, but then escaped from the sheriff's grasp. The townspeople moved quickly not only to get the two boys but also Posey, who by this time had become synonymous with all of the ill-will felt between the factions. To the townspeople, he was the living image of all Indians who were considered to be degraded or troublesome.

The newspapers played a significant role in developing this attitude, making Posey the lightning rod waiting to be struck. His name had ap-

A group of Indians associated with the "Posey War" gathered for land allotment meetings in 1921 or 1922. Posey is standing second from the left. (USHS)

peared, in either direct or indirect accusation, with almost every negative incident that had occurred, and people often cited his band of Utes as the culprits in a misdeed. Posey was said to have been the man who pulled the trigger on Joe Aiken, the white fatality in the 1915 fight; Posey reportedly killed his brother Scotty because the latter wanted a peaceful settlement of that conflict; he also killed his wife by accident, though many settlers refused to believe it was a mishap; he avoided living on the reservation; and he was such a colorful individual that his threats, cajoling, and antics for food at a cabin door or out on the range often brought a stronger reaction to what would normally have been forgiven.[85] Thus, the 1923 "war" served as the catalyst by which this "problem" could be removed.

In reality, the "war" was little more than a massive exodus of Utes and Paiutes fleeing their homes to escape into the rough canyon country of Navajo Mountain. Posey fought a rear-guard action to prevent capture, was eventually wounded, and watched his people get carted off to a barbed-wire compound set up in the middle of Blanding. He died a painful death a month later from his gunshot wound. When Posey's death was certain, some of the Utes took Marshal J. Ray Ward to where the body was located in order to certify his death. The law officer buried the corpse and disguised the grave, but to no avail—it was exhumed at least twice.[86]

Of even greater import was the solution to the question of who controlled the ranges. The Posey incident served as an excuse to force land allotments on the Utes. Hubert Work, Secretary of the Interior, issued an order in April that both Ute groups stop their nomadic life and settle on individual land holdings. Moab's *Times-Independent* reported,

> Old Posey's band, consisting of about 100 Indians will be given parcels of land located on or near Allen Canyon while Old Polk's band, numbering about 85 men, women, and children will be allotted land along Montezuma Creek. The two bands which are not friendly, will be located some distance apart.[87]

The number of allotments in Montezuma Canyon varied. Ira Hatch, who owned and operated a trading post in this area, estimated that there were twenty-three Ute camps in Montezuma and Cross Canyons.[88] Today, there are no Ute allotments in the former and only a few in the latter, the tribe having bought many of the individual holdings. In Allen Canyon, Ute families still own thirty allotments at the time of this writing.

Now that the end of a hunting-and-gathering lifestyle had reached an irreversible conclusion, agriculture became the supposed solution for the Utes. In reality, however, it faired just as badly. Ute farming efforts were on a subsistence level, failing to compete in the twentieth-century market economy with Anglos who had better land, equipment, and techniques. For instance, as late as the 1940s, the government farmer, E.Z. Black, plowed allotted lands in Allen Canyon that averaged around ten acres per family. He was also totally dependent upon the agents at Towaoc for teams, plows, seeds, and general financial backing. As soon as the funds dried up, so did the work on projects. Part of this problem arose because the Allen Canyon Utes in 1929 included only fourteen families. Their activities were so peripheral to those on the main reservation in Colorado that few people could muster sufficient funds or support for any sustained large-scale farming project.[89] How much this bothered the people of Allen Canyon is difficult to determine, but they continued to wrestle with dire poverty—living in tents and depending on rations and other government subsidies.

Sheep, cattle, and horses presented a more culturally acceptable alternative to the Utes, but the battle for the ranges that took place during the first quarter of the twentieth century put a stop to free use of Montezuma Canyon, McCracken Mesa, and the plateaus surrounding Blue Mountain. Between the U.S. Forest Service, Bureau of Land Man-

Jim Mike, who led whites to their "discovery" of Rainbow Bridge. (USHS)

agement, and private livestock companies, the lands encircling Allen Canyon were heavily controlled, forcing the Utes to keep their herds small and within certain limits. Physical and cultural restraints thus stifled the Ute economy. Clearing lands for white farmers, chopping wood for townspeople, and doing odd jobs for individual families served as only a temporary supplement in the hand-to-mouth existence of most of the area's Ute Indians.

Another shift away from traditional Ute culture came in the form of the Native American Church. As part of a pan-Indian movement shared by many tribes across the nation, the church made inroads with the People by offering a system of more generalized Indian teachings. The Native American Church has its roots in Kiowa and Comanche tribal paraphernalia of the late nineteenth century. These Plains tribes provided the tepee, feather fan, drum, waterfowl, crescent-shaped altar, fire, and poker as standardized symbols within this belief system, while peyote, a hallucinogenic button from cactus initially found in Mexico, became the driving force within the ceremony. It provided the means through which God and supernatural powers could be made manifest to the participants involved in an all-night ceremony.[90]

The Native American Church entered San Juan County from Okla-

homa via the Ute Mountain Ute Reservation. Two anthropologists, David F. Aberle and Omer C. Stewart, conducted a detailed study of this phenomenon between 1946 and 1951 and identified four phases of development of these beliefs on the Ute and northern part of the Navajo reservations. Aberle and Stewart concluded that Towaoc Utes introduced the practices in the Mancos Creek and Aneth area; this was followed by a second phase in which Navajos working alongside Utes in the Civilian Conservation Corps, as well as others traveling to Towaoc for curing rites, encountered Native American Church practices. These phases took place between 1914 and 1938. Starting in 1936, peyote priests, or "Road Chiefs," started visiting reservation communities south of the San Juan River, so that by 1951 there was an open flow of religious leaders from Oklahoma, Towaoc, and the Mancos/Aneth area throughout San Juan County. Aberle and Stewart infer that more than half of the population in the Aneth, Montezuma Creek, and region south of Bluff were practitioners in the Native American Church by this time.[91]

Not until the 1950s did a Salt Lake City law firm under the leadership of Ernest L. Wilkinson make possible real financial assistance for the Utes of Colorado and Utah. Grounds for this aid were rooted in the past, when the government dispossessed the tribe of its lands—an estimated 15 million acres—beginning in 1868. In 1938 the Utes filed a suit claiming $40 million in losses. Wilkinson won a series of legal battles that settled on a final reparation of $32 million, giving 53 percent to the Utah Utes in the north and 47 percent to the Southern and Ute Mountain Utes in Colorado. The latter payment included recompense for the White Mesa people.[92]

The federal government approved the plan for the tribal governments to pay part of this money in a per capita settlement spread over a number of years. Although there were approximately 2,500 Utes living in both states, giving about $12,500 per person, Congress felt that part of these funds needed to be held back for investment in economic development. A long-range program for improvement of tribal facilities and projects still needed to be arranged.

To the 148 Utes living near Blanding, this translated into $1,025 per person over a two-year period, or an aggregate sum of $151,700—an unheard-of amount when most family incomes were well below $800 per year. Additional funds followed on a fairly regular basis, eventually averaging a total payment of $8,000 to each man, woman, and child. The initial reaction, reported in the newspapers with an obvious tinge of jealousy, indicated the Indians' desire to own all those commodities their

Ute Indians living in Allen Canyon work with agent E.Z. Black to plant a garden. The agent's home and headquarters are in the background. (San Juan Historical Commission)

white neighbors had, such as cars, clothes, and high-priced food. Of greater import, however, were the funds set aside to improve housing, roads, and services.[93]

The Utes in Allen Canyon realized that their isolation was counter-productive, while others living on the outskirts of Blanding wanted to have better lands for farming and to use this money to build their live-stock industry. The Ute agent, Elbert J. Floyd, met with the white people of Blanding and the area Utes to discuss the problems of relocation. All

While the White Mesa Utes look forward to the future, they also retain their heritage from the past. This photo, taken in 1936 in Allen Canyon, illustrates the basket weaving skill for which the Utes are famous. Today, this tradition is passed from generation to generation. (W. R. Palmer, Special Collections, Southern Utah University Library)

three parties determined that Allen Canyon was too small for the expansion of farming and industry and that the individual allotments were too large to allow for introduction of community-owned-and-operated modern conveniences. The Westwater community, located on BLM property on the outskirts of Blanding, was situated on land too rocky for farming, while building lots within the city limits were too expensive for Indian families to afford. Eventually, Ute-owned land eleven miles south of Blanding, now known as White Mesa, attracted Utes for settlement. Close enough to Blanding for those who wished to work there, yet far enough away to foster a sense of individual identity, the White Mesa site proved to be a good choice.[94]

Starting in the mid-1950s, the Ute Mountain Rehabilitation Program, headquartered in Towaoc, provided funds for the construction of frame houses at White Mesa.[95] By 1976, fifty homes dotted the grasslands that overlooked neighboring canyons. Soon another group of twenty-five houses, equipped with water and plumbing, were added to the community. Today, more than 100 buildings are found on the mesa. Electricity arrived in 1964, a 100,000-gallon water storage tank stood sentinel at the northern end of the community by the mid-1970s, and bus service delivered Ute children to the schools in town. White Mesa had become an important social and unifying symbol of the modern Utes' presence in southeastern Utah.[96]

Modernization has taken other forms. In 1977 the people of White Mesa elected a nine-member board and with the assistance of consultants formed the community organization called the Allen Canyon Ute Council, later named the White Mesa Ute Council. Because of the distance to Towaoc and the belief that the people from White Mesa were not receiving adequate consideration and representation in the larger body politic, the Utes elevated the White Mesa Ute Council to a more prominent role. In 1978 they hired Cleal Bradford, an experienced veteran in economic development, who had enjoyed a decade of working with the Utah Navajo Development Council before joining the Utes.

It did not take long to get things started. By 1981 the White Mesa community could boast a Headstart program, day care center, adult education classes, weekly health clinics, a senior-citizen program, a full-fledged recreation program, police protection from Towaoc, a monthly visit from a tribal judge, and local employment for twenty-five to thirty people. Four years later, area residents were also able to purchase some of their traditional grazing areas on north Elk Ridge, a move that brought deep satisfaction.[97]

Still another dramatic success occurred in schooling. A study completed by the tribe in 1977 showed that approximately one-third of the school-age children were receiving no formal education; another third were in foster care or detention centers; and half of the remaining third were living in other peoples' homes under the LDS church's placement program. Only one-sixth of those eligible were actually living at home and attending public schools. By 1983 the situation had changed dramatically: 42 percent of the entire population of White Mesa—including those enrolled in headstart, kindergarten through twelfth grade, college students, and people taking adult education classes—were now receiving some type of educational benefit and living on the mesa.[98]

Even with this growth and development, difficult problems still abounded. One of these centered around the hauling of radioactive uranium mill tailings from Monticello to the Energy Fuels company's uranium mill, five miles north of White Mesa. This tentative repository site had been in operation since 1980 but had closed its doors to the processing of uranium in 1991–92. In 1994 its doors could be opened again as a storage site. To some of the people of White Mesa, other Native Americans, and some Anglos, this was unacceptable. They expressed anger over not having been consulted; they feared that the groundwater that flows to the south off of Blue Mountain to White Mesa would be contaminated; and they were concerned about the possibility of the digging of additional storage pits that would disturb Indian graves nearby. A protest march of 200 people, held on 22 September 1994, made use of the power of the media to broadcast the concerns. As a result, the tailings were never hauled to the site.[99]

While this incident proved successful, at least as far as opponents to the site were concerned, other problems have arisen. Recently, there has been a rapid series of changes in leadership since Cleal Bradford left. The people of White Mesa have struggled to find a permanent director who has both a vision of future progress and is able to work with the various factions within the community. Family groups wedded to different political agendas, combined with struggles for power between dissenters inside and outside of the community, have created a rocky political course for the present. However, if history is a good indicator of the future, the people of White Mesa will overcome these temporary setbacks as they set forth into the twenty-first century.

Today, the community of White Mesa, comprised of a population of around 350 people, has undergone substantial changes. It has modern housing with electricity and running water; some houses even sport a

satellite dish. Many of the Ute people are employed in education and service industries such as schools and motels; some work for the tribal council; others help operate a cattle company and a store at White Mesa; while still others are employed at Towaoc in farming projects and in the local casino. Many are working towards economic self-sufficiency by obtaining job skills and college educations to help them compete in a rapidly changing economy.

Future plans include increased access to water from a seven-mile pipeline extending from Recapture Reservoir to White Mesa. This will allow the two underground wells that now service the community to act as a backup to the water treatment plant during periods of heavy use. Continued self-sufficiency of the cattle company through reinvestment from its sales and a greater emphasis in local education programs to help the youth are two other endeavors that have built pride and self-sufficiency. Finally, improving relations with and acceptance by the tribal council at Towaoc will continue to lead to more and better services. As the White Mesa Utes enter the twenty-first century, they can do so with optimism.

Yet despite all the new innovations, the land remains important to the Utes. From seventy-four-year-old Stella Eyetoo, who collects willows for baskets, to Edward Dutchie, Jr., who sits on the tribal council in Towaoc in an effort to improve conditions on White Mesa, to the children who play cowboys and Indians in the canyons where their forefathers hunted and fought to stay alive, the land will remain a central concern. The Utes of southeastern Utah have always depended upon these roots as a source of life that will continue to be nurtured as long as there is a Bear Dance, as long as their language is spoken, and as long as they think of themselves as the People.

A Navajo man photographed during the 1860s. (Marriott Library, University of Utah—U of U)

The Navajos of Utah

Nancy C. Maryboy and David Begay

Introduction

Navajos have been living in the Four Corners region of the American Southwest for hundreds of years. The land of the Navajo includes areas of southeastern Utah, northeastern Arizona, and northwestern New Mexico. Navajo people traditionally and historically refer to themselves as the Diné, meaning the People. Other variations in the meaning of "Diné" also exist—for example, Child of the Holy People. Nevertheless, all the variations of meaning are an integral part of one whole, which expresses an interrelationship with the cosmos. Sacred oral stories passed down from generation to generation tell of cosmological origins and continuous evolvement through four eras or worlds, ultimately leading to what the Navajos call *Hajíinéi*, the Emergence, that brought the Navajos to their present location.

Navajos always have believed that their homeland is geographically and spiritually located within the area bounded by four major sacred mountains. Today Navajo land, held in trust by the United States government, has been set aside by treaty and executive order as an Indian reservation; however, this reservation is significantly smaller than the land that was culturally placed within the area of the four sacred mountains.

The Navajo Reservation today extends over 25,000 square miles and includes parts of nine counties. It is the largest Indian reservation in the United States, being larger than the states of Connecticut, Massachusetts, New Hampshire, and Rhode Island, combined. According to the 1990 census, there were 219,198 Navajos in the United States, with the overwhelming majority living on the Navajo Reservation.

The four sacred mountains are located in three states: *Sisnaajini*—the east mountain (Mt. Blanca, located in south-central Colorado), *Tsoodzil*—the south mountain (Mt. Taylor, located in northwestern New Mexico), *Dook'o'oosliid*—the west mountain (San Francisco Peaks, lo-

cated in northwestern Arizona) and *Dibé Ntsaa*—the north mountain (Mt. Hesperus, located in southwestern Colorado). There are two additional mountains of great signficance located in New Mexico—*Chooli'i* (Gobernador Knob) and *Dzil Na Oodilii* (Huerfano Peak). Navajos in Utah also acknowledge the cultural significance of several other mountains, including *Naatsisaan* (Navajo Mountain), *Dzil Diloi* (Abajo Peaks), and *Shash Jaa* (Bear's Ears).

The following brief history of the Navajos of Utah attempts to present the perspective of the Navajo people themselves. This history differs from most standard textbooks in that it draws on oral history as told by Navajo elders as well as providing a reexamination of written materials from a native perspective. Both general American and Navajo history largely have been written from the point-of-view of the dominant society. Books about Native American history have been influenced by a multitude of interests: written through the eyes of colonizers, military leaders, missionaries, traders, and government officials—all with their own specific interests and purposes for writing. If Navajos and other native people had a written language earlier, history books might well be different, incorporating the viewpoints of the indigenous peoples.

Many native people feel that standard history texts do not contain the indigenous point of view. There are significant discrepancies between the written materials in libraries and the histories passed down for generations by Native Americans through word of mouth. Most history books traditionally have emphasized the conflicts between native peoples and the European newcomers, primarily military and social conflicts. The native perspective instead emphasizes social interconnections and the strong relationships with nature and spirit valued by most Indian groups.

The history of Utah Navajo people begins with oral history: origin stories and early interactions with Anasazi, Pueblo, and other peoples. Written history since the 1700s has documented Spanish and Mexican relations with Navajos, followed by American military invasion and colonization of Navajo lands. The history of Utah Navajos differs somewhat from that of other Navajos due to years of their interactions with Utes and Paiutes as well as Mormon and non-Mormon settlers, ranchers, and traders. Many Utah Navajos did not go to Fort Sumner during the time of the Long Walk of the 1860s, hiding in various canyons of southern Utah and northern Arizona.

This brief Navajo history will highlight significant events that occurred from prehistoric times to the present, divided into seven main categories:

1. Traditional Oral History—Stories of the Ancestors
2. Athabaskan heritage and migration theories
3. Pueblo Indian Relations
4. Spanish and Mexican Colonial Period
5. United States Military Conquest: The Long Walk and Fort Sumner Incarceration
6. American Colonization
7. Development of the Navajo Nation as a Sovereign Entity

Traditional Oral History—Stories of the Ancestors

Navajos, like all other indigenous people, have their own stories about the creation of the world and their place in that world. These stories have been handed down for countless generations, primarily by oral history and song. Because these stories were not written in books hundreds of years ago, western historians refer to them as pre-history—essentially the time before the coming of Europeans to the Americas.

Navajo origin stories begin with a First World of darkness (*Nihodilhil*). From this Dark World the Diné began a journey of emergence into the world of the present. In this First World there was only darkness, moisture, and mist. The mists were associated with the four directions: east, south, west, and north, and they had additional associations with colors: white, blue, yellow, and black. In the world of darkness there was water and land. Insect-like people lived in the first world, along with other spiritual beings. Ant People were among the first to dwell in this world; other spiritual beings in the dark world included Underwater People, Water Spirit or Water Monster, and Fish People.

Other *Diyin Dine'é*, referred to as Holy Beings or Spirit Beings, also dwelled in the First World. They were formed of mist but had human physical attributes, as well. Among these beings, some of the notable were First Man, First Woman, First Boy, First Girl, *Beegochidii*, Black God (*Haashch'ééshzhiní*), Talking God (*Haashch'éélti'í*), Hogan God (*Haashch'ééhwaan*), and Coyote (*Ma'ii*). These beings or people lived with the Insect People.

Where white clouds and black clouds met, First Man was formed, and where blue clouds and yellow clouds met, First Woman was formed. All the beings in the First World were able to understand each other, implying a universal language by which they communicated. Eventually there was a lot of disagreement among the beings and they were forced to leave the First World, through an opening in the east. With them, however, they took all the problems they had created.

They emerged into a Blue World (*Nihodootliizh*), the home of blue-colored birds. These blue-colored beings included blue birds, blue jays, and blue herons. Other animal beings also lived in this world: bobcats, badgers, kit foxes, mountain lions, and wolves. Again, the beings quarreled and were forced to leave, going in a southern direction, taking their problems with them.

The people next emerged into a Yellow World (*Niholsoi*), meeting other animal beings: squirrels, chipmunks, mice, turkeys, deer, spider people, lizards, and snakes. The people still had their problems and quarrelsome behaviors. Eventually the men and women separated and began to live on opposite sides of the river. During the time of the separation of the sexes, the men survived by hunting and planting; however, the women did not fare as well—they were not skilled hunters and did not tend to their fields. After four years the women were starving and begged to return to the men. After the sexes were reunited, Coyote stole the Water Spirit's baby. As a result, the Water Spirit got very angry and caused a great flood.

The people escaped the flood by climbing through a huge reed, led by the locust. The last animal to climb out of the reed was the turkey. It is said that as he was climbing up, the foamy water of the flood was rising and lapped at his tail, thus creating the white-streaked tail feathers of the wild turkey. The beings emerged at a place called *Hajíínéí*, into the White, or Glittering, World—the present world. Some stories say this place of emergence was in the mountains of Colorado, near Durango.

At this point, the small group had grown to include other holy beings, including insect beings, bird beings, and animal beings—each being contributing to the planning and organization of the world. First Man formed four main sacred mountains from the soil that was taken from the lower worlds and these became the sacred boundaries of the Diné world. Each mountain was fastened to the earth in a unique way and given special adornments and empowerments.

Although each mountain was given specific natural endowments, nevertheless, all of the mountains were also endowed with all of the natural beauties and powers of the universe. The complexity of understanding nature through relationships and interrelated processes of all things is the basis and foundation of the Navajo view of the sacred mountains. The deep natural communication that is ongoing in the universe can be expressed through many concepts. In this case, it is expressed through the four sacred mountains.

There are many stories about this time related to teachings of the

A Navajo man in ceremonial mask and costume, date and
location unknown. (Utah State Historical Society—USHS)

hogan, the sweat lodge, daylight, and night. Teachings about the stars,
sun, and moon were given at this time to the people. Eight main constel-
lations were created by the Holy Beings: the Male Revolving One, which
includes the Big Dipper; the Female Revolving One, part of Cassiopeia;
the Pleiades; First Slender One, which includes Orion; Man with Legs
Spread Apart, which includes Corvus; First Big One, which includes the
upper part of Scorpius; Rabbit Tracks, which incudes the lower part of
Scorpius; and Awaits the Dawn, the Milky Way.

The Holy Beings had an orderly plan for placing the stars in the Upper Darkness and were proceeding to place the stars carefully one by one, when mischievous Coyote grew impatient and flung the buckskin holding the stars into the sky. That is why, according to the story, there are many stars placed at random in the sky. What Coyote actually did was to create chaos, but out of that chaos emerged an order.

Sometime after the emergence to the Glittering World, a few women gave birth to monsters, as a result of transgressions that had occurred in the previous world. As the monsters matured they began to prey upon the people, causing the death of children and creating a climate of fear. When the monsters had killed off most of the young children, several events occurred which eventually resulted in the placing of the earth back into harmony. One morning in the pre-dawn, a baby was found on top of Gobernador Knob. Talking God found the baby girl and brought her to First Man and First Woman to raise. She grew in a spiritual way, attaining maturity in twelve days. The baby became known as Changing Woman (*Asdzáán Nádleehé*), the spiritual mother of all Navajos. When she came of age, she had the first puberty ceremony (*kinaaldá*).

Sometime later she became impregnated by the Sun. She gave birth to twin sons, later called Monster Slayer (*Naayéé' Neezghání*) and Born for Water (*Tobájíshchíní*). As the twin boys grew up, they became curious about who their father was. Very reluctantly Changing Woman told them that their father was the Sun. Aided by spiritual beings like Spider Woman, the boys traveled to the home of the Sun. There they went through a series of endurance tests to prove that they truly were sons of the Sun. After they passed all the tests devised by the Sun, they were offered many material goods; but they refused the goods, saying they only wanted the spiritual weapons of lightning (*Atsiniltl'ish K'aa'*—male zigzag lightning arrow and *Hatsoo'alghal K'aa'*—female straight lightning arrow) to kill the monsters (*naayéé'*) on earth.

When the twins returned to earth they used their weapons and killed the monsters, beginning with the giant *Yé'iitsoh Lá'í Naaghái*, thus making the earth safe again for human beings. Several of the monsters were spared by the twins, however. These monsters pleaded for their lives, saying they carried important lessons for humans. The monsters that were allowed to live included Hunger, Poverty, Lice, Old Age, and Sleepiness.

When the world was safe, the *Diyin Dine'é* left and Changing Woman went to a home prepared for her by the Sun, somewhere in the west. She created the four original Navajo clans from her body, and later people of these four clans migrated back to the land of the four sacred mountains.

The origins of Navajo ceremonies developed from these sacred narratives, and those teachings are still honored today. There are many Navajo stories about the return from the west and how other clans were created and merged. All the stories speak of migrations and adaptations.

Athabaskan Heritage and Migration Theories

There are many theories as to where Native Americans including the Navajos actually came from. It is not known for certain where the Navajos came from before they settled in the Southwest. Most anthropologists and archaeologists believe that Navajo people came from the north or central Asia, thousands of years ago. They say that a people they call *Na-Déné* crossed the Bering Strait during the last Ice Age when there was an ice passage between the hemispheres and arrived in what is now called Alaska. Over the centuries, they migrated south, spreading out throughout Canada and the United States, even into northern Mexico. Among the *Na-Déné* people were Athabaskans and, according to this theory, these are supposedly the ancestors of the Navajo. Somewhere on their journey from the far north, Athabaskans separated into two main groups—Northern and Southern Athabaskans. Although there is little physical evidence, such as artifacts, for this anthropological theory, there is much linguistic evidence. Even today, similar words exist among Northern and Southern Athabaskans.

Other approaches to the anthropological migration theories emphasize physical human evidence, interpreted to support the Bering Strait migration theory. There are striking physical similarities between Navajo and Tibetan people, for example, as well as between Navajo and Mongolian people.

The group of people known as Southern Athabaskans migrated to the south over the course of hundreds of years, according to anthropological theory. They may have traveled south along the Pacific Coast, or they may have traveled through the Great Basin near the vicinity of present-day Salt Lake City, or through the Rocky Mountains or the western Great Plains. The migrations may have taken hundreds or thousands of years. Most probably people traveled in small nomadic groups, living primarily as hunters and gatherers. At some point, Navajos split off from other Southern Athabaskans. Some historians believe that Navajos migrated into the Southwest sometime between A.D. 200 and 1300. Some of the other Southern Athabaskans went as far south as northern Mexico, while still others were the ancestors of modern-day Apaches, Hoopa, and other tribes. Among the languages of Navajos and Apaches there are many

This Navajo sand painting shows a Yei rug. (USHS)

linguistic similarities, and, in some cases, there are even similar spiritual and ceremonial practices. Apache Sunrise ceremonies are similar to the Navajo *Kinaaldá*, for example, both being puberty ceremonies to acknowl-

edge the coming of age of young women. Both are based on oral story traditions of Changing Woman. Navajo ancestors may have intermingled with ancient Fremont Indians and with the Anasazi.

Although many Native Americans are well aware of the anthropological theories of migration, most traditional origin stories do not make any specific mention of crossing a passage like the Bering Strait and traveling south from a land of ice. Most native stories tend to emphasize how the people originated from what they now identify as their homeland. Navajos have passed down elaborate and complex origin stories describing their emergence from the earlier four worlds into the land of the four sacred mountains of the Southwest. For many Navajo students these two theories are difficult to reconcile, with schools teaching the anthropological version while at home the young people learn the traditional origin stories.

Navajo origin stories, as mentioned, speak of how Changing Woman created the original four clans and how the Navajo people returned from the west to their homeland in the Four Corners region. The stories also speak of a group separating from the main group of Navajos and traveling north. These Navajos are referred to as the *Diné Nahódlóonii*. It is said that if the two groups ever meet again, misfortune could occur. Among the complex Navajo migration stories, however, there are no stories of Navajo ancestors coming down south from the far north. Some Athabaskan groups—for example Jicarilla Apache—do have other migration stories that include references to a journey from the far north. The Mescalero Apache refer to an earlier time and place—a Land of Ever Winter—and to their journey south from there.[1] Many of the details of these oral stories are now being lost to the present generation.

Pueblo Indian Relations

After the Navajos returned from the west, according to oral tradition they settled in an large area they called Dinétah, which is located southeast of present-day Farmington, New Mexico. There is abundant archaeological evidence of Navajo occupation throughout Dinétah. Ancient hogan structures, sweathouses, and fortresses exist alongside petroglyphs and pictographs throughout the area. The rock art illustrates Navajo ceremonial arts that are clearly recognizable by Navajos today.

It is not certain when Navajos occupied Dinétah; but, based on available archaeological and anthropological data, it has been assumed that it was around A.D. 900 to 1525.[2] Navajo oral stories speak of a relationship with the prehistoric Anasazi while Pueblo Bonito in Chaco Canyon was

being built, which suggests Navajo presence in the area as early as A.D. 900. The Navajo word for corn is *naadą́ą́*, referring to an enemy's or non-Navajo's plant food.[3] This suggests that other people in the area were growing corn before the arrival of the Navajo and that there were adaptive relationships between Navajos and Anasazi. The word *Anasazi* is also a Navajo word, referring to ancient relationships with an enemy or, at the least, a non-Navajo group. Since the Anasazi are generally believed to have left the Four Corners area by 1300, this suggests that Navajos may have been in the area prior to the Anasazi migration out of the region.

Harry Walters, a Navajo scholar at Diné College, Tsaile, Arizona, writes: "Navajo oral history has no account of early Navajos living further north of the southern Colorado mountains. The emergence into this world, from three previous worlds beneath the surface of this earth took place somewhere in the mountains near La Plata, Colorado. According to the Navajo tradition, this was the beginning of the Earth Surface People."[4]

Regardless of how or when Navajo ancestors entered the Four Corners region, many sources agree that there were extensive migrations and intertribal adaptations between and among Navajos and Anasazi (ancestral Pueblo people) and among Navajos and historic Pueblo peoples. "Everywhere the Athabaskans went," comments Harry Walters, "they were influenced by people they encountered and they themselves also introduced new ideas and technology to new areas. The Athabaskans were responsible for the introduction of the woodland pottery, the hogan, tipi, shield and barbed-point bone and flint points and the moccasins to the southwest."[5]

In southeastern Utah, archaeologists suggest later dates for the arrival of the Navajos. In San Juan County, the earliest existing known Navajo site (a hogan site in White Canyon, west of Bear's Ears) has a tree-ring date of 1620. In several Spanish maps dating from the 1660s Navajo territory was described as extending "well north" of the San Juan River. Early treaties and maps made reference to Navajos occupying areas of Utah as far north as the present town of Green River.

From the early 1500s to the late 1700s Navajos occupied the area of Dinétah. This period has been generally divided into two phases: the Dinétah Phase, from 1550 to 1700, and the Gobernador Phase, from 1700 to 1775. The major difference between the two phases results from the aftermath of the intertribal Pueblo Revolt of 1680, when many Pueblo people moved into Dinétah to avoid the wrath of the returning Spaniards.

Spanish and Mexican Colonial Period

Spaniards had arrived in the Southwest in 1540 with the army of Francisco Vasquez de Coronado. Almost fifty years earlier, in 1492, Christopher Columbus had landed on an island in the Caribbean Sea, "discovering," he said, a "new world." The term New World seems ironic, since North and South America were heavily populated by native people, and had been occupied for more than 12,000 years. The Spanish conquistador Hernan Cortez landed on the eastern coast of Mexico in 1519 and conquered the Aztecs and other native groups. The Aztec leader Montezuma was killed at this time, but later legends told of his return and recapture in southern Utah. His name lives on in the present town of Montezuma Creek, Utah, and that of his people in Aztec, New Mexico. A motel in Bluff, Utah, embraces the myth with the name Recapture Lodge. The name of Cortez lives on through the town of Cortez, Colorado, just east of Montezuma Canyon.

The first Spanish expedition to come into the American Southwest was under the leadership of Coronado. He was guided by a black slave named Esteban, who was one of the few survivors of a Spanish shipwreck off the coast of Florida in 1528. Esteban journeyed throughout the southeastern part of the United States for almost eight years until he found his way to Mexico City. He later joined Coronado's expedition into the Southwest and was killed in a confrontation with Zuni Indians, ironically while proclaiming himself immortal.

Coronado spent several years roaming around the Southwest searching for gold and the fabled Seven Cities of Cibola. He visited Zuni and Hopi pueblos and undoubtedly came into contact with Navajos at this time. The Navajo name for Spaniard is *Nakai*, meaning "those who wander around," referring to the various expeditions that frequently came into Navajo country. The first recorded contact between Navajos and the Spanish invaders came in 1583 in the area of Dinétah. An expedition led by Antonio de Espejo refers to the Querechos Indians near Mt. Taylor. The Spanish also at times referred to Navajos as "Apaches de Navajo," leading to some confusion for future historians.

For the next hundred years the Spanish attempted to colonize the Southwest. Juan de Oñate came to the Rio Grande in 1595 with the intent to colonize the area. His powerful army subjugated many of the Pueblo Indians. Any Pueblo resistance was dealt with by severe and brutal measures. In one infamous incident, residents of Acoma Pueblo were attacked by Oñate's army; adult males who survived the attack were pun-

ished and tortured by having one foot cut off and being enslaved. Women also were enslaved, as were older children, some for as long as twenty-five years. Countless other stories of Spanish brutality exist among the Pueblo people, and even today Oñate's name is held in opprobrium among the Navajos and Pueblos.

Along with military colonization came forced Christianization. The native inhabitants were coerced into accepting Christianity, while their own religious practices were forbidden. Spanish records show that many thousands of Indians were baptized. Some reportedly were killed soon after the baptismal ceremony. There was an attempt at complete Spanish domination. Many Native Americans were enslaved, and some were sent to work in mines as far away as Mexico. There are no records of any returning to their own country. The king of Spain claimed the land of the Southwest, including most of present-day Utah, Nevada, Arizona, New Mexico, and California, awarding large land grants to the conquistadors, missionaries, and colonizers.

A tremendous depopulation of native peoples occurred at this time. Millions of native people died throughout the Americas from warfare, slavery, and diseases brought by the Spanish invaders. The native people had no immunity to many of the diseases, such as smallpox, brought by the Spaniards. In some cases, entire villages and tribes across the continents of North and South America were wiped out by disease.

By 1680 the Pueblo Indians, aided by various Navajo and Apache groups, had had enough of the brutality and atrocities of forced subjugation. Under the leadership of a medicine man from San Juan Pueblo named Popé, native people rose up in defense of their rights. This has been called the Pueblo Revolt by historians, but from a native perspective it might more appropriately be termed a war for independence.

The Pueblo Revolt of 1680 was an extreme reaction to an extreme situation. It is estimated that around 400 Spaniards were killed in the first days of the revolt. The rebellion became so widespread that the Spanish were forced out of the territory and returned to Mexico.

In 1693 the Spanish returned to the Rio Grande Valley. By this time the Pueblo people were no longer united and, as a result, the Spanish soon reconquered the area. Many natives fled the pueblos during this period, taking refuge among the Navajos in the Dinétah area. There was an intermixing of Navajo and Pueblo cultures during this time. Many Navajo clans are descended from Pueblo ancestry, which have their roots in this era. Other Navajo clans such as *Nakai Dine'é* acknowledge their descent from certain Spanish and Mexican ancestors.

Social interaction among the various Pueblo Indians and Navajos intensified during this time. Navajos began to rely more on farming and sheep herding as a way of life. It is believed that much cultural and spiritual sharing took place as well. Even today one can see remains of the ancient wood and stone structures that were constructed during this era. Fortresses on almost inaccessible cliffs illustrate the dangers faced by the people, while pueblitos, circular hogans built alongside square stone buildings, show the social interaction among cultures.

Eventually many of the Pueblo Indians returned to their old communities and learned to co-exist with the returning Spanish. Others remained with Navajo families, however, and gradually became adopted into the Navajo clan system.

Life became extremely dangerous in Dinétah. During the latter part of the 1700s the Spanish created alliances with the Comanches and Utes, and these combined with various French, Pawnee, and Pueblo interests were aimed at weakening and defeating the Navajos. Atrocities were committed on all sides. Constant raiding and slave-taking occurred. It is estimated that during the early 1800s more than 66 percent of all Navajo families had experienced the loss of members to slavery. Navajo children were taken from their families and sold at auction in Santa Fe, Taos, and other places. Others were sent deep into Mexico to work in the silver mines. Most never returned. Many Navajo families retell stories of slaves taken or escaping during this time.

In 1821 Mexico gained its independence from Spain; consequently, the Spanish government withdrew from the Southwest. Many of the people of Spanish origin remained, however, becoming Mexicans under the new regime. All of the people living in what became Mexican territory were proclaimed to be under the rule of the Republic of Mexico, including Navajos living in what is presently Arizona, New Mexico, and Utah. This proclamation was a unilateral declaration made without Navajo consent.

Skirmishes, slave raids, and massacres occurred with increasing frequency. The Mexicans condoned and even increased raiding and slave-taking efforts. Gradually Navajos continued to move out of Dinétah, populating areas such as Bear's Ears in Utah, Canyon de Chelly, Mount Taylor, Navajo Mountain, and as far west as the Grand Canyon.

Many treaties were hastily written and just as hastily discarded. Neither the Spanish nor the Mexicans understood the Navajo decentralized political structure, whereby no one headman could speak or sign treaties for all Navajos. Another factor contributing to the lack of cross-cultural

Two Navajos with a herd of goats near their hogan, date unknown. (U of U)

understanding was language. Few Navajos understood Spanish or English, and certainly almost no Spaniards, Mexicans, or Americans could speak or understand Navajo. Apart from the language, few Europeans could even begin to understand the Navajo worldview. European invaders had their own policies and priorities: to Christianize, to enslave, to take over the land. None was based on understanding or reciprocity between cultures.

As hostilities increased during the Mexican era, from 1821 to 1848, more treaties were written, but they all failed to bring about a lasting peace. Military expeditions were sent into Navajo country with increasing frequency. These expeditions were often accompanied by native scouts and volunteer militia from New Mexico. One of the first known expeditions entered in 1823 into what is now Utah. Jose Antonio Vizcarra commanded an expedition of 1,500 men, setting out from Santa Fe with orders to punish certain Navajos and bring about peace. Vizcarra is known to have traveled through Oljeto Creek in southeastern Utah. At the same time, another Mexican force under Don Francisco Salazar entered into Utah following the trail to Bear's Ears and fighting Navajos in Chinle

Wash.[6] Both Mexican military officers described seeing traces of Navajos fleeing north across the San Juan River into what is now Utah.

Many accounts written during the following forty years mention Navajos, Paiutes, and Utes traveling through and living in the area of southern Utah. In 1832, for example, Navajos were reported living north of the San Juan River. It is recorded that Hastiin Beyal was born at the head of Grand Gulch during this time.[7] The grandparents of a Navajo man called White Sheep were born in the 1820s, one near Bear's Ears and the other near the San Juan River. The Navajo headman K'aayelli was born around 1801 near Bear's Ears. Kigalia Spring, north of Bear's Ears, was later named after him. Another Navajo headman called Kee Diniihí was born in White Canyon in 1821. Navajos were reported living as far north as Monticello, Utah, in 1839, on a map drawn by a traveler, T.J. Farnam, and other trappers and travelers also mentioned Navajos in the area.[8]

United States Military Conquest: The Long Walk and Fort Sumner Incarceration

Although some of the following history does not directly pertain to Utah and Utah Navajos, the events are seminal in Navajo history, impacting profoundly all Navajos from the time of the Long Walk to the present. In 1846 the United States declared war on the Republic of Mexico. Colonel Stephen W. Kearny entered New Mexico in August and took over the province with no resistance from the Mexican troops there. The Navajos first thought that the Americans would be allies with them against their common enemy, the Mexicans. To their surprise, however, the Americans sided immediately with the Mexicans, declaring that they would protect Mexican colonists against all hostile Indians, including Apaches and Navajos. Kearny dispatched Colonel Alexander Doniphan to lead an armed expedition into Navajo country. This was the first U.S. military expedition into the heart of *Diné Bikéyah*, Navajo land. Part of the expedition followed the San Juan River southwest towards Chinle Wash. Utah Navajos may have seen American soldiers for the first time during this period.

By the time of the arrival of the American soldiers, hostilities were so rampant on all sides that attempts by the Americans to enter into meaningful peace treaties with the Navajo people were not worth the paper on which they were written. As was the case during the Spanish and Mexican occupation of the territory, treaties were written and broken almost immediately by one side or the other. A close reading of Spanish, Mexi-

can, and American military and governmental documents indicates that some of the Europeans shot Navajo and Apache men and women on sight, while children and babies were taken captives and sold into the slave markets.

One of the first military projects of the Americans was to build a fort—Fort Defiance—in Navajo country. There were regular negotiations between American officers and Navajo leaders. Although Navajos were not centralized in the European sense, they did come together into groups by clan and close-knit families. They were led by various leaders often referred to as *haské nahat'á* (warrior leaders) and *hozhooji nahat'á* (peace leaders). The best known leader of this time was Naabaahni (Narbona). Today these leaders are commonly known by their Spanish names, but they had various Navajo names by which they are known among traditional Navajos: Barboncito (Hastiin Dághá, Man With Mustache, and his warrior names, Haské Yil Deeyá and Hashké Yil Deswod) from Canyon de Chelly, Zarcillos Largos (Naat'áani Náádleel, Keeps Becoming Leader), and Ganado Mucho (Tótsohnii Hastiin). Manuelito (Hastiin Ch'ilhaajinii, Man of Dark Plants Emerging) also became a well-known warrior and leader. He was born in Utah, near Bear's Ears and is still known among the Navajo as Askii Diyin (Holy Boy) and Ch'il Haajin.

Navajos refer to the 1850s and early 1860s as a troubled period—*Náhonzoodáá'*—during which they had to constantly move around in defense of their livestock and families. They had to keep ahead of their enemies at all times. No permanent structures could be built, and their hogans and cornfields often were discovered and burned. Sheep and horses were stolen. Families were massacred and children were taken to be sold. Enemies came from all directions: Utes, Comanches, Jicarilla Apaches, Zunis, New Mexicans, and Americans. Alliances were constantly shifting. Americans, French, Spanish, and in some cases Mormons, reportedly furnished the Utes, Comanches, and Pawnees with guns, while the Navajos had to fight primarily with bows and arrows and spears.

With the coming of the Civil War there was a temporary withdrawal of American soldiers from the area, and many Navajos probably believed that they had seen the last of the Americans. But even before the war ended U.S. soldiers returned to subjugate the Navajos. The United States declared war on the Navajos under the military command of General James Carleton. Many Americans wanted more than a Navajo defeat—they also wanted the land of the Navajos for grazing and mining. Carleton in particular was interested in minerals. He felt that if the Navajos were removed far from their homeland, Americans could mine their territory

A Navajo hogan in Monument Valley. (USHS)

and men like himself could reap great profits. To further this scenario, Carleton immediately reserved an area in New Mexico for the removal of the Navajos. This was Bosque Redondo (Round Grove) on the Pecos River. The area was later called Fort Sumner by the Americans and *Hweeldi* by the Navajo.

Carleton hired Christopher "Kit" Carson, a former Indian fighter and Ute agent, to help carry out his plan. Carson's quite ruthless "scorched earth" policy was highly effective. Carson entered Navajo country in the summer of 1863 with a force of about 700 soldiers, Indian scouts, and New Mexico volunteers. Wherever he went, he gave orders to torch the Navajos' homes, burn their cornfields, cut down peach orchards, destroy squash and melon fields, and take the livestock. Soon food became very scarce and the Navajos began to experience starvation. Many were forced to eat the limited wild game, cedar berries, pine nuts, yucca fruits, wild potatoes, and other wild foods available that fall.[9] It was all-out war. On every side the enemies of the Navajos were pressing in and aiding the soldiers, including Ute, Hopi, Pueblo, and Zuni scouts, some disaffected Navajos, along with various Kiowas, Comanches, and Apaches. Not all the Pueblo people were enemies of the Navajo, however. Some Navajos took refuge at Jemez Pueblo as well as with other Pueblo groups where there had been centuries of intermarriage and adoption.

The Mescalero Apaches were also at war with the U.S. government and were the first group to be taken to Fort Sumner. Kit Carson made his headquarters at Fort Defiance and began to concentrate his efforts in the Canyon de Chelly area, the assumed stronghold of the Navajo.

By December 1863 the Navajos were in desperate shape. They were poor and hungry and the slave raiding had done much damage. It has been estimated that over one-third of the Navajos were enslaved in New Mexico during this era. Resentment over the slave trade was very high among the Navajos, as it was among the New Mexicans and Pueblo people who had suffered from Navajo raiding. In comparison with the thousands of enslaved Navajos, however, the number of slaves taken by the Navajos was limited.

Kit Carson continued to pursue his strategy of forced starvation. He ordered his men to destroy all waterholes and take all horses, cattle, sheep and goats. He attempted to convince the Navajos that they would be safer under his protection and that they would be well fed by the U.S. Army. Eventually many of the Navajos simply gave up and surrendered. They were ordered to gather at Fort Defiance and traveled in groups the more than 300 miles to Fort Sumner.

The winter of 1863–64 was extraordinarily cold. Most of the Navajo captives did not have adequate shoes or clothing. Carson had promised protection and food, yet what was given was grossly inadequate. The food that was provided was new to the Indians. They were not told how to prepare coffee beans and white flour, for example. People attempted to cook the beans, throwing out the water they were boiled in. People mixed flour with ash, not knowing how to cook with it. Many became sick and died from the unfamiliar food.

Almost every Navajo family has passed down stories about the horrors of the Long Walk. People were forced to walk twelve to fifteen miles a day. They were constantly fatigued and weakened by near starvation. Enemies followed the convoys, snatching captives almost at will. By the time the Navajo leader Barboncito reached Fort Sumner he had lost a son and a daughter to the slave raiders. He never saw them again. This occurred under so-called military-escort protection. The physical and psychological suffering was tremendous. The people were uprooted from their very way of life, since their life and spirituality were rooted in their land and mountains. When they passed Mt. Taylor, near present-day Grants, New Mexico, they were leaving the protection of the four sacred mountains. Oral traditions say that the Navajo people ceased to perform most ceremonies during the time of their captivity at Fort Sumner.

Clara Maryboy of White Rocks, Utah, recounted her great-grandmother's experience. She told how each night the Navajos were covered with a large tarp which was nailed down over the captives.[10] Others have told of elderly people and pregnant women who lagged behind and were shot. The weakest were left to die along the trail. The survivors were not allowed to go back and bury their family members and later told heartbreaking stories of hearing coyotes howl where their relatives had fallen.

There were several convoys of Navajo prisoners. The first convoy reached Fort Sumner fairly intact. Several other convoys which traveled later in March were hit by severe snowstorms, however, and hundreds of people died or disappeared along the way.

By November 1864 there were more than 8,000 Navajos at Bosque Redondo. It soon became evident that General Carleton's concept of a Navajo utopia of farming, education, and civilization was not going to work out in the area. He was not even able to feed the large numbers of prisoners of war. People continued to starve after they reached Fort Sumner. The rations were inadequate, and the cornfields that Navajos were forced to plant failed three years in a row, due to natural disasters such as flooding from the Pecos River, severe hailstorms, drought, and insect damage. Firewood became increasingly scarce, and in some cases people reportedly had to go twenty or thirty miles for firewood. There was little shelter from the freezing weather and hot sun except holes that people dug into the earth. Carleton wanted Navajos to live in hastily constructed homes, but this was foreign to the Navajos, who also did not want to live where others had died. In addition, the Mescaleros and Navajos did not get along in the confined area. Disease was rampant; the Navajos had little immunity to the white man's diseases such as smallpox, chickenpox, and pneumonia. Women had to prostitute themselves in order to provide food for their families, and venereal disease became another horror. The Comanches and New Mexicans were constantly raiding, raping, and taking slaves and livestock.

The military and civilian authorities in charge of the Navajo prisoners were constantly at odds. Corruption was widespread. Cattle, brought in to feed the prisoners, were sold by unscrupulous contractors for their own profit. Most of the appropriations were squandered or substituted with useless materials. Some food that was shipped in was contaminated. It was reported that flour was mixed with ground plaster and that dried bread was contaminated by rat droppings. Clothing and blankets were of poor quality. The water was highly alkaline and not good to drink or

Three Navajo horsemen make their way up a sand dune. (USHS)

to irrigate crops. The physical and mental anguish of the prisoners was great.

The conditions at Fort Sumner were so deplorable that many Navajos risked slavery and starvation to escape. Many left the reservation; some were recaptured. The Mescalero Apaches all left as a group. One winter 900 Navajos escaped. The policy of General Carleton failed miserably, at a very high cost of lives and government resources.

There were many Navajos who never went to Fort Sumner. People hid out as far west as the Grand Canyon and as far north as Navajo Mountain and Bear's Ears. Other small groups who had time to prepare were able to survive in remote canyons. Some escaped into Utah across the San Juan River. Haashkéneinii took his group from Monument Valley to a remote area of Navajo Mountain. He had learned in 1863 that both soldiers and Utes were coming to Monument Valley and had prepared his people to leave. They reportedly moved to the San Juan River, "moving at night and hiding by day."[11] Finally they reached Navajo Mountain, where they hid out until 1868. K'aayélii retreated to the area around Bear's Ears and his descendants still tell stories today with pride about how he and his people never surrendered.

One of the most influential and powerful Navajo leaders, Manuelito, who was born in Utah, hid out for several years, avoiding the soldiers but being attacked several times by Ute forces. Finally, when his force was

down to only a few wounded and starving warriors, he surrendered, his people taking pride in the fact that he was never captured.

The Black Hawk War began in central Utah in the mid-1860s, and fighting continued into the early 1870s. This was primarily a war of cattle raids, guerilla warfare, and pillaging led by Black Hawk, a charismatic Ute leader of a mixed and fluctuating coalition of Utes, Navajos, and Paiutes. Black Hawk led his forces into battle and conducted guerilla raids in order to try to feed his increasingly desperate people while also hoping to claim control of some traditional Indian lands. The Mormon settlers fought back but did not call in federal troops for aid. Brigham Young tried to minimize reports of the war, fearing that a large-scale war might lead to an increased federal presence in the region. Even today, this conflict is played down in Utah history books.[12]

Stories are told that members of other tribes came to Navajo leaders around Canyon de Chelly to ask for aid in their own fights against the white men. One even tells of a delegation of Lakota Sioux warriors who came to Navajos to request aid.[13]

By 1868 over 3,000 Navajos had perished at Fort Sumner and close to 1,000 had escaped. Finally, the corrupt administration of Fort Sumner came to the attention of high government officials and lawmakers. General Carleton was relieved of his command in August 1866 and an investigative commission traveled to Fort Sumner to see the conditions. They were horrified at the misery and corruption.

In late spring 1868 General William Sherman arrived to negotiate with the remaining Navajos at Fort Sumner. Barboncito was the chief spokesman for the Navajos. Many Navajos were ill and homesick. As a result of the negotiations, a treaty was signed on June 1 and ratified by President Andrew Johnson on August 12, 1868.

The treaty negotiations were carried out through three languages, a cumbersome interpretive process. Statements made in Navajo were translated into Spanish by Jesus Arviso, a former slave, and from Spanish to English by James Sutherland.[14] When statements were made in English, the process was reversed. Often the meaning was obscured during the translation process. Navajo and English languages are very different from one another and accurate translation is extremely difficult. It is probable that neither group completely understood the other.

Barboncito was the lead negotiator for the Navajo. Many of his statements have been preserved to the present. "Our grandfathers had no idea of living in any other country except our own," he told General Sherman. He described the living conditions of the Navajo at Bosque Redondo as a

great impoverishment. Now they had nothing to eat and nothing to wear except gunny sacks. They had sunk into absolute poverty and despair. He could no longer sleep at night because of the condition of his people and he hated the trip to the commissary for food because he did not like to be fed like a child. "I hope to God that you will not ask me to go to any other country except my own," he stated in response to the peace commission's tentative plan to send all native peoples to reservations in "the land of the Cherokee" in present-day Oklahoma.[15]

General Sherman was struck by how the Navajos had "sunk into a condition of absolute poverty and despair."[16] Much of Sherman's knowledge came from a sympathetic agent at Bosque Redondo. Agent Thomas H. Dodd had reported to Sherman that the Navajos had worked diligently at their fields but that each year the crops were destroyed by insects, floods, drought, and the unproductive alkaline soil. The peace commission finally decided to allow the Navajos to return home.

The Treaty of 1868 was and remains a very important document for the Navajo people. The treaty recognized the sovereign status of the Navajo and was a legal compact between two sovereign nations. With the signing of the treaty, Navajos were finally free to return to their homeland.

On June 18, 1868, the Navajos finally began their journey home. The column of returning Navajos was more than ten miles long, with 50 six-mule wagons. It has been said that when the people saw the peak of Mt. Taylor, the sacred mountain of the south, tears of grief and joy were shed and many prayers were said as they re-entered into the land of the four sacred mountains.

The return route led through Albuquerque. Navajos began arriving in the Fort Defiance area in late July, ending a hot, tiresome five-week journey. Overriding everything in the minds of the Navajos was the fact that they were finally allowed to return to their beloved homeland, even though it had been significantly reduced to less than one-fourth of their original holdings.

American Colonization

Although the Navajo people were free to return home, there were many difficulties ahead. The U.S. government had promised to feed the people, under the trustee status of the treaty, but the promised annuities and food did not all come as promised. Many families remained at Fort Wingate and Fort Defiance waiting for livestock and farming supplies. When sheep and goats were finally distributed to families, the people

Navajos gather to receive federal government rations in 1879. (U of U)

protected and cared for them. Even though families were hungry, they did not butcher the sheep, wanting to build up their small herds. Eventually the livestock multiplied and the people became increasingly self-reliant.

The increases in livestock required more pasture and demanded more mobility, so as not to deplete the land. Out of necessity, the Navajos began going out farther than the treaty boundaries. At the same time, white ranchers and homesteaders began to move deeper into the public domain lands, leading to continual conflicts. This was the case in southern Utah as on the rest of the reservation. Navajos began to cross the San Juan River and settle around Bluff and Montezuma Creek. They already had a long history of living near Bear's Ears, Navajo Mountain, and Monument Valley. They came into conflict with Utes in some instances and there were escalating hostilities and confrontations. There also were conflicts with whites, including ranchers, Mormon homesteaders, and some traders. Many groups were vying for the land near the San Juan River.

Land ownership was a concept foreign to the Navajo, as it was to most Native Americans. Navajos did not understand why they needed to

A Navajo weaver and her husband. (USHS)

apply for land that they felt had always belonged to them. Besides, how could you own the land any more than you could own the stars and the clouds? Furthermore, Navajo hogans and shelters did not qualify as legal land improvements, as did the buildings of the white men, so Navajos often lost control of their land. As the conflicts escalated, so too did the raiding. Manuelito was put in charge of the first Navajo police force, which was developed with the primary charge of returning livestock taken from white settlers. It was felt that a Navajo policeman could better explain the reasons behind the law enforcement to other Navajos than could a non-Navajo-speaking government authority.

The period between 1870 and 1900 saw many changes. The increased development of a barter economy began to change the dynamics of the traditional economy, and a system based on money began to develop. People began trading for outside goods. Navajo rugs were exchanged to white traders for desired goods and services. Traders built larger trading posts in the area and brought in more and varied goods. Traders also began to influence some of the patterns of rugs being woven. Brightly colored aniline dyes and Germantown yarns changed the look of Navajo rugs. In many cases, the women's rugs were the family's main trade item. Silversmiths became increasingly skilled but for some years most of their

silverwork was designed and created for their families, with little going to the trading posts.

Another force that impacted Navajo life in general (though not as much in Utah) was the construction of railroads, particularly the Atlantic and Pacific Railroad as it crossed New Mexico. Along with some wage-earning jobs, however, the railroad brought whiskey and the beginnings of a serious alcohol problem throughout the Southwest.

Many of the promises made to the Navajos in the Treaty of 1868 were never fulfilled. Most of the Indian agents were apathetic; in some cases, they were even unsympathetic to their Navajo charges. There was tremendous turnover among the agents. This was not only a Navajo problem, it was true on the majority of Indian reservations across the country. Several of the Navajo Indian agents, however, tried to get the federal government to fulfill its obligations. During several hard years with a severe shortage of food and commodities due to drought and other natural disasters, Navajos were starving. Agent Dennis Riordan was concerned and frustrated in the 1880s. In one of his reports to Washington, he described the situation:

> The reservation embraces about 10,000 square miles of the most worthless land that ever laid outdoors.... The country is almost entirely rock. An Illinois or Iowa or Kansas farmer would laugh to scorn the assertion that you could raise anything there. However, 17,000 Indians managed to extract their living from it without government aid. If they were not the best Indians on the continent, they would not do it.... No help is given to the indigent and helpless Indians, the agent being compelled to see them suffer under his eyes or else to supply the much needed articles at his own expense.... The United States has never fulfilled its promise made to them by the treaty."[17]

Indian agents could rarely cover all their assigned territory. The Navajo Reservation was large and agents could only travel by horseback. Also, many agents simply did not want to leave the safety and comfort of their posts. Consequently, many Navajos had little or no contact with agents as the years went by. Agents usually did not stay long in Navajo territory. The turnover was very high. The isolation was difficult for the agents' families and the pressures were great. Although they were backed up by the military, when necessary, they were often the only source of government authority in the area, and their resources were severely lim-

ited. Their effectiveness also was weakened by the lack of food and supplies they could obtain. In addition, not all Navajos recognized or truly consented to their authority.

As more and more Navajos began to move out of the ceded boundaries established by the treaty, agents began to realize that the reservation needed to expand in order to accommodate the growing Navajo economic needs. Several additions were made to the original treaty reservations. Lands in northern Arizona, New Mexico, and southeastern Utah were part of this expansion. A significant addition to the reservation came with an executive order of 1884, when much of what is now Utah Navajo land was added. Areas including the Aneth Expansion (1905) and the Paiute Strip (1933) were added, taken away, and then re-added according to political and economic whims, eventually resulting in the reservation boundaries of today.

Life 100 years ago in southern Utah was often uneasy, with frequent hostilities among Navajo, Utes, Mormon settlers, other Anglo ranchers and homesteaders, and, increasingly, prospectors and miners. Shootings and other physical violence were common. In some cases both Mormons and non-Mormons were accused of supplying guns to the Navajos to further their own plans. H.L. Mitchell founded the area's first white settlement in 1878, at the mouth of McElmo Canyon. Montezuma Creek was settled in 1878 and Bluff was founded by Mormon settlers in 1880. Increasingly, all the white settlers wanted the Navajos to be contained on the south side of the San Juan River. Mormons and non-Mormons alike wanted the north side of the river and all the water rights. Much of the conflict was based on greed, observed army officers who were often called in to settle armed disputes. "My sympathies are very much with the Navajos," stated a Captain Ketchum from Fort Lewis about one incident. "The people who complain against them are the very worst set of villains in existence."[18]

Other conflicts took place in the Monument Valley area, where four prospectors were murdered over a period of time, all trespassing in a sensitive area where they had been advised they did not belong. Headmen in the area did not want precious metals found in their area, because they did not want the rush of miners that would follow a find. The prospectors killed in late 1879 or early 1880 were James Merrick and Ernest Mitchell, son of H.L. Mitchell who had settled at the mouth of McElmo Canyon. In 1884 two other prospectors were killed near Navajo Mountain, triggering a hunt for the suspected Navajos. No one was ever indicted for the murders.

Another shooting took place at Rincon, several miles west of Bluff, Utah. Amasa Barton, who ran a small trading post there, was murdered by Navajos. This incident almost precipitated a war when sixty angry Navajos rode into Bluff ready for a fight. As in much of the oral history of San Juan County, the Navajo and white settlers' accounts of the incident differ somewhat.

Reformers began to emphasize the education of Indian people across the United States during the late nineteenth century. Christian denominations including Roman Catholic, Dutch Reformed, and Presbyterian churches took up the task of teaching various Indian groups. Even earlier, Navajo oral histories mention *enishoodi* (priests) working among them at Fort Sumner.[19]

Article VI of the Navajo Treaty of 1868 stipulated that education was to be compulsory for not less than ten years after the signing of the treaty. The government was to provide one schoolhouse and one teacher for every thirty Navajo pupils between the ages of six and sixteen, who could be induced or compelled to attend school. These provisions of the treaty were never fulfilled. In fact, many Navajos argue that the treaty obligations regarding education have never been fulfilled to this day.

Indian education was aimed at civilizing, "taking the savage out of the Indian." Acculturation and assimilation into mainstream society were the ultimate goals. Courts of Indian Offenses were established in the 1880s and 1890s with the purpose of abolishing all forms of Indian ceremony and "heathenish practices." Offenders (practitioners of native spiritual practices) were incarcerated through these tribunals.

Complete assimilation into mainstream society was thought to be the salvation of the tribes. The aim was to educate the younger tribal members through inculcation of the western belief system and the English language. It was believed that the younger people would assimilate the new practices more readily and that eventually the old ways would become ways of the past. Across the United States, Indian children were taken from their homes and put into government-sponsored residential schools, many not returning home for years, if ever. The first Indian residential school was the Carlisle Indian School in Pennsylvania, founded by army officer Richard Pratt in 1875. The first students included prisoners from Plains tribes. Later, Indians from across the nation attended. In 1885 there were six Navajos attending the school, among them a son of Manuelito. Only one of the Navajo students survived to return to his people. Manuelito was distraught over the loss of his son and ceased being a strong advocate of that system of education.

The residential school system of the late nineteenth century is still a topic that evokes intense bitterness and anger among many native peoples. Many of the children died of diseases such as tuberculosis. Parents were not informed that their children were ill and were devastated to learn that their children had died and had been buried so far away. The schools were highly regimented, patterned after military institutions. Children were subject to strict rule enforcement. Their hair was cut as soon as they arrived and many were forced to wear ill-fitting shoes and clothes. Ornaments and spiritual paraphernalia were taken from them. For many of the students, cutting their hair was contrary to their spiritual belief, but they had no choice. Perhaps worst of all, the children were forbidden to speak their own language, the only language many knew. Breaking the rules brought severe physical punishment. Whippings were common, as was having one's mouth washed out with soap. Some reportedly suffered sexual molestation at the schools.

The federal Indian education policy shifted several times in the late nineteenth and early twentieth centuries. More schools were built on the reservations, closer to the students' homes. The Presbyterian Board of Missions was the first religious group to be given permission to establish schools on the Navajo Reservation. The first school on the reservation was established at Fort Defiance. Parents were hesitant to send their children away to school, and it was commonly the sick, weak, and orphaned children who attended schools, leaving the healthier, more fortunate children at home to assist their parents with economic survival. Most Navajos did not know what an "English" education, as specified in the treaty, meant, and felt that what their children were learning at home was far more relevant to their lives. Since education was compulsory, however, some Indian agents tried to enforce attendance, even taking children from their homes. This naturally caused more disharmony and, in some cases, outright confrontation.

Although there was some support for education in general, there was also strong opposition to the forced attendance. Navajos began to evaluate the value of western education as they realized that the system was geared to the destruction of their traditional spirituality and ways of life. Students were told that their ceremonies were mere superstition.

Students who were educated in the system often no longer fit into the traditional society. Jobs were limited both on and off the reservation, and often the educated students were caught between two worlds, belonging to neither. They became victims of the system. Today, Navajo educators advocate the learning of one's primary language well, in order

Pouring batter into a pit for the ceremonial bread used in the Kinaalda celebration for Navajo girls when they reach womanhood. (USHS)

that the deeper thinking and consciousness of the culture can be expressed. Children who have neither a complete grasp of English or of the Navajo language have severe limitations in communication. That was often the case with the earliest Navajo students.

Day schools eventually were opened in many places on the reservation, enabling students to be educated closer to home, in accordance with their parents' desires. In 1906 the town of Bluff requested a school and a teacher for Navajo children. The Indian agency, however, was not able to fund a school. It was decided that Utah Navajo students would attend school at Shiprock, in northwestern New Mexico, which in those days before the automobile was a long journey away.

Influential Navajo leaders such as Ba'ililii reacted strongly. Ba'ililii was a spiritual leader who took an extreme position, wanting a return to the traditional teachings. He and his armed followers issued threats in reaction to the announced educational policy.

Military troops were brought in from Fort Wingate to apprehend the protestors. They attacked a hogan south of Aneth, where Ba'ililii was performing a ceremony. During the skirmish several Navajos were killed. Ba'ililii and other followers were captured and spent several years in prison

at Fort Huachuca, in southern Arizona. Later, the court decided that the Navajos had been imprisoned without due process. The case went to the U.S. Supreme Court and the Navajos were acquitted.

During this time the formation of a political structure patterned after the Euro-American political system was slowly evolving. In 1901, five governmental agencies were created, dividing the reservation into geographic districts for more effective regional governance. The Northern Agency comprising the Utah section was eventually centered at Shiprock. Utah Navajos even today are administered through the jurisdiction of the Shiprock Agency. John Hunter, Superintendant of the Leupp Agency, developed the beginnings of a chapter system of government in 1927. Today there are 110 chapters of the Navajo Nation.

The first legislative council of the Navajo people was organized in 1923, more in response to outside business interests than to Navajo desires to create their own tribal government. It had long been suspected that oil and valuable minerals were located in the Four Corners area, primarily in southeastern Utah and near Shiprock. Prospectors had been prowling around the area illegally for years looking for gold, silver, gas, and oil. The Midwest Refining Company first discovered oil in 1922, thus initiating a demand for oil leases from the tribe. Many oil companies were anxious to begin exploiting the area and pressed for a legal body that could approve business leases. The Navajo Treaty of 1868 had stipulated that no legal decisions could be made without the consent of 75 percent of all Navajo adult males.[20] Businessmen realized that it would be next to impossible to gain the consent of that many Navajo males, so they pressured the federal government to create a business council which supposedly would be representative of the Navajo males.

The first business council was a forerunner of the present-day Navajo Tribal Council. The first chairman was Chee Dodge, who was one of the few Navajos who could speak both Navajo and English. The three handpicked men who were selected to comprise the first business council were asked to sign off on the mineral leases. There were legal questions, however, as it was recognized that this small business council was not truly representative of the Navajo people. At the first meeting, the Special Commissioner to the Navajo Tribe was given the authority to sign all future oil and gas leases which the council might grant on the reservation. In addition, the U.S. Secretary of the Interior was authorized both to advertise and to approve future leases granted by the council. Everything was carried out under the supervision of the federal government. The council could not call a meeting without the approval of

A Navajo medicine man. (U of U)

the Special Commissioner to the Navajo Tribe, nor could the council meet without him. In July 1923 the tribal council met for the first time, with six serving on the council, along with six alternates.

Since the small business council had been organized primarily in response to business desires for oil leases, it was not truly representative of the Navajo people. A set of rules and regulations were drafted by the federal commissioner in 1938 which became the foundation of the tribal council of the present Navajo government. The first council that was elected under the new rules and regulations was considerably larger and more representative than the previous business councils had been.

Many Indians across the United States, including some Utah Navajos, served in World War I. Largely in recognition of their military service the federal government granted citizenship to all Indians in 1924.

Navajo women and children in front of their east-facing hogan. (USHS)

This, however, did not mean that they could vote. In many states Indians had to bring lawsuits to be able to vote. Utah was the last state to allow Indians to vote. The ruling did not come until after a lawsuit in 1957.

The exploration for gas and oil caused some problems for Navajos. Congress passed a landmark law in 1933 that became the foundation for many lawsuits being filed in Utah today. The law stipulated that if oil or gas were discovered in "paying quantities" 37.5 percent of the production royalties would go to the State of Utah to be used for the education of Indian children as well as to build roads to benefit the Indians; 62.5 percent would go directly to the Navajo Tribe. Not until 1956 would "paying quantities" be found in Aneth, however.

There was a profound shift in federal Indian policy during the 1930s, due in part to the findings of the Merriam Report, an investigative report of reservation conditions completed in 1928 by the Brookings Institute. The report highlighted the abysmal conditions in which many tribal people were living and also provided guidelines for Indian policy for the next twenty years. The Indian Reorganization Act (IRA), also known as the Wheeler-Howard Act, of 1934 was one of the outcomes of the Merriam Report.

Butchering beef to feed guests at a Navajo dance in Monument Valley. (USHS)

Under the New Deal administration of President Franklin D. Roosevelt of the 1930s and early 1940s, tribes across the United States were given increased self-determination rights and a chance to reorganize themselves with a constitution and by-laws patterned after the national constitution. Other important components of the IRA included measures to conserve and develop Indian lands and resources as well as the right to form businesses and other organizations. Tribes were given the choice of rejecting or accepting the IRA. While many tribes accepted the act and developed constitutions, Navajos rejected it, largely because they believed that it would lead to increased livestock reduction. Older Navajos still remember that vote.

In truth, livestock reduction had begun as far back as 1928, when it became apparent that there was more livestock than the land could support. Since their release from Fort Sumner Navajos had endeavored to increase their herds so as to become self-sufficient and self-sustaining. By the 1920s, however, they had become so successful that government officials felt that the land was not able to support the growing numbers of livestock. Overgrazing and soil erosion had increased as the years went by, often leading to serious land deterioration.

The resulting government-mandated livestock reduction had a traumatic economic and psychological effect on the Navajo Indians. It was particularly devastating to those whose total reliance was on their livestock, which included the majority of the Navajo people. Grazing regu-

lations were developed and enforced. Range management districts were created. John Collier took a leading role in the stock reduction as Commissioner of Indian Affairs, and even today his name is disliked among older Navajos.

Although Navajos had rejected the IRA thinking that its defeat would save them from enforced stock reduction, such was not the case. Stock reduction began in earnest in 1934 and continued throughout the decade. Government officials came on to the reservation and began to shoot sheep and horses, often right at their owner's homes. Carcasses reportedly were left to rot. The animals that Navajos had prayed for since returning from Fort Sumner were now being systematically destroyed by government agents, often without the owners understanding the reason.

Indian traders were able to buy some Navajo livestock at rock-bottom prices and keep grazing them on the reservation, creating great resentment. There was little or no understanding of the strong emotional attachment that Navajos had to their livestock, especially the sheep. Navajos say *dibe bee iina*, "sheep is life." Without sheep, people no longer had a dependable means of support and could barely sustain themselves.

Clara Maryboy remembered the stock reduction period as a time when her family was forced to take their sheep from the San Juan River grazing area south to Mexican Water. She told how every night sheep were butchered and eaten. When they reached Mexican Water, the sheep had to be sold to the trader.[21] With much of their basic means of survival stripped away, people returned home with great discouragement. Thousands of sheep were sold or destroyed at this time and many families never fully recovered. For families with small herds, even a small percentage of animals lost was difficult. More wealthy Navajos, those called *Ricos*, some with sheep herds numbering in the thousands, were also impacted but managed to survive.

While Navajos were undergoing reduction of their livestock herds, their leaders were also hearing of events going on around the world that would culminate in World War II. The Navajo Nation Tribal Council passed a resolution in 1940 supporting the U.S. government, which read in part:

> Whereas, it has become common practice to attempt national destruction through the sowing of seeds of treachery among minority groups, such as ours, and
>
> Whereas, we hereby serve notice that any un-American movement among our people will be resented and dealt with severely, and

Now, Therefore be it resolved that the Navajo Indians stand ready as they did in 1918 to aid and defend our government and its institutions against all subversive and armed conflict and pledge our loyalty to the system which recognizes minority rights and a way of life that has placed us among the greatest people of our race.[22]

In December 1941 Pearl Harbor was bombed by Japanese forces and the United States went to war against Germany, Italy, and Japan. This had a great impact on Navajo people, as many Navajos entered the military to fight for the United States. Several thousand Navajos left the reservation for the first time to work in industries related to war efforts at places such as Fort Wingate, New Mexico, and Bellemont, Arizona. This provided an impetus for a major transition from a trade to a cash economy.

Navajo "Code Talkers" played a major part in winning the war against Japan. Hundreds of Navajos were recruited by the Marines and trained to be Code Talkers. They developed a code based on the Navajo language that was used in the Pacific War Theatre. The code proved impossible for the Japanese to break. For the first time, messages sent could be secure and not intercepted. Navajo Code Talkers played a highly significant role in the winning of the war. "Were it not for the Navajos, the Marines would never have taken Iwo Jima.…The entire operation was directed by Navajo code," reported Major Howard M. Conner.[23] The efforts of the Code Talkers were top secret and did not appear publicly in print until the late 1960s, more than twenty-five years later. Even today, some Indian veterans are reluctant to discuss their service in the war effort.

Many other Navajos served in World War II besides the Code Talkers. Indian soldiers participated in some of the most famous battles of the war, including those at Guadalcanal, Bougainville, Iwo Jima, Saipan, and Okinawa. Some 3,600 of them served in the Army, Navy, Marine Corps, and even in the Women's Army Corps, and in virtually every theatre of operation.

Following tradition, Navajos were blessed at protection ceremonies before they went overseas. Maurice Knee described his ceremony, which was typical of many ceremonies held for the servicemen: "It was the Going to War ceremony. The blessing that they gave me was supposed to put a shield around me, an invisible shield, that the bullet would come right for my nose and hit that shield and go away. And it worked. I came back. If it hadn't worked I wouldn't be here!"[24]

Navajo Code Talkers during World War II at Bougainville in December 1943.
(U of U)

Seth Bigman, a Utah Navajo, served in the Pacific with the U.S. Navy for almost three years. He reported that it was a good experience, but was a major change from the dry land to a floor of water. He said that he didn't have any difficulty since he had been among white people a lot. When he came back from war his old *hataalii*, his medicine man, told him:

> The mother has send out her child to go on the warpath ... the same way as Mother Earth sent out her warriors to defend her. The rainbow is the defense of Mother Earth, where the land and water meet.... When you go through the rainbow to war, that's the defense of Mother Earth....
>
> The medicine man prayed for me when I'm going over and coming back. I was back three times on leave.... He prayed that I'll be coming home safe, come back through that rainbow. So I did, I came home safe.[25]

In 1946, shortly after the end of the war, Congress established the Indian Claims Commission, authorizing tribes to file claims against the U.S. government for lands taken without just compensation. Among the claims was the traditional homeland of the Navajo people, Dinétah. It took more than twenty years to settle many of these claims, and some are not settled yet. In order to receive monetary compensation for lost land, native people had to give up all their rights to an area.

Utah Navajos became more knowledgable about the justice system. Some residents of southeastern Utah were trying to claim Navajo lands under provisions of the Taylor Grazing Act. The State of Utah also passed a statute during this time, giving ranchers the right to dispose of any horses they claimed were abandoned. Navajos tell stories of hundreds of their horses being rounded up and sold for dog food. One story in particular mentions a round-up of over 100 horses by government agents, including charges of cruelty to the animals. Utah Navajos took this case to court and were awarded $100,000; reportedly it was the first time American Indians had successfully sued the government for intentional wrongdoing.

In 1956 Congress authorized the construction of Glen Canyon Dam, which created Lake Powell. Hundreds of Navajos were relocated from canyons on the south sides of the San Juan and Colorado Rivers. The land exchange was authorized by the Navajo Nation and the federal government—about 53,000 acres of soon-to-be-flooded reservation land was traded for public domain land on McCracken Mesa, northwest of Aneth, Utah. Little has been written about this forced relocation. The land on which the people were to be relocated was already occupied by other Navajos, whose wishes were not considered. The exchange was finalized in 1959. Some Navajos such as Jack Jones, a descendent of K'aayellii, tried to reclaim their aboriginal land rights. Although these claims reportedly were well documented, they were denied by the Department of the Interior. The Utah K'aayellii descendents requested funds to purchase additional grazing rights in 1961 but the request was denied by the courts.

In 1961 Hosteen Sakezzie and Thomas Billy sued the Utah Indian Affairs Commission on behalf of all Navajos living around Aneth. The commission had spent Navajo oil royalty money on projects which, according to the plaintiffs, did not benefit Navajos. The court agreed with Sakezzie and Billy. In 1963 Hosteen Sakezzie again sued the Utah Indian Affairs Commission for not complying with the earlier court order. He accused the commission of refusing to consult with Navajos, refusing to give Navajos information on its spending activities, and spending large

sums of money on projects that did not benefit the Aneth Navajos. Again the judge ordered the commission to comply with the court orders and spend the money on projects that would benefit the Aneth Navajos.

A series of lawsuits ensued. In 1968 the Utah Indian Commission sponsored legislation in Congress to expand the class of people who could benefit from the oil royalties. Instead of just Navajos living on the oil fields, the new bill gave benefits to all Indians living in San Juan County. The bill was passed and also included a change in the purposes for which the royalties could be used. The new wording read "health, education and general welfare." This subsequently has been loosely interpreted, and, consequently, Aneth Navajos feel they have not benefited much from the royalties, although other area Indians and county Navajos have benefited from the change.

The United States Supreme Court ruled in the case of *United States v. Jim* that the royalties granted by the 1933 congressional act were not protected by the Constitution and that Congress did have power to change the way in which the royalty funds were directed. Justice William O. Douglas wrote a strong dissenting opinion, stating that Indians are citizens and beneficiaries of the due process and just compensation clauses of the Constitution, and that Aneth Navajos have rights to the royalties, not because Congress granted the rights but because the land belongs to these Navajos because of their continuous possession of the land. He went on to say that the United States government is charged with protecting Indians and that Congress should not rob the Navajos of their rights.[26]

Utah Navajos continued to bring land-rights cases to court. Even today, there are litigations pending which will extend into the new millennium. One significant case is presently being heard in the BLM internal court system regarding the protection of sacred sites on Cedar Mesa, near Blanding, Utah. The proposal for an enlarged ranger visitor station in Kane Canyon alarmed many Navajos. The Hopi and Navajo Nations have joined in litigation aimed at protecting the cedar trees and sacred ancestral sites on Cedar Mesa.

Other Indian relocation efforts were going on across the country. Indians were encouraged to move off their reservations in a reversal of the federal Indian policy of the IRA days. Acculturation and assimilation were the desired outcomes of all relocation efforts. Beginning in the 1950s some tribes special relationships with the federal government were terminated, but Navajos were not affected. The terminated tribes were thought to have reached economic self-sufficiency and a degree of acculturation, but in every case the federal termination policy was a failure.

A group of Navajo horsemen. (USHS)

The policy began to be reversed by the 1970s, and terminated tribes have spent years trying to regain their federal trustee status. Some have been more successful than others in these efforts.

In 1956 huge quantities of oil were discovered in the Aneth area, certainly in "paying quantities," according to the earlier royalty stipulations. By 1961 approximately 350 oil wells were pumping on Navajo land. Utah was catapulted into the top ten oil-producing states. Oil companies made fortunes, but some Navajos began to suffer as a result of the oil explorations. Some artesian wells that had served Navajo families for generations became polluted. Rangelands were damaged. The general health and physical well being of people and their livestock were adversely affected. People reportedly became sick from eating cattle and sheep that had consumed contaminated water. Detrimental effects have been long term.

As the years went on, a wide range of cases were brought to court by the Utah Navajos. The Utah Affairs Commission often was chastized by the presiding judge for mismanagement of the Utah oil royalties, yet the Navajo requests were never granted.

Uranium mining became big business in Utah in the late 1940s and throughout the 1950s. The Cold War and the nuclear power race provided increased demand and momentum to the uranium mining industry into the 1970s. The Four Corners area was covered with miners seeking to make their fortunes. A Navajo, Luke Yazzie, is often credited with

the discovery of a major uranium deposit in Monument Valley, Utah. According to a story told by trader Harry Goulding, Yazzie had seen samples of uranium ore on the counter of Goulding's Trading Post. Later, he showed the trader some samples he had found. In return he received only a free lunch. The site where Yazzie's samples were found turned into one of the largest uranium mines on the Navajo Reservation. Although it generated tremendous wealth for the owners, all Luke Yazzie received was $130 per month for the the next fifteen years, the minimum wage.[27]

The Navajos, in general, did not receive much more than wage work for their contributions to the uranium mining industry. When Luke Yazzie was seventy-two he was interviewed, parts of which follow.

> I was born here where I still live. As a child I herded sheep. By the time I was ten years old I had explored the cliffs, the hills, the trees around here.... I also collected rocks and stones.... Among them I found some uranium. I didn't know what it was: it just felt heavy to me. I drew pictures of animals and I painted them with these rocks. Finally I found a place where there was a lot of uranium. I found a strange heavy stone.... I discovered a yellow strip in the rocks.... I thought these rocks might be gold, so I hid them carefully and checked on them to be sure they were still there.
>
> Then, many years later, during the war, I heard there were some minerals among the Navajos that might be used to make ammunitions. When I was in Goulding's Trading Post I noticed that there were all kinds of rocks lying on the counter, and I asked Dibé Neez [Tall Sheep, Harry Goulding] about them.... He said they cost a lot of money. "If you find these rocks, bring them in."
>
> A few weeks later I took the rocks I'd been keeping to Dibé Neez. He looked at them very carefully and said, "That's it! These are the rocks. They're worth a lot of money."
>
> He put them on a scale to weigh them. He was amazed. He asked where I had found the rocks and if there was a road leading to the place.... I was kind of hesitant to tell him where I had found them because I thought he might get all the glory and money from it. He already knew what they were and I didn't....
>
> He gave me free pop and asked me to have lunch with him.... He told me if I showed him where the rocks were, I would not have to do any of the work, that I'd probably just get paid for

showing them, that starting today I would receive payment for the rocks. Up to this day I have never received any payments from those rocks or the place where the rocks were.... He said the rocks that I had were worth a lot of money and that I would get most of the money from the minerals....

Harry Goulding contacted Denny Viles, an official from the Vanadium Corporation, the first uranium mining corporation on the Navajo Reservation, and they followed Luke Yazzie out to the area where he had found the rocks. When they tested the rocks they were astonished. Luke Yazzie did not receive what he had been promised, however. He was asked to help survey the area, and later related more of the events:

After this they sort of ignored me. In another year they started mining. They gave me a pick, a shovel, a big jackhammer, and a wheelbarrow. Instead of being one of the owners, I was just one of the laborers.... Altogether I must have worked for about fifteen years.

What they promised me at the beginning was a lie. I was told that I'd get paid for the mine discovery, which I never did. Instead I worked hard for the money I was given from the mine. My salary was about $130 a month. What Dibé Neez and Denny Viles did was they took advantage of me. It seems like they profited the most from the mine. Many Navajos from here and other parts of the country worked here. Yes, they benefited from the uranium mine.... But I still feel that I was taken advantage of. I feel like I helped everyone else, including Window Rock and the United States Army.[28]

Chee Dodge, chairman of the Navajo Tribal Council at the time, urged better royalty arrangements for individual Navajos who found valuable ore deposits. In 1948 a resolution was passed in the Tribal Council to reward the Navajos who found sites. This resolution, however, was passed too late to reward Luke Yazzie.

Harry Goulding claimed that he also received nothing from the discovery. He said he was only interested in assisting the Navajos with economic development after the war. Goulding was also noted for opening up Monument Valley to the motion picture industry. Movies made by directors such as John Ford, starring John Wayne and other famous actors, brought some revenues to the Navajos of the region.

Uranium mining held many hazards. Although it brought much-needed funds to individual Navajo miners and the tribal treasury, the cost in human suffering was tremendous. Most Navajo miners were completely ignorant of the dangers inherent in the mining process and also were not informed of either the short-term or long-term consequences. Navajo miners would come home wearing clothes saturated with uranium dust. In essence, the entire family became exposed to high radiation levels. The uranium mining town of Halchita, Utah, contained many Navajo homes that were built on uranium tailings, thus becoming highly radioactive. Since the 1950s, most of the uranium miners have become sick and many have died from related diseases. Almost every miner's family has lost at least one member due to the effects of radiation. Even children have died from the radioactive contamination. "As children, we used to play in the golden sands," reported Sarah Police, a resident of White Rocks, a Utah community. "My dad died from uranium poisoning and my sister passed away from it too. So far we have received absolutely no compensation from the federal government."[29]

Navajo children living near Bluff played in the mines on a regular basis. Sarah Police remembers that children in her family were told to take a bucket into a nearby mine every night to get water for dinner. For years the federal government denied all claims brought by Navajo survivors. Recently, in the late 1990s, with the intervention of U.S. congressional leaders, widows of Navajo miners began receiving compensation, but most Navajos felt it was too little and too late. The bureaucratic process was cumbersome, and in many cases widows who had been married in traditional Navajo weddings could not produce a valid state marriage certificate as required by law for compensation.

The legacy of uranium mining continues. Presently the federal government is funding the Superfund cleanup program at selected sites on and off the reservation in an attempt to clean up the radioactive mine tailings. Today many Navajos regard the uranium mining negatively. "To open up Mother Earth, to take those rocks out of her, it should never have been done," states Clara Maryboy, the widow of a uranium miner. "Now we have to pay the price. And it's much too high a price."[30]

Development of the Navajo Nation as a Sovereign Entity

The 1960s brought about another major shift in the federal Indian policy. Federal policies swung away from termination and began again to recognize the sovereignty of Indian tribes. This was philosophically similar to the Indian Reorganization Act of the 1930s in that tribal sover-

A Navajo medicine man. (USHS)

eignty and self-determination were once again recognized as the foundation of Indian policy. The movement towards sovereignty and self-determination coincided with the civil rights movement that was sweeping the country. Minorities everywhere were claiming the rights to which they felt entitled. Civil liberties, basic fundamental rights, had been long denied minorities according to such national leaders as Martin Luther King, Jr., and John F. Kennedy. Under the leadership of President Lyndon B. Johnson, many social programs were extended into minority areas, including the reservations.

The Navajo tribal government began to administer programs in coordination with federal agencies. Navajo officials increased their visits to Washington to testify and lobby for a multitude of causes. In 1965 the Navajo Tribal Council established the Office of Navajo Economic Opportunity (ONEO) and Peter MacDonald became its first executive director. ONEO had substantial federal funding and was able to take advantage of many economic opportunities. The Navajo Tribal Council began to assume more power and authority as well as attain greater economic self-sufficiency and prestige.

In 1970 Peter MacDonald was elected Navajo tribal chairman, the

A Navajo woman at her rug loom. (Utah Publicity Department and U of U)

first university-educated chairman in the history of the tribe. He went on to be elected chairman four times, serving the Navajo Nation effectively in terms of social and economic development. However, his successes were mixed with some controversy. He was eventually accused of mismanagement of funds and conspiring to overthrow the Navajo government and later was sentenced to federal prison.

During the 1970s, 1980s, and 1990s, increasing emphasis was placed on Navajo education, social services, and economic development. Native Americans across the country began to take increasing control of their own economic development. Peter MacDonald was the primary leader of the Council of Energy Resources Tribes (CERT), a consortium of twenty tribes that was founded to gain equity in the payment of natural resource royalties.

Other Navajo leaders also had a great impact on Navajo life. Peterson Zah was elected twice as chair of the Navajo Nation. Albert Hale was elected president of the Navajo Nation under a tribal reorganization. He promoted tribal sovereignty across the country as well as local governmental development at the chapter level. In 1999 Kelsey A. Begaye began serving as president of the Navajo Nation.

Three Navajo women exhibit their fine woven rugs. (USHS)

At the present time, more than 54 percent of the population of San Juan County is Native American. Navajos make up the majority, with small groups of Paiutes and Utes. The county was redistricted on orders of the U.S. Justice Department in 1986 to provide more equal representation based on population. It was the only county in Utah that was ordered to be redistricted. There was a massive voter registration drive on the reservation to register Utah Navajo voters. Students from universities came to aid in the effort. There was an influx of media on the reservation in search of human-interest stories. Many Navajos felt invaded and resented the media attention; others felt the publicity was positive, bringing national attention to the voter registration drives. With the redistricting, a young Navajo Democrat, Mark Maryboy, was elected one of three county commissioners, the first Native American to hold an elected position in Utah.

In 1990 the Utah Democratic party nominated an all Native American slate for San Juan County offices. This had never occurred anywhere before in the United States. The candidates ran under the slogan *Niha Whool Zhiizh*, which roughly translates, "It's Our Turn." Jean Melton and Mark Maryboy provided the leadership for the campaign, which drew national attention. All the native candidates were defeated with the ex-

ception of Maryboy, who was running for a second term; but the result was that the state and county were forced to take notice of the increasing political strength of the 7,500 Native Americans in southeastern Utah.

Maryboy, a Democrat in a traditionally Republican-dominated state, was supported by the national Democratic party, including presidential candidate Bill Clinton. At the 1992 Democratic National Convention he became the first Native American to give the opening prayer in his own native language.

In 1991 a coalition of Navajos, Utes, mixed-blood Utes, and other Indians orchestrated the passage of a landmark bill that gave them increased representation in Utah politics. Legislation was passed that established governance of the Utah Navajo Trust Fund. This legislation took the responsibility from the Division of Indian Affairs and gave it to the State of Utah, under the oversight of Utah officials such as the state treasurer. The legislation came about as a result of an investigation and subsequent report issued by the Utah State Legislative Auditors that described the mismanagement of the trust fund. The auditors' report stated that over $200 million had been mismanaged over the past thirty years, although some people disagree with the findings and this interpretation.

Two years later, in 1993, the legislative act was revised and mandated the creation of the Diné Advisory Committee, which gave the rightful representation to the Utah Navajos to oversee the distribution and safeguards of the trust fund. During the remainder of the 1990s Utah Navajos assumed increasing responsibility for the management of the fund. Today, litigation continues as Utah Navajos seek to be reimbursed for the earlier mismanagement of the funds. No easy solution seems to be in sight. Governor of Utah Michael Leavitt has asked the Utah Navajos to take $2 million and drop the lawsuit, but the Navajos have no inclination to settle for such a sum.[31]

Education issues had assumed increasing importance during the 1970s. In 1975 Navajo parents brought suit against the Utah state school boards and San Juan County to force the building of schools on Utah's Navajo lands. Until then, many Utah Navajo children had had to attend often-distant boarding schools. Charles Wilkinson and attorney Eric Swenson took leading roles in the lawsuit, which was decided in favor of the Navajo parents. As with so many other Navajo lawsuits, however, the State of Utah did not enforce the ruling. Twenty-five years later, in 1997, the issue was taken back to court; again the Navajos won. It was mandated that the State of Utah build schools on the Utah part of the reservation for local Navajo children.

A Navajo medicine man (right, stooping) gathers up donations tossed onto a blanket by spectators. (USHS)

Mark Maryboy continues to be a leader of his people today. He has been elected to the San Juan County Commission four times and has served on the Navajo Nation Tribal Council as chairman of the Budget and Finance Committee. He was named the "Most Valuable Council Delegate" of the tribal council by his fellow delegates and staff in 1998.

Health care continues to be an issue today among Utah Navajos. The only large medical facility on the Utah part of the Navajo Reservation, the Monument Valley Hospital, has been closed. There are plans to build a large clinic at Montezuma Creek, but nothing has materialized as of 1999. Today, in the year 2000, some Navajos still have to transport water to their homes. Many families on the reservation still do not have electricity, telephones, or running water.

Environmental issues also are in the forefront of concerns today. The Navajo Environmental Protection Agency recently gained its own separate status, which means that it can enter into environmental cases as a separate entity, giving it greater impact. Issues of reforestation, conservation, and the dumping of waste into the San Juan River greatly concern Utah Navajos.

Hunting rights are another concern, with court cases pending. Utah Navajos wish to be able to exercise their treaty rights to hunt game as they have traditionally hunted without being cited for treating deer carcasses in a non-western way. Navajo culture teaches that the deer must

A Navajo weaver in Blanding. (USHS)

be honored in a prescribed manner. Having to tag the deer and take the head away from the place it was killed, in accordance with Utah Fish and Game Department rules, is contrary to traditional customs that are intended to show respect for deer and honor the animals' continuing willingness to be hunted. Questions also exist over the amount of hunting permitted.

San Juan County began negotiations with the federal government in the mid-1990s in regards to developing a Monitored Retrievable Storage site, a nuclear waste dump. Two of the county commissioners voted for the establishment of a waste dump on the border of the reservation. Mark Maryboy was the only county commissioner who opposed it. This dump would store spent nuclear rods, which remain highly radioactive. Navajos did not want this nuclear waste dump in their backyards and entered the fight to stop it. At the time of this writing, the nuclear waste dump plans have been halted.

Utah Navajos were featured in the national news during the summer of 1998 when three armed men killed a law officer in Cortez, Colorado, and were believed to be hiding northeast of Bluff. One was shot near St. Christopher's Mission. One of the largest manhunts in the history of the Four Corners area ensued. The Navajo Nation contributed skilled trackers and specially trained officers to the manhunt. Due to fears and re-

This Navajo grandmother, the widow of Hosteen Cly, watches her grand-daughter win a girl's foot race. (USHS)

ported sightings on the reservation, many Navajos were moved out of their homes into safer quarters, such as the high school at Red Mesa. Others remained in their homes but armed themselves. Months later, the body of one of the two remaining fugitives was found in the area; the other is considered to be still at large.

Many Utah Navajos feel that they continue to be the stepchildren of the State of Utah as well as of the Navajo Nation. Each political entity seems to believe that the other one should be responsible for the Utah Navajos. Many essential services that most people take for granted, such as telephones and electricity, are still not available to most people on the reservation. It is probable that some of the very complex issues discussed earlier will continue to be major issues in southern Utah; however, many of the new leaders are likely to be Utah Navajos. The younger generation is becoming more educated and more involved in local economic and political issues. They will undoubtedly have a major impact on the continuing history of San Juan County and the state of Utah.

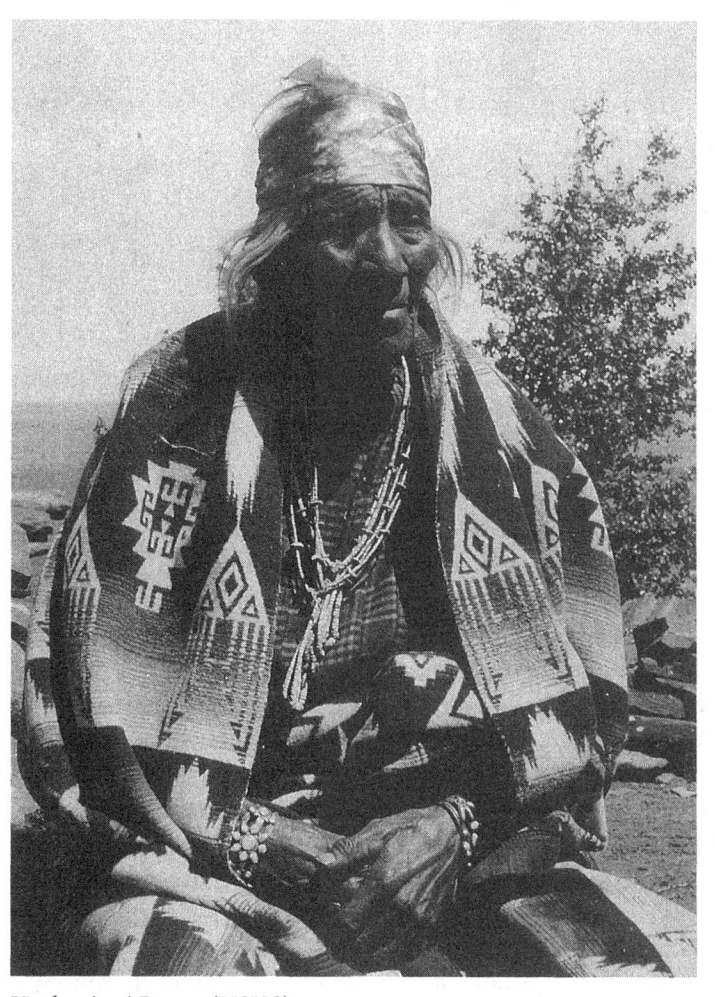

Hoskaninni Begay. (USHS)

Conclusion: The Contemporary Status of Utah Indians

Robert S. McPherson

The preceding tribal histories have brought the reader through the period of termination to more contemporary times. But what direction has Indian affairs taken over the past decade or so, and what does the future promise? Significant adjustments have been made in the past to accommodate the shifting economic, social, and political events and developments that have inundated the tribes following white contact. The direction and rate of change increased in tempo as fresh challenges confronted Native Americans. The only element that appears to have remained constant is that something new seemed to rear its head each year.

In the fast-paced world of contemporary Indian America, one looks for basic themes that have remained consistent through history and into the present. This concluding chapter points out that even though the type and nature of the problems from the past have been altered, they are still very visible in a modern form. The physical battles of the nineteenth century have been moved from the canyons, hills, and basins of Utah to the legal courts and government offices of the city. Still, many of the same issues are at stake. For Native Americans, the safeguarding of lands, the maintenance of an economy, and the preservation of tribal goals and individual ethnic identity are just as real now as they were fifty or 150 years ago. There remains just as much determination to hold on to these cultural ideals and autonomy as there was in the past. The difference lies in how it is done.

Traditional Native American ties to the land through religious beliefs and practices are well known. Every tribe has its sacred sites as defined in their teachings and history. Today, many of these places have felt the pressure of increased use by the dominant culture that does not know or care to recognize the spiritual importance attached to these sites.

One of the finest examples of this problem is the controversy surrounding Rainbow Bridge, a national monument created in 1910. To the

Navajos, this 290-foot-tall and 275-foot-long sandstone bridge is spiritually powerful, associated with rain-producing ceremonies, supernatural protection, and curative powers.[1] Until the completion of the Glen Canyon Dam and the creation of Lake Powell in the mid-1960s, access to this remote area was limited to intrepid river runners or saddle-sore tourists on horseback. The numbers were small, their impact minimal.

Today, however, the National Park Service estimates that 1,000 people a day arrive by boat at the area's docking facilities for a leisurely stroll to the monument and the mandatory picture-taking ritual. Navajo medicine men believe these activities have greatly reduced the spiritual power that once resided at the site. That is why on 11 August 1995 a small group of Navajos called Protectors of the Rainbow closed the monument to any outside interference, then held a cleansing ceremony for four days. The National Park Service enforced the group's wishes, re-routing scheduled boat tours and closing down any activities beyond the dock facility. It has also implemented policies to remove graffiti and to prevent climbing on the bridge.[2]

While this was a peaceful resolution of the problem, it was only temporary. Underlying the issue is the question of how much and what type of protection can be afforded such sacred sites. And it is not just Rainbow Bridge: rangers at Devil's Tower National Monument in Wyoming have discouraged rock climbers from ascending its face; Chaco Canyon National Park in New Mexico closed its Great Kiva after Pueblo people and Navajos complained of the site being defiled; and park rangers now prevent tourists from going to the Lion's Shrine at Bandelier National Monument in New Mexico for the same reason.[3] Indian people do not want to see their sacred sites profaned.

Part of the problem is in trying to fit Native American practices into Anglo-American law. While the National Park Service is able to grant temporary closure of these sites, it cannot totally prevent general public use of them. One court ruling said, "We do not believe [the Navajos] have a constitutional right to have tourists visiting the Bridge 'in a respectful and appreciative manner.' Were it otherwise, the monument would become a government-managed shrine," an obvious infringement of First Amendment rights separating government from religion.[4]

Certainly some of these concerns to maintain the sacredness of a site from outside interference were part of the Northwestern Band of Shoshones' decision to leave the Bear River Massacre site alone. Located two miles north of Preston, Idaho, this 120-acre area holds the bones of the 250–400 Shoshone killed in that tragic fight. The band's vice-chair-

A Ute father with two children. (Marriott Library, University of Utah—U of U)

man, Tom Pacheco, said that the "Number one [priority] is to leave the site undisturbed," since to do otherwise would bother the ancestors.[5] Therefore, the National Historic Landmark remains undeveloped.

In 1997, Box Elder County, Utah, opened a landfill in the Little Mountain area, twenty miles west of Brigham City, in spite of Shoshone protests. The Indians' claim that some of their people were buried there was

not enough to prevent the building of the dump.[6] At the same time, the Kanosh Band of Paiutes protested a Bureau of Land Management (BLM) chaining of "tens of thousands of acres of fire damaged federal land" in the Richfield area. Preservation of archaeological sites, pictographs, and human remains are the reason for these complaints. The court ordered a ten-day work stoppage, which, because of the limited seeding time, prevented the BLM from continuing with its chaining and planting project. At this time, the project has been abandoned, although reapplication to work on specific locations may be considered in the future.[7]

The issue of burial remains is not limited to those in the ground. In November 1990, President George Bush signed into law the Native American Graves Protection and Repatriation Act (NAGPRA). Its purpose was to protect burial sites, artifacts associated with those sites, and Indian remains now in the custody of museums and other repositories. A major part of this law directs that skeletal remains be returned to the appropriate tribe when origin can be determined.

This law set in motion a flurry of events by various agencies. The Utah Museum of Natural History, for instance, has 1,500 pieces that fall under the jurisdiction of the repatriation law. In 1993 the Utah legislature appropriated $60,000 to pay for reburial costs of Northwestern Shoshone remains recovered from public lands throughout the state. The money purchased a burial vault, located in Pioneer State Park in Salt Lake City, that could hold up to 500 wooden caskets.[8]

An increased sensitivity towards the reburial of Indian skeletons has also captured the attention of much of the public. One Boy Scout for his Eagle project became interested in Black Hawk, Ute leader during the 1865–68 conflict with the Mormons. No one knew where the Native American leader's remains were located after they had been removed from their original burial site at Spring Lake in Utah County. Eventually, because of the scout's persistence, what is believed to have been Black Hawk's skeleton was found in the LDS Historical Department's holdings. The bones were transferred to the museum at Brigham Young University and have recently been reinterred near Payson under the direction of the U.S. Forest Service.[9]

The issues of repatriation are not always so nicely resolved. What seems to be a straightforward solution to problems created in the past has proven to be far more complex. To begin with, there are only two tribes—the Northern Utes and the Navajos—in Utah who have cultural preservation offices and museums to deal with returned artifacts and remains. Second, once one moves beyond clearly identified historic tribal

Members of the Northwest Shoshone Band on board a Salt Lake City sightseeing bus, actual date unknown but probably in 1920s. (Courtesy Mae Parry)

remains, a gray area of ownership arises. Anasazi and Fremont skeletons and artifacts have been claimed by modern-day Hopis, Paiutes, Utes, and Navajos, who live in areas once used by these prehistoric groups. The acknowledged relationship to the earlier peoples now holds political and economic ties to land that extend beyond the moral and geneaological questions of ancestry.[10]

Native Americans have always recognized the pragmatic side of making a living from the land, a view entwined with religious, economic, and political values. Today, as in the past, tribal groups continue to depend on their land holdings for survival. And, as in the past, these rights are often challenged. One of the most interesting—and as yet still unresolved—examples of these issues is found on the Uintah and Ouray Ute Reservation. The complexity of the questions raised would give even King Solomon pause to consider.

Twenty-one years after President Abraham Lincoln established the initial reservation in 1861, the federal government added more land to the tribe's control, boosting Ute holdings to more than 4 million acres. Around the turn of the century, substantial lands were lost through the effects of the Dawes Allotment Act and the creation of national forest lands. Added to this was the loss of territory on the western part of the reservation for the Strawberry Reservoir Project and acreage given to mixed-blood Utes as part of the termination settlement during the 1950s.

A young Navajo in Monument Valley, 1938. (Utah State Historical Society—USHS)

It can thus be seen how the reservation by 1970 had shrunk to a quarter of its original size.[11]

Beginning in 1975, questions concerning jurisdiction, boundary rights, and land control led to ten years of litigation and a final court decision that pushed Ute tribal boundaries back to the 4 million acre mark. Rather than solving the issues of jurisdiction with white neighbors, however, new ones arose, adding to some of the old issues never resolved. All of these questions, however, spring from use rights of the land for those who live on it.

At present, the complexity of these issues can be categorized into three general related areas. The first one is jurisdiction. There are about 40,000 people who live in the Uinta Basin, and only about 3,200 (8 percent) of them are Utes. However, 90 percent of Duchesne County and 60 percent of Uintah County are within the reservation boundaries. The Anglos living on previously homesteaded lands that are now located within the reservation want to have a clear understanding of what their relationship is going to be with the Ute tribal government. According to one report, while "homesteaded lands fall under the laws of local and state government, former Indian lands—no matter who owns them today—are under tribal jurisdiction."[12]

The question of taxation and control of non-Indians is still a thorny issue. The tribe has suggested that its members remain exempt from paying taxes throughout these counties and that it be responsible for handling all of its members who become involved in misdemeanor cases on homestead lands, which includes the city of Roosevelt. To the Anglos, this could be the first steps taken to return some of their lands to a reservation status—what they view as a form of creeping control.[13]

A second issue that the Utes face is that of water rights. The federal government and the Central Utah Water Conservancy District in 1965 agreed with the tribe to use some of its water in exchange for the building of a water-control project on the reservation. By 1992, the government admitted that it had not followed through on its word and wanted to make amends by building the water project and settling past wrongs. After thirty years of promises, however, the Utes are slow to enter a deal that could turn against them in the future. They fear that anything that will give the state more control over Ute resources will do nothing but harm their chances for future use of the resource. In 1994 they presented the Central Utah Water Conservancy District with a bill for $33 million for water lost in the past. As Ron Wopsock, member of the tribal council, pointed out, "History tells us we can't trust white people. The trust just isn't there, and probably never will be."[14]

That is the third point of contention—beyond the land and water issues, beyond the question of jurisdiction—how much trust and good will can each contending side muster, given the friction and conflicts of the past. A recent newspaper article summarized underlying attitudes between the two groups in the Uinta Basin, maintaining that the real problems are between two conflicting sets of values—those of the Indian and those of the white man. Some Utes have suggested that there be separate Indian and non-Indian school districts, that voting should be

done in "blocs" for those candidates who voice a pro-Ute campaign platform, and that at least one county commission seat be occupied either by an Indian or someone who will work for Indians. Where these issues will go from here may be a question as much of attitude as of the letter of the law. But as Roland McCook, vice chairman of the tribe, said, "The white settlers came here by choice. They live here today by choice. They should be the ones to get along with us."[15]

The Goshutes in Skull Valley have their own problems in getting along, but this time it is with the state government. They have chosen to make 450 acres of their 18,000-acre reservation the home for 10,000 metric tons of nuclear waste. If the federal government builds a repository there, radioactive materials will come by road and rail from as far away as Minnesota. The Monitored Retrievable Storage (MRS) sites are expected to be in use for about fifty years until a more permanent facility can be built in Nevada. In the meantime, the approximately 130 members of the tribe would participate in the hiring for the 1,500 temporary and 500 permanent jobs derived from the construction and maintenance of the site.[16]

Many people outside of the tribe see the MRS as a threat to the environment that is far greater than the chemical and biological weapons being stored and now destroyed at nearby Dugway Proving Ground, also in Tooele County. The two commercial hazardous-waste incinerators, the hazardous waste dump, and the low-level radiation dump found near Tooele, as well as a private company that test-burns rocket motors on the reservation, do nothing to calm the fear of environmentalists and state officials. They envision the nuclear repository as an even greater threat to the quality of life than already exists in the area.[17]

But many Indians feel that they are forced by their poverty and neglect to take advantage of such economic opportunities. In the words of U.S. Senator Ben Nighthorse Campbell, a Cheyenne Indian from Colorado: "It's like the old treaties. The government is playing the same game. If you're hurting bad enough, you'll sign anything."[18] On 7 February 1997 the Skull Valley Band signed an agreement with ten utility groups to build the repository. Governor Michael Leavitt has been quoted as saying, "Over my dead body," and state agencies have claimed the right to close roads and the transportation system that would start bringing the radioactive materials to the reservation.[19] The Goshutes have examined the idea of building their own roads. Beyond the most obvious part of the disagreement lies the important issue of sovereignty of the tribe as well as issues of state's rights versus federal control. Thus, the roots of this conflict

extend far back to the nineteenth century, but the branches from the main stem of Goshute history have a very contemporary posture.

There is disagreement among Native Americans on environmental issues, just as there is in society as a whole. There are many Indian groups who oppose nuclear waste dumps and want reservations to remain nuclear waste free. The international Indigenous Environmental Network, as well as the national group Native Americans for a Clean Environment, the National Environmental Coalition of Native Americans, and the Southwest Research and Information Center encourage resistance to what they consider environmental exploitation. All of these groups point to the history of abuse and mismanagement of federal, state, and corporate use of reservations as dumping grounds for problems in the society at large.

That is why, when the White Mesa Utes protested certain aspects of a federal clean-up of mill tailings from a site thirty miles north of the Indians' land, the protest received widespread attention. The storage facility for this waste was already in place, at a closed uranium mill next to the Utes' reservation. Still, the people of White Mesa feared that the estimated 110,000 dump truck round-trips over a three-year period would endanger tribal members traveling the road, contaminate underground water, place more radioactive materials in the air that would be carried downwind to their lands, and disturb ancestral burial sites. Whether or not these concerns were totally justified can be debated, but the 200 people who marched in protest drew many Native Americans and part of the white community together long enough for the Department of Energy to change its mind and bury the tailings near the original mill site.[20] The people at White Mesa can now breathe easier, literally.

South of the Ute Reservation lie the oil-producing lands of the Navajo Strip in the Montezuma Creek–Aneth area. In December 1997 an explosion at a Mobil Oil pumping station raised once again the issue of the oil company's relationship with the people who live nearby. Reminiscent of the 1978 "takeover" that closed 800 wells for two weeks and the 1993 blocking of a road used by another oil company to drill on a nearby mesa, the protesters set up a tepee in the parking lot of the Mobil Oil offices near Aneth. Their concerns, echoes from past demonstrations, centered on environmental degradation, health problems, employment opportunities, and renegotiating leases.

Mobil Oil officials reacted calmly. The company set about negotiating the reopening of sixty-three wells closed by request of the demonstrators. There were other people just as anxious to see the closure end. With 500 oil wells on the Utah strip annually producing around $16

A World War II Navajo code talker on Saipan in July 1944. (USHS)

million for the Utah Navajo Trust Fund and $1.5 million in San Juan County property taxes, many area residents—both Navajo and Anglo—wished to have the problems solved quickly.[21] Albert Hale, president of the Navajo Nation, arrived in time to play an important part in the negotiations.

Seventy-two hours later the various factions had signed a thirty-two-point agreement. In addition to paying partial salaries for two Navajo public liaison specialists, Mobil pledged to follow Navajo hiring practices and to settle further issues in the tribe's "peacemaker" courts, which follow a community-level conflict resolution format. Hale promised to have more of the tribe's royalties (approximately two-thirds of all of the money that comes to the Navajo Indians from the oil field) go to the Utah Navajos.[22] With that, the Aneth oil field resumed normal operations.

In addition to contemporary issues surrounding usufruct rights, there are also issues concerning religion. One of the most interesting questions to be raised recently involves the status of Indians in prison. This has proven to be a national concern as well, there having been over fifty lawsuits in various states since 1970.[23] Utah has had more than its share

of the controversy. Starting in 1986, when the correctional facility in Draper denied nineteen Navajo inmates access to a sweat lodge, the prison system came under increasing fire. The protesters invoked their rights under the Native American Religious Freedom Act (1978), claiming that the government denied their entitlements and had not consulted with traditional practitioners as it should. These denied rights came in many forms—not providing space to hold ceremonies, an absence of sweat lodges, forbidding prisoners to grow their hair long, restricting paraphernalia necessary for ceremonies in the prison, and treating Indian religious leaders who performed the ceremonies suspiciously and differently than ministers from other faiths.[24]

Advocacy groups continued to form. Beyond a national network of protesters, there developed a number who became particularly representative of Indians in Utah, including the Native American Brotherhood Organization, the Aboriginal Uintah Nation of Utah, the Navajo Inmate Spiritual/Social Development Organization, and the Navajo Nation Corrections Project. In 1993 the United States Congress passed the Religious Freedom Restoration Act, which encouraged litigation on behalf of Native American inmates if their rights were not honored during incarceration. What this meant in layman's terms is that: (1) prisoners have equal access to Native American religious ceremonies that are comparable to what is allowed for Judeo-Christian practitioners; (2) prisoners can wear their hair according to tribal customs; (3) there can be no discrimination against those who practice these beliefs; and (4) non-Indian workers within the penal system must receive training to increase their sensitivity to these rights and their obligations.[25]

In 1996 the Utah Legislature passed Senate Bill 128, "Indian Worship at Correctional Facilities," which guaranteed the state's commitment to equality. One section itemized some of the objects permitted for use in ceremonies: cedar, corn husks, corn pollen, corn meal, eagle and other feathers, sage, sweet grass, willows, drums, gourds, lava rock, medicine bundles, bags or pouches, staffs, pipes, and tobacco.[26]

This last object has raised the eyebrows of some prison officials. Tobacco, as contraband, cannot be used by inmates. The fear now is that it will become a black market item and that the allowing of it shows favoritism to a small sector (in 1996, 1.4 percent) of the state's prison population.[27] Native Americans counter that tobacco is an integral part of their traditional religious practices and is used in the rehabilitative process to combat substance abuse. Leonard Foster, Director of the Navajo Nation Corrections Project, argued, "Approximately 95 percent of those Native

Americans incarcerated are serious substance abusers and under the influence of alcohol while committing a crime and this rate is 30–50 percent higher than that of other ethnic groups in the institutions." He indicated elsewhere that when Indians participate in indigenous religious
rituals while in prison only 7 percent become repeat offenders, compared with the 30–40 percent who do not.[28]

Issues still arise involving the contents of medicine bundles, the type
of tobacco to be used, and whether pipes or cigarettes are acceptable.
Guards have interrupted the middle of some ceremonies to perform ac-
countability or contraband checks, thus killing the spirit of the rite. Also,
spiritual advisors often are not consulted when an interpretation of what
is or is not acceptable is made by prison officials.[29] While many things
have improved for Native American inmates, there is room for greater
progress.

The same can also be said for the treatment of members of the Native American Church (NAC). This organization's history, even after it
was officially formed and recognized in 1918, has seen it be the object of
attacks and litigation. Central to the conflict is peyote, a hallucinogenic
drug whose use is viewed by participants as a sacrament. Estimates of
membership in this loosely organized church vary within each reservation, ranging from 90 percent of Southern Utes, to 50 percent of Goshutes,
to 2 percent of Western Shoshone in 1972. Even with the passage of the
U.S. Drug Abuse Act (1972), which exempted peyote from prosecution
when used by members of the NAC, and the American Indian Religious
Freedom Act (1978), harassment and persecution of NAC members have
continued.[30]

For instance, Indians serving in the military during the 1970s and
1980s were not allowed to practice NAC ceremonies. As late as 1996 the
Marines rejected for reenlistment a Navajo member of the church when
they learned that he had participated in a ceremony. It was not until
April 1997 that the barrier was dropped and the stigma removed for practitioners.[31] From a Utah standpoint, this and the acceptance of other
aspects of Indian religion have come in support of the Religious Freedom Restoration Act (1993), championed by both the Mormon church
and U.S. Senator Orrin Hatch (R-Utah).[32]

To some people in the Native American community, the involvement of the LDS church as an advocate on behalf of Indian religious
practices is somewhat strange. The long history of Mormon and Indian
relations in Utah has been discussed in previous chapters and has not
often been a very positive one. However, one program that has only been

lightly touched upon is that of the LDS Indian Placement Program, officially inaugurated in 1954 after some tentative first steps.

In order to qualify for the program, a child that was to be placed in an Anglo home in a white community needed to be a member of the LDS church, accepted for placement, have a physical examination, obtain written consent from his or her biological parents, and show a basic understanding of English. It was a strictly voluntary program. Once a person was accepted, he or she would arrive at their new home, where they would stay for nine months of the year to attend school. The adopting family would cover the costs of food, clothing, and other expenses, without reimbursement. The child might return to the same family for a number of years until either the educational process was completed or a necessary change was made.

During the first year of the program in 1954, 253 children entered foster homes; fifteen years later, an estimated 4,500 students from thirty-two tribes were placed with Mormon families in thirty states and two provinces in Canada.[33] By 1978 there were 2,000 Navajos from New Mexico and Arizona alone being placed in LDS homes, with another 500–700 from the Utah portion of the reservation.[34] This growing number of students coincided with the cultural activism of the 1960s and 1970s and turned what started as a benevolent educational endeavor into a hot-bed of contention. Spokespeople from various tribes began accusing the program of cultural genocide, as a prisoner exchange for free labor, and as a violation of the Indian Child Welfare Act (1978). Those in favor of the program pointed out its voluntary nature, the academic progress of those who participated as contrasted with those who did not, and the success of graduates who returned to the reservation to help their people. Both groups freely admitted that there were problems.

The LDS church's position on the issue changed with the times. The previous age of eligibility of eight years old was raised to students entering the ninth grade, some fourteen or fifteen years old. Beginning in 1990 the program took on such a selective spin that it was reduced to 450 participants; by 1996 it had dwindled to fifty. Enrollment is now described as only a "handful" who are completing their course of study.[35] No new students have been enlisted recently; thus, for all intents and purposes, the program has ended.

Unfortunately, some of the animosity towards the Mormons has not. This became particularly apparent as the state celebrated its centennial anniversary of statehood in 1996 and then, the following year, its pioneer sesquicentennial festivities, marking 150 years since the Mormon

Mae T. Parry of the Northwest Shoshone Band, who has worked tirelessly to preserve the history and heritage of her people. (Courtesy Mae Parry)

pioneers arrived in Utah. Larry Cesspooch, public relations director for the Ute Tribe, described the latter as not being a celebration for Utes. "It's a celebration for [non-Indians] taking over our culture and land."[36] Even though the LDS church and state agencies encouraged Indian participation in the events, little was done to effect it, nor was there much participation from Indians.

While the Mormons, because of their conspicuous presence in Utah, may take the blame for some of the wrongs committed in the past against Native Americans, their chastisement is mild compared to what the state and federal government have received. The number and complexity of issues of each tribe as it interacts with state and federal agencies is bewildering and worthy of an entire volume to sort them out. What can be

Wallace Zundell of the Northwest Shoshone Band scraping a deer hide. (Courtesy Mae Parry)

said, however, is that these dealings are best characterized as a "love-hate" relationship that has existed from the beginning. Tribal groups are dependent upon the trust relationship established by the federal government, from which comes economic aid and a special "domestic, dependent" status that allows a certain autonomy. At the same time, the tribes want to enjoy a freedom that at times conflicts with what state and federal agencies would like to see accomplished. Money and power reside at the root of the turmoil.

While each tribe has its own history of relationships with various government entities, one example may illustrate the complexity of what they face. The Utes on the Uintah and Ouray Reservation have 490 oil wells that have produced almost a steady 1,250 barrels per day over the last ten years.[37] They, along with the Navajos and White Mesa Utes, are among the Utah tribes that have filed a suit against the government for money that has been misplaced, mismanaged, or lost through the federal trust-fund system. The Utah tribes joined national Indian leaders in applying for some $450 million that has been controlled by the government for over one hundred years.

A Navajo woman at an outdoor loom with an exhibit of native
vegetable dyes used in Navajo rug making. (U of U)

There are two types of accounts in question—the tribal trust funds
that come mostly from lawsuits and the tribal and individual accounts
that come from royalties on natural resources, land leases, and invest-
ments. The exact amount of money that the government held for various tribes is unknown. As one reporter explained, "The amount of money
tied up in all the various trust funds is mind boggling.... The Office of
Trust Funds Management in Albuquerque said in 1995 that it handled
$2.6 billion in American Indian trust funds, about $2.1 billion for 1,500
tribal accounts and $453 million for nearly 390,000 individual American
Indian accounts."[38] The latter is what is in question.

The Government Accounting Office is struggling to solve the question of who gets what. Bad accounting practices and the sheer volume of transactions have led to a confusing mess that will only be settled through litigation. How much money the Utah tribes may receive at the conclusion is unknown, but the whole controversy breeds mistrust. Robert Allan, an attorney for the Navajo Nation, summarized the hope of all the Native Americans when he said, "We might stand to get money rightfully ours, but wrongfully taken."[39]

Another example of how mistrust colors Anglo and Indian relationships is found in the talk of splitting San Juan County into two entities. The division, if accepted, would create an Indian (primarily Navajo) and a non-Indian county. The friction that has existed on both sides for many years came to a head through deliberations on whether or not this split was feasible. The contention focused on a myriad of issues but can be summarized as two different social, economic, and political philosophies at odds with each other.

The roots of the conflict reside in questions of Navajo tribal sovereignty, which creates problems that the county cannot solve by itself. Who is supposed to pay for services on the reservation, support the schools, define school district policy, maintain the roads, determine the jurisdiction of tribal courts and law enforcement, and so on? Some of these questions have been satisfactorily answered, but others have not. In 1996 Navajo Nation President Albert Hale signed a memorandum of understanding to work with Utah's newly established Native American Legislative Liaison Committee to try to find solutions. Founded in 1995, this organization's purpose is to work with reservations throughout the state to formulate answers to problems and then propose appropriate bills to Utah's legislature.[40] While the splitting of a county was a huge issue, similar problems of sovereignty existed with most Utah tribes.

Fundamental to this type of political issue is an economic issue. In San Juan County, property owners felt they had paid, and would continue to have to pay, taxes to solve reservation problems. Since Navajos living on the reservation do not pay county property taxes, it did not seem fair that the white minority (though only by a small percentage fewer than the Indians) should have to support the growing Navajo population.[41] Some people expressed the feeling that everyone should be treated equally and that the special status of the reservation should be done away with entirely.

This was the environment that the Center for Public Policy and Administration, an independent arbitrator from the University of Utah,

stepped into. Its task was to form a blue-ribbon committee to study the issue and then present its findings. That was in 1995. By 1997 the final report was available to county residents; but it held nothing very surprising. It stated that if the split were carried out the southern county (Indian) would have a difficult time meeting its financial obligations, since most of the businesses are in the north. The report did not recommend any particular course of action, but, in order for the split to be accomplished, it would require 25 percent of the voters in San Juan County to sign a petition to get the process underway.[42] At this point, the issue appears dead. What is important, however, are the feelings engendered by the trust relationship and special status of reservations. Similar questions and feelings have existed since the beginning of the federal government's program of establishing enclaves for Indian people.

The special status afforded Native Americans has led to other questions on a state, local, and tribal level. For instance, a Navajo man, Loren Crank, recently filed a lawsuit against the Seventh District Court, claiming that the number of Indians represented on juries was far below what it should be. The court claimed that because of a reservation Indian's special status, such Native Americans could not be required to serve on a jury the same way that other people could. The court's findings indicated that jury lists should be expanded to include those living on the reservation, and the tribe agreed to help enforce the ruling that these people fulfill their obligation as jurors.[43]

Litigation also led to a court order requiring the San Juan School District to build a small high school (at an estimated cost of $4.1 million) for students living in the Navajo Mountain area. Although there were only thirty-five student enrollees as of October 1997, the county and the state have committed to this outreach project to eliminate bussing and boarding students.[44]

The Uintah Utes were not as fortunate in having a recent school problem solved: the placement of a Ute on the Uintah School Board. Although there was an opportunity to have a Native American serve in a vacated position, none of the three Indian candidates was selected, sending signals to the tribe of mistrust and prejudice. Talk of boycotting three Uintah County schools that have a significant number of Indian children did not bring results. At the time of this writing, there is no Native American on the school board.[45]

Even the most basic issue—who is an Indian—has become a question. To be eligible for BIA services, a person must be a member of a federally recognized tribe and have one-fourth or more Indian ancestry.

On the other hand, the tribes define their own membership requirements. In Utah, this means that the Utes insist on one having one-half Indian blood; the Goshute, Navajo, and Paiute require one-quarter Indian blood; and the Shoshone one-eighth.

This appears to be straightforward. However, if what is happening in the rest of the nation is any indication of what the future holds for Utah's Native Americans, there will be a gradual shift in acceptance. Some tribes in the East have dropped the bloodline issue (for example, for the Pequot in Connecticut it is one-sixteenth) and have moved to insisting that applicants for tribal status prove their relationship to a member on the census rolls of 1900 or 1910.[46] The Southern Utes in Colorado and the Shoshone Indians in Wyoming report an ever-increasing number of people trying to have their names placed on the tribal roles, even though some of these people do not know where the tribes are located or the names of their grandparents.[47]

Why is there suddenly a high interest in Indian ancestry? Part of it can be explained through the increasingly positive image of Native Americans in film and literature. It is generally considered an honor to be a member of a tribe. Just ask Karl Malone, star player for the Utah Jazz basketball team, who emotionally accepted the name of "The Bear Who Leads with Dignity" given him by the White Mesa Utes.[48] Another reason is that more people are claiming Indian ancestry on census data; the figure of 800,000 Indians found on the 1970 census record jumped to some 1.9 million twenty years later—an increase of 140 percent.[49] And finally, there are economic advantages that can come from money specially earmarked for Native American education or disbursement from royalties or tribal earnings. This is particularly true with eastern groups, where the profits from tribally owned casinos have proven to be substantial.

Tied directly to the issue of tribal status is that of marriage. Until 1997, Native Americans had to be married by a duly recognized authority figure of the dominant society. This person could be a justice of the peace, a Mormon bishop, a minister or priest from another Christian denomination, or a Jewish rabbi. Many Indians were offended by the fact that spiritual leaders from their own tribe were not given the same status and that often a traditional wedding needed to be followed by a ceremony with one of the other "recognized" authorities.

Utah House Bill 186 changed all of that in 1997. Now, an Indian religious leader—defined as one who "leads, instructs or facilitates a Native American religious ceremony or service and is recognized as a

John Duncan, a leader of the Uintah Band of the Ute Tribe, in ceremonial dress. (U of U)

spiritual advisor by a federally recognized Native American tribe"—can perform the service.[50] The certificate provided at the end of the ceremony is just as binding in a court of law as any other provided by an already accepted source.

One of the most vocal advocates of Native American rights and a player in the midst of most issues is the Utah Division of Indian Affairs (UDIA). Established in 1953, it serves as the official organization in voicing concerns of the tribes. It has four legislatively created committees that represent and unify efforts on behalf of Utah's approximately 25,000 Indian people.[51] These committees are: (1) the Utah Indian Cooperative Indian Council, (2) the Outreach Subcommittee, (3) the Native American Remains Review Committee, and (4) the state Native American Coordinating Board.

The activities of this organization are so far-ranging that just to name the eighty different projects listed in its annual report for 1996 is beyond the scope of this chapter. Suffice it to say, it has assisted tribes with everything from grant writing to collecting oral histories, from assessing health care to supervising construction of the Indian Burial Repository, and from training Job Service staff in hiring Indian employees to assisting the BLM in producing an educational video.[52] The UDIA's work is felt throughout the state.

As people think of Utah's diverse Native American population, they often envision life on a reservation. The scene is almost stereotypical, with elders huddled around a woodburning stove, youngsters herding livestock on horseback, and the ubiquitous pickup truck hauling wood, water, or the family to town. While these are all very real images, they ignore a growing sector of Utah's Indian community. According to the 1990 U.S. Census, the second largest group of Native Americans in the state—6,111—live in Salt Lake County, the largest group being in San Juan County (6,859), with the third largest in Uintah County (2,335).[53]

What this means is that the urban Indian population, at 25 percent of the state's total Indian population, is growing and will play an important part, now and in the future, in determining the direction of Utah's Native American cultural heritage. While individuals may get lost in the sea of other cultures found in the city, their presence becomes particularly noticeable when they come together.

There are some two dozen organizations along the Wasatch Front that are designed to do just that—bring Native Americans together. They include Native American Community Services (LDS Social Services), Indian Christian Center (non-denominational), Utah Inter-tribal Veter-

ans Association, American Indian Resource Center, Intertribal Students Association (University of Utah), and Native American Educational Outreach (Brigham Young University). All of these organizations help bring together Native Americans to either receive specific services or to celebrate their unique heritage.

A look at two organizations helps one appreciate the importance of this type of institution in fostering a pan-Indian environment in an urban setting. One is the Indian Walk-In Center. Having now been established for twenty-three years, this non-profit organization supported by the United Way Agency has a mission to materially assist, promote cultural values and heritage, and strengthen the families and communities of Native Americans.

The volume and scope of the Center's accomplishments are impressive. In 1996 more than 18,000 people, half of whom were under the age of eighteen, received help with emergency food. While this service is available to all low-income families, members from all of Utah's tribes as well as forty-three other tribes who had members living along the Wasatch Front were among the recipients of this aid. The Center also provides counseling services, cultural enrichment programs for Indian youths, an elders program, and a rehabilitation program for alcohol abuse. Each month there is a powwow that draws an average of 400–500 participants, while at Christmas time an average of 600 needy people receive a Christmas dinner and toys for the children.[54]

To support many of these activities, the Center sponsors a variety of fund-raising activities. For instance, it rents parking space for Salt Lake Buzz baseball games, the fees from which go to its programs. Indian arts and crafts shows raise money while giving talented Native American artists an opportunity to gain public exposure. Local businesses and individuals are canvassed for support of special programs such as the Christmas dinner. Auctions bring in yet another group of contributors.[55] One reason that the Center has remained viable for so long, when many similar programs blossom and die within a short period of time, is its flexibility to reach many different parts of both the Indian and non-Indian community of Salt Lake City.

Five blocks south of the Walk-In Center is another organization, the Indian Training Education Center (ITEC), which has enjoyed similar success. This Utah-based, private non-profit corporation, funded in part by a federal grant, was established in 1988 to provide short-term (usually three to nine months) job training and education for Native Americans. An applicant must be over the age of fourteen, economically disad-

Members of the Northwest Shoshone Band Tribal Council. (Courtesy Mae Parry)

vantaged, and living off reservation in Utah. Programs available include adult basic education, GED preparation, high school completion, occupational skills training, and assisting in the acquiring of short-term college certificates or degrees.

ITEC conducted a study of its first five years (1989–1994) of operation to determine who was using its services and what kind of barriers and successes they had encountered. An interesting profile emerged, based upon the 1,044 individuals served by that time. The "typical" person who walked through the door was a Navajo (71 percent) male who was twenty-seven years old, supported a family of two, earned less than $8,000 per year, held a high school diploma but was unemployed, and who, at the end of the program, entered unsubsidized employment that provided a wage per hour increase.[56] Subsequent data essentially confirms this profile.

Upon entering the program, the new enrollee encounters personalized counseling and placement services. Monitoring of progress in the form of class attendance and satisfactory grades is tied to a monthly stipend for living expenses. At the end of the training, the participant is assisted in job search and placement. During the past eight years, ITEC has achieved an 80 percent success rate, meaning that its graduates have either "finished their programs successfully and/or entered into the job

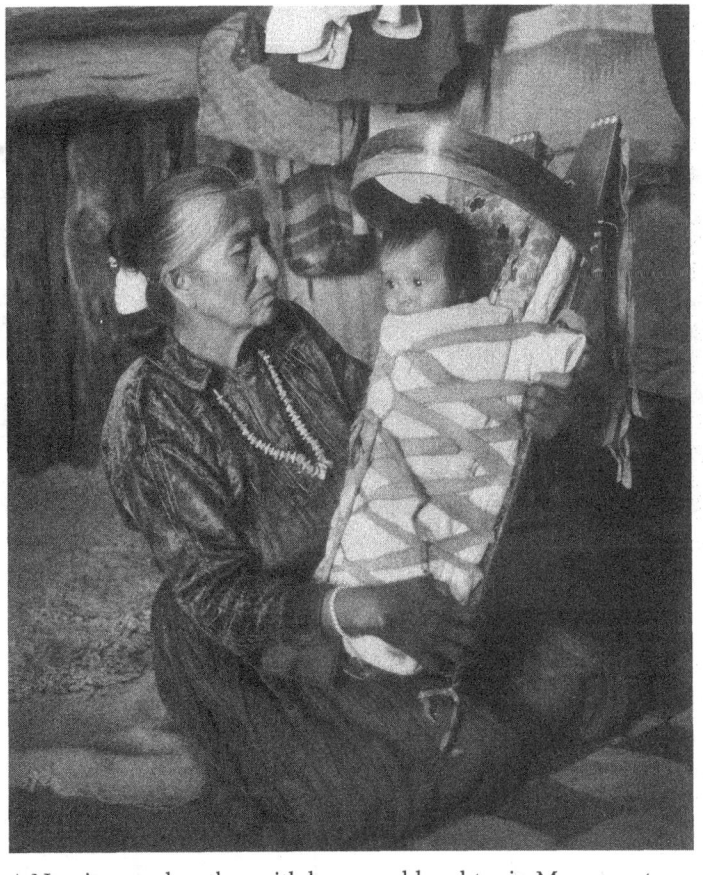

A Navajo grandmother with her granddaughter in Monument Valley. (USHS)

market better prepared than when they started."[57] All through this experience, cultural sensitivity ensures an open dialogue between students and counselors.

Thus, the present situation in Utah for the urban as well as the reservation Indian is one of change. As Native Americans enter the twenty-first century, they can look back with pride at the obstacles they have overcome and the progress that has been made. Their values and heritage at times may have been at odds with those of the dominant culture, but they nevertheless provided a firm support when grasped. Native peoples today still retain those values. Although there may be changes on the surface, there still remains the bedrock foundation that ties people to the land, to their families, and together as a community.

Photograph taken about 1880 of the Ute leader Guero,
one of many Indians who can be looked back upon
with pride by contemporary Native Americans. (USHS)

It is upon this bedrock that the future reposes. The challenges and changes ahead most likely will be just as disquieting and rapid as those in the past. They will take new forms and create obstacles never before imagined. Most of them probably will not be life-threatening but will tend to remove future generations from those principles that have been such a strong support in the past. The "new and improved" world of modern America will entice the youth as never before to stray from the traditional past.

But it will be their choice. Just as their elders made their choices as young people in the past, so will today's youth. The hope is that they will make these decisions based upon the wisdom of the past seasoned with a view to future generations. As they do so, the momentum will move them through the present and into the future, providing for the next generation a solid foundation of example upon which to live and build.

A Navajo woman with a child partially visible behind her. (USHS)

Notes to Chapters

Notes—Setting the Stage: Native America Revisited

[1] Calvin Martin, ed., *The American Indian and the Problem of History* (New York: Oxford University Press, 1987), 27, 33.

[2] Peter Iverson, "Indian Tribal Histories," in *Scholars and the Indian Experience*, ed. W.R. Swagerty (Bloomington: University of Indiana Press, 1984), 205–22.

[3] It is problematic to discuss Native American beliefs in general terms, since each tribe has specific ways of explaining the sacred. Even within the tribe or band there may be differences. For the reader who wishes to explore published works on the worldview of some of the tribes in Utah, the following books are suggested: Fred Conetah, Norma Denver, Daisy Jenks, Kathryn MacKay, Floyd O'Neil, *Stories of Our Ancestors—A Collection of Northern-Ute Indian Tales* (Salt Lake City: Uintah-Ouray Tribe, 1974); Trudy Griffin-Pierce, *Earth is My Mother, Sky is My Father* (Albuquerque: University of New Mexico Press, 1992); Gerald Hausman, *The Gift of the Gila Monster—Navajo Ceremonial Tales* (New York: Simon and Schuster, 1993); Ake Hultkrantz, "Mythology and Religious Concepts," *Handbook of North American Indians— Great Basin*, volume 10 (Washington: Smithsonian Institution, 1986): 630–40; Franc Johnson Newcomb, *Navaho Folk Tales* (Albuquerque: University of New Mexico Press, 1990); Karl W. Luckert, *Navajo Mountain and Rainbow Bridge Religion* (Flagstaff: Museum of Northern Arizona, 1977); Robert S. McPherson, *Sacred Land, Sacred View—Navajo Perceptions of the Four Corners Region* (Provo: Brigham Young University, 1992); William R. Palmer, *Pahute Indian Legends* (Salt Lake City: Deseret Book, 1946); Anne M. Smith, *Ethnography of the Northern Utes*, University of New Mexico Anthropological Papers 17, 1974; Anne M. Smith, *Ute Tales* (Salt Lake City: University of Utah Press, 1992); Colin F. Taylor, *Native American Myths and Legends* (London: Salamander Books, Ltd., 1994); and Paul G. Zolbrod, *Dine bahane* (Albuquerque: University of New Mexico Press, 1984).

⁴ McPherson, *Sacred Land, Sacred View*, 67–68.

⁵ See John W. Van Cott, *Utah Place Names* (Salt Lake City: University of Utah Press, 1990).

⁶ Jesse D. Jennings, "Prehistory: Introduction," *Handbook of North American Indians—Great Basin*, 113.

⁷ C. Melvin Aikens and David B. Madsen, "Prehistory of the Eastern Area," *Handbook of North American Indians—Great Basin*, 149–54.

⁸ Ibid., 154–57.

⁹ Ibid., 157–60.

¹⁰ There is a profusion of literature concerning the Anasazi. A good general overview may be obtained from Jesse D. Jennings, *Prehistory of Utah and the Eastern Great Basin*, University of Utah Anthropological Papers 98 (Salt Lake City: University of Utah Press, 1978): 95–153; and Winston B. Hurst, "The Prehistoric Peoples of San Juan County, Utah," *San Juan County, Utah*, ed. by Allan Kent Powell (Salt Lake City: Utah State Historical Society, 1983), 17–44.

¹¹ For further information see John P. Marwitt, "Fremont Cultures," *Handbook of North American Indians—Great Basin*, 161–72.

¹² See McPherson, *Sacred Land, Sacred View*, 77–127.

¹³ Jennings, *Prehistory of Utah*, 235.

¹⁴ See Wick R. Miller, "Numic Languages," *Handbook of North American Indians—Great Basin*, 98–106.

¹⁵ Brian D. Stubbs, "The Native American Languages of San Juan County," *Blue Mountain Shadows* 13 (Summer 1994): 63–67.

¹⁶ Julian H. Steward, *Basin-Plateau Aboriginal Sociopolitical Groups*, Bureau of American Ethnology Bulletin 120 (Washington: Smithsonian Institution, 1938): 235.

¹⁷ Ibid., 238.

¹⁸ See Brigham D. Madsen, *The Shoshoni Frontier and the Bear River Massacre* (Salt Lake City: University of Utah Press, 1985).

¹⁹ See Dan Vogel, *Indian Origins and the Book of Mormon* (Salt Lake City: Signature Books, 1986); Leonard J. Arrington and Davis Bitton, *The Mormon Experience—A History of the Latter-day Saints* (New York: Random House, 1979): 145–60; and Juanita Brooks, "Indian Relations on the Mormon Frontier, *Utah Historical Quarterly* 12, nos. 1-2 (1944): 1–48.

²⁰ Howard A. Christy, "Open Hand and Mailed Fist: Mormon Indian Relations in Utah, 1847–52," *Utah Historical Quarterly* 46 (Summer 1978): 216–61.

²¹ Richard D. Poll, Thomas G. Alexander, Eugene E. Campbell, and

David E. Miller, *Utah's History* (Provo: Brigham Young University Press, 1978), 689.

[22] Ibid., 357.

[23] Ibid., 730.

[24] Compare and contrast the previously cited works by Arrington, Brooks, and Christy for examples of the variety in interpretation scholars have made concerning Native Americans and their relations with white immigrants to Utah.

[25] See Robert S. McPherson, *The Northern Navajo Frontier 1860–1900: Expansion through Adversity* (Albuquerque: University of New Mexico Press, 1988), 10–12.

[26] Morris Shirts, "Mountain Meadows Massacre," *Utah History Encyclopedia*, Allan Kent Powell, ed. (Salt Lake City: University of Utah Press, 1994), 384–85.

[27] Richard O. Clemmer and Omer C. Stewart, "Treaties, Reservations, and Claims," *Handbook of North American Indians— Great Basin*, 544.

[28] See James S. Olson and Raymond Wilson, *Native Americans in the Twentieth Century* (Provo: Brigham Young University Press, 1984), 131–56. See also R. Warren Metcalf, "Lambs of Sacrifice: Termination, the Mixed-Blood Utes, and the Problem of Indian Identity," *Utah Historical Quarterly* 64 (Fall 1996): 322–43.

Notes—Shoshone

[1] See *Handbook of North American Indians*, Volume 11, *Great Basin* (Washington: Smithsonian Institution, 1986); Brigham D. Madsen, *The Northern Shoshoni* (Caldwell, ID: Caxton Printers, 1980); Robert H. Lowie, "The Northern Shoshone," *Anthropological Papers of the American Museum of Natural History*, Vol. 2 (New York, 1909); Omer C. Stewart, "Shoshoni History and Social Organization," *Idaho Yesterdays* 9 (Fall 1965); David B. Madsen and David Rhode, eds., *Across the West: Human Population Movement and the Expansion of the Numa* (Salt Lake City: University of Utah Press, 1994). These works describe the territory of the Shoshone bands and their social organization and relationships to other Great Basin region inhabitants prior to white contact. Indian Agent Frederick W. Lander reported to the Commissioner of Indian Affairs in February 1860 (United States National Archives, M234: Utah) the different bands of the Shoshone: the "Shoshonees or Eastern Snakes" (Washakie's Eastern Shoshones), the "Salmon River Snakes, Bannacks

and Snakes and Sheep Eaters" (the mixed band of the Lemhi Valley), the "Western Snakes," (the Northwestern Shoshone bands including Pocatello's), the "Bannacks, or Panackees or Pannacks" (the mixed buffalo-hunting bands of the Fort Hall region), "Bannacks of Fort Boise" (probably the mixed group which became known as the Boise Shoshones), the "Salt Lake Diggers, Lower or Southern Snakes" (the Northwestern Shoshone bands that lived among the Mormon settlements of northern Utah), and the "Warraricas, ['Sun-Flower Seed Eaters'] or Diggers or Bannacks, Below Fort Boise, West of the Blue Mountains" (probably the Paiute speakers known as "Snakes" in Oregon).

² Scott R. Christensen, "Sagwitch: Shoshoni Chieftain, Mormon Elder, 1822–1884" (Master's thesis, Utah State University, 1995), 11–12.

³ Ibid., 13–14. Chief Washakie (1804–1900); Chief Pocatello (ca. 1815–1884); Chief Sagwitch Timbimboo (1822–1884); Chief Bear Hunter (d. 1863) Chief Sanpitch (d. 1863); Chief Lehi (dates unknown). Sagwitch and Bear Hunter were cousins. The LDS leadership decided in their earliest encounters with native tribes against attempting to "buy" land. A policy of feed rather than fight with local tribes was decreed by Brigham Young in the earliest days of settlement and continued to be semi-official doctrine through the 1850s and 1860s, even though many individual Latter-day Saints complained about being forced to bear the economic hardship the policy entailed.

⁴ See Wick Miller, "Numic Languages," in *Handbook of North American Indians*, Volume 11, *Great Basin*, 98–106; Beverly Crum and John Dayley, "Western Shoshone Grammar," *Occasional Papers and Monographs in Cultural Anthropology and Linguistics*, Vol. 1 (Boise: Boise State University, 1993); Robert and Yolanda Murphy, "Shoshone-Bannock Subsistence and Society," *Anthropological Records* 16 (Berkeley: University of California Press, 1960).

⁵ According to May Parry research, Hitope Joshua related stories of Navajos and Utes trading horses for skins and buckskins with the Northwestern Shoshones. See Francis Haines, "Where Did the Plains Indians Get Their Horses?" *American Anthropologist* 40 (1938): 112–17; Francis Haines, "The Northward Spread of Horses Among the Plains Indians," *American Anthropologist* 40 (1938): 429–37; Dmitri B. Shimkin, "The Introduction of the Horse," in *Handbook of North American Indians*, Volume 11, *Great Basin*, 6–7; The spread of horses among Native American tribes, the arrival of the horse in the Great Basin, and the impact of horse ownership is well documented in these sources.

⁶ Mae Parry research. Traditional building methods of the "green-

houses" have been preserved through continued use; Kippie and Positze Norigen and other community residents built a traditional "greenhouse" each summer at Washakie, Utah.

[7] Mae Parry research. Annie Camasovah owned one of these blankets at Washakie, Utah, and showed construction methods.

[8] The author's grandmother Yampatch Wongan Timbimboo taught her grandchildren the traditional methods of food gathering and preparation.

[9] Mae Parry research. Moroni and Yeager Timbimboo showed their descendants (and photographed) the remnants of sagebrush corrals used during their and their parents' lifetimes. Diamond Wo me hup and Grouse Creek Jack related stories of large animal hunts.

[10] Mae Parry research. Annie Camasovah related this custom; and Wallace and Hazel Zundel attended a ceremony of this type.

[11] Brigham D. Madsen, *The Shoshoni Frontier and the Bear River Massacre* (Salt Lake City: University of Utah Press, 1985), 185. A California newspaper reporter accompanying Colonel Conner on the expedition which resulted in the Bear River Massacre in 1863 reported hastily dug entrenchments in both the ravine embankment and by the river. In the days following the massacre those who inspected the site concluded that neither was the case. On the ravine side, what were reported as foxholes were actually shallow steps to facilitate climbing up out of the ravine to the horse pasturage area, and those "entrenchments" by the river were judged to be natural depressions.

[12] Mae Parry research. Tribal history was passed to current generations of Northwestern Shoshones in this way. Survivors of the Bear River Massacre, including the author's direct ancestor Chief Sagwitch and his children, handed down the Indian account of what happened that day.

[13] Christensen, "Sagwitch: Shoshoni Chieftain," 34–36; Madsen, *The Shoshoni Frontier*, chapter 9; Mae Parry resesarch. Northwestern Shoshone oral tradition holds these three men from the Northwestern Shoshone camp on the Bear River as responsible for one of the key events that precipitated the army's attack in January 1863; Christensen and Madsen place the mens' actions in a larger context of events which began in late 1862 and continued through December.

[14] Brigham D. Madsen, *Chief Pocatello: The White Plume* (Salt Lake City: University of Utah Press, 1986), 54–55; Madsen cites the author's report of Northwestern Shoshone oral tradition which claims the men responsible for these murders were from Pocatello's band.

[15] Madsen, *The Shoshoni Frontier*, 154. Madsen relates the growing

tensions on both sides, writing, "The Mormon settlers of Cache Valley played their part. Tensions with neighboring Northwestern bands increased after the July 1860 killing of Chief Pagumap at Smithfield and the loss of two of the Saints at the hands of the revenge-seeking natives. Fighting seemed to be the rule during the next two years. Cache Valley residents mounted guard over their herds and fields and Chief Bear Hunter skillfully sought provisions for his people while negotiating with the Mormon leaders, but anger and frustration escalated on both sides as their impossible situation grew worse."

[16] Oral tradition passed through the author's family describes this event.

[17] Mae Parry research. As a direct descendant of Chief Sagwitch and Yeager Timbimboo, the chief's youngest surviving son of the massacre, the author was told stories of what happened that morning.

[18] See Brigham D. Madsen, *Glory Hunter: A Biography of Patrick Edward Connor* (Salt Lake City: University of Utah Press, 1990); Madsen, *The Shoshoni Frontier*, 167. Colonel Connor's intent of broad retribution to discourage further Indian aggression is well documented through Nevada and Utah in 1862–63. Before a similar punitive engagement in Nevada in late 1862, Connor ordered Major Edward McGarry to "destroy every male Indian whom you may encounter in the vicinity of the late massacres." As in Nevada, in the heat of fighting no distinction was made between men, women, children, young or old during the Bear River Massacre.

[19] Madsen, *The Shoshoni Frontier*, chapter 9. Madsen gives a point by point reconstruction of the course of the day's fighting and aftermath from army records and eyewitness accounts from white settlers and army participants.

[20] Mae Parry research. Ray Diamond lived at Washakie and was a family friend and neighbor of the author.

[21] Mae Parry research. Yeager Timbimboo is the author's grandfather.

[22] Madsen, *The Shoshoni Frontier*, chapter 9.

[23] Ibid., 193, 200.

[24] Mae Parry research. Oral tradition from family and other survivors.

[25] Ibid.

[26] Two monuments now are found at the site. The first, erected by the Daughters of Utah Pioneers, describes the conflict as a battle and celebrates the bravery of the soldiers and praises the aid offered by Cache

Valley residents to the wounded soldiers. The second, erected by the National Park Service, describes the conflict as a massacre and relates the basic facts of the Northwestern Shoshone and army positions on that day.

[27] The Treaty of Box Elder in 1863 officially ended conflict with the Northwestern Shoshone bands. The treaty did not set aside a land base for the bands, though it did outline a territory to which Chief Pocatello claimed ancestral right for his band. The treaty also promised an annuity of $5,000 a year with an immediate $2,000 in goods given to relieve hardships.

[28] Mae Parry research. Forty public domain allotments were entered under the Homestead Act for Indian families. Existing records for these are located at the tribal offices on the Fort Hall Indian Reservation in Idaho. See Christensen, "Sagwitch: Shoshoni Chieftain, Mormon Elder." Christensen includes in his appendices a typescript of Chief Sagwitch Timbimboo's homestead affadavit.

[29] Christensen, "Sagwitch: Shoshoni Chieftain, Mormon Elder," 154–60. After the disaster at Corinne the LDS church more carefully designed the Malad farm to guard against the types of accusations leveled against Hill and the Indians by Corinne townspeople.

[30] Ibid. Christensen discusses in detail the Washakie farm and the administration of the farm by the LDS church.

[31] The author was born and raised at Washakie. Her family, including her great-grandfather Sagwitch, grandfather Yeager Timbimboo, and father Moroni Timbimboo, held land at Washakie and homesteaded adjacent land to the farm. The description of the settlement and its history comes from family knowledge and the oral traditions of the community.

[32] Christensen, "Sagwitch: Shoshoni Chieftain, Mormon Elder," 182. The Samaria sawmill was founded to provide wood for the completion of a canal needed for Washakie. The sawmill also produced lumber used to build the first dwellings at Washakie.

[33] Frank Timbimboo, interview, 1967, Doris Duke Oral History Project, Special Collections, Marriott Library, University of Utah.

[34] Fullmer Allred and Newel J. Cutler, interviews, 1967, Doris Duke Oral History Project, Special Collections, Marriott Library, University of Utah. Both men were LDS church employees at the Brigham City farm. Allred discusses church involvement in teaching Washakie residents building trades. Cutler discusses buildings and the general standard of living on the farm.

[35] Mae Parry research. Existing records for homesteads are located at

the tribal offices on the Fort Hall Indian Reservation in Idaho.

[36] Moroni and Mrs. Timbimboo, interview, 1967, Doris Duke Oral History Project, Special Collections, Marriott Library, University of Utah. Moroni Timbimboo (father of the author) speaks of the sheep herd and his memories of working on the Washakie farm as a boy.

[37] Mae Parry research. The author gathered this information from Washakie community members and from her own experience in the Washakie school.

[38] Mae Parry research; typescript held by author

[39] Dan Egan, "Shoshone Hoping to Reestablish Tribal Homeland in Northern Utah," *Salt Lake Tribune*, October 31, 1999, A-1.

Notes—Goshutes

[1] Captain J.H. Simpson, *Report of Explorations across the Great Basin of the Territory of Utah for a Direct Wagon-Route from Camp Floyd to Genoa, in Carson Valley, in 1859* (Washington, D.C.: Government Printing Office, 1876), 35–36.

[2] An Act to vacate and sell the present Indian Reservation in Utah Territory and to settle the Indians of said Territory in the Uinta Valley, May 5, 1864, *Statutes at Large*, vol. 13, chap. 77, p. 63.

[3] Sir Richard Francis Burton, *The City of the Saints and across the Rocky Mountains to California* (New York: Harper, 1862), 457; U.S., Department of Interior, Office of Indian Affairs, *Annual Report of the Commissioner of Indian Affairs for the Year 1870* (Washington, D.C.: Government Printing Office, 1870), 96, hereafter referred to as *Report of the Commissioner* (plus date); George M. Wheeler, "Report upon United States Geographical Surveys West of the One-hundredth Meridian," *Archaeology*, vol. 7 (Washington, D.C.: Government Printing Office, 1879), 410; Julian H. Steward, *Basin-Plateau Aboriginal Sociopolitical Groups* (1938; reprint, Salt Lake City: University of Utah, 1970), 132.

[4] Gloria Griffen Cline, *Exploring the Great Basin* (Norman: University of Oklahoma Press, 1963), 9.

[5] Carling I. Malouf, "The Gosiute Indians," *The Shoshone Indians* (New York: Garland Press, 1974), 35–36.

[6] Ibid., 36–37.

[7] Steward, *Basin-Plateau*, 48

[8] Ibapah is an anglicized form of the Goshute word "Ai-bim-pa," which means something like "white clay water." The water in Deep Creek

is often heavy with fine white clay materials. For more information see John W. Van Cott, *Utah Place Names* (Salt Lake City: University of Utah Press, 1990), 197.

[9] The meaning of the word Tooele is still in dispute. One source says it is the name of a Goshute Indian leader named "Tuilla"; other sources state it is a reference to the rushes and reeds that are sometimes called "tules." For more information see Van Cott, *Utah Place Names*, 372. Oquirrh is a Goshute word which has several meanings, some of which are "wooded mountain," "cave mountain," "west mountain," and "shining mountain." See also Van Cott, *Utah Place Names*, 282.

[10] Jesse D. Jennings, Elmer R. Smith, and Charles E. Dibble, *Indians of Utah: Past and Present* (Salt Lake City: University of Utah, 1959), 27.

[11] A number of works relating to human expansion into the Great Basin have been produced in the last decade. Previously held assumptions have undergone major revisions, and some new, controversial hypotheses have been developed. It appears that ancestors of the Goshute could have arrived in the Great Basin as recently as 1,000 years ago, or in a distant past of perhaps 8,000 to 12,000 years, or any time in between. For additional information on the controversy see David B. Madsen and David Rhode, eds., *Across The West: Human Population Movement and the Expansion of the Numa* (Salt Lake City: University of Utah Press, 1994).

[12] Ralph V. Chamberlin, "Place and Personal Names of the Gosiute Indians of Utah," *Proceedings of the American Philosophical Society* 52 (January–April, 1912): 2.

[13] Jennings, Smith, and Dibble, *Indians of Utah*, 17.

[14] Pierre-Jean De Smet, *Life, Letters and Travels of Father Pierre-Jean De Smet*, edited by Hiram M. Chittenden and Alfred T. Richardson, vol. 3 (New York: F.P. Harper, 1905), 1033.

[15] Jennings, Smith, and Dibble, *Indians of Utah*, 17; Malouf, "Gosiute Indians," 1974, 3–4.

[16] Ralph V. Chamberlin, "The Ethnobotany of the Gosiute Indians" *Philadelphia Academy of Natural Science Proceedings* 53 (1911): 337–44.

[17] Jennings, Smith, and Dibble, *Indians of Utah*, 17.

[18] Ibid.

[19] Ibid., 19.

[20] Information provided by Goshute tribal members Milton Hooper and Vyrie Grey, April 1996.

[21] Jennings, Smith, and Dibble, *Indians of Utah*, 17.

[22] Ibid., 36.

[23] Ibid., 37.

[24] Ibid.

[25] Carling I. Malouf and Elmer R. Smith, "Some Gosiute Mythological Characters and Concepts," *Utah Humanities Review* 1 (1947): 369–78.

[26] Anne M. Smith, ed., *Shoshone Tales* (Salt Lake City: University of Utah Press, 1994), 42.

[27] Malouf, "Gosiute Indians," 101.

[28] Dale L. Morgan, *Jedediah Smith and the Opening of the West* (Lincoln: University of Nebraska Press, 1964), 23.

[29] Maurice S. Sullivan, *The Travels of Jedediah Smith* (Santa Ana, CA: Fine Arts Press, 1934), 19–20.

[30] Charles Kelly, "Jedediah S. Smith on the Salt Desert Trail," *Utah Historical Quarterly* 3 (January 1930): 26.

[31] Malouf, "Gosiute Indians," 103.

[32] Osborne Russell, *Journal of a Trapper 1834–1843*, edited by Aubrey L. Haines (Lincoln: University of Nebraska Press, 1955), 121–22.

[33] For more information see LeRoy R. Hafen and Ann W. Hafen, *Old Spanish Trail: Santa Fe to Los Angeles* (Glendale, CA: Arthur H. Clark Company, 1954), and C. Gregory Crampton and Steven K. Madsen, *In Search of the Spanish Trail: Santa Fe to Los Angeles, 1829–1848* (Layton, Utah: Gibbs Smith, Publisher, 1994).

[34] Hafen and Hafen, *Old Spanish Trail*, 41.

[35] Eleanor Frances Lawrence, "The Old Spanish Trail from Santa Fe to California" (M.A. thesis, University of California, 1929), 101–2.

[36] *Acts, Resolutions, and Memorials passed at the several annual sessions of the Legislative Assembly of the Territory of Utah* (Great Salt Lake City: Henry McEwan, 1866), 102–3.

[37] John U. Terrell, *Pueblos, Gods and Spaniards* (New York: Dial Press, 1973), 246–47.

[38] Simpson, *Report of Exploration*, 54.

[39] A.R. Mortensen, ed., *West From Fort Bridger* (Salt Lake City: Utah State Historical Society, 1951), 186.

[40] Allan Nevins, *Fremont: Pathmarker of the West*, vol. 1 (New York: Frederick Ungar Publishing Co., 1961), 175–90.

[41] Andrew Love Neff, *History of Utah 1847 to 1869* (Salt Lake City: Deseret News Press, 1940), 370–82.

[42] Milton R. Hunter, *Brigham Young the Colonizer* (Salt Lake City: Deseret News Press, 1940), 234–42.

[43] *Inventory of the County Archives of Utah, No. 23, Tooele County* (Ogden, Utah: W.P.A. Historical Records Survey, 1939), 16–17, 35–36.

[44] Hunter, *Brigham Young*, 240–42.

[45] Ibid., 241–42.

[46] *History of Tooele County* (Salt Lake City: Daughters of Utah Pioneers, 1961), 311–12, 325.

[47] *County Archives*, 35–37.

[48] Malouf, "Gosiute Indians," 114–15; Major Howard Egan and Howard R. Egan, *Pioneering the West, 1846 to 1878* (Salt Lake City: H.R. Egan estate, 1917), 222–23.

[49] Malouf, "Gosiute Indians," 116–17.

[50] Daniel W. Jones, *Forty Years Among the Indians* (Salt Lake City: Bookcraft, 1960), 157.

[51] Malouf, "Gosiute Indians," 88.

[52] James B. Allen and Ted J. Warner, "The Goshute Indians in Pioneer Utah," *Utah Historical Quarterly* 39 (Spring 1971): 164.

[53] *County Archives*, 18–19; Edward W. Tullidge, *Tullidge's Histories*, vol. 2 (Salt Lake City: Juvenile Instructor Press, 1889), 83–86.

[54] Quoted in Carling I. Malouf, "A Study of the Gosiute Indians of Utah" (M.S. thesis, University of Utah, 1940), 70.

[55] Peter Gottfredson, *Indian Depredations in Utah*, reprint edition (Salt Lake City: n.p., 1969), 79.

[56] *Report of the Commissioner, 1858*, 561–65. See also Dale L. Morgan, "The Administration of Indian Affairs in Utah, 1851–1858," *Pacific Historical Review* 17 (November 1948): 406.

[57] *Report of the Commissioner, 1859*, 730–41.

[58] Ibid., 745–47.

[59] Ibid., 377–79; Jack D. Forbes, *Nevada Indians Speak* (Reno: University of Nevada Press, 1967), 37–39.

[60] *Report of the Commissioner, 1859*, 737.

[61] *Report of the Commissioner, 1861*, 130.

[62] See Simpson, *Report of Explorations*.

[63] Malouf, "Gosiute Indians," 95.

[64] *Report of the Commissioner, 1861*, 130.

[65] Ibid.

[66] Mark Twain, *Roughing It* (New York: New American Library), 118.

[67] Burton, *City of the Saints*, 559.

[68] Ibid., 540.

[69] Ibid., 558–71; Malouf, "Gosiute Indians," 129.

[70] Egan, *Pioneering the West*, 263–64; Albert B. Reagan, "Shoshoni-Goshute Indians and the Deep Creek Region, Utah," *Improvement Era* 22 (October 1919): 33.

[71] Amos Reed to William P. Dole, December 30, 1862, in "Letters Received by the Office of Indian Affairs, 1824–1881," National Archives, Microcopy M-243), hereafter referred to as "Letters Received."

[72] Allen and Warner, "Gosiute Indians," 167; Hubert Howe Bancroft, *History of Nevada, Colorado and Wyoming, 1540–1880* (San Francisco: A.L. Bancroft & Company, 1890), 219.

[73] James Doty to William P. Dole, April 22, 1863, in "Letters Received."

[74] *Report of the Commissioner, 1863*, 116–18.

[75] An Act to vacate and sell the present Indian Reservations in Utah Territory and to settle the Indians of said Territory in the Uinta Valley, May 5, 1864, *Statutes at Large*, vol. 13, chap. 77, p. 63.

[76] Allen and Warner, "Gosiute Indians," 168.

[77] U.S., *Statutes at Large*, 13 Stat. (1866).

[78] *Report of the Commissioner, 1864*, 319.

[79] O.H. Irish to William P. Dole, November 28, 1864, in "Letters Received."

[80] U.S., *Statutes at Large*, 13 Stat. 432 (1866).

[81] William P. Dole to O.H. Irish, March 28, 1865, in *Report of the Commissioner, 1865*, 149.

[82] O.H. Irish to William P. Dole, June 29, 1865, in *Report of the Commissioner, 1865*, 150–51.

[83] F.H. Head to N.G. Taylor, August 22, 1867, in *Report of the Commissioner, 1868*, 117.

[84] F.H. Head to Ely S. Parker, August 1, 1869, in *Report of the Commissioner, 1869*, 20–21; *History of Tooele*, 29.

[85] J.E. Tourtellotte to Ely S. Parker, September 20, 1869, in *Report of the Commissioner, 1869*, 230–31.

[86] J.E. Tourtellotte to Ely S. Parker, March 28, 1870, in "Letters Received."

[87] J.E. Tourtellotte to Ely S. Parker, April 31, 1870, in "Letters Received."

[88] H. Douglas to Ely S. Parker, September 20, 1870, in *Report of the Commissioner, 1870*, 560; John V. Dougherty to J.J. Critchlow, October 18, 1871, in "Letters Received."

[89] William Lee to J.J. Critchlow, April 23, 1871, in "Letters Received."

[90] George W. Dodge to F.A. Walker, February 2, 1872, in "Letters Received"; George W. Dodge to F.A. Walker, August 31, 1872, in "Letters Received." Dodge justified this recommendation by stating that the Shoshone-speaking Indians in Utah and Nevada were related to the Shoshone-speaking Comanches in Oklahoma.

[91] Allen and Warner, "Goshute Indians," 174.

[92] John W. Powell and George W. Ingalls, *Report of the Commissioner, 1873*, 51, 63.

[93] John W. Powell to John Q. Smith, November 26, 1875, in "Letters Received."

[94] William Lee to Edward P. Smith, March 17, 1877, in "Letters Received."

[95] Hunter, *Brigham Young*, 299.

[96] *Deseret Evening News*, June 2, 1874.

[97] Malouf, "Gosiute Indians," 146–47.

[98] Egan, *Pioneering the West*, 283.

[99] Edward H. Anderson, "Apostle Lyman's Mission to the Indians," *Improvement Era* 3 (1900): 515.

[100] Malouf, "Gosiute Indians," 154–55.

[101] Larry H. Godwin and Bruce D. Smith, eds., *Special Symposium 1994 on Economic Mineral Resources of the Goshute Indian Reservation, Nevada-Utah* (Golden, Colorado: Bureau of Indian Affairs, 1994), 1.

[102] Ronald R. Bateman, *Deep Creek Reflections: 125 Years of Settlement at Ibapah, Utah, 1859–1984* (Salt Lake City: Bateman, 1984), 367–68.

[103] Ibid., 370.

[104] Godwin and Smith, *Special Symposium 1994*, 4.

[105] Information provided by Utah State Division of Indian Affairs.

[106] Godwin and Smith, *Special Symposium 1994*, 3

Notes—Paiutes

[1] Mae Parashonts, interview with Ronald Holt, October 7, 1982, Holt fieldnotes, in authors' possession.

[2] Ronald L. Holt, *Beneath These Red Cliffs: A Southern Paiute Ethnohistory* (Albuquerque: University of New Mexico Press, 1992), 6–11. Also see Isabel Kelly and Catherine Fowler, "Southern Paiute," in *Handbook of North American Indians*, vol. 11, *Great Basin*, Warren d'Azevedo, ed. (Washington, D.C.: Smithsonian Institution, 1986), 368–70.

[3] Isabel T. Kelly, *Southern Paiute Ethnography* (Salt Lake City: University of Utah Press, 1964, 95. Also see LaVan Martineau, *The Southern Paiutes* (Las Vegas: KC Publications, 1993).

[4] Robert C. Euler, *Southern Paiute Ethnohistory* (Salt Lake City: University of Utah Press, 1966), 61–98.

[5] Robert J. Franklin and Pamela Bunte, *The Paiute* (New York: Chelsea House Publishers, 1990), 15–16.

[6] See Juanita Brooks, *Journal of the Southern Indian Mission: Diary of Thomas D. Brown* (Logan: Utah State University Press, 1972).

[7] See, for example, Juanita Brooks, *The Mountain Meadows Massacre* (Palo Alto: Stanford University Press, 1950), and Juanita Brooks, *John Doyle Lee: Zealot, Pioneer Builder, Scapegoat* (Glendale, CA: Arthur H. Clark Company, 1962. Numerous articles also have been written, many of which can be found at the Utah State Historical Society Library, Salt Lake City, Utah.

[8] See files of Paiute Tribe, Cedar City, Utah, Geneal Anderson, Chairwoman.

[9] Ibid.

[10] Richard W. Stoffle and Michael J. Evans, *Kaibab Paiute History: The Early Years* (Fredonia, AZ: Kaibab Paiute Tribe, 1978), 57.

[11] Ibid., 57–58. See also Brooks, *Mountain Meadows Massacre*, ix–xii.

[12] Holt, *Beneath These Red Cliffs*, 22–31.

[13] Inter-Tribal Council of Nevada, *Nuwuvi: A Southern Paiute History* (Salt Lake City: University of Utah Printing Service, 1967), 78.

[14] O.H. Irish, Articles of Agreement and Convention made and concluded at Pinto Creek, unratified treaty, National Archives, RG 75, 1865.

[15] Anthony W. Ivins, Journal, papers of Ronald L. Holt, Special Collections, Marriott Library, University of Utah. Also see Anthony Ivins, "Traveling over Forgotten Trails," *Improvement Era* 29 (1916): 350–56.

[16] William Manning, My Work Among the Indians, Journal, papers of Ronald L. Holt, Special Collections, Marriott Library, University of Utah.

[17] Ibid.

[18] William R. Palmer, "The Wahnquint Indians," 1946, Palmer Collection, Special Collections, Southern Utah University, Cedar City, Utah.

[19] Lyman S. Tyler, *A History of Indian Policy* (Washington, D.C.: Government Printing Office, 1973), 63–64.

[20] Mary J.T. Jacobs, "Termination of federal supervision over the Southern Paiute Indians of Utah" (M.S. thesis, University of Utah, 1976), 22.

[21] Holt, *Beneath These Red Cliffs*, 73–76.

[22] Gary Orfield, *A Study of the Termination Policy* (Denver: National Congress of American Indians, 1965), 4.

[23] Harry Stevens, Letter to Rex Lee, 1954, BIA files, Cedar City, Utah.

[24] Frank Scott, Action Taken Report, 1956, BIA files, Cedar City, Utah.

[25] Francis Prucha, *The Great Father*, abridged ed. (Lincoln: University of Nebraska Press, 1986), 351.

[26] See Y.T. Witherspoon, "Interim Report for the Educational-Vocational Survey of the Ute, Kanosh, Koosharem, Indian Peaks, and Shivwits Indians" (Salt Lake City: University of Utah, Extention Division, 1955).

[27] David J. Whittaker, "Mormons and Native Americans: A Historical and Bibliographical Introduction," *Dialogue* 18 (1985): 39.

[28] John W. Cragun, Letter to Philleo Nash, 1964, papers of Ronald L. Holt, Special Collections, Marriott Library, University of Utah, 3.

[29] Leonard M. Hill, "Social and Economic Survey of Shivwits, Kanosh, Koosharem, Indian Peaks, and Cedar City Bands of Paiute Indians," papers of Ronald L. Holt, Special Collections, Marriott Library, University of Utah, 2.

[30] Lafollette Butler, Letter to Wade Head, 1965, papers of Ronald L. Holt, Special Collections, Marriott Library, University of Utah.

[31] Holt, *Beneath These Red Cliffs*, 126–32.

[32] Ibid., 132–34.

[33] Paiute Indian Tribe of Utah, Proposed Paiute Indian Tribe of Utah Restoration Plan [draft], 1982, papers of Ronald L. Holt, Special Collections, Marriott Library, University of Utah.

[34] Quoted in Stephen Trimble, *The People: Indians of the American Southwest* (Santa Fe: SAR Press, 1993), 344.

[35] Holt, *Beneath These Red Cliffs*, 150–51.

[36] Ibid., 151.

[37] Ronald L. Holt, field notes, in author's possession.

Notes—Northern Utes

[1] Some of this history is based on information in Fred A. Conetah, *A History of the Northern Ute People* (N.p.: Uintah-Ouray Ute Tribe, 1982).

[2] *Deseret News*, December 13, 1851.

[3] Conetah, *A History of the Northern Ute People*, 27.

[4] *Dominguez-Escalante Journal*, 60.

[5] Hubert H. Bancroft, *History of Utah*, 278.

[6] *Deseret News*, October 25, 1861.

[7] *Commissioner of Indian Affairs Annual Report*, 1866, 144.

[8] See Kathryn L. MacKay, "The Strawberry Valley Reclamation Project and the Opening of the Uintah Indian Reservation," *Utah Historical Quarterly* 50 (1982).

Notes—White Mesa Utes

¹ Billy Mike, interview with Aldean Ketchum and Robert S. McPherson, October 13, 1993, transcript in possession of author.

² Don D. Fowler and Catherine Fowler, *Anthropology of the Numa: John Wesley Powell's Manuscripts on the Numic People*, Smithsonian Contributions to Anthropology 14 (Washington, D.C.: Smithsonian Institution, 1971), 78.

³ Pamela A. Bunte and Robert J. Franklin, *From the Sands to the Mountains: Change and Persistence in a Southern Paiute Community* (Lincoln: University of Nebraska Press, 1987), 227.

⁴ James A. Goss, "Culture-Historical Inference from Utaztekan Linguistic Evidence," paper presented at Plenary Symposium on Utaztekan Prehistory of the Society for American Archaeology and the Great Basin Anthropological Conference, May 1966, 11, 27.

⁵ Ibid., 28.

⁶ Alan D. Reed, "Ute Cultural Chronology," *An Archaeology of the Eastern Ute: A Symposium*, ed. Paul R. Nickens, Colorado Council of Professional Archaeology Occasional Papers Number 1 (Denver: 1988), 80–81; Winston Hurst, conversation with author, September 9, 1992.

⁷ Robert C. Euler, "Southern Paiute Archaeology," *American Antiquities* 29 (January 1964): 380; Reed, "Ute Cultural Chronology," 82; C.S. Fowler and D.D. Fowler, "The Southern Paiute: A.D 1400–1776," *The Protohistoric Period in the North American Southwest, A.D. 1350–1700*, D.R. Wilcox and W.B. Masse, editors, Arizona State University Archaeological Research Papers Number 24, 129–62.

⁸ C. Melvin Aikens and Younger T. Witherspoon, "Great Basin Numic Prehistory Linguistics, Archaeology, and Environment," *Anthropology of the Desert West: Essays in Honor of Jesse D. Jennings*, University of Utah Anthropological Papers Number 110 (1986), 9–20; Stephen C. Jett, "Testimony of the Sacredness of Rainbow Natural Bridge to Puebloans, Navajos, and Paiutes," *Plateau* 45 (Spring 1973): 54.

⁹ Goss, "Culture-Historical Inference," 29–30.

¹⁰ Ibid., 33–34.

¹¹ S. Lyman Tyler, "The Yuta Indians Before 1680," *Western Humanities Review* 8 (Spring 1951): 157, 160.

¹² Donald G. Callaway, Joel C. Janetski, and Omer C. Stewart, "Ute," in *Handbook of North American Indians*, Volume 11, *Great Basin* (Washington: Smithsonian Institution, 1986), 339.

[13] Ibid., 366. The entire issue about use of Weenuche and Weeminuche · is still very unclear. One elder explained that Weeminuche was fine and that Weenuche referred more to the prehistoric Ute peoples, while author Mary Jane Yazzie felt more comfortable with the name Weenuche.

[14] Isabel T. Kelly and Catherine S. Fowler, "Southern Paiute," in *Handbook of North American Indians*, Volume 11, *Great Basin*, 368, 396.

[15] William R. Palmer, "Utah Indians Past and Present—An Etymological and Historical Study of Tribes and Tribal Names from Original Sources," *Utah Historical Quarterly* 1 (April 1928): 52.

[16] Omer C. Stewart, *Culture Element Distributions: Ute-Southern Paiute* (Berkeley: University of California Press, 1942), 236.

[17] William R. Palmer, "San Juan Indians," Palmer Collection Notes, Special Collections, Southern Utah University, Cedar City, 32.

[18] Bunte and Franklin, *Sands to the Mountains*, 183, 232. Historic accounts by careful observers underscore these differences by saying that at times the Utes from the Montezuma Canyon-southwestern Colorado area would help whites control the Allen Canyon group and that the general term of "Paiute" was given to the latter, while those people nearer Colorado were called "Utes." See Lyman Hunter, interview with Michael Hurst, February 21, 1973, Charles Redd Center for Western Studies, Brigham Young University, Provo, Utah, 2; Kumen Jones manuscript, Utah State Historical Society, Salt Lake City, 106; Stella Eyetoo, interview with Aldean Ketchum and Robert S. McPherson, December 21, 1994, tape in possession of authors.

[19] E.L. Hewitt, "Field Notes 1906–09," photocopy, Edge of the Cedars Museum, Blanding, Utah; Mike, interview; Chester Cantsee, Sr., interview with Aldean Ketchum and Robert S. McPherson, September 6, 1994, transcript in possession of author; John W. Van Cott, *Utah Place Names* (Salt Lake City: University of Utah Press, 1990), 264.

[20] Julius S. Dalley, "Mancos Jim Mesa—San Juan County," Utah Writers' Project, August 11, 1942, Utah State Historical Society Library.

[21] Fowler and Fowler, *Anthropology of the Numa*, 67–76.

[22] See William R. Palmer, "The Pahute Fire Legend," *Utah Historical Quarterly* 6 (April 1933): 62–64; Albert B. Reagan, "Mother Nature," Albert B. Reagan Collection, Special Collections, Harold B. Lee Library, Brigham Young University, 64–65; Uintah Ouray Tribe, *Stories of Our Ancestors: A Collection of Northern Ute Indian Tales* (Salt Lake City: University of Utah Press, 1974), 22.

[23] Carla Knight, "The Utes and Their Environment," unpublished paper, used with permission, in possession of author.

[24] Terry Knight, spiritual leader of the Ute Mountain Utes, interview with Mary Jane Yazzie and Robert S. McPherson, December 19, 1994, tape in possession of authors.

[25] Marvin Kaufman Opler, "The Southern Ute of Colorado," in *Acculturation in Seven American Indian Tribes* (New York: D. Appleton-Century Company, 1940), 141–42; Fowler and Fowler, *Anthropology of the Numa*, 66; Knight, interview.

[26] Harold Lindsay Amoss, Jr., "Ute Mountain Utes" (Ph.D. diss., University of California, 1951), 90.

[27] Frank Silvey, "Information on Indians," September 26, 1936, Utah State Historical Society Library, 1–2. While Silvey's work addresses this topic specifically, many of the sites mentioned are known from a scattering of historical documents that span one hundred years

[28] Frank Silvey, "Indians in San Juan," June 10, 1940, Silvey Files, Utah State Historical Society, 4.

[29] Amoss, "Ute Mountain Utes," 55–61; Ralph V. Chamberlain, "Some Plant Names of the Ute Indians," *American Anthropologist* 2 (January-March 1909): 27–37.

[30] Amoss, "Ute Mountain Utes," 49–51.

[31] Opler, "The Southern Ute," 141–45; Amoss, "Ute Mountain Utes," 36–38.

[32] Amoss, "Ute Mountain Utes," 37–38; Chamberlain, "Some Plant Names," 27–40; James Jefferson, Robert W. Delaney, and Gregory Thompson, *The Southern Utes: A Tribal History* (Ignacio, CO: Southern Ute Tribe, 1972): 72–73.

[33] Mary Jane Yazzie, "Life and Traditions of the Utes of Avikan," unpublished manuscript, in possession of author; Joseph G. Jorgensen, *The Sun Dance Religion: Power for the Powerless* (Chicago: University of Chicago Press, 1972), 23–25.

[34] David J. Weber, *The Taos Trappers: The Fur Trade in the Far Southwest* (Norman: University of Oklahoma Press, 1968), 23.

[35] See G. Clell Jacobs, "The Phantom Pathfinder: Juan Maria Antonio de Rivera and His Expedition," *Utah Historical Quarterly* 60 (Summer 1992): 201–23.

[36] Donald C. Cutter, "Prelude to a Pageant in the Wilderness," *Western Historical Quarterly* 8 (January 1977): 4–14; F.A. Barnes, "A Journey to the Rio del Tizon," *Canyon Legacy* 9 (Spring 1991): 16–22; F.A. Barnes, "Update—Rivera's 1765 Expedition," *Canyon Legacy* 10 (Summer 1991): 31.

[37] Joseph J. Hill, "Spanish and Mexican Exploration and Trade North-

west from New Mexico into the Great Basin, 1765–1853," *Utah Historical Quarterly* 3 (January 1930): 5, 27–31.

[38] Ibid., 90.

[39] Ibid., 101–4.

[40] Ted J. Warner, ed., *The Dominguez-Escalante Journal: Their Expedition Through Colorado, Utah, and New Mexico in 1776* (Provo: Brigham Young University Press, 1976): 33.

[41] Weber, *Taos Trappers*, 27; L.R. Bailey, *Indian Slave Trade in the Southwest* (Los Angeles: Westernlore Press, 1966), 143.

[42] Bailey, *Indian Slave Trade*, 144; Hill, "Spanish and Mexican Exploration," 17–18.

[43] J. Lee Correll, *Through White Men's Eyes: A Contribution to Navajo History*, volume 3 (Window Rock: Navajo Heritage Center, 1979): 141, 147, 149, 154, 179–80.

[44] C. Gregory Crampton, "Utah's Spanish Trail," *Utah Historical Quarterly* 47 (Fall 1979): 361–82; Steven K. Madsen, "The Spanish Trail Through Canyon Country," *Canyon Legacy* 9 (Spring 1991): 23–29. For a detailed account of the trail see Leroy R. Hafen and Ann W. Hafen, *The Old Spanish Trail: Santa Fe to Los Angeles* (Glendale, CA: Arthur H. Clark Company, 1954).

[45] G. Douglas Brewerton, "A Ride with Kit Carson," *Harpers New Monthly Magazine* 8 (April 1854): 312–13; Conway B. Sonne, *World of Wakara* (San Antonio: Naylor Company, 1962), 135.

[46] U.S., Congress, Senate, *Report of the Secretary of War*, John Garland to Army Headquarters, January 31, 1858; J.G. Walker to Commander, September 20, 1859, S. Ex. Doc 2, 36th Cong., lst Sess., 339–40.

[47] William Brooks to Assistant Adjutant General, July l and 15, 1858, Record Group 98, Records of the United States Army Commander, Department of New Mexico, 1858, National Archives, Washington, D.C.

[48] Dixon Miles to Nichols, September 3 and 8, 1858, Record Group 98, National Archives.

[49] Electus Backus to William Lane, November 19, 1858, Record Group 98, National Archives; "Return of Spies and Guides," *Santa Fe Gazette*, January 15, 1859, cited in Correll, *Through White Men's Eyes*, 239.

[50] Thomas T. Fauntleroy to Winfield Scott, January 29, 1860, Record Group 98, National Archives.

[51] Paul Jones, interview with Aubrey Williams, January 19, 1961, Duke #712; George Martin, Sr., interview with David Brugge, March 22, 1961, Duke #913; Maggie Holgate, interview with Gary Shumway, June 13, 1968, Duke #956.

[52] Major Albert Pfeiffer to A.K. Graves, December 10, 1866; Felipe Delgado to Office of Indian Affairs, January 7, 1866, Record Group 75, Letters Received by Office of Indian Affairs, New Mexico Superintendency, 1866 and 1868, National Archives.

[53] "Report of Special Agent J.K. Graves," 1866, *Report of the Secretary of the Interior*, 39th Cong., 2nd Sess, House Ex. Doc. l, 132; Archuleta to Graves, January 1, 1866, ibid., 141.

[54] W.F.M. Arny to A.B. Norton, "Abiquiu Agency Report," June 24, 1867, *Report of the Commissioner of Indian Affairs*, 206.

[55] W.F.M. Arny to Charles Mix, October 3, 1868, Letters Received, Office of Indian Affairs—New Mexico Superintendency, 1868 (hereafter cited as Letters Received—NM).

[56] John Ayers, Abiquiu Agency Annual Report, August 16, 1869, Report of the Commissioner of Indian Affairs (hereafter cited as RCIA), 240–43; Ayers, Abiquiu Agency Annual Report, September 3, 1870, RCIA, 618–20. For a fuller treatment of this period for both the Utes and the Navajos see Robert S. McPherson, *The Northern Navajo Frontier, 1860–1900: Expansion through Adversity* (Albuquerque: University of New Mexico Press, 1988).

[57] J.B. Hanson, Abiquiu Agency Annual Report, September 11, 1871, RCIA, 408.

[58] Calloway, Janetski, and Stewart, "Ute," 355.

[59] "Treaty Between the United States of America and the Navajo Tribe of Indians" (Las Vegas: KC Publications, 1973), 22, 24. See McPherson, *Northern Navajo Frontier* for further information.

[60] "Cattle Companies," General File, Monticello Ranger District, Monticello, Utah, 2.

[61] Edmund S. Carlisle to W.M. Clark, October 1, 1884; Carlisle to Major Hall (Fort Lewis, Colorado) November 8, 1884; John F. Tapping to William Clark, December 16, 1884, Record Group 75, Consolidated Ute Records, Denver Record Center (hereafter cited as Consol. Ute).

[62] George M. Williams to Post Adjutant, December 11, 1889, National Archives, Record Group 75, Letters Received, 1881–1907, Bureau of Indian Affairs (hereafter cited as Letters Received—BIA).

[63] Ibid.; Silvey, "Indians in San Juan," 42.

[64] Charles A. Bartholomew to David L. Shipley, October 13, 1890, Consol. Ute; Bartholomew "To the Navajo Indians," November 11, 1890, Letters Received-BIA.

[65] For further information see Faun McConkie Tanner, *The Far Country—A Regional History of Moab and La Sal, Utah* (Salt Lake City:

Olympus Publishing Company, 1976): 105–46; Don D. Walker, "Cowboys, Indians, and Cavalry—A Cattleman's Account," *Utah Historical Quarterly* 34 (Summer 1966): 255–62; Cornelia Perkins, Marian Nielson, and Lenora Jones, *Saga of San Juan* (Salt Lake City: Mercury Publishing Company, 1957), 234–44; and Albert R. Lyman, "History of San Juan County, 1879–1917," manuscript, Harold B. Lee Library, Brigham Young University, 22–23, 41–42.

[66] Edmund S. Carlisle to William M. Clark, October 1, 1884, Ute Agency Files, Federal Record Center, Denver.

[67] Edmund S. Carlisle to William M. Clark, December 30, 1884, DRC —Ute Agency. See Walker, "Cowboys, Indians, and Cavalry," 255–62.

[68] Larabee to Thomas McCunniff, June 17, 1889, Consol. Ute Agency; "Report of Brigadier-General Crook," *Report of the Secretary of War*, 1887, 1st Sess., 50th Cong., 133.

[69] Frank Moss Papers, Special Collections, Marriott Library, University of Utah, Salt Lake City, 55.

[70] Ibid., 198.

[71] Ibid., 202.

[72] Christian L. Christensen, "When the Utes Invaded Utah," *Times-Independent* (Moab), August 3, 1933, 4.

[73] Report of Agency in Colorado—Southern Utes, *RCIA*, 1898, 140.

[74] Report of Agent in Colorado—Southern Ute Agency, *RCIA*, 1896, 132.

[75] Report of Agent for Southern Ute Agency, *RCIA*, 1900, 213–14; Report of Agent for Southern Ute Agency, *Annual Report of Department of the Interior Fiscal Year Ending June 30, 1901*, 205.

[76] For a detailed explanation of this event and others surrounding it see Forbes Parkhill, *The Last of the Indian Wars* (New York: Crowell-Collier Publishing Company, 1961).

[77] "Armed Posse is After Renegade," *Grand Valley Times*, February 19, 1915, 1.

[78] "1 White and 3 Piutes Are Killed," *Grand Valley Times*, February 26, 1915, 1.

[79] "Scott Captures Renegade Indians," *Grand Valley Times*, March 26, 1915, 2.

[80] James C. Wilson to Agent A.H. Symons, January 5, 1917, James McLaughlin Papers, Microfilm #8, Denver Public Library (hereafter cited as McLaughlin Papers).

[81] James McLaughlin to Indian Commissioner Cato Sells, January 18 and 20, 1917, McLaughlin Papers.

[82] Undersigned of Bluff to Major James McLaughlin, January 12, 1917, McLaughlin Papers.

[83] A.H. Symons to Major James McLaughlin, February 3, 1917, McLaughlin Papers.

[84] For a lengthier treatment of the Posey incident see "Paiute Posey and the Last White Uprising," *Utah Historical Quarterly* 53 (Summer 1985): 248–67; and Albert R. Lyman, *The Outlaw of Navaho Mountain* (Salt Lake City: Publishers Press, 1986).

[85] "Piute Indian Chief Slays His Brother," *Grand Valley Times*, March 5, 1915, 7; "Indians Refuse to Go to Reservation, Is Report," *Grand Valley Times*, June 4, 1915, 1; "Posey at Bluff," *Grand Valley Times*, June 11, 1915, 1.

[86] Ibid.; "Forest Ranger First to Find Posey's Body," *Grand Valley Times*, May 17, 1923, 1.

[87] "Government Allots Farms and Livestock to San Juan Paiutes," *Times-Independent*, April 19, 1923, 1.

[88] Mr. and Mrs. Ira Hatch, interviewed by Floyd A. O'Neil and Gregory C. Thompson, September 10, 1970, Doris Duke Oral History Project, Special Collections, Marriott Library, University of Utah, 9.

[89] See "Farmers Reports: Allen Canyon, 1925–27," Record Group 75, Consolidated Ute Agency, National Archives, Denver; Agent E.J. Peacore to Commissioner of Indian Affairs, March 12, 1929, Record Group 75, Letters Received, Bureau of Indian Affairs, National Archives.

[90] For a detailed explanation of the growth of the Native American Church see David F. Aberle, *The Peyote Religion Among the Navaho* (Chicago: University of Chicago Press, 1982).

[91] David F. Aberle and Omer C. Stewart, *Navaho and Ute Peyotism— A Chronological and Distributional Study*, University of Colorado Studies Number 6 (Boulder: University of Colorado Press, 1957), 25–27, 90.

[92] "Utes Agree on Money Division," *Desert Magazine* 13 (June 1950): 38; "Ute Indians Awarded $31,000,000 Settlement," *San Juan Record*, July 20, 1950, 1; "Ute Indians to Receive Payment," *San Juan Record*, September 6, 1951, 5.

[93] "San Juan Piutes Have Pay Day," *San Juan Record*, April 24, 1952, 3; "Ute Land Settlement Fund Allocation Set by Council," *San Juan Record*, June 26, 1952, 1.

[94] "Indian Meeting at Blanding Takes up Many Problems Facing Tribe Including Living Conditions in the Area," *San Juan Record*, 6 November 1952, 1; "Rehabilitation of Indians to Be a Reality," *San Juan Record*, 19 December 1952, 1.

[95] "Ute Indian Tribe Building New Homes," *San Juan Record,* October 14, 1954, 6.

[96] "Progress on White Mesa," *San Juan Record,* 29 January 1976, 8.

[97] "White Mesa Council Celebrates," *San Juan Record,* 9 April 1981, 6; "White Mesa Council Nominated for International Exposition," *San Juan Record,* 21 July 1983, 1; Cleal Bradford, conversation with author, 27 June 1996.

[98] Cleal Bradford, conversation with author, 27 June 1996.

[99] "White Mesa Community Marches to Protest Mill Tailings Truck Haul—Washington Judge Hears Case," *Blue Mountain Panorama,* 28 September 1994, 1; "Ute, Navajos Protest Tailings Plan," *San Juan Record,* 28 September 1994, 12.

Notes—Navajos

[1] Claire R. Farrer, *Living Life's Circle: Mescalero Apache Cosmovision* (Albuquerque: University of New Mexico Press, 1991), 28.

[2] Caroline B. Olin, *Early Navajo Sandpainting Symbols in Old Navajoland: Visual Apects of Mythic Images* (Albuquerque: Albuquerque Archaeological Society, 1984), 43.

[3] Harry Walters, "A New Perspective on Navajo History," manuscript, 1991, Goddard College, 5.

[4] Ibid.

[5] Ibid., 9.

[6] Jose Antonio Vizcarra, Journal, June 18–August 31, 1823, from J. Lee Correll, *Through White Men's Eyes: A Contribution to Navajo History* (Window Rock, AZ: 1976), 112–55.

[7] Ibid., 130.

[8] Clyde Benally, with Andrew O. Wiget, John R. Alley, and Garry Blake, *Dinéjí Nákéé' Nááhane' A Utah Navajo History* (Monticello, UT: San Juan School District, 1982), 99.

[9] Ruth Underhill, *The Navajos* (Norman: University of Oklahoma Press, 1956), 118.

[10] Clara Maryboy, interview, July 10, 1999.

[11] Benally, *Dinéjí Nákéé' Nááhane',* 138.

[12] See John Alton Peterson, *Utah's Black Hawk War* (Salt Lake City: University of Utah Press, 1999) for the most comprehensive study of this conflict, its causes, and participants—including Navajos.

[13] Paul Tolakai, interview, July 9, 1999.

[14] Gerald Thompson, *The Army and the Navajo: The Bosque Redondo Reservation Experiment: 1863–1868* (Tucson: University of Arizona Press, 1976), 153.

[15] Ibid., 154.

[16] Ibid., 152.

[17] *Report of Commissioner of Indian Affairs, 1883*, 119–20.

[18] Benally, *Dinéjí Nákéé' Nááhane'*, 151.

[19] Clara Maryboy, interview, June 6, 1992,

[20] Navajo Treaty of 1868, Article 10: "No future treaty for the cession of any portion or part of the reservation herein described, which may be held in common, shall be of any validity or force against said Indians unless agreed to and executed by at least three-fourths of all the adult male Indians occupying or interested in the same."

[21] Clara Maryboy, interview, February 20, 1997.

[22] Doris A. Paul, *The Navajo Code Talkers*, Philadelphia: Dorrance, 1973), 2–3.

[23] Samuel Moon, *Tall Sheep, Harry Goulding, Monument Valley Trader* (Norman: University of Oklahoma Press, 1992), 171–72.

[24] Ibid., 172.

[25] Ibid., 173–74.

[26] Mark Maryboy, interview, May 5, 1996; see also *United States v. Jim*, case 409-US-80, 1972. Other cases of importance to the interested reader include *Sakezzie and Billy v. Utah Indain Affairs Commission*, 1961; *Sakezzie v. Utah Indian Affairs Commission*, 1963; and *State of Utah v. United States*, in Tenth Circuit Court, 1962.

[27] Moon, *Tall Sheep, Harry Goulding*, 177–80.

[28] Ibid., 179–80.

[29] Sarah Police, interview, May 20, 1999.

[30] Clara Maryboy, interview, February 20, 1999.

[31] Marilyn Ellingson, interview, July 10, 1999.

Notes—Conclusion: The Contemporary Status of Utah Indians

[1] See Karl W. Luckert, *Navajo Mountain and Rainbow Bridge Religion* (Flagstaff: Museum of Northern Arizona, 1977).

[2] "Navajos Blockade Bridge During Tribal Ceremonies," *Deseret News*, August 12, 1995, B-1; "Rainbow Bridge Closed for 'Cleansing Ceremony,'" *San Juan Record*, August 16, 1995, 1; "Rainbow Bridge Open After Four-day Closure," *Navajo Times*, August 17, 1995, A-5.

[3] Chris Smith and Elizabeth Manning, "The Sacred and Profane Collide in the West," *High Country News*, May 26, 1997, 1–4.

[4] Ibid., 4.

[5] "Reverent Thoughts Bring Tears on Visit to Massacre Site," *Deseret News*, September 26, 1995, A-13.

[6] "Box Elder Opens Landfill Despite Protests," *Deseret News*, August 10, 1997, B-6.

[7] Karl Cates, "Wilds Advocates Join Paiutes Against Chaining," *Deseret News* (Web edition), March 23, 1997, 1–2; Jerry Goodman, BLM District Manager, telephone conversation with author, November 6, 1997.

[8] "U. of U. Catalogs Artifacts In Case Tribes Want Them," *Salt Lake Tribune*, November 16, 1995, A-18; "Appropriation for Indian Burial Repository," *Utah Legislative Report 1993*, H.B. No. 368, March 19, 1993, 645. See also the Native American Graves Protection and Repatriation Act (25 U.S.C. 3001), Public Law 101-601, November 16, 1990.

[9] "Boy Scout Tracks Down the Bones of Black Hawk in LDS Basement," *Indian Trader* (October 1995): 7; Joel Janetski, Director of the Museum of Peoples and Cultures, Brigham Young University, telephone conversation with author, December 19, 1997.

[10] Joe Bauman, "Native Artifacts are Still Buried in Controversy," *Deseret News* (Web edition), December 8, 1996, 1–3.

[11] Daniel McCool, "Utah and the Ute Tribe Are at War," *High Country News*, June 27, 1994, 1–3; Shiela R. McCann, "Uniting the Basin: Utes and Their Neighbors Are Cooperating," *Salt Lake Tribune*, May 25, 1997, A-1, A-13.

[12] McCann, "Uniting the Basin," A-13. See also Lucinda Dillon and Bob Bernick, "Clash of 2 Cultures Divides Uintah Basin," *Deseret News*, September 20, 1997, A-1, A-9; Brett DelPorto, "Ruling Giving Utes Control of Land Troubles Residents," *Deseret News*, December 3, 1986, B-1.

[13] Lezlee Whiting, "Top Court Ruling Sought in Ute Land Dispute," *Deseret News*, September 2, 1997, E-2.

[14] McCool, "Utah and the Ute Tribe," 3.

[15] Dillon and Bernick, "Clash of 2 Cultures," A-1, A-9.

[16] "Apaches and Goshutes Looking at Nuclear Waste Storage," *Navajo Times*, September 2, 1993, 9.

[17] Cherie Parker, "NSP's Skull Valley Duggery," *Twin Cities Reader*, January 1997, 1–2.

[18] "Apaches and Goshutes," 9.

[19] Parker, "NSP's Skull Valley Duggery," 1; "Taking a Road to Untold Hazards," *Deseret News*, December 9, 1997, B-1.

[20] "White Mesa Utes Beat Back Superfund Tailings," *High Country News*, January 23, 1995, 5; Neil Joslin, "White Mesa Community Marches to Protest Mill Tailings Truck Haul—Washington Judge Hears Case," *Blue Mountain Panorama*, September 28, 1994, 1, 13.

[21] "Stakes Are High for Mobil Oil, Navajo Nation, and San Juan County," *San Juan Record*, January 15, 1997, 1; "Navajos Prevail as Mobil Closes Wells," *Salt Lake Tribune*, January 10, 1997, A-1.

[22] "Oil's Well that Ends Well as Tepee Talks Pay Off," *Salt Lake Tribune*, January 13, 1997, A-1.

[23] Chris LaMarr, "Free Exercise of Religion by Native American Prisoners: A Plan of Action," *NARF Legal Review* 1 (1996): 10–15.

[24] "Indians Fight for Religious Freedom," *Navajo Times*, April 7, 1986, 1–2; "Utah Wardens Nix Use of Sweatbaths," *Navajo Times*, May 22, 1986, 1.

[25] Attorney General Directive, "Providing for the Free Exercise of Religion by Native American Prisoners," 1995, in handout received from Leonard Foster, Director of Navajo Nation's Correctional Project, Navajo Studies Conference, Albuquerque, April 1996.

[26] "Indian Worship at Correctional Facilities," *Utah Legislative Report 1996*, S.B. No. 128, February 27, 1996, 1025–26.

[27] "Does Prison Stifle Indian Worship?" *Salt Lake Tribune*, November 12, 1996, B-1, B-4.

[28] Leonard Foster, "Written Testimony of Len Foster, Director/Spiritual Advisor Navajo Nation Corrections Project, Window Rock, Arizona," given at the Missouri State Capitol in support of House Bill 325, March 4, 1997, 2, in possession of author; "Bill Would Protect Inmate Rites," *Salt Lake Tribune*, February 8, 1996, B-1.

[29] "Does Prison Stifle Indian Worship?", B-4.

[30] Omer C. Stewart, "The Peyote Religion," *Handbook of North American Indians*, volume 11, *Great Basin* (Washington: Smithsonian Institution, 1986), 673, 677–81.

[31] "NAC vs Marines," *Navajo Times*, July 28, 1986, 5; "Navajo Rejected From Marines," *Navajo Times*, October 17, 1996, 7; "Military to Allow Peyote Use by Indian Soldiers," *Deseret News*, April 16, 1997, B-4.

[32] "Justices Deal Blow to Religious Freedom," *Deseret News*, June 25, 1997, B-1.

[33] Leonard J. Arrington, "The Mormons and the Indians: A Review and Evaluation," paper delivered to the Friends of the Library, Washington State University, October 2, 1969, manuscript in possession of author, 28.

[34] Beth Wood, "The Mormon Southwest: LDS Indian Placement Program," *Akwesasne Notes* 10 (Winter 1978): 16.

[35] Tona J. Hangen, "A Place to Call Home: Studying the Indian Placement Program," *Dialogue: A Journal of Mormon Thought* 30 (1997): 57.

[36] "Utah Tribes Reluctant to Join in Mormon Pioneer Celebration," *Indian Trader* (January 1997): 16.

[37] "Uintah and Ouray Indian Reservation," web site information, 29 August 1997, 1-2.

[38] "No Telling How Much U.S. Owes Utah Tribes," *Deseret News*, July 23, 1996, A-1.

[39] Ibid.

[40] "Hale Working on Utah Agreement," *Navajo Times*, March 21, 1996, 1; "Native American Legislative Liaison Committee," *Utah Legislative Report 1995*, H.B. 316, March 1, 1995, 458–59.

[41] "Blue Ribbon Committee Meets to Study Creation of New County," *San Juan Record*, November 8, 1995, 1.

[42] "New Study Investigates the Issues Involved in Splitting San Juan County," *San Juan Record*, July 9, 1997, 1.

[43] "Settlement Reached in Jury Selection Bias Case," *San Juan Record*, June 19, 1996, 1.

[44] "Another School Year Begins This Week," *San Juan Record*, August 20, 1997, 1; enrollment figure from secretary, San Juan School District, telephone conversation with author, December 30, 1997.

[45] "School Board Selection Angers Utes in Uintah," *Deseret News*, March 26, 1997, B-2.

[46] "Tribes' Quandary: Who's a Real Indian," *Salt Lake Tribune*, January 27, 1997, 1.

[47] "Utes Are Getting a Lot More Calls from Prospective Members, *Indian Trader*, March 1997, 21; "Controversy Continues Over Those Claiming to Have Shoshone Blood," *Indian Trader*, October 1995, 30.

[48] "Mailman Gets Yet Another Name: 'Bear Who Leads With Dignity,'" *Deseret News*, July 26, 1997, B-10.

[49] "More People Are Saying They Are Indian," *Indian Trader*, May 1995, 22.

[50] "Native American Performance of Marriages," *Utah Legislative Report 1997*, H.B. No. 186, February 11, 1997, 295–96.

[51] "1990 County Population by Race," U.S. Bureau of the Census, handout provided by the Utah Division of Indian Affairs.

[52] "Utah Division of Indian Affairs Report to the Appropriations Subcommittee," February 1997, Utah Division of Indian Affairs Office.

53 "1990 County Population by Race."

54 "Native Community Connections," Indian Walk-In Center quarterly newsletter, Spring 1996, 1; Gail Russell, Executive Director of the Indian Walk-In Center, conversation with author, November 13, 1997.

55 "Native American Connections," Indian Walk-In Center quarterly newsletters, Spring 1996 and Spring 1997.

56 Burton S. White and Robert D. Peterson, "Indian Training and Eduction Center Statistical Study 1989–1994," on file in the Indian Training and Eduction Center, Salt Lake City, Utah.

57 Robert D. Peterson to Robert S. McPherson, September 10, 1997, letter in possession of author.

Selected Bibliography

Aberle, David F. *The Peyote Religion Among the Navaho.* Chicago: University of Chicago Press, 1982.

Aberle, David F., and Omer C. Stewart. *Navaho and Ute Peyotism—A Chronological and Distributional Study.* University of Colorado Studies Number 6, 1957.

Aikens, C. Melvin, and David B. Madsen. "Prehistory of the Eastern Area." In *Handbook of North American Indians,* vol. 11, *Great Basin,* Warren d'Azevedo, ed. Washington, D.C.: Smithsonian Institution, 1986.

Aikens, C. Melvin, and Younger T. Witherspoon. "Great Basin Numic Prehistory Linguistics, Archaeology, and Environment." In *Anthropology of the Desert West: Essays in Honor of Jesse D. Jennings,* University of Utah Anthropological Papers Number 110 (1986).

Alexander, Thomas G., and Leonard J. Arrington. "The Utah Military Frontier, 1872–1912: Forts Cameron, Thornburgh, and Duchesne." *Utah Historical Quarterly* 32 (1964): 330–54.

Allen, James B., and Ted J. Warner. "The Goshute Indians in Pioneer Utah." *Utah Historical Quarterly* 39 (Spring 1971): 162–77.

Amoss, Jr., Harold Lindsay. "Ute Mountain Utes." Ph.D. diss., University of California, 1951.

Anderson, Edward H. "Apostle Lyman's Mission to the Indians." *Improvement Era* 3 (1900): 510–16.

Arrington, Leonard J. "The Mormons and the Indians: A Review and Evaluation." Paper delivered to the Friends of the Library, Washington State University, October 2, 1969.

Arrington, Leonard J., and Davis Bitton. *The Mormon Experience—A History of the Latter-day Saints.* New York: Random House, 1979.

Bancroft, Hubert Howe. *History of Nevada, Colorado and Wyoming, 1540–1880.* San Francisco: A.L. Bancroft & Company, 1890.

———. *History of Utah.* San Francisco: History Company, 1890.

Barnes, F.A. "A Journey to the Rio del Tizon." *Canyon Legacy* 9 (Spring 1991): 16–22.

———. "Update—Rivera's 1765 Expedition." *Canyon Legacy* 10 (Summer 1991): 31.

Bateman, Ronald R. *Deep Creek Reflections: 125 Years of Settlement at Ibapah, Utah, 1859–1984.* Salt Lake City: Bateman, 1984.

Beeton, Beverly. "Teach Them to Till the Soil: An Experiment with Indian Farms, 1850–1862." *American Indian Quarterly* 3 (1977–78): 299–320.

Benally, Clyde, with Andrew O. Wiget, John R. Alley, and Garry Blake. *Dinéjí Nákéé' Nááhane' A Utah Navajo History.* Monticello, UT: San Juan School District, 1982.

Board of Indian Commissioners. Annual Reports, various years.

Brewerton, G. Douglas. "A Ride with Kit Carson." *Harpers New Monthly Magazine* 8 (April 1854): 312–13.

Brooks, Juanita. "Indian Relations on the Mormon Frontier." *Utah Historical Quarterly* 12 (1944): 1–48.

———. *John Doyle Lee: Zealot, Pioneer Builder, Scapegoat.* Glendale, CA: Arthur H. Clark Company, 1962.

———. *Journal of the Southern Indian Mission: Diary of Thomas D. Brown.* Logan: Utah State University Press, 1972.

———. *The Mountain Meadows Massacre.* Palo Alto: Stanford University Press, 1950.

Bunte, Pamela A., and Robert J. Franklin. *From the Sands to the Mountains: Change and Persistence in a Southern Paiute Community.* Lincoln: University of Nebraska Press, 1987.

Burton, Richard Francis. *The City of the Saints and across … to California.* New York: Harper, 1862.

Callaway, Donald G., Joel C. Janetski, and Omer C. Stewart, "Ute." In *Handbook of North American Indians*, volume 11, *Great Basin.*

Campbell, Eugene E. "Brigham Young's Outer Cordon—A Reappraisal." *Utah Historical Quarterly* 41 (1973): 220–53.

Carvalho, Solomon Nunes. *Incidents of Travel and Adventure in the Far West with Colonel Fremont's Last Expedition.* New York: Denby and Jackson, 1856.

Chamberlin, Ralph V. "The Ethnobotany of the Gosiute Indians." *Philadelphia Academy of Natural Science Proceedings* 53 (1911): 337–44.

———. "Place and Personal Names of the Gosiute Indians of Utah." *Proceedings of the American Philosophical Society* 52 (January–April 1912): 2.

———. "Some Plant Names of the Ute Indians." *American Anthropologist* 2 (January-March 1909): 27–37.

Christensen, Scott R. *Sagwitch: Shoshoni Chieftain, Mormon Elder, 1822–1884.* Logan: Utah State University Press, 1999.

Christy, Howard A. "Open Hand and Mailed Fist: Mormon Indian Relations in Utah, 1847–1852." *Utah Historical Quarterly* 46 (1978): 216–35.

———. "The Walker War: Defense and Conciliation as Strategy." *Utah Historical Quarterly* 47 (1979): 395–420.

Clemmer, Richard O., and Omer C. Stewart. "Treaties, Reservations, and Claims." In *Handbook of North American Indians—Great Basin.*

Cline, Gloria Griffen. *Exploring the Great Basin.* Norman: University of Oklahoma Press, 1963.

Coleman, Ronald G. "The Buffalo Soldiers: Guardians of the Uintah Frontier 1886–1901." *Utah Historical Quarterly* 47 (1979): 421–39.

Collins, Thomas W. "The Northern Ute Economic Development Program: Social and Cultural Dimensions." Ph.D. dissertation, University of Colorado, 1971.

Commissioner of Indian Affairs, Annual Reports, various years.

Conetah, Fred A. *A History of the Northern Ute People.* N.p.: Uintah-Ouray Ute Tribe, 1982.

Conetah, Fred, Norma Denver, Daisy Jenks, Kathryn MacKay, Floyd O'Neil. *Stories of Our Ancestors—A Collection of Northern-Ute Indian Tales.* Salt Lake City: Uintah-Ouray Ute Tribe, 1974.

Correll, J. Lee. *Through White Men's Eyes: A Contribution to Navajo History,* volume 3. Window Rock: Navajo Heritage Center, 1979.

Covington, James Warren. "Relations Between the Indians and the United States Government, 1848–1900." Ph.D. dissertation, University of Oklahoma, 1949.

Crampton, C. Gregory. "Utah's Spanish Trail." *Utah Historical Quarterly* 47 (Fall 1979): 361–83.

Crampton, C. Gregory, and Steven K. Madsen. *In Search of the Spanish Trail: Santa Fe to Los Angeles, 1829–1848.* Layton, Utah: Gibbs Smith, Publisher, 1994.

Creer, Leland H. *The Founding of an Empire—The Exploration and Colonization of Utah, 1776–1856.* Salt Lake City: Bookcraft, 1947.

Culmsee, Carlton. *Utah's Black Hawk War.* Logan: Utah State University Press, 1973.

Cutter, Donald C. "Prelude to a Pageant in the Wilderness." *Western Historical Quarterly* 8 (January 1977): 4–14.

Dalley, Julius S. "Mancos Jim Mesa—San Juan County" (1942). Utah State Historical Society Library.

De Smet, Pierre-Jean. *Life, Letters and Travels of Father Pierre-Jean De Smet*, vol. 3. New York: Harper, 1905.

Downing, Finis E. "With the Ute Peace Delegation of 1863, Across the Plains and at Conejos." *Colorado Magazine* 22 (1945): 202–3.

Egan, Major Howard, and Howard R. Egan. *Pioneering the West, 1846 to 1878*. Salt Lake City: H.R. Egan estate, 1917.

Emmitt, Robert. *The Last War Trail*. Norman: University of Oklahoma Press, 1954.

Euler, Robert C. "Southern Paiute Archaeology." *American Antiquities* 29 (January 1964): 379–81.

———. *Southern Paiute Ethnohistory*. Salt Lake City: University of Utah Press, 1966.

Farrer, Claire R. *Living Life's Circle: Mescalero Apache Cosmovision*. Albuquerque: University of New Mexico Press, 1991.

Fowler, C.S., and D.D. Fowler. "The Southern Paiute: A.D 1400–1776." In *The Protohistoric Period in the North American Southwest, A.D. 1350–1700*, ed. by D.R. Wilcox and W.B. Masse. Arizona State University Archaeological Research Papers Number 24.

Fowler, Don D., and Catherine Fowler. *Anthropology of the Numa: John Wesley Powell's Manuscripts on the Numic People*. Smithsonian Contributions to Anthropology 14 (1971).

Franklin, Robert J., and Pamela Bunte. *The Paiute*. New York: Chelsea House Publishers, 1990.

Gibbs, Josiah F. "Blackhawk's Last Raid." *Utah Historical Quarterly* 4 (1931): 99–108.

Godwin, Larry H., and Bruce D. Smith, eds. *Special Symposium 1994 on Economic Mineral Resources of the Goshute Indian Reservation, Nevada-Utah*. Golden, CO: Bureau of Indian Affairs, 1994.

Gottfredson, Peter. *Indian Depredations in Utah*. Salt Lake City: Shelton Publishing Company, 1919.

Griffin-Pierce, Trudy. *Earth is My Mother, Sky is My Father*. Albuquerque: University of New Mexico Press, 1992.

Washington: Smithsonian Institution, 1986.

Hafen, Ann W. "Efforts to Recover the Stolen Son of Chief Ouray." *Colorado Magazine* 16 (1939): 53–62.

Hafen, Leroy R. "The Fort Pueblo Massacre and the Punitive Expedition Against the Utes." *Colorado Magazine* 4 (1927): 49–58.

———. "Historical Summary of the Ute Indians and the San Juan Min-

ing Region." In *Ute Indians II*. New York: Garland Publishing Inc., 1974.

Hafen, LeRoy R., and Ann W. Hafen. *The Old Spanish Trail: Santa Fe to Los Angeles*. Glendale, CA: Arthur H. Clark Company, 1954.

Haines, Francis. "The Northward Spread of Horses Among the Plains Indians." *American Anthropologist* 40 (1938): 429–37.

———. "Where Did the Plains Indians Get Their Horses?" *American Anthropologist* 40 (1938): 112–17.

Hangen, Tona J. "A Place to Call Home: Studying the Indian Placement Program." *Dialogue: A Journal of Mormon Thought* 30 (Spring 1997): 53–69.

Hart, Gerald T. "Confederated Ute Indian Lands." In *Ute Indians II*.

Hausman, Gerald. *The Gift of the Gila Monster—Navajo Ceremonial Tales*. New York: Simon and Schuster, 1993.

Hill, Alice P. *Tales of the Colorado Pioneers*. Denver: 1844.

Hill, Edward E. *The Office of Indian Affairs, 1824–1880: Historical Sketches*. New York: Clearwater Publishing Co., 1974.

Hill, Joseph J. "Spanish and Mexican Exploration and Trade Northwest from New Mexico into the Great Basin, 1765–1853." *Utah Historical Quarterly* 3 (January 1930): 5–31.

History of Tooele County. Salt Lake City: Daughters of Utah Pioneers, 1961.

Holt, Ronald L. *Beneath These Red Cliffs: A Southern Paiute Ethnohistory*. Albuquerque: University of New Mexico Press, 1992.

Hultkrantz, Ake. "Mythology and Religious Concepts." *Handbook of North American Indians—Great Basin*.

Hunter, Milton R. *Brigham Young the Colonizer*. Salt Lake City: Deseret News Press, 1940.

Hurst, Winston B. "The Prehistoric Peoples of San Juan County, Utah." In *San Juan County, Utah*. Salt Lake City: Utah State Historical Society, 1983.

Inventory of the County Archives of Utah, various vols. Ogden, Utah: W.P.A. Historical Records Survey, 1939.

Ivins, Anthony. "Traveling over Forgotten Trails." *Improvement Era* 29 (1916): 350–56.

Jacobs, G. Clell. "The Phantom Pathfinder: Juan Maria Antonio de Rivera and His Expedition." *Utah Historical Quarterly* 60 (Summer 1992): 200–23.

Jacobs, Mary J.T. "Termination of Federal Supervision over the Southern Paiute Indians of Utah." M.S. thesis, University of Utah, 1976.

Jefferson, James, Robert W. Delaney, and Gregory Thompson. *The Southern Utes: A Tribal History.* Ignacio, Co.: Southern Ute Tribe, 1972.

Jennings, Jesse D. "Prehistory: Introduction." In *Handbook of North American Indians—Great Basin.*

———. *Prehistory of Utah and the Eastern Great Basin.* University of Utah Anthropological Papers 98 (1978).

Jennings, Jesse D., Elmer R. Smith, and Charles E. Dibble. *Indians of Utah: Past and Present.* Salt Lake City: University of Utah, 1959.

Jett, Stephen C. "Testimony of the Sacredness of Rainbow Natural Bridge to Puebloans, Navajos, and Paiutes." *Plateau* 45 (Spring 1973): 54.

Jones, Daniel W. *Forty Years Among the Indians.* Salt Lake City: Juvenile Instructor Office, 1890.

Jones, Kevin T., and Kathryn L. MacKay. "Cultural Resources Existing Data Inventory, Vernal District, Utah." BLM, 1980.

Jorgensen, Joseph G. *The Sun Dance Religion: Power for the Powerless.* Chicago: University of Chicago Press, 1972.

Kelly, Charles. "Jedediah S. Smith on the Salt Desert Trail." *Utah Historical Quaterly* 3 (January 1930): 23–27.

Kelly, Isabel T. *Southern Paiute Ethnography.* Salt Lake City: University of Utah Press, 1964.

Kelly, Isabel T., and Catherine Fowler. "Southern Paiute." In *Handbook of North American Indians, Great Basin.*

Lang, Gottfried O. "The Ute Development Program: A Study in Culture Change in an Underdeveloped Area within the United States." Ph.D. dissertation, Cornell University, 1954.

Larson, Gustave O. "Walkara's Half Century." *Western Humanities Review* 6 (1952): 235–59.

Lawrence, Eleanor Frances. "The Old Spanish Trail from Santa Fe to California." Master's thesis, University of California, 1929.

Lister, Robert H., and Florence C. Lister. *Those Who Came Before.* Southwest Parks & Monuments Association, 1983.

Lloyd, John B. "Uncompahgre Utes: A Contribution of Data to the History of the Uncompahgre Ute." Master's thesis, Western State College, 1932.

Luckert, Karl W. *Navajo Mountain and Rainbow Bridge Religion.* Flagstaff: Museum of Northern Arizona, 1977.

Lyman, Albert R. "History of San Juan County, 1879–1917." Manuscript, Harold B. Lee Library, Brigham Young University.

———. *The Outlaw of Navaho Mountain.* Salt Lake City: Publishers Press, 1986.

MacKay, Kathryn L. "The Strawberry Valley Reclamation Project and the Opening of the Uintah Indian Reservation." *Utah Historical Quarterly* 50 (1982): 68–103.

McPherson, Robert S. *The Northern Navajo Frontier 1860–1900: Expansion through Adversity.* Albuquerque: University of New Mexico Press, 1988.

———."Paiute Posey and the Last White Uprising." *Utah Historical Quarterly* 53 (Summer 1985): 248–67.

———. *Sacred Land, Sacred View—Navajo Perceptions of the Four Corners Region.* Provo: Brigham Young University, 1992.

Madsen, Brigham D. *Chief Pocatello: The White Plume.* Salt Lake City: University of Utah Press, 1986.

———. *Glory Hunter: A Biography of Patrick Edward Connor.* Salt Lake City: University of Utah Press, 1990.

———. *The Northern Shoshoni.* Caldwell, ID: Caxton Printers, 1980.

———. *The Shoshoni Frontier and the Bear River Massacre.* Salt Lake City: University of Utah Press, 1985.

Madsen, David B. *Exploring the Fremont.* Salt Lake City: Utah Museum of Natural History, 1989.

Madsen, David B., and David Rhode, eds. *Across The West: Human Population Movement and the Expansion of the Numa.* Salt Lake City: University of Utah Press, 1994.

Madsen, Steven K. "The Spanish Trail Through Canyon Country." *Canyon Legacy* 9 (Spring 1991): 23–29.

Malouf, Carling I. "A Study of the Gosiute Indians of Utah." Master's thesis, University of Utah, 1940.

———. "The Gosiute Indians." In *The Shoshone Indians.* New York: Garland Press, 1974.

Malouf, Carling I., and Elmer R. Smith. "Some Gosiute Mythological Characters and Concepts." *Utah Humanities Review* 1 (1947): 369–78.

Martin, Calvin, ed. *The American Indian and the Problem of History.* New York: Oxford University Press, 1987.

Martineau, LaVan. *The Southern Paiutes.* Las Vegas: KC Publications, 1993.

Marwitt, John P. "Fremont Cultures." In *Handbook of North American Indians—Great Basin,* 161–72.

Metcalf, R. Warren. "Lambs of Sacrifice: Termination, the Mixed-Blood Utes, and the Problem of Indian Identity." *Utah Historical Quarterly* 64 (Fall 1996): 322–43.

Miller, David H. "The Impact of the Gunnison Massacre on Mormon-

Federal Relations: Colonal Edward Jenner Steptoe's Command in Utah Territory, 1854–1855," Master's thesis, University of Utah, 1968.

Miller, Wick R. "Numic Languages." In *Handbook of North American Indians—Great Basin.*

Moon, Samuel. *Tall Sheep, Harry Goulding, Monument Valley Trader.* Norman: University of Oklahoma Press, 1992.

Morgan, Dale L. "The Administration of Indian Affairs in Utah, 1851–1858." *Pacific Historical Review* 17 (November 1948): 383–409.

———. *Jedediah Smith and the Opening of the West.* Lincoln: University of Nebraska Press, 1964.

Mortensen, A.R., ed. *West From Fort Bridger.* Salt Lake City: Utah State Historical Society, 1951.

Neff, Andrew Love. *History of Utah 1847 to 1869.* Salt Lake City: Deseret News Press, 1940.

Nevins, Allan. *Fremont: Pathmarker of the West,* vol. 1. New York: Frederick Ungar Publishing Co., 1961.

Newcomb, Franc Johnson. *Navaho Folk Tales.* Albuquerque: University of New Mexico Press, 1990.

Nuwuvi: A Southern Paiute History. Reno: Inter-Tribal Council of Nevada, 1976.

Olin, Caroline B. *Early Navajo Sandpainting Symbols in Old Navajoland: Visual Apects of Mythic Images.* Albuquerque: Albuquerque Archaeological Society, 1984.

Olson, James S., and Raymond Wilson. *Native Americans in the Twentieth Century.* Provo: Brigham Young University Press, 1984.

O'Neil, Floyd A. "An Anguished Odyssey: The Flight of the Utes, 1906–1908." *Utah Historical Quarterly* 36 (1968): 315–27.

———. "A History of the Ute Indians of Utah until 1890." Ph.D. dissertation, University of Utah, 1973.

O'Neil, Floyd A., and Kathryn L. MacKay. "A History of the Uintah-Ouray Ute Tribe." Occasional Paper No. 10. American West Center, University of Utah.

O'Neil, Floyd A., and Stanford J. Layton. "Of Pride and Politics: Brigham Young as an Indian Superintendent." *Utah Historical Quarterly* 46 (1978): 236–50.

Orfield, Gary. *A Study of the Termination Policy.* Denver: National Congress of American Indians, 1965.

Palmer, William R. "The Pahute Fire Legend." *Utah Historical Quarterly* 6 (1933): 62–64.

———. *Pahute Indian Legends.* Salt Lake City: Deseret Book, 1946.

————. "San Juan Indians." Palmer Collection Notes, Special Collections, Southern Utah University.

————. "Utah Indians Past and Present—An Etymological and Historical Study of Tribes and Tribal Names from Original Sources." *Utah Historical Quarterly* 1 (April 1928): 35–52.

Papanikolas, Helen Z. *The Peoples of Utah.* Salt Lake City: Utah State Historical Society, 1976.

Parkhill, Forbes. *The Last of the Indian Wars.* New York: Crowell-Collier Publishing Company, 1961.

Paul, Doris A. *The Navajo Code Talkers.* Philadelphia: Dorrance, 1973.

Perkins, Cornelia, Marian Nielson, and Lenora Jones. *Saga of San Juan.* Salt Lake City: Mercury Publishing Company, 1957.

Peterson, John Alton. *Utah's Black Hawk War.* Salt Lake City: University of Utah Press, 1998.

Poll, Richard D., Thomas G. Alexander, Eugene E. Campbell, and David E. Miller, eds. *Utah's History.* Provo: Brigham Young University Press, 1978.

Prucha, Francis. *The Great Father,* abridged ed. Lincoln: University of Nebraska Press, 1986.

Reagan, Albert B. "Shoshoni-Goshute Indians and the Deep Creek Region, Utah." *Improvement Era* 22 (October 1919): 33.

Reed, Alan D. "Ute Cultural Chronology," *An Archaeology of the Eastern Ute: A Symposium,* ed. by Paul R. Nickens. Colorado Council of Professional Archaeology Occasional Papers Number 1 (1988).

Remington, Newell C. "A History of the Gilsonite Industry." Master's thesis, University of Utah, 1959.

Rockwell, Wilson. *The Utes: A Forgotten People.* Denver: Sage Books, 1956.

Ruffner, Lieut. E.H. *Report of a Reconnaissance in the Ute Country Made in the Year 1873.* Washington, D.C.: GPO, 1874.

Russell, Osborne. *Journal of a Trapper 1834–1843.* Lincoln: University of Nebraska Press, 1955.

Schroeder, Albert A. "A Brief History of the Southern Utes." *Southwestern Lore* 30 (1965): 55.

Shimkin, Dmitri B. "The Introduction of the Horse." In *Handbook of North American Indians, Great Basin.*

Shirts, Morris. "Mountain Meadows Massacre." In *Utah History Encyclopedia,* Allan Kent Powell, ed. Salt Lake City: University of Utah Press, 1994.

Simpson, Captain J.H. *Report of Explorations across the Great Basin of the Territory of Utah … in 1859.* Washington, D.C.: GPO, 1876.

Smith, Anne M. *Ethnography of the Northern Utes*. Papers in Anthropology No. 17. Santa Fe: Museum of New Mexico Press, 1974.

———. *Shoshone Tales*. Salt Lake City: University of Utah Press, 1994.

———. *Ute Tales*. Salt Lake City: University of Utah Press, 1992.

Sonne, Conway B. *World of Wakara*. San Antonio: Naylor Co., 1962.

Sprague, Marshall. "The Bloody End of Meeker's Utopia." *American Heritage* 8 (1952): 36–39.

Steward, Julian H. "Aboriginal and Historical Groups of the Ute Indians of Utah: An Analysis." In *Ute Indians I*. New York: Garland Publishing Inc., 1974.

———. *Basin-Plateau Aboriginal Sociopolitical Groups*. Bureau of American Ethnology Bulletin 120 (1938).

Stewart, Omer C. *Culture Element Distributions: Ute-Southern Paiute*. Berkeley: University of California Press, 1942.

———. "The Peyote Religion." In *Handbook of North American Indians*, volume 11, *Great Basin*.

———. "Shoshoni History and Social Organization." *Idaho Yesterdays* 9 (Fall 1965).

———. *Ute Peyotism, A Study of a Cultural Complex*. University of Colorado Anthropological Series No. 1, (1948).

———. "Ute Indians: Before and After White Contact." *Utah Historical Quarterly* 34 (1966): 38–61.

Stoffle, Richard W., and Michael J. Evans. *Kaibab Paiute History: The Early Years*. Fredonia, AZ: Kaibab Paiute Tribe, 1978.

Stubbs, Brian D. "The Native American Languages of San Juan County." *Blue Mountain Shadows* 13 (Summer 1994): 63–67.

Sullivan, Maurice S. *The Travels of Jedediah Smith*. Santa Ana, CA: Fine Arts Press, 1934.

Swagerty, W.R., ed. *Scholars and the Indian Experience*. Bloomington: University of Indiana Press, 1984.

Tanner, Faun McConkie. *The Far Country—A Regional History of Moab and La Sal, Utah*. Salt Lake City: Olympus Publishing Company, 1976.

Taylor, Colin F. *Native American Myths and Legends*. London: Salamander Books, Ltd., 1994.

Terrell, John U. *Pueblos, Gods and Spaniards*. New York: Dial Press, 1973.

Thompson, Gerald. *The Army and the Navajo: The Bosque Redondo Reservation Experiment: 1863–1868*. Tucson: University of Arizona Press, 1976.

Trimble, Stephen. *The People: Indians of the American Southwest*. Santa Fe: SAR Press, 1993.

Turner, Katharine C. *Red Man Calling on the Great White Father.* Norman: University of Oklahoma Press, 1951.

Tyler, S. Lyman. "Before Escalante: An Early History of the Yuta Indians and the area north of New Mexico." Ph.D. dissertation, University of Utah, 1951.

———. *A History of Indian Policy.* Washington, D.C.: Government Printing Office, 1973.

———. "The Myth of the Lake of Copala and the Land of Teguayo." *Utah Historical Quarterly* 20 (1952): 313–30.

———. "The Spaniard and the Ute." *Utah Historical Quarterly* 22 (1954): 343–61.

———. "The Yuta Indians Before 1680." *Western Humanities Review* 8 (Spring 1951): 157–60.

Uintah Ouray Ute Tribe. *Stories of Our Ancestors: A Collection of Northern Ute Indian Tales.* Salt Lake City: University of Utah Press, 1974.

Underhill, Ruth. *The Navajos.* Norman: University of Oklahoma Press, 1956.

U.S. Congress, House. "The Ute Indian Outbreak." House Misc. Doc. 38, 46th Cong., 2nd Sess., 1880.

U.S. Unratified Treaty Files.

U.S. Statutes at Large, various volumes.

The Ute System of Government. Salt Lake City: Uintah-Ouray Ute Tribe, 1977.

Ute Ways. Salt Lake City: Uintah-Ouray Ute Tribe, 1977.

Van Cott, John W. *Utah Place Names.* Salt Lake City: University of Utah Press, 1990.

Vogel, Dan. *Indian Origins and the Book of Mormon.* Salt Lake City: Signature Books, 1986.

Walker, Don D. "Cowboys, Indians, and Cavalry—A Cattleman's Account." *Utah Historical Quarterly* 34 (Summer 1966): 255–62.

Walters, Harry. "A New Perspective on Navajo History." Manuscript, 1991, Goddard College.

Warner, Ted J., ed. *The Dominguez-Escalante Journal.* Provo: BYU Press, 1976.

The Way It was Told. Salt Lake City: Uintah-Ouray Ute Tribe, 1977.

Wardle, James W. "Reluctant Immigrants of Utah, the Uncompahgre Utes." Master's thesis, Utah State University, 1976.

Weber, David. *The Taos Trappers: The Fur Trade in the Far Southwest, 1540–1846,* Norman: University of Oklahoma Press, 1971.

Wheeler, George M. "Report upon United States Geographical Surveys

West of the One-hundredth Meridian." *Archaeology*, vol. 7. Washington, D.C.: Government Printing Office, 1879.

White, Eugene S. *Experiences of a Special Indian Agent.* Norman: University of Oklahoma Press, 1965.

Whittaker, David J. "Mormons and Native Americans: A Historical and Bibliographical Introduction." *Dialogue* 18 (1985): 33–64.

Wood, Beth. "The Mormon Southwest: LDS Indian Placement Program." *Akwesasne Notes* 10 (Winter 1978): 16.

Wright, Coulsen, and Geneva Wright. "Indian-White Relations in the Uintah Basin." *Utah Humanities Review* 2 (1938).

Yazzie, Mary Jane. "Life and Traditions of the Utes of Avikan." Unpublished manuscript.

Zolbrod, Paul G. *Dine bahane.* Albuquerque: University of New Mexico Press, 1984.

Notes on Contributors

David H. Begay is the Dean of Instruction for the Arizona Campus and Centers of Dine College, the tribal college of the Navajo Nation, and Coordinator of Higher Education Programs of the Navajo Nation. He received his Ph.D. from the California Institute of Integral Studies, San Francisco, California, in Integral Studies, with a concentration on the articulation and application of indigenous knowledge to contemporary education. Dr. Begay is a member of the Navajo Nation and has lived on the Navajo Reservation most of his life. He is a combat veteran who served in Vietnam. He resides in Ganado, Arizona, with his family.

Forrest S. Cuch was born and raised on the Uintah and Ouray Ute Indian Reservation in northeastern Utah. He graduated from Westminster College in 1973 with a Bachelor of Arts Degree in Behavioral Sciences. He served as education director for the Ute Indian Tribe from 1973 to 1988. From 1988 to 1994 he was employed by the Wampanoag Tribe in Gay Head, Massachusetts, first as a planner and then as tribal administrator. In 1994 he was appointed head of the Social Studies Department at Wasatch Academy in Mt. Pleasant, Utah. Since October 1997 he has been director of the Utah Division of Indian Affairs.

Dennis R. Defa holds undergraduate degrees in history and anthropology and graduate degrees in history and economics. A Utah native, he has spent most of his life studying, researching, and traveling through the Great Basin. A denizen of the West Desert, he has come to know and work with many people who live in this arid region of the state. He currently works as an administrator at the University of Utah, in Salt Lake City, where he lives with his wife and three children.

Clifford Duncan was born and raised on the Uintah and Ouray Ute Res-

ervation. He served in the U.S. Army during the Korean conflict, after which he returned to the Uinta Basin. He owns a ranch in Neola. He has been active in various positions in Ute tribal government, including serving as museum director for the Ute Tribe. A talented artist, his paintings and illustrations document Ute heritage. He has dedicated his life to preserving Ute culture and traditions and is recognized as a spiritual leader among the Ute people.

Dr. Ronald L. Holt is Professor of Anthropology at Weber State University in Ogden, Utah. He received his Ph.D. in Cultural Anthropology from the University of Utah in 1987. He has conducted anthropological fieldwork in the Middle East as well as with several Native American tribes, and he is currently studying martial arts and Shinto in Japan. He is the author of *Beneath These Red Cliffs: An Ethnohistory of the Utah Paiutes*, published by the University of New Mexico Press. He began his association with the Utah Paiutes in 1981.

Robert S. McPherson teaches at the College of Eastern Utah—San Juan Campus and has lived and worked with Navajo and Ute people for over thirty years. He earned his Ph.D. in history from Brigham Young University in 1987. Among his published works are: *The Northern Navajo Frontier, 1860–1900* (1988); *Sacred Land, Sacred View: Navajo Perceptions of the Four Corners Region* (1992); and *The Journey of Navajo Oshley: An Autobiography and Life History* (2000). Bob and his wife Betsy have six children and live in Blanding, Utah.

Nancy C. Maryboy is the Director of the Office of Institutional Research and Accreditation for Dine College, the tribal college of the Navajo Nation. She received a Ph.D. from the California Institute of Integral Studies, San Francisco, California, in Integral Studies, with a concentration on the application and articulation of indigenous knowledge to contemporary education. Dr. Maryboy is Cherokee and Navajo. Her family lives in Oregon and on the Navajo Reservation in southeastern Utah.

Dallin Maybee is the artist of the drawings used on the front cover, the frontispiece, and the tailpiece of this book. He was born in 1974 and is a member of the Arapaho-Seneca Tribe. A native of New York state, he has been in Utah for about five years and is presently a student at the University of Utah.

Mae Parry, a member and leader of the Northwestern Band of the Shoshone Nation, was born at Washakie, Utah. She has served the Northwestern Shoshone Band in many offices and capacities including secretary, vice-chairperson, and acting chairperson. She has also worked hard to preserve the history and culture of the Shoshone people through her research, writing, and bead work. A dedicated mother and grandmother, she was named Honorary Mother of the Year for Utah in 1987.

Allan Kent Powell is the Public History Coordinator at the Utah State Historical Society. He received his Ph.D. in History from the University of Utah in 1976. In addition to his own work as a historian and writer, he has served as editor of *The Utah History Encyclopedia* and as general editor of the twenty-nine-volume Utah Centennial County History Series.

Gary Tom grew up on the Kaibab Paiute Reservation and has family ties to the Shivwits and Indian Peak Paiute Bands. He earned his Master's degree in education from Northern Arizona University in 1975 and has been Education Director for the Paiute Indian Tribe of Utah since 1976. He currently lives in Cedar City and has worked as a consultant for a number of films and publications. He performs traditional Indian flute music and since 1992 has been a board member for the International Organization for Folk Arts, headquartered in Vienna, Austria.

Mary Jane Yazzie was born in Blanding, Utah, and has lived most of her life on White Mesa, where she worked for the White Mesa Ute Tribe for more than twenty years. She is an enrolled Ute Mountain tribal member and serves on the Ute Mountain Indian Gaming Commission. She is also chairperson of the White Mesa Ute Board and has served on the governor's Utah Indian Cooperative Council and other committees and commissions. She attended public schools in Blanding and graduated from the College of Eastern Utah, San Juan Center. She and her husband are parents to three children and grandparents of four grandchildren.

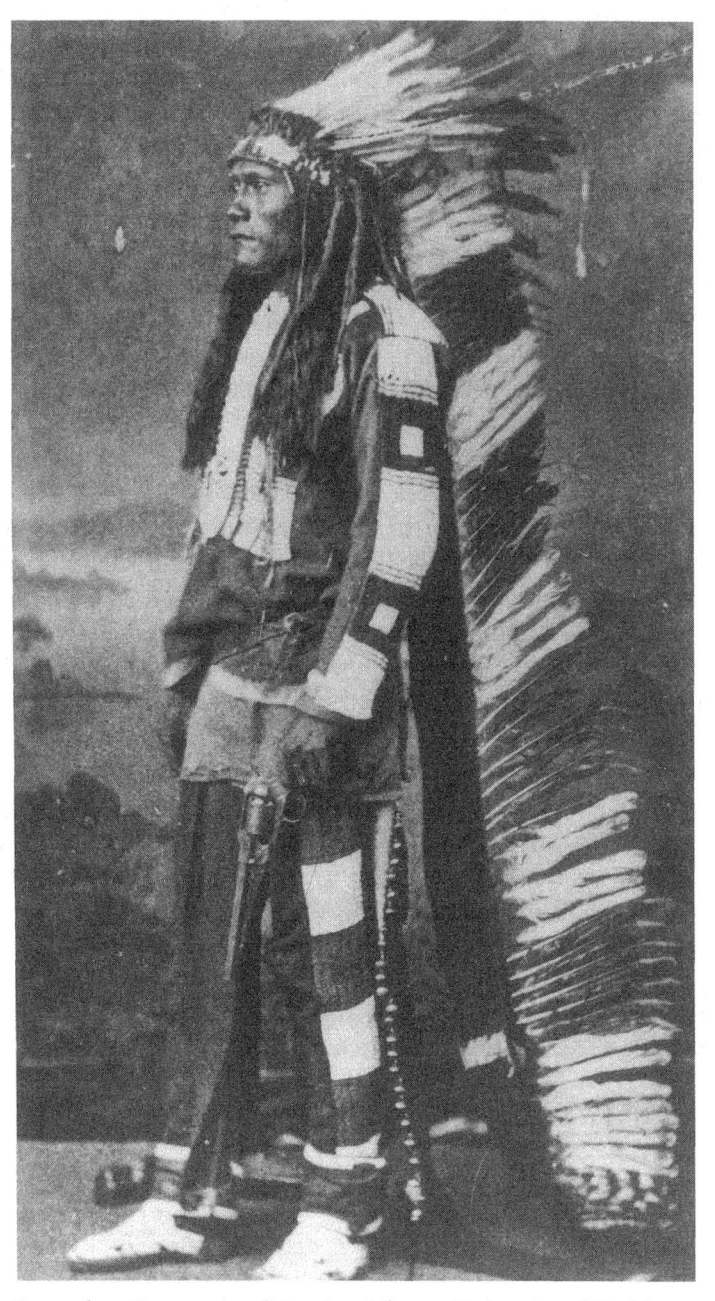

Powatch, a Ute warrior. (Marriott Library, University of Utah)

Index

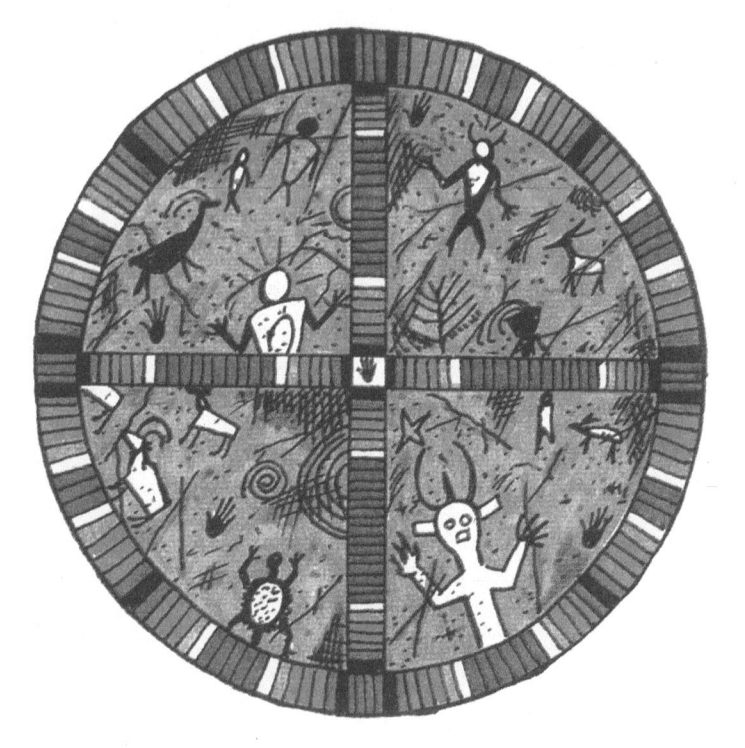

Medicine wheel. (Contemporary drawing by Dallin Maybee)